The Rationalizing Voter

Human beings are consummate rationalizers, but rarely are we rational. Controlled deliberation is a bobbing cork on the currents of unconscious information processing, but we have always the illusion of standing at the helm. This book presents a theory of the architecture and mechanisms that determine when, how, and why unconscious thoughts, the coloration of feelings, the plausibility of goals, and the force of behavioral dispositions change moment by moment in response to "priming" events that spontaneously link changes in the environment to changes in beliefs, attitudes, and behavior. For from the consciously directed decision making assumed by conventional models, political behavior is the result of innumerable unnoticed forces, with conscious deliberation little more than a rationalization of the outputs of automatic feelings and inclinations.

Milton Lodge is a Distinguished University Professor of Political Science at Stony Brook University. He is the author of three books and numerous research articles in political science and psychology, a Fulbright Research Scholar (Nepal), a Research Scholar at the Netherlands' Institute for Advanced Study, and a member of the American Academy of Arts and Sciences.

Charles S. Taber is a Professor of Political Science and Dean of the Graduate School at Stony Brook University. He has written several books and many articles on political psychology and computational modeling in the social sciences. He is the winner of nine research grants from the National Science Foundation. Professor Taber is a past editor of the journal *Political Psychology* and serves on several editorial boards in political science.

Cambridge Studies in Public Opinion and Political Psychology

Series Editors

Dennis Chong, *Northwestern University*
James H. Kuklinksi, *University of Illinois, Urbana-Champaign*

Cambridge Studies in Public Opinion and Political Psychology publishes innovative research from a variety of theoretical and methodological perspectives on the mass public foundations of politics and society. Research in the series focuses on the origins and influence of mass opinion; the dynamics of information and deliberation; and the emotional, normative, and instrumental bases of political choice. In addition to examining psychological processes, the series explores the organization of groups, the association between individual and collective preferences, and the impact of institutions on beliefs and behavior.

Cambridge Studies in Public Opinion and Political Psychology is dedicated to furthering theoretical and empirical research on the relationship between the political system and the attitudes and actions of citizens.

Books in the series are listed following the Index.

The Rationalizing Voter

MILTON LODGE
Stony Brook University

CHARLES S. TABER
Stony Brook University

CAMBRIDGE
UNIVERSITY PRESS

32 Avenue of the Americas, New York NY 10013-2473, USA

Cambridge University Press is part of the University of Cambridge.

It furthers the University's mission by disseminating knowledge in the pursuit of education, learning, and research at the highest international levels of excellence.

www.cambridge.org
Information on this title: www.cambridge.org/9780521176149

First published 2013
Reprinted 2013 (twice)

A catalog record for this publication is available from the British Library.

Library of Congress Cataloging in Publication data
Lodge, Milton, author.
The rationalizing voter / Milton Lodge, Stony Brook University, Charles S. Taber, Stony Brook University.
    pages   cm. – (Cambridge studies in public opinion and political psychology)
Includes bibliographical references and index.
ISBN 978-0-521-76350-9 (hardback) – ISBN 978-0-521-17614-9 (paperback)
1. Political psychology.   2. Public opinion.   3. Voting.   I. Taber, Charles S., author.
II. Title.
JA74.5.L62   2013
320.01′9–dc23   2012021024

ISBN 978-0-521-76350-9 Hardback
ISBN 978-0-521-17614-9 Paperback

Contents

List of Tables

List of Figures

Preface

This is a book about unconscious political thinking and the subterranean forces that determine how citizens evaluate political leaders, groups, and issues. It is the culmination of a twenty-year collaboration to chart the stream of information processing, which constructs political deliberation and behavior, and the impact of early, unnoticed feelings. This is a book about why the first 100 milliseconds of thought matters. It is about rationalizing, rather than rational, citizens.

This book was a long time in the making, in part because of teaching and administrative obligations, but more because of the explosion of research on unconscious thinking and on implicit attitudes and measures (see reviews in Gawronski and Payne, 2010; Petty, Fazio, and Brinol, 2009). In just the first quarter of 2011, five large volumes were published that apply implicit measures to a broad range of social phenomena: social conflict and aggression (Forgas et al., 2011); moral emotions (Giner-Sorolla, 2011); social identity and intergroup relations (Kramer et al., 2011); social judgment and decision making (Krueger, 2011); and, perhaps most importantly, the summing up and theoretical reconceptualization of a Nobel-winning research program on judgmental heuristics (Kahneman, 2011). While all of this is to the good, the sad fact is that it has become nearly impossible to keep up!

Virtually all the research reported here was carried out in Stony Brook's Laboratory for Experimental Research in Political Behavior, supported by grants from the National Science Foundation (SES-0550629, SES-0241282, SES-0300419, SES-0201650, SES-9975063, SES-9310351, SES-9102901, SES–9010666, and SES–9106311). We of course absolve NSF for any and all errors and thank our Stony Brook students and colleagues for saving us from even more grievous mistakes and miscalculations. Over the years Stony Brook's departmental "wine and cheese" seminar series has been especially helpful, and we would like to extend our deepest gratitude to our colleagues, Stanley Feldman, Leonie Huddy, and Howie Lavine, who forced us to confront our penchant as motivated reasoners to skim over and sidestep weaknesses in theory, experimental design, and analyses. We are also deeply indebted to former colleagues and seminar members Ruth Hamill, Bob Huckfeldt, Kathleen McGraw, and Marco Steenbergen. Our research program survived more blunders than we would like to admit because of the unwillingness of these past and present colleagues to tolerate slipshod thinking and magical assumptions. We have also benefited from the pointed criticisms of numerous fellow political psychologists, chief among them Rick Lau, George Marcus, Dave Redlawsk, and the Cambridge University Press editors Dennis Chong and Jim Kuklinski.

Much of the work reported herein was conducted in collaboration with our many bright, hard-working graduate students, to whom we owe our deepest debt. Chapter 4 developed as an extension of our most basic *hot cognition* hypothesis to political and social group identifications and contains research we did with Inna Burdein, some of which became the basis of her dissertation on racial attitudes and political principles. Brad Verhultz worked with us on the *affect transfer* studies reported in Chapter 5 and was an invaluable sounding board on experimental design for other studies conducted while he was a student at Stony Brook. Chapter 6, testing our critical *affective contagion* hypothesis, is based on a collaboration with Cengiz Erisen, and some of these studies are reported in his dissertation on the same topic. One of the *motivated reasoning* studies in Chapter 7 began as a group project in Taber's Political Psychology Foundation class and was completed with Damon Cann and Simona Kucsova. Finally, the computational model described in Chapter 8, which is a working, comprehensive, formal model of our theory of motivated political reasoning, *John Q. Public (JQP)*, and which we apply empirically to the 2000 U.S. presidential election campaign and to experimental data collected by David Redlawsk and Rick Lau, was conducted with Sung-youn Kim. This last work was a massive effort and was the centerpiece of Sung-youn's dissertation. More generally, a number of other graduate students commented on research contained in this book, and we are especially grateful to those who worked with us in the Laboratory for Experimental Research in Political Behavior, which we codirect: Dan Cassino, Katie Donovan, Chris Johnston, Mary Kate Lizotte, David Martin, Ben Newman, Dave Perkins, Martijn Schoonvelde, Eser Sekercioglu, Nick Seltzer, Marco Steenbergen, April Strickland, Patrick Stroh, Chris Weber, Ben Woodson, Julie Wronski, Sanser Yener, and Everett Young. April Strickland and Alexa Bankert assisted in preparation of the references and index.

Much of this research has appeared in previous articles or chapters, including in the *American Political Science Review*, *American Journal of Political Science*, *Political Psychology*, and *Political Behavior*, and we are grateful to reviewers and editors for helpful advice and direction. This work is acknowledged by citation where appropriate in text.

Despite all this help we are fully aware of the soft underbelly of our theory and gaps in our empirical tests. Wish we could have done better.

Stony Brook, NY

Unconscious Thinking on Political Judgment, Reasoning, and Behavior

We are told by the astrophysicist Michio Kaku that 6.4 percent of the universe is visible, with another 23 percent unseen but measurable, leaving much of the universe in the dark. It is much the same in our inner world, where most thinking occurs outside of awareness, available to neither introspection nor direct observation. Humans are designed to process rapidly and *implicitly* enormous quantities of environmental and internal data. But our ability to focus *explicit* thought is severely limited. By and large, the social sciences are not well prepared to understand this duality of cognition, and political science is no exception. Grounded in an Enlightenment view of Rational Man, political science has been dominated by models of conscious control and deliberative democracy. Rational and intentional reasoning, in this conventional view, *causes* political behavior.

This is a book about unconscious thinking and its influence on political attitudes and behavior. It is a book about powerful affective and cognitive forces that motivate and direct deliberation and political action outside of conscious awareness and control. It is a book about rationalizing, rather than rational, citizens.

What people think, feel, say, and do is a direct function of the information that is momentarily accessible from memory – be it the recall of facts and feelings, the recollection of experiences, or the turning of goals into action. Political behavior and attitudes are very much a function of the unconscious mechanisms that govern memory accessibility. But we political scientists know very little about the processes that underwrite individual variation in beliefs and behavior. We know about variation in public opinion as indicated by verbal self reports. We routinely ask respondents for their party and candidate preferences, their approval of policy proposals, and how warmly they feel toward one or another group, and we are often able to relate these explicit measures through sophisticated multivariate analyses that we interpret as revealing underlying causal processes. There has also been considerable growth in the use of controlled experiments to determine causality, but most of these also rely on overt verbal responses that may not reveal an underlying implicit process. This reliance on direct, explicit measures of political beliefs and attitudes is intensely problematic, assuming as it does that people have accessible beliefs and attitudes, that they are willing and able to voice them, and that these self-reports are causally related to their political behaviors.

Though it has gone largely unnoticed in political science, we are witnessing a revolution in thinking about thinking. Three decades of research in the cognitive sciences, backed by hundreds of well-crafted behavioral studies in social psychology and now evidence from the neurosciences, posit *affect-driven, dualprocess modes* of thinking and reasoning that directly challenge the way we political scientists think about, measure, and interpret political beliefs and attitudes. Central to such dual-process models is the distinction between the unconscious ("System 1," "implicit") and conscious ("System 2," "explicit") processing of judgments, preferences, and decisions. System 1 processes are spontaneous, fast, effortless, and operate below conscious awareness, whereas System 2 processes are slow, deliberative, effortful, and self-aware.

Given the serious real-time limitations of conscious processing, we humans have evolved compensatory heuristics, including a System 1 *likeability heuristic* that automatically links positive and/or negative affect to familiar social objects in long-term memory. Once associated, this felt positivity or negativity strongly influences downstream thinking and reasoning. What especially attracts our interest as political scientists to such dual-process models is the finding that unconscious processes are continually at work, with effects that appear to be most influential when the most knowledgeable among us think hard about an issue and carefully weigh the pros and cons when forming opinions and making choices.

The Ubiquity of Unconscious Thinking

Cognitive scientists estimate that the human capacity for processing sensory experience is about 11 million bits per second (Norretranders, 1998). The visual system takes up about 90 percent of this total capacity, processing roughly 10 million bits of visual information per second. No more than 40 bits per second of this visual information enters conscious working memory, so we become aware of only 1/250,000 of what we see! Similarly, a healthy human brain processes 1 million bits of tactile information and 100,000 bits of auditory information, while we at best become aware of just 5 bits of tactile and 30 bits of auditory information per second. When we read (with or without moving our lips) we process a maximum of 45 bits per second. More limited still is our capacity to consciously think and reason, where we are able to keep in the focus of attention only about 7 ± 2 chunks of information (Miller, 1956).

About 98 percent of what we experience, our very connection to the outside world, are whispers that come and go unnoticed.

What are the consequences of this colossal difference between conscious and unconscious experiences for thought and action? What types of information activate unconsciously when citizens watch a candidate debate, see a campaign ad, argue politics with friends, ruminate about a political issue, answer a pollster's question, or enter the voting booth? Where, when, and why will conscious and unconscious processes reinforce one another? What happens when unconscious influences are at odds with conscious control? When and how can unconscious influences be overridden (Bodenhausen and Todd, 2010)?

Research across the cognitive and neurosciences demonstrates the profound impact of unconscious processing on the content of our thoughts, how we reason, and consequently the choices we make (Ferguson and Porter, 2010; Hassin, Uleman, and Bargh, 2005; Perugini, Richetin, and Zogmaister, 2010). To place this empirical literature in perspective, and reassure readers that the "unconscious" explored here and in the contemporary psychological literature is not the subterranean id, ego, or superego of Freud, or the psychoanalytic analyses popular in the mid-twentieth century (Erikson, 1950; George and George, 1956; Lasswell, 1930), let us operationalize the unconscious in terms of objective and subjective thresholds of perception.

An objective threshold, as can be measured by brain-wave patterns, must be passed for an external stimulus event to enter one of the sensory systems. A subjective threshold is passed if the stimulus event enters conscious awareness. There are three possibilities:

- If the objective threshold is not passed, perception does not occur and there is no registration of the event on the senses. Essentially, a nonevent with no impact on information processing.
- If the objective threshold is passed but the subjective is not, we have unconscious perception – a sensory experience passes objective thresholds without ever entering conscious awareness. Such *Consciously Unnoticed Events* (Type 1 CUEs or interchangeably called Type 1 primes) escape notice; seen, registered, but consciously unnoticed. An objectively perceived stimulus may not reach conscious awareness for many reasons: because it occurred too rapidly or too peripherally to be noticed, or one is momentarily distracted.
- If the subjective threshold is passed, we have explicit conscious perception, the stuff of everyday experience. But – this very common – we may "see" the stimulus without realizing its influence on our thoughts, feelings, preferences, and choices. For such *Consciously Unappreciated Events* (Type 2 CUEs or interchangeably Type 2 Primes), the individual is consciously aware of the stimulus, say the American flag in the background of a candidate's speech, but its impact on thought, reasoning, and choice is not seen as being influential.

Unconscious primes are ubiquitous in the real world (Bargh, 1997), the play-things of advertisers selling detergents and presidential candidates, where the men and women in beer and car commercials are unusually attractive and fun loving; the smokers in cigarette ads look preternaturally healthy; the men tout-ing erectile dysfunction medications appear uncommonly virile. Laugh tracks in situational TV comedies, although widely bemoaned, nonetheless enhance audience enjoyment. Worse yet, all types of humor, whether real or feigned, are commonly used to mask deceptive advertising (Shabbir and Thwaites, 2007). And as we will show in multiple experimental demonstrations, such "inciden-tal," more-often-than-not diagnostically irrelevant Type 1 and Type 2 primes prove to be powerful influences on how people think about and evaluate polit-ical leaders, groups, and issues.

Unconscious events and processes can drive political behavior in two ways: they may directly trigger a snap judgment or response entirely out of awareness, or they may indirectly drive behavior through their influence on conscious thought processes. A great deal of psychological research has demonstrated the direct causal process, but there has been comparatively little research on the mediated impact of implicit processes.

Implicit Cues in the Real World and in the Laboratory

Because citizens are confronted with more information than they can con-sciously handle, it should come as no surprise that they take mental shortcuts to arrive at their vote decisions, including endorsements, opinion polls, phys-ical attractiveness, elite opinion, and feelings toward social groups (Mondak, 1994) – and of course party identification (Bartels, 2000; Goren et al. 2009; Jackman and Sniderman, 2002; Lau and Redlawsk, 2006; Riggle et al., 1992; Sniderman, 2000; Sniderman, Brody, and Tetlock, 1991). Reliance on one or another heuristic seems a reasonable strategy to the extent that it helps align a candidate's issue positions and attributes with the voter's interests and values (Lau and Redlawsk, 2006) or more generally improves the quality of decisions (Kahneman, Slovic, and Tversky, 1982).

But we believe and hope to demonstrate another, even faster, more readily available and general heuristic exists that may provide quicker and "better" candidate evaluations: a System 1 *likeability heuristic* stored as an implicit attitude unconsciously guides preferences in accord with the citizen's history of information processing. Implicit attitudes or feelings about individuals, social groups, and ideas can exist outside of subjective awareness, affective tallies capture the evaluative implications of prior conscious and unconscious thinking about these objects, and these feelings come spontaneously to mind when their associated objects become targets of thought.

A great deal of psychological research shows the impact of implicit attitudes on a variety of social behaviors (Gawronski and Payne, 2010; Petty, Fazio, and Briñol, 2009), though the relationships among implicit and explicit attitudes remain controversial (De Houwer, 2009). For example, implicit racial attitudes have been repeatedly shown to influence social behaviors, though they often diverge from explicit self-report measures of racial attitudes (Dovidio et al., 2009; Greenwald and Nosek, 2009; Nosek and Smyth, 2007). We believe that it would be a serious error to make a too-sharp distinction between implicit and explicit attitudes and we resist doing so (Sherman, 2009). Our view is that implicit and explicit attitudes are different responses from a single underlying memory system. Explicit attitudes are consciously considered responses for which one has the time and motivation to form a response. They will be influenced by myriad unnoticed factors, but somewhere in the decision stream will be an opportunity for control and consciously reasoned thought. Implicit attitudes are affective responses to stimuli that one cannot control or consciously reason about. It is more likely that an implicit response reflects affect stored directly with a memory object (what has been called an online tag in the research literature), but these too will be influenced by extraneous factors. It is a mistake to think of one as more "true" than another, and both are subject to bias, though of a different kind.

Is it possible to like someone or something without any conscious awareness of how or why this preference came to be? In his presidential address to the American Psychological Association, Robert Zajonc (1980) provides a simple experimental example for how "Preferences Need No Inferences." A sample of non-Chinese Americans were briefly shown a number of Chinese ideographs and later asked to evaluate how aesthetically pleasing they were. The ideographs were shown zero, one, two, or three times, though participants were not aware of the multiple exposures and could not later identify which characters in a test set had been presented to them. Nevertheless, the more often they were shown a symbol the more they found it pleasing, a finding labeled the "mere exposure effect." Preferences were altered without the objects even being recognized. In a final definitive demonstration that the mere exposure effect operates unconsciously, Murphy and Zajonc (1993) replicated the study using subliminal exposures to the ideographs (i.e., presentations too rapid for conscious perception).

Mere exposure can also influence other types of social judgments. Jacoby, Kelley, Brown, and Jasechko (1988) found that judgments of whether a name is that of a famous person (i.e., Is Sebastian Weisdorf famous?) are influenced by previous exposure to the name, even when it was presented on a list explicitly labeled Nonfamous People. Names were accurately judged to be nonfamous immediately after exposure to the list, but twenty-four hours later as recall of the source of information faded from memory, the residue memory trace was sufficient for many of those on the list to become famous overnight. Mere exposure, bolstered by this sleeper effect, changed the accessibility of names, making them appear more familiar and hence mistakenly identified as famous. This effect mimics what is routinely found in studies of persuasion where familiar arguments are judged more believable (Eagly and Chaiken, 1993), where in advertising repetition builds brand name identification (Warshaw and Davis, 1985), and where candidate name recognition is, after money, the most critical step in winning an election (Kleinnijenhuis, van Hoof, and Oegema, 2006). Here again, conscious and unconscious processing may go their separate ways.

Unconsciously processed cues operating in the political realm can impact the evaluations of known candidates and their electoral success. The 1960 Nixon-Kennedy preelection debate is a well-known political example of noticed-but-unappreciated effects: seventy million people watched the first televised presidential debates in American history between Richard Nixon and John Kennedy. Nixon, recently out of the hospital, refused make-up; Kennedy had been campaigning in California and had the tan to show for it. Television viewers, apparently distracted by Nixon's pallid look and five-o'clock shadow, thought Nixon shifty and untrustworthy, while radio listeners, who had little to go on but the substance of the debates, thought Nixon the clear winner. The familiar version of this story is used to illustrate how image can dominate substance in politics; in our terms, how System 1 implicit processing can lead voters astray from the solid moorings of conscious deliberation. But as Malcolm Gladwell (2005) points out, the familiar version of the story has it backwards: Nixon did indeed turn out to be shifty and untrustworthy. Viewers' implicit, affective responses to the candidates' appearances proved to be more accurate than judgments based presumably on a less-biased, more careful consideration of issue positions and policies.

Similarly, facial expressions of news broadcasters influence the political judgments of viewers. In coverage of the 1976 presidential election campaign, Friedman, DiMatteo, and Mertz (1980) found discernable differences in the perceived positivity of broadcasters' facial expressions when they uttered different candidates' names. Mullen and colleagues (1986) replicated this result with the 1984 presidential election and demonstrated further that a broadcaster's facial expressions influenced voters' political preferences. Specifically, voters came to favor the candidate for whom the broadcaster exhibited more positive facial expressions. The same effect in a different modality: Gregory and Gallagher (2002), analyzing the voice frequencies of candidates in nineteen nationally televised American presidential debates, found that this auditory cue signaled a candidate's relative social dominance within a debate and predicted his vote share in the election. Media effects without message – more accurately, media effects through implicit rather than explicit channels of communication.

Babad (1999, 2005) obtained similar noticed-but-unappreciated results in the domain of political interviews. She found, not only that TV newscast interviewers exhibited differential levels of positive and negative nonverbal behaviors toward the politicians they were interviewing, but that an interviewer's nonverbal behavior impacted the viewers' perceptions of the politician. In particular, a politician's image suffered when the interviewer appeared hostile rather than friendly.

Here is an even more subtle effect of an unappreciated cue on choice: Berger, Meridith, and Wheeler (2008) showed that budgetary support for education varied as a function of where people voted – whether in schools, churches, or firehouses – with voters more likely to favor raising state taxes to support education when voting in schools, even controlling for their political views. Clearly, the voters knew what building they were in but were not consciously aware of its influence on their vote choice. Ballot order effects provide another political case in point, where being listed first increased the vote count for 80 percent of candidates (Schneider, Krosnick, Ofir, Milligan, and Tahk, 2008).

Some cues seem so obvious it is hard to imagine an implicit effect, but the inference is nevertheless made unconsciously. Race messages in campaign advertising, for example, are more effective when they remain covert. Tali Mendelberg demonstrates this effect in *The Race Card* (2001) via an experimental analysis of the infamous Willie Horton campaign ads, in which presidential candidate Michael Dukakis used pictures and sounds to implicitly associate African Americans with crime with. When the race cues are made fully explicit in Mendelberg's study (that is, when subjects are alerted to their presence) they lose their power to influence political judgments. Another case in point was a 2004 MoveOn.org TV ad that showed images of Hitler before a photo of Bush raising his hand to take the oath of office, accompanied by the voice over, "A nation warped by lies. Lies fuel fear. Fear fuels aggression. Invasion. Occupation. What were war crimes in 1945 is foreign policy in 2003." Republican groups and Jewish organizations expressed outrage over the ad, which was quickly removed from the MoveOn.org website. Research suggests, however, that subtle propaganda would be more effective; an implicit message more powerful still.

In the mid-1990s, Mayor Rudolph Giuliani of New York City adopted a "quality of life" campaign fashioned on James Q. Wilson and George Kelling's (1996) "broken windows theory." In this theory, signs of disorderly and petty criminal behavior signal neighborhood decay and deterioration, which trigger more disorderly and petty criminal behavior. Giuliani's change in policy had more cops walking beats, city work crews painting over graffiti, sweeping streets and cleaning subways, towing abandoned cars, ticketing jaywalkers, punishing vandals, and rousting the homeless from city streets and parks. After the introduction of the campaign, petty crime rates in New York City dropped dramatically and polls showed an uptick in perceived quality of city life (which became a major talking point for Giuliani's later political campaigns). A change in policy that was essentially cosmetic eventually had real effects on the compliance behavior of citizens, in our interpretation because of the replacement of implicit cues of neighborhood decay with cues of orderliness and civic control.

Political judgments can be directly affected by irrelevant, nonpolitical cues as well. While theories of retrospective voting suggest voters should reward or punish incumbents for the things they can control (in particular, wars and the economy), it is hard to imagine why voters should hold politicians accountable for such "acts of God" as earthquakes or floods. And yet in their analysis of retrospective voting in Woodrow Wilson's 1916 reelection, Achen and Bartels (2006) find that a string of shark attacks in the summer months before the 1916 election cost Wilson about ten percentage points in New Jersey beach communities, with no effect inland. Closer to home is the Healy, Malhotra, and Mo (2010) finding that local college basketball and football wins impacted the vote for Obama. Such findings are hard to square with conventional normative models of conscious deliberation, but are compatible with the implicit effects of affective cues on candidate preference.

A major area of research pointing to robust effects of unconscious influences on snap judgments is the effect of facial attractiveness on evaluations, attitudes, and behavior. Here, as in the stereotypic inferencing of traits from gender, age, and race, the face is rapidly registered and spontaneously triggers stereotypic assumptions about the individual's character, attitudes, and behavior. Three large meta-analyses covering more than 1,000 peer-reviewed psychological studies of physical attractiveness confirm significant experimental and correlational effects on a broad range of social attitudes and behaviors (Eagly, Ashmore, Makhijini, and Longo, 1991; Feingold, 1992; Langlois, Kalakanis, Rubenstein, Larson, Hallam, and Smoot, 2000). Whether a person is seen as attractive or unattractive, assumptions are brought into play. Across cultures, what is beautiful is assumed to be good, and all manner of negative traits may be attributed to those less physically blessed. As Langlois and colleagues point out, this research shows that implicit responses debunk the descriptive if not the normative validity of three popular folk maxims:

Whereas it is said that *beauty is in the eye of the beholder*, the empirical evidence shows widespread consensus as to who is or is not attractive, with correlations suggesting near unanimity: within culture, $r = .90$; across ethnic groups, $r = .88$; and across cultures, $r = .94$. Such levels of agreement support the probability of rather uniform implicit responses to the appearances of political candidates or opinion leaders.

While we are admonished to *never judge a book by its cover*, hundreds of studies report stereotypical attributions advantaging attractive children in school and adults in their everyday lives and careers. It is routinely found that physical appearance exerts a strong influence on character perception, with scores of studies reporting a "beautiful-is-good" halo effect. The meta-analyses document that physically attractive people are perceived to be more sociable, dominant, extraverted, popular, and warm. Even among strangers a one second glance is enough to trigger an inference that an attractive man is more interesting, successful, intelligent, and virtuous. Strong correlations between attractiveness and particular attitudinal and behavioral characteristics have been found across cultures for both adults and young children, implying that a large part of this beauty-is-good projection effect is inborn and supplemented by nurture (Rhodes, 2006).

In general, a mere glance at an attractive face promotes a one-half standard deviation enhancement on positive personality traits, with about 64 percent of attractive people but only 36 percent of less attractive people perceived as having a better-than-average personality, the attractive seen as being more socially competent (70 percent vs. 30 percent), more worthy of attention (74 percent vs. 26 percent), more successful (68 percent vs. 32 percent), and if in need more likely to receive help (59 percent vs. 41 percent). Even in death the attractive are "advantaged," their demise judged more tragic (Callan, Powell, and Ellard, 2007).

Finally, if it were true that *beauty is only skin deep*, there would not be a robust influence of self-rated attractiveness on measures of popularity, sociability, or objective measures of mental health. Physically attractive individuals have more sexual partners, find better-looking mates, become more professionally successful, make more than their fair share of decisions, and are happier than those of us below the median of physical good looks (Dion, Walster, and Berscheid, 1972). This "beauty premium" has been shown by Biddle and Hamermesh (1998) to positively impact attorneys' wages, and – this unimaginable for elected office to political science associations – good-looking scholars are more likely to be voted into leadership positions of the *American Economics Association*.

The impact of physical appearance extends beyond attractiveness. A study by Mueller and Mazur (1996) found that ratings of facial dominance of West Point cadets (rectangular face, strong brow, square jaw) predicted later military rank. A follow up study (Little, Burriss, Jones, and Roberts, 2007) graphically manipulated facial dominance of alleged politicians and found that facial dominance affects voting decisions. Moreover, changing the context from peacetime to wartime promoted an even larger advantage for the dominant candidate.

What is important here is that physical appearance is registered but its inferential impact on character perceptions, evaluations, and behavior remains covert for those making the judgments. When this influence is pointed out, it is routinely denied. Given that facial appearance is one of the very first things we see in another person and that there are specific brain structures designed to detect and characterize faces, it is not surprising that attractive people prompt positive attributions which, entering the evaluation early, anchor and bias subsequent evaluations. Routinely, humans make positive attributions to attractive people without consciously realizing it, yet the magnitude of these effects is roughly the same as other variables in the social sciences (Eagly, 1996).

"Beautiful-is-good" stereotyping is alive in the political domain as well, where many of the same effects of attractiveness on snap judgments found in nonpolitical domains are matched in impressions of politicians, with attractive candidates seen as possessing more integrity, competence, likeability, and being better suited for public office (Rosenberg et al., 1986). For example, a large-scale study of the 2003 parliamentary and 2004 municipal elections in Finland collected ratings by more than 10,000 web-survey respondents on a host of dispositional traits for a total of 1,900 facial photos of real political candidates. The finding: a one standard deviation increase in attractiveness was associated with a 20 percent increase in the number of votes over the average nonincumbent (Berggren, Jordahl, and Poutvaara, 2010). Similarly, in a study of the 2004 Australian election, where voting is compulsory and voters are handed a "How to Vote" card with pictures of the candidates, the more attractive of the two was associated with a 1.5 percent to 2 percent change in vote share, with this effect even larger in electorates with a higher share of apathetic voters (King and Leigh, 2010). Rosar, Klein, and Beckers (2008) found the same result for the state-wide elections in the largest German Bundesland, North Rhine-Westpahlia, where campaign posters feature pictures of the candidates: attractive candidates – especially when their opponents are unattractive – garnered not only a larger vote share but also an increase in turnout.

While most of these studies have experimental participants view photos at their leisure in a contextually relevant frame, a great deal of information in addition to facial attractiveness can be gleaned in the blink of an eye (Gladwell, 2005). Here's an "experiment" to try. On the next page are side-by-side photos of a pair of adult males, both candidates for the U.S. Senate (Figure 1.1). Turn the page, take no more than one second to scan the photos and return here.

Now which of the two candidates would you say is more competent?

In an important series of experiments reported in *Science*, Alex Todorov and his colleagues (2005; see also Olivola and Todorov, 2010) demonstrated that competence ratings based on a one-second exposure to paired photos of competing candidates predicted the 2004 House and Senate election outcomes at significantly better than chance levels (67.7 percent and 68.8 percent, respectively). Competence in the Todorov studies is modeled as a direct predictor of vote choice, and ratings were made of *unfamiliar* candidates by *naive* experimental participants *before* the 2004 congressional elections and the predictions are to the *actual* electoral outcomes, not vote intention. In other analyses, in addition to making competence judgments, participants evaluated the paired candidates on attractiveness, likeability, trustworthiness, and other dispositional judgments, all well-known to be important in the evaluation of political candidates (Kinder, Peters, Abelson, and Fiske, 1980; Funk, 1999). Now postdicting the 2000 and 2002 Senate races, Todorov and colleagues found what is also true in the National Election Studies: competence trumps the other trait assessments in accurately discriminating winners from losers. The inescapable implication of this research is that people can make substantively important attributions on a mere one second exposure to the facial photos of unfamiliar political candidates, and what is more, these snap judgments (typically taking little more than one second) discriminate winners from losers without any information or contextual cue other than being told the photos were of politicians. All this predictive power without party identification, ideological

FIGURE 1.1. A Pair of Senate Candidates from Todorov and Colleagues (2005)

proximity, or any of the traditional predictors of vote choice! Of course, it is possible that these more traditional levers of political judgment would be as or more influential on vote choice if they were available for respondents in these studies. But this fact does not overturn the importance of the finding that mere exposure to faces is sufficient to generate snap trait judgments and thereby alter vote choice.

A number of additional studies have replicated the general finding that appearance-based competence judgments predict election outcomes, while ruling out the alternative hypothesis that competence judgments simply reflect media-induced familiarity with the politicians. Lenz and Lawson (2007) asked American participants to make facial competence judgments of Mexican politicians. Their judgments predicted Mexican election outcomes and accounted for 18 percent of the variance in vote shares, though these participants were never exposed to the Mexican media. Experiments by Antonakis and Dalgas (2009) are especially revealing here because they address the possible confound between competence and incumbency and raise the question as to how facial appearance predicts vote choice. Judgments collected from a sample of 1,106 Swiss adults predicted the winner and runner-up from the run-off stages of the 2002 French parliamentary elections and their competence ratings predicted the margin of victory.

Antonakis and Dalgas pushed the research question deeper by asking 681 children aged 5 to 13 years to play a computer game simulating a voyage on a difficult seagoing mission in which they chose which person (from the paired photos of French parliamentarians) they would want to captain the boat from Troy to Athens. The premise for this study dates back to Plato's *Republic* (2000: 153): "Imagine then a fleet or a ship in which there is a captain who is taller and stronger than any of the crew, but he is a little deaf and has a similar infirmity in sight, and his knowledge of navigation is not much better." Plato argues that the crew (voters) cannot select a competent captain (ruler) because the crew is beguiled by appearances. The children in Antonakis and Dalgas's experiment (mean age 10.3 years) predicted the French election outcome from their choice of ship captain with a correlation 0.71, which was indistinguishable from the adults' predictive success. These findings tell us that appearance-based trait inferences develop quite early and are surprisingly stable across age cohorts. Whatever the underlying process, both children and adults use facial cues rather than any in-depth processing.

Let's take the process one level deeper than cognitive deliberation can fathom. Social scientists may find it hard to believe but there are many experiments in developmental psychology that show the effects of attractiveness on infants and toddlers younger than the adolescents engaged in the sea-faring adventure of Antonakis and Dalgas (see Pascalis and Slater, 2003). Because infants cannot tell you what they find attractive or tell you much of anything, researchers use a "preferential-looking technique" in which two faces are shown side by side for ten-second exposures while a video camera records the time the infant spends gazing at each of the pictures. The consensual assumption is that the longer the fixation the more the infant is attracted to, or ostensibly "likes" the face. In one of many such experiments, Langlois and colleagues (1987) showed 6-month-olds images of female faces previously rated by college students as more to less attractive. For each pairing of faces (none were "drop-dead gorgeous" or "grotesque"), they found that the infants fixed their gaze longer on the more attractive face. Pushing the paradigm to its limits, the Langlois team (1991) next examined the preferences of 3-month-old infants to four types of faces – Black men and women, White men and women – all previously rated on attractiveness. Results confirm earlier, less-well controlled studies, in showing that preference for attractive faces holds across genders and races.

But what is it about the faces of politicians that causes people to perceive the winners as more competent than the losers? From our viewing of C-Span it is certainly not the case that the real-world competence or intelligence of politicians is reliably related to facial appearance. Perhaps there is a negative relationship. Todorov and colleagues (as well as other experiments from here and abroad) show that attractiveness and age, along with competence are proximate predictors of vote choice, but they do not rule out the possibility that competence simply mediates the causal effect of attractiveness and age on vote choice. Working from the "beautiful-is-good" literature, Verhulst, Lodge, and Lavine (2010) reconsidered the Todorov (Todorov et al., 2005; Olivola and Todorov, 2010) analyses to test the hypothesis that competence ratings are

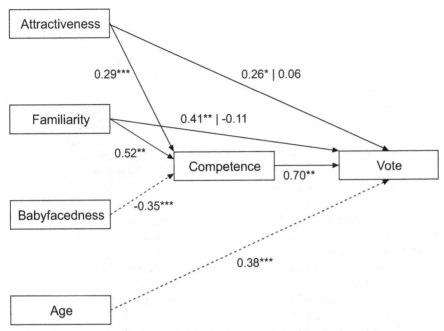

FIGURE 1.2. A Mediation Model of the Todorov and Colleagues (2005) Data

themselves derived from perceptions of facial attractiveness (as well as several other theoretically prior trait attributions).

Figure 1.2 reports the Todorov findings, rearranged into a mediational causal analysis to explain vote choice with four independent variables, three of which are mediated through competence attributions. Following the traditional mediational logic of Baron and Kenny (1986), Figure 1.2 shows three separate stages of regression analyses: first, we report the unmediated effect of each of the independent variables on vote choice, finding that attractiveness, familiarity, and perceived age all have a significant effect on vote choice, while babyfacedness does not have a direct effect; second, we report the effect of each independent variable on the mediator, finding that attractiveness, familiarity, and babyfacedness all significantly predict attributions of competence; finally, we report the effect of the mediator on the dependent variable while controlling for all four independent variables, finding that competence is the strongest predictor of vote choice, while the direct effects of attractiveness and familiarity drop out (the second coefficients reported for those paths in Figure 1.2). In short, Todorov's data show that the causal pathways from attractiveness and familiarity to vote choice travel indirectly through the more proximate, causally later assessments of competence. In fact, 70 percent of the effect of attractiveness on vote choice, and 89 percent of the total effect of familiarity is mediated through competence. Perceptions of candidate age exert a direct causal influence on vote choice without any indirect effect through competence, while babyfacedness has only an indirect influence.

Judgments of competence are clearly related to vote choice as Todorov and colleagues suggest (and as is shown repeatedly in the National Election Surveys), but the spontaneous process of making competence judgments appears to be preceded by an even earlier automatic assessment of attractiveness and familiarity. Given the emerging consensus that judgments of attractiveness have a biological basis, with specific brain structures engaged in the recognition of faces and facial expressions (Ekman, 2007), it is not surprising that these thin-sliced, one-second evaluations of political candidates are influenced by an even more primary evaluation of attractiveness. In addition to predicting higher levels of competence, physical attractiveness of politicians significantly predicts higher levels of likeability, integrity, and trust, all of which have also been repeatedly linked to the evaluation of political candidates and vote choice (Kinder, Peters, Abelson, and Fiske, 1980).

A cautionary note: neither we nor Todorov claim that the momentary effects of attractiveness on vote choice trump incumbency, party identification, issue proximity, or the many other factors known to predict congressional elections. Nor is anyone arguing that this bias cannot be corrected (Hart, Ottati, and Krumdick, 2011), although not easily, requiring as it does the conjunction of cognitive capacity to recognize the influence of physical attractiveness on one's judgment, the belief that the bias is inappropriate, and the motivation to correct the evaluation downward for an attractive candidate and upward for an unattractive contender. Rather, the point is that a simple glance generates inferences that have political import. Not surprisingly, a Todorov-like study by Atkinson, Enos, and Hill (2009) shows that political parties running candidates in competitive congressional elections selectively choose challengers with "higher quality faces." Across the ninety-nine Senate elections the authors found a significant "face quality" effect for both independent and partisan voters, but no instance where face effects in competitive elections changed the electoral outcome.

The question asked for millennia but still a puzzle today is why we are predisposed to find attractive faces so interesting (it cannot be a familiarity or socialization effect) and why preschoolers, youngsters, teenagers, and adults go beyond attractiveness to infer "beauty is good" given that these inferences appear not to facilitate accurate social judgments. One possibility consistent with the existing empirical evidence is that such inferences are based on cues that have adaptive significance (Todorov et al., 2008; Zebrowitz, 2004; Zebrowitz and Montepare, 2008). There is a dark side to the attractiveness-competence relationship, of course, in that the intelligence of adults cannot be predicted from facial appearance (Zebrowitz, Hall, Murphy, and Rhodes, 2002), and – this is admittedly a leap of faith – some politicians may actually be more competent than others.

Nonverbal cues have impact even in situations where decisions are made thoughtfully with due deliberation: Zebrowitz and McDonald (1991), for example, found judicial decisions to be influenced by the facial features of defendants and plaintiffs: mature-looking defendants were required to pay larger penalties in small claims courts when the plaintiffs were babyfaced. The robust effects of attractiveness on perception and behavior lend credence to Blaise Pascal's claim in his *Pensees* (1660; 2010): "Cleopatra's nose, had it been shorter, the whole face of the world would have been changed" (180).

In addition to unconscious trait attributions and the pronounced halo effects of attractiveness, there are countless examples of even more "incidental" influences on political information processing. Here is a perfect example of what we see as a not-so-subtle attempt to manipulate political inferences. In a televised, thirty-second, 2007 Christmas message by presidential candidate Michael Huckabee to Iowans a week before the caucuses. A single frame of this campaign ad is presented on the next page (Figure 1.3). Glance at it quickly, and then come back here.

Did you notice the bookcase over Hucklebee's right shoulder? Did the bright white separators of the bookcase form a cross? Note that the bookcase/cross may or may not be noticed. Perhaps the bookcase-as-cross would be more likely noticed by evangelicals and register as positive, while for others the implications might be negative, perhaps seen as a right-cross jab at Mitt Romney's square jaw or a poke at his Mormon religion. There is also the possibility that the symbol would escape conscious awareness, but be registered unconsciously, and thereby not be open to critical appraisal.

Such "incidental" priming is of course commonplace in the world of commercial and campaign advertising and given the research demonstrating that even brief exposures can impact preferences, it was to be expected that "thin-sliced" exposures much too fast to be reliably noticed would find their way into advertising as "hidden persuaders" and then into the selling of the president.

In his prophetic novel *1984*, George Orwell (1949/2003) foretold of a future in which our thoughts, attitudes, and behaviors would be controlled by government-directed media. This prophecy gained plausibility in the late 1950s after the advertising executive James Vicary reported significant increases in Coke and popcorn sales after flashing three-hundredth-of-a-second directives to "Drink Coke" and "Eat Popcorn" during a movie. The results seemed staggering: movie sales of Coke and popcorn increased 18 percent and 58 percent, respectively. People were understandably appalled at this insidious mind-control technique. If it could be used to persuade people to buy snacks and soft drinks, what other behaviors might be subliminally manipulated? There is a problem with the results of the study, however: it never actually took place. Vicary made it up as a publicity stunt to generate interest in his struggling advertising agency. Hoax or not, most people are fearful of the possibility of being influenced by subliminal messages (Wilson and Brekke, 1994), and many countries prohibit it in advertising.

FIGURE 1.3. Huckabee Campaign Ad Image (2007)

Of course, the fact that Vicary's claim was a hoax did not establish that subliminal messages do not influence attitudes. Karremans, Stroebe, and Claus (2006) conducted two experiments to examine whether subliminal priming of a drink can affect people's choices for the brand, and, importantly, whether this effect is moderated by individuals' feelings of thirst. Both studies demonstrated that subliminal priming of a brand name (here, Lipton Iced Tea) positively affected participants' choice for, and their intention to drink the primed brand, but only for participants who were already thirsty. "You can lead a horse to water but...."

As any self-respecting free marketeer would predict, the priming of hidden persuaders would find its way into the selling of the president. In the 2000 presidential election campaign, the Republican National Committee aired a TV ad nationwide attacking Gore's prescription drug plan 4,400 times, costing the RNC $2,576,000. When the final segment of the ad is run in slow motion, we can see the word "RATS" pop out of the phrase "Bureaucrats Decide." At the exposure speed of one thirtieth of a second, "rats" has likely not crossed the borderline of subjective perception and should not consciously register. The ad's creator said it was not his intention to create a subliminal ad, but rather to make the ad more visually interesting by flashing part of the word "bureaucrats" on the screen. "It was," he said, "just a coincidence" that the letters popping centerscreen out of "bureaucrats" spelled out the negative prime "rats." Such denials notwithstanding, Weinberger and Westen's (2008) experimental test shows an "affective contagion" effect such that on exposure to the subliminal "rats" prime candidates are evaluated negatively. In a follow up experiment, a photo of Bill Clinton primed evaluations of Governor Gray Davis in his 2003 recall election, with Republicans evaluating Davis more negatively than Democrats. Both inside the lab and in the real world, unconscious priming effects like these are proving to be influential in how information is encoded, retrieved, interpreted, evaluated, and acted upon.

While the use of subliminal primes (Type 1 CUEs) in the laboratory provides the strongest experimental control and clearest demonstration of the automaticity of beliefs and attitudes and allows the researcher to rigorously test for the causal effects of unconscious events on both implicit and explicit attitudes and behavior, our endorsement of subliminal priming stops at the lab door, not on the airwaves or the campaign trail. Moreover, the use of truly subliminal priming in advertising is undoubtedly exceedingly rare. But the effects of consciously noticed but unappreciated (supraliminal) primes (Type 2 CUEs) are common throughout the social world and most obviously manipulated in the advertising realm.

The Stream of Political Information Processing

In the following chapters we set forth our affect-driven, dual-process model of the architecture and mechanisms that account for when, how, and why thoughts, feelings, and behavioral intentions come to mind automatically to promote the rationalization of political beliefs and attitudes. At this juncture let us outline our model in broad strokes, leaving for Chapter 2 a detailed description of the architecture and processes that promote motivated reasoning. We take a constructionist approach whereby the content of one's thoughts and coloration of feelings change moment by moment in response to both noticed and unnoticed "priming" events that link changes in the immediate environment to changes in political beliefs, attitudes, and behaviors.

When an individual is exposed to a communication, the concepts in the message – whether consciously attended to or not – begin to activate the attendant concepts in *long-term memory*. Once a concept is activated, its activation spreads to all its related concepts (Collins and Loftus 1975), whether that connection is semantic or affective. As political communications generally involve a large number of concepts coming into perception in rapid succession (think of television ads combining still images, words, or video with a voice over narration, all of which would simultaneously activate associations in long-term memory), individual concepts become activated and reactivated in real time as they, and concepts related to them, are perceived. Then, in a matter of moments, the activation levels of current concepts and their associated concepts decrease to make ready for what information comes next.

At this point in the process, the second type of memory becomes relevant. In contrast with long-term memory, *working memory* has a severely limited capacity: only about seven concepts can coexist in working memory simultaneously (Barsalou, 1992; Rumelhart and Ortony, 1977; Simon, 1967). These concepts in working memory, in a very real sense, are what the individual is consciously thinking about at that time. Researchers have envisioned the process of moving concepts from long-term memory to working memory through a pandemonium model (Larson, 1996; Neisser, 1967; Ratcliff and McKoon, 1996) in which activation is seen as a competition between all of the activated concepts, with those that are most activated, for whatever reason, being selected for further processing in working memory.

It is at this point that the parallel nature of the affective and semantic connections becomes critical. Those concepts that are most semantically implicated by the communication are of course likely to win the competition, and move into working memory. So, if an individual is reading a message about tax policy, the concept of taxes is going to be constantly activated and reactivated, as many of the concepts in the communication will either be about taxes directly, or about concepts closely related to taxes that will cause its further activation. However, the concepts related to taxes that are most likely to be brought into working memory, and therefore potentially enter the conscious awareness of the individual as relevant considerations, are those that are *both* semantically and affectively related to the concept. Suppose that taxes are viewed negatively, but there are an equal number of positively and negatively evaluated concepts that are semantically related to taxes (public works projects and tax refunds might be seen positively, while IRS audits and tax preparation might have a negative affective connection). Because the activation of the concept of taxes spreads both affectively and semantically, those concepts that are both semantically and affectively connected with the concept of taxes will most likely pop into working memory. So, when a message mentions taxes, a negatively viewed concept, the other associations that come into working memory are going to be biased in favor of other negatively viewed concepts. IRS audits rather than positively perceived public works projects are likely to win out.

Figure 1.4 presents an overview of our account of the stream of information processing from the initial unconscious registration of an event to the generation of an evaluative response. *The fundamental assumption driving our model is that both affective and cognitive reactions to external and internal events are triggered unconsciously, followed spontaneously by the spreading of activation through associative pathways which link thoughts to feelings, so that very early events, even those that remain invisible to conscious awareness, set the direction for all subsequent processing.* It is only at the tail end of this stream of processing that we become consciously aware of the associated thoughts and feelings generated moments earlier. It is at this moment that we experience what subjectively seems to be consciously initiated thinking and reasoning (Custers and Aarts, 2010; Libet, 1985).

Most of the key concepts and processes in our theory are represented in Figure 1.4, starting with the left to right causal directionality of processing through time. A stimulus event triggers the stream of processing, proceeding through affective and then cognitive mediators, and perhaps leading to the construction of evaluations of political objects and conscious deliberation. As a function of time, attention, and other factors, the likelihood of subjective

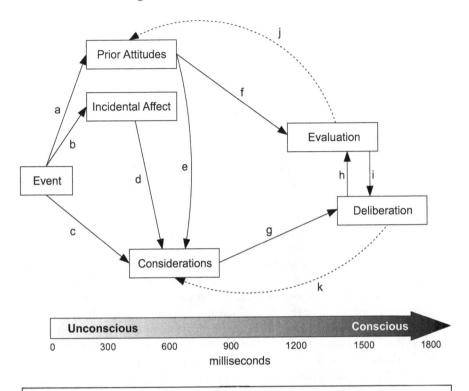

FIGURE 1.4. A Dual Process Model of Political Evaluation

awareness also increases left to right. Each arrow in the figure represents a theoretical process hypothesis. It is worth noting before we introduce these hypotheses that the conventional model of political reasoning involves only the c-g-h sequence in Figure 1.4: an event triggers the retrieval of cognitive considerations from memory, from which conscious deliberations are constructed, yielding reasoned evaluations.

While such controlled political cognition may sometimes occur, our dual process model claims that all thinking is suffused with feeling, and these feelings arise automatically within a few milliseconds (in our data as little as thirteen milliseconds) of exposure to a sociopolitical object or event. This is the *hot cognition* hypothesis that stands at the center of our theory of motivated political reasoning. Affect is primary in our theory because it arises first in the stream of processing, is unintentional, and is difficult to control. Almost immediately, the decision stream becomes affectively charged, viscerally "hot," and thereupon embodies our thoughts, providing proprioceptive feedback to mental processing (as shown, for example, by Damasio, 1994). Some of these feelings are attitudes that are intrinsic to the stimulus object (arrow a), while others are incidental or semantically unrelated to the stimulus (arrow b). Any subsequent considerations, deliberations, and evaluations are necessarily influenced by spontaneous affect. In terms of Figure 1.4, conventional political reasoning (causal path c-g-h) can occur only in the context of hot cognition.

Shortly after the arousal of positive and/or negative feelings, activation will spread along well-traveled associative pathways from, say, Obama to president to African-American to Democrat, thereby enriching our semantic understanding of the original stimulus. This is the *spreading activation* hypothesis (arrow c), well-established in cognitive psychology as the primary mechanism of memory retrieval. Note that many considerations may receive and send activation and thereby influence the stream of processing, but only a small number of highly activated considerations will reach conscious awareness – perhaps the 7 ± 2 chunks suggested in early psychological research (Miller, 1956).

In the context of just-aroused feelings, the retrieval of considerations will be biased in the direction of the valence of initial affect. This is the *affective contagion* hypothesis (arrow d) and the *motivated bias* hypothesis (arrow e). A flag, emotive music, an attractive candidate, or a celebrity spokesperson all influence the character of thought by favoring the retrieval of affectively congruent considerations while suppressing incongruent ones. Though it is possible for strongly associated concepts to reverse the direction of initial affect (as when initial positive affect triggered by a picture of John Edwards becomes strongly negative upon semantic recognition and retrieval of memories of his adulterous affair), it is more likely that initial feelings will "snowball" through the retrieval of increasingly congruent considerations, eventually driving deliberations and evaluations through indirect causal pathways. Spontaneous feelings can also cause evaluations directly through *affect transfer* (arrow f). A sunny day reliably drives more positive evaluations of life satisfaction (Schwartz and Clore, 1988). We have described how facial attractiveness directly drives positivity in addition to favoring the retrieval of more positive considerations. For evangelicals, Huckabee's cross will promote a positive evaluation as well as prompting positive and more religious thoughts. The "rats ad" transferred negative affect directly onto evaluations of Al Gore. The twin influences of affect contagion and affect transfer are, we believe, among the most powerful and underappreciated sources of unexplained variation in studies of political evaluation.

With sufficient time and motivation, the retrieval of a set of considerations can trigger the construction of conscious deliberative reasoning given the motivation, opportunity, and cognitive wherewithal to query the immediate affective response (Devine, 1989; Gawronski and Bodenhausen, 2007; Olson and Fazio, 2009). This process, labeled *argument construction* (arrow g) in Figure 1.4, will depend heavily on the earlier processes of hot cognition, spreading activation, and affect contagion. The central processes of motivated reasoning, including disconfirmation biases and the active counterarguing of counterattitudinal evidence, invoke these affective biases on memory retrieval (Taber, Cann, and Kucsova, 2009; Taber and Lodge, 2006). Conventional models of political thought view the conscious construction of arguments and reasoning as the foundations of public opinion and the guideposts to rational political behavior. We are skeptical.

Out of the grist of deliberation, citizens might *construct evaluations* (arrow h). That is, they might consciously build their evaluations of political figures, groups, or ideas from well-reasoned foundations, as in the conventional c-g-h model. In the context of hot cognition, affect contagion, and affect transfer, however, such cold evaluations will be exceedingly rare. The central place accorded to intentional rational evaluation in political science, a vestige of Enlightenment mythology in our view, continues to mislead our discipline, despite the valiant efforts of a few critics (David Sears and George Marcus come to mind).

Far more common, we believe, will be the reverse causal pathway from evaluation to deliberation. This *rationalization* hypothesis (arrow i) asserts that the causal pathways in Figure 1.4 that travel through unconscious affect, and in particular the affect-driven evaluation processes, cause most of our deliberation about politics. It is not our claim that citizens are incapable of rational thought in the traditional sense defined by links c-g-h. Evidence is accumulating, however, that attitudes and behavioral intentions – even behavior itself – arise from automatic, uncontrolled processes and are often set before we begin seriously "thinking" about them. This the case, deliberation serves to rationalize rather than cause.

The two dashed arrows in Figure 1.4 represent updating processes through which affect and considerations may be stored back to memory for future use. *Affect updating* (arrow j) allows the feelings and evaluations associated with current unconscious and conscious thought to be linked to objects in memory, where they can be the source of future hot cognition. For example, upon processing a newspaper story about Barack Obama's handling of the BP Gulf oil spill, a citizen who was initially very positive about Obama may update her affect to be less positive or perhaps more ambivalent. *Belief updating* (arrow k) allows new beliefs or semantic associations to be stored in memory. This might include the creation of new memory objects (BP oil spill perhaps) or new linkages among objects (Obama and BP oil spill).

Notably absent from Figure 1.4 is any mention of emotions. In our theory, the appraisal of emotions follows and is directed by the arousal of valence affect and the motivating push of the concept's somatic linkage. Appraised emotions (for a review of the appraisal literature, see Scherer, Shorr, and Johnstone,

2001) can be important mediators between aroused affect and subsequent processing, but for reasons detailed in Chapter 2 we will focus our attention on the causally prior processes of unconscious valence affect.

Most of this processing – the establishing of affect, meaning, and intentions – is subterranean, each process following one upon the other in about a second of time. An inkling of conscious awareness begins 300–400 milliseconds after stimulus exposure with a felt sense of positive and/or negative feeling, followed by a rudimentary semantic understanding of the concept, both of which are based entirely on prior unconscious processes. People can report simple like-dislike judgments in about 500–800 milliseconds and make simple semantic categorizations in 700–1,000 milliseconds, depending in part on whether the priming context for the categorization facilitates or inhibits comprehension. It takes somewhat longer (1,000–2,500 milliseconds) to provide a scaled response, and even longer to answer open-ended questions. Were we to ask a committed Republican to evaluate Secretary of State Clinton using a simple like/dislike button response, it would take about 700 milliseconds to press the dislike button. It would take significantly longer to report any cognitive associations to Hillary Clinton, that, for example, she is a woman, a Democrat, or mother. Affect precedes and contextualizes cognition.

Finally, given sufficient time and motivation, people may think self-consciously and reflectively about the object of evaluation and their own reactions. A point about conscious deliberation bears repeating: though deliberation will trigger new rounds of unconscious processing, it cannot go back and alter earlier processes and responses. In short, though we may feel we direct our thoughts and behaviors through conscious reasoning, deliberation is a product of unconsciously determined, affectively driven processes. Conscious deliberation and rumination is from this perspective the *rationalization* of multiple unconscious processes that recruit reasons to justify and explain beliefs, attitudes, and actions. It is possible, though difficult, to override implicit responses, as when we explicitly censor our socially unacceptable group stereotypes (Devine, 1989; Greenwald and Banaji, 1995), though it is not clear how fully we can control the "cognitive monster" of unconscious processing (Bargh, 1999). Our key argument and justification for the book title begins with, but then goes well beyond this primitive form of rationalization, to show how citizens' snap judgments of likeability *as well as* their systematic thinking about political candidates and issues is motivated reasoning – a rationalization process driven by unconscious affective biases (for a parallel argument through the quite different lens of Affective Intelligence Theory, see Marcus, 2002). Emotions, like beliefs and attitudes, are reconstructed from what is made accessible to consciousness from unconscious memory processes, and in our model the positive and/or negative evaluative tally linked to an attitudinal object anchors the construction process.

For these and many more reasons, we are skeptical of the ability of citizens to reliably access or veridically report their beliefs and attitudes. Our discipline's reliance on verbal self-report introduces a bushel basket of conceptual and measurement problems. In addition to well-known problems with the survey response (Tourengeau, Rips, and Rasinski, 2000), there is the obvious fact that the interview context, by design a sterile environment, is nothing like the immediate, situationally rich context that sparked the attitudinal response. In fact, it may well be the case that the simple act of asking questions promotes an intellectualization process that dampens the affective connection between thoughts and feelings (Epstein, 1972; 1992). These reasoned responses are no longer heartfelt, but affect negative *beliefs about the experience, not the experience itself*. Absent a somatosensory connection to the experience itself, the response is not embodied. Without a visceral boost the response is what Paula Neidenthal and her colleagues call a "cold, as-if emotional response" (Niedenthal, Halberstadt, and Setterlund, 1997; Niedenthal, Halberstadt, and Innes-Ker, 1999).

That the visceral experience need not be heart palpitating is demonstrated in a series of experiments carried out by Risen and Critcher (2011) testing a "visceral fit" hypothesis, the prediction that one's current bodily state – warmth, thirst, hunger – that "fits" the evaluation of a worldly event – here specifically aspects of global warming – will be judged more credible and likely. So, for example, feeling hungry will strengthen your estimate of the likelihood of famine, being thirsty makes droughts more probable.

In Study 1 on the Cornell campus during the months of September and October (with outside temperatures ranging from 49° F to 89° F) participants were taken outdoors for a psychophysical experiment ostensibly to measure the perceived height of various campus landmarks, then responded to a series of issue questions on eleven point scales, chief among them a CNN Poll question: "Which of the following statements comes closest to your view of global warming?" with the scale ranging from "Global warming is a proven fact" to "Global warming is a theory that has not yet been proven." Next, they reported their party ID and ideological self-placement (combined into a left-right index), and finally checked those terms they believed applied to their current physical state: hungry, thirsty, warm, tired, and chilly, while the experimenter measured the ambient outside temperature. Regressing belief in global warming on the outside temperature, left-right index, and the interaction term, ambient temperature proved to be as strong a predictor of belief in the validity of global warming, $\beta = .24$, t(63), as ideology, $\beta = .22$, t(63), and was not qualified by an interaction, with both liberals and conservatives reporting greater belief on warmer days.

In Study 2, to break the obvious diagnosticity of outdoor temperature to global warming, participants were randomly assigned to complete the survey in either a small heated room (81° F) or in an identical nonheated room (73° F). As in Study 1, both liberals and conservatives in the warmer environment were significantly more likely to believe that global warming was a proven fact, again without an interaction with ideology, although here ideology was a stronger predictor than room temperature, ostensibly because the temperature indoors was not as readily associated with the outside weather. In other studies in this project pictures on the computer screen of desert scenes or snowy weather produced the expected viscera-fit effects. The favored explanation for the effects is that the bodily response makes it easier for people to imagine and simulate the belief. These "embodiment" effects are subtle and not readily recognized as influential and easily misattributed (Payne et al., 2005).

The Rationalizing Voter

Before turning to the empirics supporting this opinionation-as-rationalization argument, let us flesh out our line of reasoning for seeing citizens as rationalizing voters. Our model asserts that motivated reasoning – the systematic biasing of judgments in favor of automatically activated, affectively congruent beliefs and feelings – is built into the basic architecture and information processing mechanisms of the brain (Gazzaniga, 1992; 1998). Because both the spreading of semantic associations and biases favoring the retrieval of affectively congruent thoughts and feelings operate below awareness, the conscious, systematic construction of beliefs, attitudes, and intentions is necessarily dependent on those considerations and feelings that have been made available through unconscious processes. When called on to make an evaluation, state a preference, recount or justify an opinion, conscious introspection will not have access to the operative unconscious causal processes or many of the considerations that entered the decision stream unconsciously. Respondents, if pressed to account for their beliefs or attitudes, will as natural storytellers generate rationales that are more plausible than veridical (Clore and Isbell, 2001).

While the general principles guiding the role of accessibility and retrieval of information are well-known (Anderson, 1983), the implicit versus explicit distinction goes to the heart of our discipline's problems in accounting for how, when, and why citizens think, reason, and act as they do. We expect that people will routinely rely on their spontaneously generated thoughts and feelings to explain their responses and behaviors, unless confronted by irrefutable evidence, social pressure, challenges to self-image, or interviewer pressure. And even here they will only experience these challenges as filtered through preconscious processes that have a built-in capacity for motivated bias. The experimental literature presents clear evidence that automatic processes underlie *all* conscious processing and are especially powerful determinants of top-of-the-head evaluations when

- affectively charged cognitions are available and strong;
- explicit measures are tainted by social desirability, deceit, or prejudice;
- one is under time pressure;
- attentional resources are otherwise engaged or distracted;

- an environmental event is noticed but not recognized as being influential; and
- one's behavior is not so consequential as to trigger such questions as "why did I think, feel, say, or do that?"

These situational and contextual factors appear to characterize the world of politics for many of us most of the time, where, typically, the consequences of our political beliefs and attitudes are distant and indirect, where uncertainty reigns, rumination is rarely called for, where one is easily distracted by rapid-fire TV images, and via selective media attention we infuse our thoughts with congenial cues.

Sometimes, of course, there is a feeling of unease with the considerations that come to mind, or a sensed dissociation of implicit from explicit thoughts, feelings, and intentions. If consciously conflicted, one may make the effort to resolve the conflict among and between thoughts and feelings (Gawronski and Bodenhausen, 2007). But there is now reason to believe that spontaneous activations are difficult to correct, even when people are encouraged to stop, think, deliberate, or actively try to work their way through a problem (Erisen, Lodge, and Taber, 2008; Forgas, 1995; Wilson, 2002). When constructing a response, the sample of retrieved considerations will likely be skewed in favor of affectively congruent associations. Because we are but dimly aware of the reasons for the thoughts that come to mind, those recollections entering the decision stream feel right, cannot be directly fathomed, do not typically produce a sense of dissonance, and consequently are not readily open to disconfirmation unless directly challenged.

While this argument of cognition as rationalization may seem radical, it is hardly new (see Achen and Bartels, 2006; Russell, 2003; Zajonc, 2000). Pioneering experimental work by Benjamin Libet (1985; 1993; 2004) demonstrates how consciousness lags behind even the intention to act. In a series of experiments, participants were asked to watch a sweeping clock hand, and report the moment when they made the decision to move a finger, while the researcher recorded their brain waves. Analysis of the EEGs revealed that a "readiness potential" to move the finger began approximately half a second before the conscious intention to move, but – and here is where the illusion of control comes in – the subjects retroactively predated their conscious experience by almost the exact amount of time it took the decision to reach consciousness (Libet, 2004), making the illusion of conscious control over these actions compelling. If the conscious decision to perform a physical action comes well after the intention has been formed, the notion that an individual's considered opinion precedes an automatic process is as likely an "illusion of conscious will" (Wegner, 2002).

These same processes apply to judgments. Zajonc (1980, 1984) found that even when people are able to give a reason for their judgments, the reasons they give are often not the ones that informed the decision. This can be seen in the aforementioned "mere exposure" effect, in which subjects are found to prefer Chinese ideograms to which they had been previously exposed, without realizing that they had seen them before. Familiarity breeds liking. For our purposes, the most interesting aspect of the mere exposure effect is that, just as Libet's subjects mistook when they had consciously initiated a simple physical motion so as to match it with the onset of unconscious initiation, Zajonc's participants were able to give sensible reasons for liking one ideogram over another. Though they were consciously unaware of having seen some of the ideograms more frequently than others, they readily misattributed their preferences to the aesthetic value of the more frequently presented ideograms, rather than to the mere exposure effect where familiarity itself spurred liking. People are experts at rationalizing unconscious judgments. Moreover, even when explicitly told that they have been primed to evaluate the images in a pro or con way, people were still unable to overcome their automatic affective response (Winkielman, Zajonc, and Schwarz, 1997).

These effects – broadly speaking, the unconscious linking of feelings to thoughts to preferences to behavioral intentions – conspire to promote our view of the individual as more rationalizer than rational decision maker. Treating the citizen as a motivated reasoner will require a revolution in how we think about and model citizens' mental representations of the world and the processes involved in the formation and expression of their political beliefs, attitudes, and behavior. When we limit ourselves to equating cognition with conscious awareness and the expression of preferences with the conscious integration of costs and benefits, as is the practice in political behavior research, it proves impossible to understand contemporary social, cognitive, and neuropsychology, and consequently makes it impossible to understand how, when, and why citizens think, reason, and act as they do.

At this juncture, we are highly skeptical of the ability of citizens to reliably and veridically access the sources of their beliefs, the reasons for their attitudes, their past, present, future intentions, and actions. Much if not most of our experience takes place outside our conscious awareness, and as our recollections fade from memory they are replaced by socially constructed rationalizations about how and why we as well as others think and behave. What recollections are activated depends on the set of preconditions operative in the environment *at the moment* and what's going on inside the individual's head *at the moment*. The key here is that once triggered, once the extant attitude enters the decision stream, thoughts are linked to feelings, feelings to intentions, and intentions to choices without necessarily triggering conscious or deliberative guidance.

Looking Ahead

Chapter 2 will detail our affect-driven, dual-process theory of motivated reasoning, and ensuing chapters will show how, when, and why the automatic activation of affect spontaneously impacts the way citizens evaluate political leaders, groups, issues, and events. A basic finding, demonstrated in multiple experiments, is that feelings enter the evaluative process before cognitive considerations and immediately influence what thoughts and preferences will enter the decision stream. As we have already argued, this finding challenges the way we political scientists conventionally model the relationship between beliefs and attitudes — for most people most of the time the causal arrow flies spontaneously from affect to cognition, from preferences to thinking, from feeling to action.

As is common to the human condition, this "affect heuristic" is both a benefit and a problem, sometimes working well, at others leading us astray: on the plus side the primacy of affect promotes coherent thinking and attitudinally consistent behavior, but at one and the same time it is responsible for deep-rooted processes that bias how we think and reason. Where, when, how, and for whom conscious processing will successfully override the automatic intuitive response is the critical unanswered question that goes to the heart of all discussions of human rationality and the meaning of a responsible electorate. We leave a discussion of this paradox to the Conclusion but must forewarn the reader that we see no obvious resolution to the dilemma and cannot in good faith counsel as to when to follow the dictates of the heart.

The *John Q. Public* Model of Political Information Processing

In this chapter we set forth our theory of the architecture and mechanisms that determine when, how, and why unconscious thoughts, feelings, and goals come to mind to guide downstream political behavior. We take a constructionist approach whereby the content of one's thoughts, the coloration of feelings, the plausibility of goals, and the force of behavioral dispositions change moment-by-moment in response to "priming" events that spontaneously link changes in the environment to changes in beliefs, attitudes, and behavior. Far from the consciously directed decision-making assumed by conventional models, we see political behavior as the result of innumerable unnoticed forces, with conscious deliberation little more than a rationalization of the outputs of automatic affective and cognitive processing.

The Architecture of Memory

How we picture the world – our mental representation of self, other, and what is out there – is "the residue of a lifetime of observation, thought, and experience," both conscious and unconscious (Carlston, 2010: 38). A cornerstone of any model of political reasoning then is the citizen's preexisting knowledge and predilections. These long-term factors, functionally speaking, require a *long-term memory* (LTM) for storing facts, beliefs, images, feelings, habits, and behavioral predispositions, plus a mechanism for "moving" such conceptual objects as leaders, groups, events, and issues from LTM into *working memory* (WM) where they can be attended to (Barsalou, 1992; Rumelhart and Ortony, 1977; Sanford, 1987; Simon, 1969). Conscious attention is very limited, hence the need for heuristics, habits, and other simplifying mechanisms for thinking, reasoning, and doing (Cialdini, 2001; Lau and Redlawsk, 2006; Lupia, McCubbins, and Popkin, 2000; Kuklinski and Quirk, 2000). The important point is that those concepts and their connections processed in working memory are strengthened and the resulting representation modifies the linkages in LTM.

The primary bottlenecks of consciousness, which stand in stark contrast to our much greater capacity for unconscious thought, are: (1) the small capacity of WM, which allows us to hold 7±2 chunks of information in awareness at any one time (Miller, 1956); (2) the necessary displacement of old information in order to bring new information into conscious WM; and (3) strictly serial conscious processing, in which information must be processed sequentially (Payne, 1982). By contrast, LTM is vast and capable of highly parallel processing. The limits on conscious awareness are the primary reason for our being "bounded rationalists."

Associative Memory. LTM is organized associatively, and it is useful to think of knowledge structures in LTM metaphorically as configurations of *nodes* linked one to another in a network of associations (Anderson, 1983; 1993), or if you prefer as neurons "bundled" together by weighted connections (Read and Miller, 1998; Smith, 1999). Were we able to tap into a citizen's full political knowledge structure, there might be tens of thousands of conceptual objects (among them surely a node for Barack Obama), with a complex network of linked associations along well-trod pathways to the presidency, the Democratic Party, his characteristics and perceived traits, perhaps his stand on a few issues, and maybe an inferential abstraction or two, that, for example, he is somewhat liberal. Concepts are linked associatively to form beliefs (conceptual relations) and attitudes (affective relations), the strength of both varying from weak to strong. Moreover, memory objects vary in their *accessibility* – the ease with which a stored object lying dormant in LTM can be activated to influence information processing or even retrieved into conscious WM (Fazio, 2007).

Figure 2.1 sketches the architecture of a hypothetical citizen's political knowledge structure, denoting different types of memory objects by shape, object accessibility by border thickness, and strength of association between nodes by the thickness of links. Here and throughout "object" refers to any sort of concept in LTM, be it a person, event, abstract idea, image, or your left foot. This particular example depicts knowledge about Barack Obama of a white American citizen, who identifies with the Republican Party. A variety of associations to Obama are shown, including perceived attributes or characteristics (ovals), groups or political persons (rectangles), emotions (rounded rectangles), and behavioral intentions (diamonds). Darker shaped borders signify more accessible objects. Links between conceptual objects represent beliefs, with darker links showing stronger beliefs; links to affective objects represent feelings or attitudes. All objects carry positive and/or negative affect, denoted by plus and minus signs respectively, and darker plus/minus signs represent stronger affect.

Attitude is a central concept, both historically and in contemporary research, of this and virtually all social-psychological models of human behavior, with attitude defined simply as the expression of one's likes and dislikes, what one

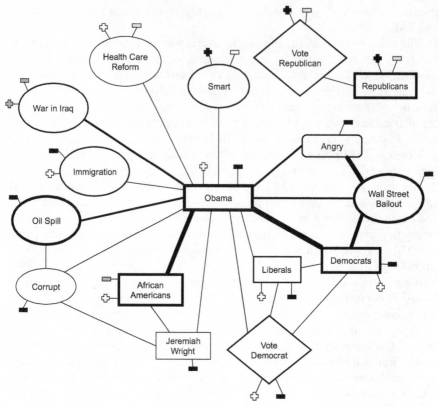

FIGURE 2.1. The Structure of Political Beliefs, Attitudes, and Intentions for a Hypothetical Citizen

favors or opposes, views positively or negatively (Petty and Briñol, 2010: 335). Here, following Fazio's lead (2007), we define attitude as an evaluative tally attached to an object in long-term memory. The hypothetical citizen in Figure 2.1 is generally negative or at best ambivalent toward President Obama. Obama is most strongly associated with Democrats and African Americans, and is appraised negatively for the oil spill recovery. This citizen is unlikely to vote for Obama, is especially angry (an appraised emotion that has been stored back to memory) for the Wall Street bailout, is ambivalent about the war in Iraq, and she has a weak voting preference for Republicans.

Our model, named *John Q. Public (JQP)* departs significantly from earlier node-link associative models (Anderson, 1983; Lodge and Stroh, 1993) in directly integrating positive and negative affect and goal-directed behavioral dispositions (in our example, the vote intention) into the model. From this Dewey-like "thinking-is-for-doing" vantage point, thought, feeling, and action are linked together, sometimes loosely, other times strongly, depending on one's history of experience.

Strong, affectively charged objects (in Figure 2.1, Obama, Democrats, African Americans, and to a lesser extent Wall Street) are routinely formed by evaluative (Pavlovian) conditioning where a previously neutral object is repeatedly paired with such affectively charged unconditioned stimuli as "evil," "dangerous," a frown, or a curse. Once formed, such evaluative associations can be activated spontaneously on mere exposure, without conscious consideration of their validity, and then prove to be remarkably resistant to countervailing information. The second type of relationship depicted in this knowledge structure are beliefs linking one concept to another, here for instance, that Democrats were responsible for the Wall Street bailout. Such propositions are more cognitively based and less resistant to disconfirmation, *if* the individual is aware of a contradiction, confronts strong countervailing evidence, is motivated to challenge the spontaneously activated positive or negative responses, and has the opportunity and cognitive wherewithal to adjust the attitude. As we will soon see, when concepts are affectively charged, as is the case for all self-related social concepts, attitude change is difficult at best.

It is worth emphasizing that implicit and explicit beliefs, attitudes, and goals are represented in much the same way in this memory architecture (Carlston, 2010; Gawronski and Bodenhausen, 2007; Ferguson and Porter, 2010). From this perspective – now the consensual view (Petty, Fazio, and Briñol, 2009; De Houwer and Moors, 2010) – explicit beliefs and attitudes require some level of deliberation and can be measured directly, typically by simply asking if the individual likes him/her/it. In contrast, people are either unaware of holding implicit beliefs or attitudes (Wilson, Lindsey and Schooler, 2000) or far more common they are unaware of the factor(s) that create, maintain, or change their beliefs or attitudes. Implicit and explicit beliefs, attitudes, or intentions are not different in how they are represented in long-term memory, but they do require different measurement strategies. Unlike the direct approach used for measuring explicit attitudes, measures of implicit attitudes or beliefs must be more indirect. Early approaches included the unobtrusive observation of bodily gestures, eye contact, and a variety of physiological responses (Webb et al., 1966). Now-a-days implicit beliefs or attitudes are routinely inferred from response latencies – the time it takes for a respondent to indicate a like or dislike, belief, preference, or intention (Fazio, 2007; Huckfeldt, Levine, Morgan, and Sprague, 1999; Lavine, Borgida, and Sullivan, 2000; Lodge, Taber, and Verhulst, 2011; Teige-Mocigemba, Klauer, and Sherman, 2010; Wentura and Degner, 2010).

Spreading Activation. But how is information moved from LTM into conscious WM? Spreading activation provides the mechanism. An object node in LTM switches from being dormant to a state of readiness with the potential to be moved into WM when it is activated, either by direct recognition or because it is linked to an associated object of thought. Figure 2.2 depicts the activation process, with the Y-axis representing the level of activation of a given node in LTM and the X-axis representing time in milliseconds. The rise time from

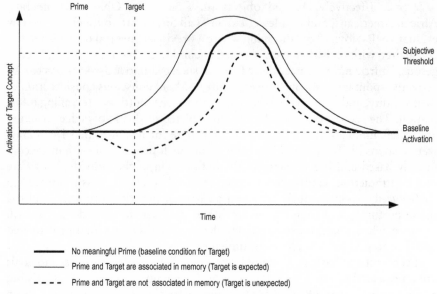

FIGURE 2.2. Activation of a Node in LTM

dormant-state to activation threshold is almost instantaneous (100–200 milliseconds). Were you thinking of George Washington's false teeth? Are you now? Activation decays quite rapidly so that an energized node will drop back to its baseline level of potentiation in less than a second if there is no further source of activation.

In Figure 2.2, the distinction between unconscious and conscious processing corresponds to moving across the subjective threshold. All processes below that line involve LTM or other nonconscious processes, while processes above the line involve WM and conscious awareness. Imagine a person reading "President Obama" in a newspaper headline. Without perceptible effort, the concept Barack Obama is activated and energizes the network of links to related concepts (as seen earlier in Figure 2.1), where Obama primes our respondent's strong semantic associations to Democrat and African American, as well as to her beliefs (he favors the war in Iraq), traits (he's smart but corrupt), feelings ("he makes me mad"), and behavioral intentions ("I will vote against him"). For a few hundred milliseconds, these associated concepts remain in a heightened state of arousal.

It is useful and appropriate to think of priming through spreading activation as producing *pre*conscious expectations. Figure 2.2 shows the activation of associations under different stimulus priming contexts. Consider again the activation of the concept Obama from a newspaper headline. Concepts associated with Obama in LTM receive spreading activation, thereby raising their potential so that any subsequent processing that passes activation to these energized concepts may well drive them over the threshold into consciousness. If the citizen depicted in Figure 2.1 were primed by exposure to the concept Obama, it would facilitate (i.e., speed up) subsequent retrieval of African American or Wall Street Bailout (the "expected" activation curve in Figure 2.2). Priming concepts has several predictable effects on information processing: "expected" associations take substantially less processing time to activate and consequently will have a better chance of getting into WM, of being processed faster, and thereby of "framing" the perception, recognition, and interpretation of subsequent information down the processing stream.

Conversely, spreading activation can *inhibit* the processing of *un*expected categories (the slowest activation curve in Figure 2.2). When a concept is encountered unexpectedly, more bottom-up processing is necessary before it may pass threshold and enter WM. If the word "Einstein" were heard immediately before reading a newspaper headline about Barack Obama, this would surely inhibit the recognition of such semantically unrelated concepts as Obama, Democrat, or oil spill, which would consequently take more time to recognize and more effort to process. Finally, the middle course in Figure 2.2 represents a neutral or baseline case in which no "expectations" are created by a prime. The nonword letter string BBB, for example, conveys no semantic expectations, so would neither facilitate nor inhibit the recognition and categorization of subsequent concepts.

The long and the short of it: the closer the connections among and between beliefs, feelings, and intentions the more quickly coactivated associations pass threshold. This is the rationale for reaction time measures – the retrieval of related concepts are speeded up, distant concepts slowed down. Specific to attitudes, the activation of affectively congruent concepts is facilitated, incongruent pairings inhibited.

The strong implication of this architectural model is that all beliefs and attitudes will be constructed in real time from whatever cognitive and affective information is momentarily accessible from LTM. Keep in mind our earlier cautionary note against treating each conceptual node as a crystallized "point" in memory. Beliefs, attitudes, predilections, and intentions – all the stuff of consciousness – are constructed on the fly, in real time, at the moment of perception from whatever associations – whether conscious or not – make their way into Working Memory.

The best evidence for this construction process comes from neurological studies of patients with brain lesions showing that the naming, comprehension, evaluation, and functional use of concepts is distributed in different areas of the brain. So, listening to Mozart's 40th *Symphony* activates hundreds of thousands of coordinated firings in the brain, with pitch processed in one set of neural regions, tempo in another, the timbre of a violin in another, all coming together seamlessly in a fraction of a second. Consider something more tangible – a tea cup. Visual agnosia is the inability of the brain to make sense of or make use of some part of an otherwise normal visual stimulus and is typified by the inability to recognize familiar objects or faces. This is distinct from blindness, which is a lack of sensory input to the brain due to damage to the eye, optic nerve, or the primary visual cortex. Visual agnosia is often due to stroke affecting the posterior occipital and/or temporal lobe(s) in the brain. The specific dysfunctions vary depending on the type of agnosia. Some sufferers are unable to copy drawings but are able to manipulate objects with good dexterity. Commonly, patients can name the object, here a tea cup, categorize it, but cannot describe its function; or the reverse, be able to drink from it appropriately but not know its name or describe its uses. Lesion studies clearly demonstrate that even crystallized objects, your left foot, or here a tea cup, are not "things" in long-term memory but are concepts constructed from multiple brain modules at the moment of perception (Farah, 1999).

What is critical here is that neither implicit nor explicit beliefs or attitudes represent a solitary "point" in memory but are constructed in real time by the spreading of activation to cognitive, affective, and behavioral associations. People do not store in memory associative links for every conceivable category, subtype, or situation encountered in the past. The direction and strength of links to people, places, and things varies by one's accumulated experiences across time and the immediate context. A puppy is generally not so "cute" when caught peeing on the rug. Intelligence is generally a positive trait but negative when seen in an enemy rather than a friend. If immediately prior to an assessment of George W. Bush a survey respondent were asked to evaluate the statement "All politicians are crooks," the negative link to politician would predictably make the evaluation of Bush more negative.

Given that one cannot store attitudes in memory corresponding to every object in every conceivable context and because of the attitude construction processes for integrating affective associations, people reason and behave in ways that reflect the mechanics of spreading activation (Anderson, 1983; Boynton and Lodge, 1994; Gawronski and Sritharan, 2010). The effect of subtle contextual factors like question wording, question order, and interviewer effects on explicit beliefs and attitudes is well documented (Bishop, 2004; Tourangeau, Rips, and Rasinski, 2000) and is exactly what one should expect from this constructionist perspective where the momentary activation of cognitive, affective, and motivational associations will influence how objects and events are first implicitly and perhaps later explicitly perceived, conceived, and acted upon.

Seven Postulates Drive the Formation and Expression of Political Attitudes

Our theory can be captured by seven central claims: information processing is largely automatic, it is infused with feelings, it is embodied in physiological systems, it is impelled by affect, it is responsive to the environment through online updating processes, and it builds momentum through affect transfer and affective contagion.

Postulate 1, Automaticity. What people think, feel, say, and do is a direct function of the information that is momentarily accessible from memory – be it the recall of facts and feelings, a recollected experience, or the turning of goals into action (Greenwald and Banaji, 1995). Feelings of pride and in-group solidarity that swell when flags wave and patriotic music plays in the background of political events, the subtle confidence felt in the presence of tall political candidates or infatuation for attractive or charismatic ones, or the unease experienced by some voters at the prospect of an African American or female president can influence political thinking outside conscious awareness.

Research on automaticity demonstrates that beliefs, feelings, and behavioral intentions will, if "contiguously activated," become so strongly connected in memory as to become *unitized* in a network of interdependent associations that enter the decision stream spontaneously on mere exposure to a "triggering event." Automatic processes, in which thoughts, feelings, and intentions come to mind unconsciously, on a time scale of milliseconds, contrast with the more effortful processes people engage in when they have sufficient time, motivation, awareness, and the cognitive resources to deliberate. Process matters: with the repeated association of thought to feeling, beliefs become affectively charged; feelings motivate intentions, and plans direct behavior. From this perspective, Antonio Damasio (1999) is right in seeing the brain as a "thinking machine for feeling."

Realizing that humans process information both consciously and uncon-sciously, theorists have proposed a conceptual distinction between attitudes that are the products of introspection and those that occur implicitly, outside of conscious appraisal. The labeling of one mode of processing as "conscious" emphasizes the reflective, deliberative character of responses to an "object" – whether person, place, event, thing, or idea – which generally (but not necessar-ily) involves verbal reasoning. Deliberative processes are cognitively effortful, demanding of attention, time consuming, and presumed to be based on an intentional search of memory for relevant facts and considerations. Such pro-cesses rely on the intensive use of WM, which as we have seen is severely limited in capacity and characterized by slow, one-chunk-at-a-time serial pro-cessing. Conversely, automatic processes – whether the immediate activation of cognitive associations (for example, Obama is a Democrat), the spontaneous activation of feelings (Republicans are evil; Democrats are dumb), or those habitual actions that operate "mindlessly" – are involuntary, fast, immediate, top of the head, and unlike conscious processes can be activated even when the individual's conscious attention is focused elsewhere. These processes rely on the spreading of activation to associated cognitive, affective, and behavioral connections in LTM, which is vast and based on rapid parallel processing. People are frequently unaware of the specific situational and contextual factors that bring to mind the thoughts, feelings, and intentions that appear introspec-tively to be the outcome of a deliberative evaluation of the evidence (Wegner, 2002). Implicit processes, moreover, can, and oftentimes do, produce sound decisions, sometimes better than those based on careful deliberation (Dijkster-huis and van Olden, 2006; Hofmann and Wilson, 2010; Verhulst, Lodge and Taber, 2010).

Triggering effects, whether consciously recognized or not, are ubiquitous in everyday life. Virtually all mental representations – be they words, pictures, sounds, or smells – appear to be "primeable," that is, activated incidentally or unobtrusively in one context to influence one's thoughts, feelings, goals, and even complex behaviors in another context, without the person necessarily being aware of having been influenced (Gawronski and Sritharan, 2010).

To call a process "automatic" it must satisfy four criteria (Bargh, 1997). It must be *spontaneous*, that is, the process or response must be triggered even if the individual is not consciously engaged in making an evaluation. The automatic influences on the judgment task must be *unconscious*. The response must be *uncontrollable*; once triggered, the process runs its course without conscious monitoring or guidance. And the process must *expend few cognitive resources*. In many familiar situations, as well as in such uncommon settings as a survey interview, automatic processes will directly impact the expression of evaluations, judgments, goals, decisions, and actions with little or no conscious or deliberative guidance. Given that implicit attitudes operate below conscious awareness, they cannot be measured directly, as typically by verbal self-report (De Houwer and Moors, 2010).

Unconscious priming effects have been demonstrated experimentally on vir-tually all higher mental processes:

- in making social judgments (Greenwald and Banaji, 1995);
- in attitude formation (Betsch, Plessner, Schwieren, and Guetig, 2001);
- the expression of beliefs (Neely, 1977);
- the expression of attitudes (Fazio, Sanbonmatsu, Powell, and Kardes, 1986);
- liberal – conservative ideology (Jost, Nosek, and Gosling, 2008);
- religious appeals (Albertson, 2011);
- trait inferencing (Newman and Uleman, 1989);
- self-esteem (Dijksterhuis, Albers, and Bongers, 2009);
- in-group and out-group identifications (Perdue, Dovidio, Gurtman, and Tyler, 1990);
- racial and gender stereotyping (Craemer, 2008; Devine, 1989; Dovidio, Evans, and Tyler, 1986);
- such national symbols (Butz, 2009) as the American (Ferguson and Hassin, 2007; Schatz and Lavine, 2007), confederate (Ehrlinger et al., 2011), and Israeli (Hassin et al., 2007) flags;
- such judicial symbols as a gavel, lady justice, and a judge's robes (Gibson, Lodge, and Woodson, 2010);
- the making of moral judgments (Haidt, 2001);
- decision making across a variety of domains (Loewenstein and Lerner, 2003);

- the behavioral expression of egalitarian values in a competitive game (Bargh, Gollwitzer, Lee-Chai, Barndollar, and Troetsghel, 2001);
- corruption and the abuse of power (Chen, Lee-Chai and Bargh, 2001);
- evaluations of political candidates (Verhulst, Lodge, and Taber, 2010) and groups (Burdein, Lodge, and Taber, 2006);
- health decisions (Wiers, Houben, Roefs, de Jong, Hofmann, and Stacy, 2010);
- deliberate, reasoned belief systems such as political ideology (Jost, Nosek, and Gosling, 2008);
- deliberation about political policy issues (Erisen, Lodge, and Taber, 2007); and
- on a range of overt, goal-driven behaviors (Gollwitzer and Bargh, 1996), including consumer preferences and behavior (Perkins and Forehand, 2010).

Bargh (2007) draws an important distinction between *pre*conscious and *post*conscious automaticity. In postconscious automaticity one is aware of the stimulus but not cognizant of its influence on thoughts, feelings, or behaviors, whereas in preconscious automaticity the stimulus is experienced below the threshold of conscious awareness so that the observer is not aware of having been exposed to the priming stimulus let alone able to appraise its costs and benefits.

Telltale evidence of postconscious automatic processing is routinely discerned in public opinion surveys, showing up most obviously as question-wording and question-order effects (Tourangeau, Rips, and Rasinski, 2000). For example, a *Washington Post* opinion poll asked a national sample of Americans in November of 2002, when President Bush's approval rating was in the mid-sixties, whether the country was headed "in the right direction" or "was seriously off in the wrong direction." Immediately before or after this question, they asked whether the respondent approved or disapproved of the job Bush was doing as President. A postconscious "Bush effect" is implied by the finding that 42 percent of those asked the Bush approval question first believed the country was headed in the right direction, whereas only 34 percent felt that way when the Bush question was asked second. Outside of conscious awareness, respondents' positive feelings toward Bush influenced their assessments of the state of the nation. One suspects that this postconscious "Bush effect" would be more horns than halo by mid-2004, when approval ratings had dropped twenty points.

Our theory predicts that priming effects – whether sparked by a President's name, upbeat music in the background of a commercial, the sound of prison doors slamming shut in the Willie Horton ad, or even having "rats" jump out of the word "bureaucRATS" – would produce the same biasing effect on information processing. As with flags and other symbols in the backdrop of presidential speeches, the more subtle and unobtrusive the "manipulation" the stronger the effect is expected to be as it would not trigger conscious reflection

(Gibson and Caldeira, 2009; Mendelberg, 2001; Schwarz and Bless, 1992; Schwarz and Clore, 1983).

Greenwald and Banaji's (1995) Implicit Association Test (IAT) is currently the most popular postconscious procedure for measuring automaticity (see demonstrations of the IAT at http://implicit.harvard.edu). A meta-analysis by Greenwald, Poehlman, Uhlmann, and Banaji (2009) compared implicit to explicit measures (184 independent samples, 14,900 experimental subjects), finding that correlations vary widely – from 0.18 to 0.68, with an average implicit-explicit correlation across attitudinal, judgmental, and behavioral measures of 0.27. When the implicit and explicit measures were collected in the same session (156 of the 184 samples), this average correlation rose to 0.36. These low-to-moderate correlations carry much the same power as do explicit-to-explicit measures on the same variables (Nosek and Smyth, 2007).

Latent-variable structural models on these data demonstrate that a two-factor model, with implicit and explicit attitudes as separate factors, is superior to a single-factor specification. "That is, despite sometimes strong relations between implicit and explicit attitude factors, collapsing their indicators into a single factor resulted in a relatively inferior model fit. We conclude that these implicit and explicit measures assess related but distinct attitudinal constructs" (Nosek and Smyth, 2007: 1). Support for the distinct contribution of implicit and explicit measures of political attitudes was found by Roccato and Zogmaister (2010) in their two-wave panel study of the 2004 Italian National Election. Employing both a comprehensive survey of explicit political attitudes and the Implicit Association Test, they found consistent relationships between both measures and vote intention, with the IAT in the first wave showing a significant, though modest, improvement in prediction to the actual vote.

The consensual view is that implicit and explicit attitudes are different processes working from a single underlying memory system (Gawronski, Strack, and Bodenhausen, 2009). It is not the case that implicit attitudes are stored in one way and explicit in another. The clear distinction is between conscious versus unconscious awareness. Explicit attitudes are consciously considered responses for which one has time to form a response. They will be influenced by lots of unnoticed factors, but there will be an opportunity for control and consciously reasoned thought. Implicit attitudes are affective responses to stimuli generated outside conscious awareness that one cannot control or consciously reason about. It is more likely that an implicit response reflects affect stored directly with a memory object (i.e., OL tag), but here too the response will be influenced by lots of extraneous factors. We think it is a mistake to think of one as more "true" than another. Although both are subject to certain types of bias, we will show that there is more opportunity for motivated bias when people explicitly consider and evaluate the considerations in mind, but this doesn't make explicit attitudes less "true" because motivated biases are likely to move in the direction of underlying affect.

The wide range of correlations between implicit and explicit attitude mea-sures found by social psychologists is precisely what dual-process models pre-dict, and what we expect given *JQP*'s architecture and built-in processes. That is, in some processing contexts or on some issues one may become consciously aware of the feelings and beliefs that drive a downstream behavior, while in other contexts these currents of thought will remain unavailable to explicit reporting. We will critique the extensive literature analyzing the relations between implicit and explicit measures of attitude at the end of this chap-ter, once the logic and measures of implicit processing have been set forth and in the conclusion following our empirical demonstrations.

More recent research goes beyond the automaticity of beliefs and attitudes to focus on the postconscious activation of complex social behaviors. In a now classic experiment, Bargh, Chen, and Burrows (1996) primed the concept "elderly" by having participants in the treatment group unscramble five word strings such as "bank sweater a knit she" and "lives Florida water in he" into grammatically correct four word sentences as quickly as possible. In addition to "knits" and "Florida," the stereotypic elderly primes (both positive and nega-tive) were: worried, old, lonely, gray, selfishly, careful, sentimental, wise, stub-born, courteous, withdraw, forgetful, retired, wrinkle, rigid, traditional, bitter, obedient, conservative, dependent, ancient, helpless, gullible, cautious, alone, and of course, bingo. In the neutral treatment, the elderly prime words were replaced in scrambled sentences with words unrelated to the elderly stereotype (e.g., thirsty, clean, private). The behavioral dependent variable was the time, measured in seconds, it took subjects on completing the sentence unscrambling task to leave the lab and walk to the elevator. Those primed by the concept elderly took significantly longer than control subjects to walk the thirty meters to the elevator, even though none of the Type 2 primes for elderly referenced slowness of gait and the study participants were college students, not old folks. Yet, their mental representations of the elderly activated a rich behavioral script that included slow walking. Another study (among dozens of similar "ideomotor" demonstrations) primed one group of subjects to the concept "professor" and another to "soccer hooligan" and found (sigh of relief?) that the professor-primed group correctly answered more *Trivial Pursuit* questions than did those exposed to the hooligan primes (Dijksterhuis and van Knippen-berg, 1998).

While much of the priming literature is focused on the stereotyping of others (in the United States, most commonly Jews before WWII, then African Amer-icans, women, homosexuals, and more recently Muslims, the obese... and the list goes on [King, Shapiro, Hebl, Singletary, and Turner, 2006]), cur-rent research has taken an inward turn to examine the effects of one's own group identity on self-perceptions, expectations, and behavior. Here, for exam-ple, priming minorities' own group identifications has been demonstrated many times over to significantly lower their performance on standardized tests (Steel and Aronson, 1995). Called "stereotype threat," simply having African

Americans check off their race on a test form before taking a standardized test will result in a lower grade than if the identification question was asked after the test.

The same effect holds for women taking science tests. In a clever experiment demonstrating the subtle, insidious power of stereotype threat, Shih, Pittinsky, and Ambady (1999) worked with two stereotypes acknowledged commonly in the academy – Asians are good at math, and women are not. In their study, one group of Asian women completed a brief survey of attitudes toward coed dorms (which primed their gender identity), a second group was asked questions about their family history, language spoken at home, and such (to activate their ethnic identification), while the control group was asked neutral questions. Test performance on an objective math test matched the stereotype-threat expectation: performance was best in the Asian-identity condition, moderate in the control condition, and worst in the gender-identity condition. Here again, we see a postconscious effect: the women knew the cultural stereotype that was activated in the priming questions but were unaware of its potent effects on their performance.

In another series of remarkably subtle experiments suggesting the everyday importance of postconscious priming, Kay and colleagues (2004) investigated the effects of simple business Type 2 primes (for example, pictures of boardroom tables, men and women's business suits, attaché cases) on competitive behavior. Their hypothesis: common objects carry implicit psychological meaning (i.e., business is competitive) that will prime the behavior of experimental subjects who are in the unobtrusive presence of these objects. The design across studies was to first engage participants in a postconscious business-related priming task, and then in an ostensibly unrelated second study engage participants in one or another behavioral task in which they could act cooperatively or competitively.

Study 1 asked treatment subjects to match business-related pictures to word labels, while control subjects performed the same priming task for such non-business objects as a kite, sheet music, and a toothbrush. All subjects were then asked to complete twenty-four word fragments, nine of which connoted competition, among them (w)in, (p)ower, wa(r), and one ambiguous fragment, "c_ _ p_ _ _tive." While none of the participants reported awareness of the relevance of the priming task to the word fragment task, those primed with business objects completed significantly more competitive word fragments than the control group. Moreover twenty-four of thirty-four treatment subjects saw "competitive" in the fragment c_ _ p _ _ _ tive, compared with just thirteen of thirty three in the control group, who were slightly more likely to see "cooperative."

The next study looked beyond judgment to behavior. Following a similar postconscious picture-priming task, subjects were now asked to play an Ultimatum Game, in which one player chooses how to split $10 with another player in a one-time, take-it-or-leave-it proposition. Here too, the results show strong priming effects, even though the participants were consciously unaware of any connection between the picture primes and their subsequent behavior. All but one of the control subjects offered an even split, but seven of the eleven participants primed with business images offered significantly less.

The third study saves the best for last. The Ultimatum Game again, with all subjects in the role of choosing how much of $10 to offer another (unseen) player, but now there is no picture-priming task. Instead, subjects write down their take-it-or-leave-it offer in one of two settings: half made their offer in a room with a long wooden conference table on which lay at the far end a leather briefcase and before them a black leather portfolio and wide-barrel, silver, executive style pen to write down their offer and then place the sheet in the briefcase. The other half of the participants performed the same Ultimatum Game task in the same room, but now a student's backpack replaced the brief-case at the far end of the table, a cardboard box substituted for the executive portfolio, and the take-it-or-leave-it bid was made using a wooden pencil. After making their offer, all were asked to list the factors that contributed to their offer. None indicated being influenced by any of the objects in the room, yet the results show significant effects of condition on offer, with all ten subjects in the backpack condition opting for a 50:50 split, while only six of twelve in the business setting did so. A significant priming effect was also found in the dollar amounts offered: on average, the paltry sum of $3.89 was offered by those in the business setting, while a cooperative $5 was offered by those in the scruffy student setting.

These studies and many more demonstrate the influence of unappreciated priming events on perceptions, social judgments, and behavior (Bargh, 2007). Of special note here is that in each case, study participants were consciously aware of the environmental primes, but were unaware of their biasing effects. Similar processes, we expect, permeate everyday life outside the laboratory (Bargh, 1997), especially so in commercial and campaign advertising, which are geared to promote positive messages without being heavy-handed (Singer, 2010).

In contrast, *pre*conscious automatic responses – whether thoughts, feelings, motivations, or overt behaviors – occur spontaneously, within 300 to 500 milliseconds of a triggering event without conscious attention, awareness, intention, or monitoring. But who cares what happens in the blink of an eye? To answer this question, let us describe a trio of experiments by Dijksterhuis and Aarts (2003) that usher in themes that we will focus on when describing our own studies of automaticity in the evaluation of political leaders, groups, and issues. Dijksterhuis and Aarts set out to test the hypothesis, rooted in evolutionary theories of automatic vigilance, that people process negative stimuli more quickly than positive stimuli. Many studies have shown that negative events and objects demand more attention than do positives, but these Dutch studies looked one step earlier in the process in asking whether negative stimuli are detected faster and easier at the *pre*conscious level.

Study 1 tested whether participants would be able to detect positive or negative words flashed on a screen at the subliminal speed of 13 milliseconds, which is far too fast for conscious recognition. For half the trials, a positive or negative word appeared, for the other trials a nonword appeared. The subjects, who were fully informed in advance about the expected 50:50 frequency of words and nonwords but not of their valence, were asked after each trial whether they thought a word had or had not been presented. Not surprisingly at this subliminal exposure time, none of the subjects could consciously discriminate whether the stimulus flashed on the screen was a word or nonword, yet they correctly guessed significantly more of the negative than positive words. In short, what participants reported subjectively to be pure guesswork turned out to be systematically biased in favor of detecting negative stimuli.

But at what level did they perceive this negativity? Study 1 showed that negative words were detected faster, but it did not ask whether subjects preconsciously recognized the valence of the words. Studies 2 and 3 take this next step, asking participants to press one key when guessing positive words and another for negative. Again, words were presented at thirteen milliseconds, but now either a positive or negative word was flashed on every trial, without nonword foils. Results confirmed expectations: the proportion of correctly identified negative words was significantly higher than correctly identified positive words, despite the fact that participants believed they were shooting in the dark. But can we yet be sure that this preconscious vigilance for negative stimuli was truly affective? Perhaps the semantic meaning of negative words is somehow processed faster than positive words.

Study 3 eliminated this possibility by asking participants to guess which of two same-valenced words presented explicitly on the screen was a synonym of the subliminally presented word. The results were striking: although subjects were significantly better able to detect negative than positive words, they were unable to reliably identify the synonym. The valence of concepts was identified preconsciously but not the semantic meaning of the concepts. This then is a clear demonstration of preconscious affective processing and telltale evidence of a disjuncture between affective and semantic processing, with people able to "sense" that something is good or bad even though they are unable to tell you what it was they saw.

After five decades of well-replicated research, it is simply no longer tenable for those interested in understanding political attitudes, public opinion, campaigns, media, or vote decisions to ignore the effects of automaticity. Many, if not most, political scientists cling to an outmoded notion of rational behavior, in which citizens *cause* their issue stances, candidate preferences, and vote decisions through careful, intentional reasoning. Our research paints a very different portrait of the citizen as subject to the eddies and currents of innumerable priming events, some of which carry the potential to significantly alter the course of information processing in ways that the citizen does not notice and cannot control.

Postulate 2, Hot Cognition. Conventionally, political scientists like their fellow social scientists have viewed the "holy trinity" of cognition, affect, and behavior as conceptually distinct and analytically separable, with cognition primary in causing both affect and behavior (Eagly and Chaiken, 1993; Kinder, 1998). Now a half century into the cognitive revolution (Eysenck and Keane, 1995; Lackman, Lackman, and Battlefield, 1979; Lindsay and Norman, 1977), we are finding it impossible to reliably tease apart thinking from feeling from behavioral intentions. Central to our affect-driven dual process model of attitude is the *hot cognition postulate* (Abelson, 1963), which brings feelings center stage in human information processing in claiming that all socio-political concepts are affect-laden (Bargh, 1997; Fazio et al., 1986; Sears, 2000). Fazio's (1989) attitude theory, which is built into our theoretical architecture as represented in Figure 2.1, treats attitudes as object-evaluation associations stored in LTM memory, with their strength of association determining the likelihood that the evaluation will be activated on encountering the attitude object. Just as attitude objects can differ in the strength of their evaluative associations, people can differ in their chronic accessibility of evaluations (Lau, 1989). Specific to politics, all political leaders, groups, issues, symbols, and ideas thought about and evaluated in the past become affectively tagged – positively, negatively, or both – and with repeated coactivation an evaluative charge is linked directly to the concept in long-term memory. Affective tags represent the value of social objects as good, bad, or ambivalent.

With repeated evaluations an affective tag is linked to a concept and springs to mind spontaneously upon mere exposure to the associated object, thereby signaling the concept's affective coloration. By election eve, most citizens will have formed impressions of the major candidates, parties, and issues and these feelings will be inescapably activated on their mere mention and will predictably come to mind most strongly and rapidly for those citizens who have given the most thought to the campaign. At the moment the president's image on the TV screen passes threshold, one's feelings about him come immediately to mind followed by his strongest cognitive associations. These accumulating positive and/or negative affective charges stimulate somatic changes in the body that will be experienced as positive or negative affect and then if strong enough to call for an answer to the question "why do I feel this way?" be labeled as a discrete emotion (for example, anger, fear, joy), with or without conscious awareness (Westen and Blogov, 2007).

The impact of context on evaluations follows directly from the *JQP* model. If "jobs" is primed for a working class citizen, "business" may be seen in a positive light, while in the context of "Wall Street," "business" will likely be evaluated negatively. Note too that one is ambivalent when there are links to both positivity and negativity, as with "health care reform" and "the war in Iraq" in Figure 2.1. From our constructionist perspective, the evaluation of

an object represents the integration of multiple sources of affective information from the object itself (Obama is negative) as well as from its strongest
associations (Democrats is negative).

The direct linking of feelings to concepts to goals and to behavioral intentions has profound implications for our conception of human information
processing. The associative strength between an object (for example, politician) and its evaluation is conceived as varying along a continuum from nil –
an object with little or no affective association, a "nonattitude" (Converse,
1964) – to a "crystallized attitude," that is, an object with a strong, chronically
accessible, univalent evaluation. Whereas weak and nonattitudes require effortful, piecemeal, bottom-up construction, the stronger the association between
an object in memory and its affective tally the less time and effort needed to
bring the attitude to mind, with objects carrying strong affective links activated
automatically on mere exposure, without the observer necessarily being aware
of even having perceived the triggering event (see Bargh, Chaiken, Govender,
and Pratto, 1992).

Hot cognition helps solve the problem posed by the fourteenth-century
French scholastic Jean Buridan, a student of William of Occam, who argued:
"If a hungry ass were placed exactly between two hay-stacks in every way
equal, it would starve to death, because there would be no motive why it
should go to one rather than to the other" (quoted in Brewer, 1898, *Dictio-
nary of Phrase and Fable*). Most humans, unlike Buridan's ass, are equipped
to solve such "equilibrium problems" by tagging the valence of goals which
thereupon facilitates the making of quick, intuitive, directional choices (Wilson, 2002). Because affect permeates the entire decision-making system, beliefs,
feelings, and actions will typically cohere (Thagard, 2000; 2006). When things
go wrong, of course, there is a good chance that both thoughts and feelings
will conspire to promote a misguided response.

This constructionist perspective implies that the evaluations a citizen might
report in an opinion poll or vote choice reflect the integration of thoughts and
feelings associated with one's history of conscious and unconscious political
evaluations. Immediately and without intentional control, a perceived candidate, issue, group, or idea is classified as either good or bad (Lodge and
Taber, 2005; Morris, Squires, Taber, and Lodge, 2003), and in a matter of
milliseconds, this evaluation facilitates a behavioral disposition toward the
stimulus.

Note, again, that because unconscious processes are extraordinarily sensitive to contextual factors that easily escape conscious appraisal (Hofmann
and Wilson, 2010; Niedenthal et al., 2005), the expression of beliefs and attitudes is context dependent (whether more or less so than conscious appraisals
remains an unanswered question), and as will be demonstrated in upcoming
chapters preconscious processes prove to be capable of integrating much more
information into the decision stream than can be handled consciously. One
consequence is that explicit attitudes appear to be (and are expected to be)

unstable over time and across situations because far more information has entered the decision stream than can be consciously processed.

Postulate 3, The Somatic Embodiment of Affect: In direct contrast to much of Western thought, which treats affect, feelings, and emotion as irrational intrusions that befuddle decision making, *JQP* follows the lead of recent neuro and social psychological evidence in connecting positive and negative feelings aroused by external events and internal thoughts to attitudes, goals, choices, and behavior. Hot cognition, the link from valence affect to cognition to preference to behavior, is viscerally monitored. Gut-level feelings automatically signal whether a person, situation, event, or option is seen as good or bad, threatening or rewarding. This embodiment of affect may be felt below conscious threshold as an intuition, or in other cases it may be experienced as intense arousal, demanding immediate cognitive appraisal for what and why I'm feeling this way. However it is experienced, whether consciously appraised or not, the immediate visceral response ensures that options will accompany perception, thereby facilitating approach or avoidance behaviors by signaling the prospect of pleasure or pain. Without the direct linking of feelings to thought to action, our beliefs and preferences would be cool, "as-if" experiences and as such likely to be weak, unstable, and poorly predictive of behavior (Niedenthal, Halberstadt, and Innes-Ker, 1999; Niedenthal, Halberstadt, and Setterlund, 1997).

Like so many advances on body-brain connections, contemporary research took its lead with patients who suffered damage to a particular area of the brain through accident, lesion, or stroke (Damasio, 1994; 1996; Damasio, Tranel, and Damasio, 1991). Those so afflicted provide us with analytic leverage for understanding what areas of the brain correspond to what functions: if you want to know what a particular area of the brain does, a time-honored starting point is to see what happens when it is damaged. In this case, the area of the brain of interest is the ventromedial prefrontal cortex (VMPC: in the middle of the brain on both sides, behind the eyes, right in front of the amygdalae). Individuals whose ventromedial cortexes are damaged retain their language and memory functions, all everyday cognitive abilities, but lose the ability to make use of their emotions to guide their social behaviors. They know what role emotions should play in such circumstances – how they and others should react – but simply don't feel the visceral tug pulling them in one direction or another. They live an "as-if" emotional life.

The VMPC is especially important because of its role associating knowledge about the environment with changes in bio-regulatory emotional states. In a social situation, the ventromedial prefrontal cortex associates similarities between the current situation and previous circumstances with the emotional context of the associations, creating what Antonio Damasio and his colleagues call a "body loop" (Bechara, Damasio, and Damasio, 2000). In essence, anticipatory visceral responses tell the individual that if she does *that*, she will likely feel *this*: if you criticize your partner's outfit, you'll regret it sooner, later, or forever. This anticipatory affect is then used to guide behavior. So armed, the individual avoids behaviors that would have negative emotional consequences, and pursues those that have led to positive outcomes in the past. This process can be completely obscure to the individual experiencing it. In some cases, you may know and be able to articulate exactly why you like or dislike a particular person or choice, but often body-loop feedback simply takes the form of a good or bad gut feeling, the causes of which remain murky.

One of the earliest demonstrations of a disassociation of emotion from cognition dates to 1911 when the Swiss neurologist Claparede concealed a pin in his hand on greeting one of his amnesic patients with a handshake. The patient quickly withdrew her hand, but within minutes forgot the encounter. Shortly after, when Claperede reintroduced himself and offered his hand, the amnesic patient refused to shake, but when asked why could not remember being pricked with the pin. A contemporary demonstration of this disassociation of feeling from memory was carried out by Feinstein, Duff, and Tranel (2010), again with amnesic patients with damage to the hippocampus. Here patients, on watching sad and happy film clips showed the normal range of appropriate emotional expressions (smiling and laughing, frowning and crying), and continued to experience the emotion for as long as did the counterbalanced control participants, but they were unable just minutes later to recall much of anything about the film clips, and certainly not the reasons for their feelings.

A now-classic example of the disassociation of emotion from cognitive awareness comes from the Iowa Gambling Task (Bechara, Damasio, Damasio, and Anderson, 1994; Bechara, Damasio, Tranel, and Damasio, 2005). In this experimental procedure, participants choose 100 cards, one at a time (though they are not initially told how many cards they will draw), from four decks laid before them. On the face of each card, revealed only after it is chosen, is a monetary gain or loss, which is then added to or subtracted from the dollar amount accumulated. Two of the decks feature large payoffs, $100 per card, but larger occasional losses of $1,250. In the other two decks, the gains are smaller, only $50 per card, but so are the losses: just $250 per ten cards. On average, drawing ten cards from the two high-payoff, high-risk decks results in a net loss of $250, while drawing from the low-risk, lower-payoff decks results in a net gain of $250.

As would be expected, nearly all brain-intact participants begin by drawing cards in a relatively random order from the four decks. After about fifty draws, these players report having a hunch about which decks are better. After about eighty draws, they are typically able to articulate an understanding of the structure of the game and can explain their choice of cards in terms of a positive expectation about two of the decks. This is what we would expect from a deliberative solution to the game, and if this were the only mechanism through which players could intuit the game, they would after the eighty or so draws experience substantial losses. But this was clearly *not* the only mechanism at work, *nor even the one that actually drove behavior*, since these same players avoided the risky decks long before they arrived at their first conscious glimmer of a hunch, beginning on average after just ten cards. Somehow, the Iowa gamblers (and participants in dozens of replications) were able to act on their real-time affective experiences in the game, without realizing they were doing so. How? The Iowa team suggested that physiological responses, monitored in the VPMC provide this mechanism, and they collected data to test their body-loop hypothesis.

While playing the gambling game, the Iowa team measured their participants' galvanic skin conductance, which tracks to the millisecond the participants' physiological stress levels outside of awareness and conscious control. In a striking confirmation of their hypothesis, after about ten cards stress levels rose sharply when participants considered the two high-risk decks. Most telling, this bodily response was precisely timed to their behavioral adaptations long *before* they could report a hunch about the risky decks. They were not consciously aware of what would likely be a good or bad outcome, yet these implicit impulses guided their behavior long before they became consciously aware of the relative costs and benefits of the card decks. At this early stage of the game, participants begin to play sensibly without even realizing that they're drawing from the good decks more than bad.

Individuals with damage to their VMPC simply don't get these somatic-induced hunches, and thus are unable to make use of the information about their visceral experience that others assemble unconsciously. Like the normal participants, those with bilateral damage to the VPMC begin by sampling a few cards from each deck, but unlike intact participants they don't gravitate towards the better decks as the game progresses. Instead, the longer the game continues, the more they draw from the high risk decks, which give them clearly observable higher payouts but large long-term losses. The critical difference seems to come from the anticipatory bodily reactions experienced by the normal participants: these somatic signals of stress do not occur among the impaired respondents (Damasio, 1996).

Findings like this are important to us not so much for what they tell us about the VMPC, but more for what they tell us about how people learn from their own visceral experiences: what is known as the *somatic marker hypothesis*. In essence, the brain uses feelings that have become associated with objects or behavioral options through good or bad past experiences as a visceral signal for the likely positive or negative consequences of an action. The intact participants in the Iowa Gambling experiments do not have a bad feeling about the high-risk decks because they calculated their expected values; rather they avoided these decks because they *felt* a stressful somatic response when they so much as moved a hand toward those decks. These intact participants decided "advantageously before knowing the advantageous strategy" (Bechara, Damasio, Tranel, and Damasio, 1997).

Our visceral embodiment postulate (with the somatic marker hypothesis a specific instance) is a 180 degree turnabout from the way most of us understand the relationship between consciousness and actions. Rather than

controlling our actions, consciousness often functions to interpret and rationalize the actions and processes that have already been carried out unconsciously.
Nor is Damasio alone in putting forward such a model: Daniel Dennett (1991)
and Douglas Hofstatdter (2007) both arrived at similar conclusions from rad-
ically different starting points, as did Libet (1985, 2004) in his classic experiments involving conscious control of the timing of a simple motor behavior
such as moving a finger. This sort of unconscious processing is troubling to
many of us in political science and social psychology steeped in the belief that
conscious thought precedes and dictates preference.

The visceral embodiment of affect allows the brain to use affect as real-time
information to promote quick, efficient, spontaneous responses to what should
be approached and what avoided. Over time, body-loop feedback helps to
structure political knowledge, though by "structure" we have in mind associated connections among concepts rather than strict ideological constraint. It
now appears that affect and cognition are *inter*dependent systems, only separable in pathological cases. Among those of us with intact brains, all thinking,
reasoning, and intentions, whether conscious or unconscious, are embodied by
feelings of good or bad, like or dislike. Ironically, oftentimes tragically, the very
same affective processes that contribute to rational action are also responsible
for promoting bias in human thought, a theme we will pursue in following
chapters.

Postulate 4, The Primacy of Affect. It is now well-documented that feelings
enter the decision stream *before* any cognitive considerations come consciously
to mind (Zajonc, 1980; 2000). Neurological studies of both mice and men suggest that the "affect system" follows a "quick and dirty" pathway that prepares
organisms for approach-avoidance behavioral responses within 200–300 milliseconds of exposure and appear to enter the evaluation process spontaneously
moments before cognitive considerations come to mind (Burdein, Lodge, and
Taber, 2006; LeDoux, 1994; 1996; Morris, Squires, Taber, and Lodge, 2003).
People feel their opposition to the Iraq and Afghan wars before any facts about
the war (thousands dead and counting) come to mind, and these positive or
negative feelings influence what cognitive considerations come consciously to
mind. Even when one's attention is focused elsewhere, automatic evaluative
processes prepare the individual to make an affectively congruent response
(Bargh and Chartrand, 1999).

The temporal primacy of affect over cognition seems perverse because it
reverses causality in the conventional social science model and undermines the
deliberative foundations of Enlightenment rationality. Feeling *before* cognition
threatens normative and empirical standards for our understanding of political
behavior because, if we are right, conscious deliberation is the wake behind the
boat, while automatically stimulated affective and cognitive processes control
the rudder. Rationale becomes rationalization.

As a preview of more to come, consider this clever demonstration of the
direct link between feelings and approach-avoidance behavior: Chen and Bargh

(1999) instructed half their subjects to pull a joystick toward themselves when positive words appeared on the computer screen and push the lever away for negative words, while the other half received the opposite push-pull instructions. Results confirmed that subjects were faster to pull the joystick toward themselves for pleasant concepts and push away for unpleasant concepts, this a result we see as telltale evidence for the central role played by affect in triggering basic approach-avoidance behaviors.

The affective link to evaluations and choices helps prevent decision calculations from becoming so complex and cumbersome that choices would be impossible. Indeed, it is the primacy of affect that makes timely and effective decision making possible (Thagard, 2000). Feelings provide feedback about the unconscious processes that precede conscious consideration. Because automatic brain processing capacity is greater and faster than conscious appraisals, this "affect heuristic" (Slovic, 1999; Slovic et al., 2004; 2007), or better yet a "likeability heuristic" (Sniderman, Brody, and Tetlock, 1991) precedes and impels conscious processing. Without the weighting of goals by feelings no option would be more important than another and we would consequently end up like Buridan's ass, unable to choose among preferences. But how are these feelings updated and in response to what?

Postulate 5, Online Updating of Evaluations. Benjamin Franklin (1779) proposed a classic decision-making strategy when advising his grand nephew on choosing a marriage partner:

Follow your own judgment. If you doubt, set down all the reasons, pro and con, in opposite columns on a sheet of paper, and when you have considered them two or three days, perform an operation similar to that in some questions of algebra; observe what reasons or motives in each column are equal in weight, one to one, one to two, two to three, or the like, and when you have struck out from both sides all the equalities, you will see in which column remains the balance. It is for want of having all of the motives for and against an important action present in or before the mind at the same time, that people hesitate and change their determinations backwards and forwards day after day, as different sets of reasons are recollected or forgot, and if they conclude and act upon the last set, it is perhaps not because those were the best, but because they happen to be present in the mind, and the better absent. This kind of Moral Algebra I have often practiced in important and dubious concerns, and tho' it cannot be mathematically exact, I have found it to be extremely useful. I am your ever affectionate Uncle.

Note the commonsense wisdom of "Franklin's Rule." Making a list of pros and cons and checking them twice, he would probably expand the number of considerations entering the mix, perhaps stop himself from jumping to conclusions, and conceivably (although we think not) weigh and integrate the most important considerations most heavily into the equation. Kelley and Mirer (1974: 574), mirroring Franklin's Rule, state the case for such *memory-based* models of vote choice: "The voter canvasses his likes and dislikes of the leading candidates and major parties involved in an election. Weighing each like and dislike equally, he votes for the candidate toward whom he has the greatest number of net favorable attitudes. . . . "

Nearly all theories and empirical studies of public opinion assume memory based processing. While they differ in what memory "considerations" come to mind – whether a candidate's partisan affiliation, endorsements, personality traits, or policy preferences – they all suppose that a citizen's evaluation is a straightforward function of consciously retrieved thoughts. Were this generic account of the evaluation process a faithful representation of how citizens actually construct their preferences, it would indeed make the pollster's life simpler. If citizens could provide a more or less veridical account of what campaign events led them to favor one candidate over another, we could simply ask respondents for their likes, dislikes, and reasons for preferring one candidate over another and not bother examining the on-going psychological processes that convert campaign events into political preferences and vote choice. All we would need to do is have respondents recount the considerations that come to mind, which is exactly what is done in the National Election Studies.

To go beyond the tautological "voters vote for the candidate they like best," the analyst must assume that the mix of recollections evoked by the open-ended, like-dislike, and issue-proximity responses stand as valid expressions of beliefs, attitudes, and reasons for vote intentions. True enough, across hundreds of survey-based studies, we do find a positive correlation between the self-report measures and candidate preferences. Respondents regularly vote for the candidate they tell us they like best and/or is closest to them on one or a few issues. If the criterion for success is prediction (or more commonly in practice, postdiction), all is well and good. If, however, the aim is to work our way out of the black box, to learn when and how citizens go about forming and updating their impressions of candidates and issues, the first question to be asked is how much credence can be placed in the citizen's recall of likes and dislikes or placements of self and candidates on issue proximity scales as bona fide descriptions of how preferences and choices are formed and updated.

A major difficulty with memory-based models based on survey responses is that they are unable to distinguish among various psychological mechanisms underlying the judgment process and consequently cannot tease out the causal ordering of effects. There's an oddity in the evidence that alerts us to the problem: in contrast to the survey results, experiments in social and cognitive psychology routinely report weak correlations between the mix of pro and con evidence recalled from memory and the direction and strength of various social evaluations (Anderson and Hubert, 1963; Hastie and Park, 1986; Lichtenstein and Srull, 1987; Lodge and Stroh, 1993; Lodge, Steenbergen, and Brau, 1995). When the researcher knows exactly what information respondents actually see, as is the case in these experiments, we find that the considerations people remember about other people, places, and events and the reasons they give for their preferences provide a poor fit to their evaluations. People tend to recall their good-bad, like-dislike global assessments, *not* the specific considerations that actually went into their evaluations. At the very best, the recollections represent a biased sampling of the actual causal determinants (McGraw, Lodge, and Stroh, 1990; Reyes, Thompson, and Bower, 1980). At worse, recollections may simply reflect rationalizations dredged up to support the global judgment constructed earlier in the information processing stream (Pratkanis, 1989). In both cases the correlation between memory and judgment is spurious, and causal "explanations" based on these explicit "recollections" have the arrow going the wrong direction.

There is now a great deal of evidence showing that people form impressions of others automatically, anchor on this early impression, and adjust insufficiently to later information (Uleman and Bargh, 1989). By contrast, the recall of considerations is most strongly influenced by the most recently processed information. Information that comes early in a political campaign will more strongly influence the reception, interpretation, and evaluation of new campaign information, even though later information is typically better remembered (Lodge, McGraw and Stroh, 1989; Zaller and Feldman, 1992). This pattern of primacy effects on spontaneous impression formation but recency effects on explicit memory renders recall-based measures suspect as indicators of why people favor one person or idea over another.

The failure to find empirical support for the memory-causes-judgment hypothesis across a broad range of topics and tasks under experimental conditions where the researcher has control over the content of the message has sparked interest in what is called *online processing*. Online (OL) models hold that beliefs and attitudes are constructed in real time, at the moment of comprehension, when an object is before your eyes, so to speak (Anderson, 1965; Hastie and Park, 1986; Lodge, Steenbergen, and Brau, 1995). When people form or revise their overall impressions of persons, places, events, or issues, they are found to spontaneously extract the affective value of the message, and then within milliseconds integrate their appraisal of the object into their prior evaluation, all without any conscious query of memory for a set of considerations on which to compute an updated evaluation, as prescribed in Franklin's Fable. This "running" OL tally, representing an automatic integration of all prior evaluations of the object, is then restored to long- term memory where it is readily available for subsequent evaluations (Cassino and Lodge, 2007). From this OL constructionist perspective, affect infuses the encoding, retrieval, and comprehension of information, its expression as a preference, and readies us to act aversively or appetitively in accord with our feelings (Ito and Cacioppo, 1999). The OL tally is an elemental processing heuristic, more "primitive" we think than other such heuristics as partisan identification and the stereotyping of others known to guide impressions.

Because the online updating of attitudes necessarily moves forward in time, with existing feelings ever-present to influence subsequent processing, early information will have a greater impact on attitudes than later information. This powerful effect of primacy on impressions was first suggested by Solomon Asch

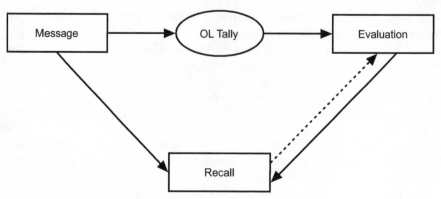

FIGURE 2.3. Online Model of Evaluation Processes

(1946), who argued that the very same descriptors of a person would produce a different holistic impression, depending on their order of presentation. Try the following thought "experiment" for yourself: On a scale that ranges from "highly favorable" (+4) to "highly unfavorable" (−4) evaluate person A, who is described as:

Faultfinding, awkward, cool, sentimental, athletic, and smart.

Now, to clear working memory count backwards by 7s from 100 until you reach 65, then evaluate person B, who is described as:

Smart, athletic sentimental, cool, awkward, and faultfinding.

Experimental participants evaluated person A as "slightly unfavorable" (−0.7) and person B as "moderately favorable" (+1.4), despite the fact that only the order of the trait descriptors changed (Anderson and Banios, 1961). First impressions count.

From this online perspective, as depicted in Figure 2.3 (adapted from Lodge, Steenbergen, and Brau, 1995), the appraisal of campaign messages is directly integrated into a summary evaluation (OL Tally), which directly informs the candidate evaluation. The recall of campaign messages contributes only weakly to the summary evaluation (dashed line) and is likely to reflect tally-driven rationalizations of the OL impression (the solid arrow from evaluation to recall).

Summary impressions bias recall in two distinct ways, which we will document in ensuing chapters. First, as noted earlier, an affective tally enters the processing stream earlier than do a concept's semantic associations (you feel you like or dislike Barack Obama before you remember he is a Democrat), and consequently affect anchors judgments, which trigger why-do-I-feel-this-way rationalizations. This is the indirect path from the OL tally through the evaluation to recall in Figure 2.3. A second, more direct influence on memory is the "affective contagion effect" in which one's OL tally biases the sampling of recalled information in tally-consistent ways (Erisen, Lodge, and Taber, 2008; Rahn, Krosnik, and Breuning, 1994). This would be a direct arrow from the OL tally to recall in Figure 2.3. Moreover, semantic information is subject to an exponential forgetting curve (Ebbinghaus, 1885; 1913), while evaluations of an object are relatively stable over longer periods of time. In short, affective associations tend to persist in long-term memory and over time will outlive the semantic associations to an object leading to an ever-increasing infusion of affect.

To make their central point, early descriptions of online information processing drew too sharp a dichotomy between memory-based and online processing (e.g., Lodge, McGraw, and Stroh, 1989; Lodge, Steenbergen, and Brau, 1995). An either-or view is theoretically flawed and empirically untenable (Kim, Taber, and Lodge, 2010; Lavine, 2002; Redlawsk, 2001; Taber, 2003). The confusion stems from the failure to clearly discriminate encoding from retrieval effects. Recall the semantic network model in Figure 2.1, where affect is linked directly to concepts in LTM. Affective tags are attached when an object (person, group, place, event, issue, or abstract concept) is first evaluated and strengthened with each replication through the automatic online process we have just described. After but one or two evaluations, a concept is "hot," affective charged (Lodge and Taber, 2005). From this point onward, affect and cognition are unitized in memory and difficult (we believe impossible) to disentangle in practice, though they remain conceptually distinct.

In a survey context the measurement of OL processing of candidate evaluations proceeds in stages. First, participants are asked to evaluate all the information that will subsequently be presented in a candidate message, plus many other pieces of information that will not appear in the message so as to later check for rationalization effects in recall. Next, there is a distracter task, perhaps questions asking for demographics, to thwart short-term rote memory of the items and their evaluations. Then, participants read about one or more candidates or issues, typically embedded in narrative form as a newspaper article or newscast. This is the candidate message. Fourth, participants are asked to evaluate the candidates. And finally, after another distracter or better yet a longer delay, participants are asked to recall the information in the article, followed by probes of recognition-memory asking for details about the candidate's demographics, issue positions, and any trait inferences they may have inferred. Compute the correlation between an integration of the likes/dislikes for *all* the information presented in the candidate message and the reported candidate evaluation. Compute the correlation between an integration of the likes/dislikes for the *recalled* information and the reported candidate evaluation. To the degree that the first correlation is stronger than the second (or that the first statistical relationship survives inclusion of the second in a multivariate model), there is evidence of online processing.

Note that within this survey context the measurement of the OL evaluation is explicit; participants are asked directly for their preferences. But there is now

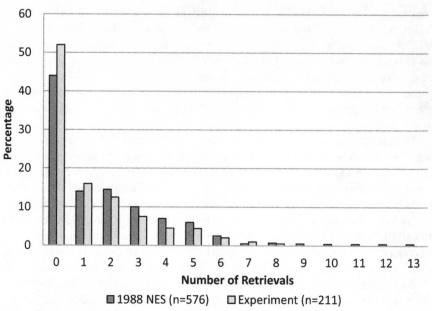

FIGURE 2.4. Memory Retrieval in Two-Candidate Election

empirical evidence and theoretical rationale for believing that OL processing is automatic, that people evaluate, update, and integrate their evaluations into a summary judgment effortlessly, outside of conscious awareness.

A well-replicated finding (Bassili, 1989; Hastie and Park, 1986; Lodge, Steenbergen, and Brau, 1995) is that whereas people can integrate lots of complex information in real time, even without being explicitly instructed to evaluate the object (e.g., candidate), they prove unable to recall much of this information after a short distracter task. And a day or two later the number and accuracy of recall no longer predicts either the information in the message or the summary evaluation. When Lodge, Steenbergen, and Brau (1995) looked at how much of the presented campaign messages their experimental participants could recall, the results were consistent with the findings from public opinion surveys. As shown in Figure 2.4, citizens forget... a lot, with about 54 percent of our respondents unable to recollect a single issue that either of the two candidates had addressed. The modal number of recalls for the policies' gist meanings (for example, "Candidate Williams opposes abortion") was zero, while recall for his more complex issue position ("... except in the case of rape or incest") was worse still, with more than 75 percent of the subjects unable to recall even one qualifier for either of the two candidates.

This dismal level of recall of campaign information by our subjects is not different from what researchers typically find in surveys about real-life candidates (Delli Carpini and Keeter 1991; Erskine, 1963; Neuman 1986; Smith,

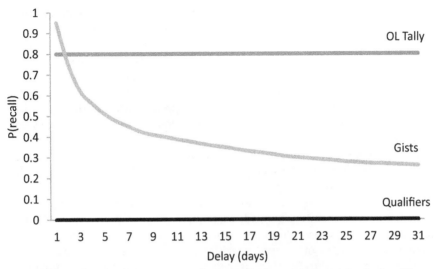

FIGURE 2.5. Online and Memory-Based Forgetting Curves for Democratic Candidate

1989). For instance, as shown in Figure 2.4, when we contrasted the number of recalls in our 1995 experiment with those for congressional candidates in the 1988 NES, we found a striking congruence. The loss-curves are virtually identical. In both samples the modal number of recalls is zero, with very few people providing more than two recollections of the campaign. Voters appear to forget much of the campaign information to which they were exposed, even after year-long campaigns.

Recall how severely limited conscious processing is compared to the much greater capacity of unconscious processes. Over the last decade or so experimental evidence has accumulated to suggest, if not yet demonstrate to everyone's satisfaction, that unconscious processing allows people to take in far more social information than can be processed consciously. The experiment by Lodge, Steenbergen, and Brau (1995) included a variety of manipulations to check for what goes into the OL Tally and so provides evidence as to the relative capacities of unconscious and conscious processing. To examine the effects of recall, all subjects were re-interviewed, this time by phone, one to thirty-one days after the experiment. Two striking results stand out in Figure 2.5: memory of the affective tally persisted over the thirty-one-day period, while recall of the candidates' gist policy proposals decayed exponentially and any specific policy details were essentially zero from day one.

Now to the key point from the Lodge, Steenbergen, and Brau experiment: in every case subjects' average like/dislike ratings of the candidates' seven policy statements in the brochure (i.e., their OL tally) strongly predicted their candidate evaluations, while the information they could recall did not predict their candidate evaluations, even for those who were instructed to think hard about the candidates while they read the brochures. What is even more problematic for memory-based processing, the considerations subjects voiced when asked for their likes, dislikes, and reasons for their preferences are strongly biased by their summary attitudes, and many of their "memories" prove to be little more than rationalizations and projections stemming from their OL-based tally favoring one candidate over the other. What we see here is evidence that people are able to integrate far more information into preferences than they can recall and more importantly more complex information than presumably they can process consciously.

A compelling test of postconscious automaticity in online processing was carried out by a team of German social psychologists (Betsch et al., 2002) who had their subjects watch a series of thirty videotaped TV commercials, which they were told they would have to later recall and evaluate. Simultaneously, these subjects performed a second, cognitively demanding "distractor" task: they were asked to read aloud the changing stock prices of five hypothetical companies presented on a crawler at the bottom of the TV screen. Though participants were led to believe that their ability to remember and evaluate the TV commercials under pressure of an irrelevant distraction was the primary purpose of the study (their recall of the commercials proved to be very good), the researchers were actually interested in how the viewers would track the stock ticker outside their focal attention. In a surprise test, subjects were asked their preferences for the five companies. As predicted by the online processing model, participants were unable to recall much if any of the pertinent stock information, yet their summary, rank-ordered evaluations correlated positively and strongly with the actual performance of the 5 companies as had been reported in the stock ticker prices they could not remember. These results point to the spontaneity of online evaluations: subjects accurately evaluated the companies' stock performance even when their attention was actively focused on an unrelated, attention-demanding task.

In sum, the evidence is now clear that people automatically update their attitudes toward a variety of social and political objects at the time they encounter relevant information. The process is autoregressive: the summary judgment is not based on a fresh look at all the evidence, but rather on the OL tally and the biased assessment of messages at the instant they are received (Huckfeldt et al., 2011). This updating process does not require conscious intervention and appears to engage our substantial capacity for the unconscious processing of large amounts of information. As such, citizens may be more responsive to the complex, high-volume information available in the political environment than conventional memory-based models suggest. This greater responsiveness, however, may come at the price of motivated bias in perceptions and judgments.

Postulate 6, Affect Transfer. The direct linking of positive and negative feelings to objects in memory is often the result of *affect transfer*, in which current affective states become associated with currently activated objects. The simple pairing of positive or negative cues with an object will tend to transfer affect to the object in a form of classical conditioning that operates below conscious awareness. The sunny day effect is an oft-noted case in point. Life and love seem sweeter on a beautiful day, and even mundane objects may gain cachet. Advertisers routinely exploit affect transfer to manipulate feelings about candidates or commodities. Positive cues work by making the perceived object more likeable, while negative responses follow quickly upon exposure to negative cues. The effects are simple, direct, immediate, and spontaneous. Other responses, say an emotional appraisal, may or may not follow upon the immediate affective response.

The sunny day effect is a good example of *extrinsic* affect transfer in which feelings generated by an event *un*related to the object are transferred to the object. Common also is *intrinsic* affect transfer, in which positive or negative feelings that are relevant to an object become associated with it through simple pairing. For example, when a friend takes an issue position or wears a lapel pin supporting a political candidate, one's affect toward that position or candidate may become directly transferred to the friend (or vice versa). Similarly, when a presidential candidate announces his running mate he is likely hoping for some affect transfer from the bottom to the top of the ticket. Note that because affect transfer occurs on mere association of two objects or events, it can move in either direction, though a reasonable prediction would be that affect would more likely transfer from a strongly to a weakly felt object. The distinction between extrinsic and intrinsic affect transfer is in many ways a normative one, because the relevance of objects or events to each other is somewhat subjective, while the underlying simple conditioning process is the same.

It is important to recognize that our theory goes beyond a simple good-bad bipolar response in allowing for people to hold *both* positive and negative affect toward a political leader, group, or issue. The theoretical rationale here is the independence of positive and negative affect (Cacioppo, Gardner, and Berntson, 1997). One's evaluation can be ambivalent, with both positive and negative reactions activated, if not simultaneously, then triggered within milliseconds of one another. As will be demonstrated repeatedly in the upcoming experiments, this ambivalence has important consequences for how objects are evaluated and how information is processed.

A head's up is appropriate here: several scholars of the affective intelligence school (Brader, 2005; Marcus, Neuman, and MacKuen, 2000) argue against the affect-transfer hypothesis in claiming that positive and negative emotions, in particular enthusiasm versus anxiety, promote different behavioral responses above and beyond their valence. Perhaps. But our claim is that affect enters the decision stream first and subsequent emotional appraisals are heavily anchored by the initial valence response; such appraisals are often part of a postbehavioral rationalization process rather than the impetus for said behavior. Moreover, the empirical evidence provided in support of the causal importance of enthusiasm and anxiety may be better explained by affect transfer. When valence is controlled for in these analyses there is little left-over variance to be explained

by like-valenced discrete emotions. We will return to this debate in the conclusion after showing multiple experimental demonstrations of the direct effects
of positive and negative affect on the evaluations of political leaders, groups,
and issues, and on the in-depth processing of campaign information.

Postulate 7, Affect Contagion. In our theory, the affective tallies tagged
to social concepts and updated through online processes inevitably color all
phases of the evaluation process, sometimes explicitly, other times not, sometimes for good, other times not. Hot cognition and affect transfer provide two
direct mechanisms. If these transitory effects were the full extent of the influence of affective online tallies on evaluations they would still be important if
that momentarily activated affect is integrated in real time into evaluations and
thereafter anchors subsequent judgments. However, hot cognition and affect
transfer are not the only ways that feelings alter thought processes. *Affect contagion* will also influence political reasoning and behavior by altering the memory
processes through which politically relevant considerations are retrieved.

When called on to express a judgment, given sufficient time to think and
the motivation to query memory, the considerations that make their way into
the conscious decision stream will be biased. As we will show in upcoming
chapters, what comes to mind when voicing an opinion – as when responding
to an NES open-ended question asking for likes and dislikes of the candidates
and parties – will reflect what information is readily accessible from long-term
memory, and this accessibility is strongly influenced by affective congruence.

Information in LTM that is congruent with the valence of current feelings
will be favored in memory retrieval while affectively incongruent information
will be inhibited. This means that the sampling of new considerations from
LTM will generally support initial affective reactions, and as currently experienced feelings strengthen, the set of considerations retrieved into conscious
WM will likely become more one-sided. In this way, reasoning processes that
may seem to the citizen to provide reasons for one's evaluative reactions may
more often rationalize the initial affect one felt toward the object of evaluation.
This "snowballing" of affect over time will be most pronounced for people who
have strong, univalent affect tagged to the object of thought and who have a
substantial number of congruent considerations stored in LTM. In the political
realm, it may be knowledgeable partisans who best fit this description.

As with affect transfer, affect contagion may be the product of extrinsic or
intrinsic feelings. That is, affective tags already associated with political candidates, parties, issues, or other objects of thought – prior attitudes – will bias the
retrieval of considerations and thereby alter the character of thought. When
one is asked to produce and justify an opinion on affirmative action, for example, the prior attitude stored in affective tags linked to the affirmative action
node in LTM will inevitably (and appropriately) color the response. One may
have a variety of pro and con considerations on affirmative action, but the ones
that are congruent with prior affect will more likely be retrieved. Such affect
contagion is intrinsic to the object of thought. Unrelated or extrinsic feelings

can also bias the retrieval of considerations, using the same affect contagion processes. A bad mood, for example, or an unrelated negative prime (perhaps the word RATS subliminally presented in a campaign ad) will influence one's responses to the affirmative action question, reliably leading to the retrieval of more negatively valenced considerations.

We will show in upcoming empirical tests evidence of the systematic biasing effects of affective contagion on how citizens evaluate political leaders, groups, and issues, and how they judge policy proposals.

Given the seven postulates operating on a network of cognitive and affective associations, our expectation is that most citizens most of the time will be *motivated reasoners* who find it difficult if not impossible to evaluate attitude-relevant information in an evenhanded way. Challenged by attitudinally incongruent information, people will routinely rationalize the facts, figures, and arguments that they cannot effortlessly discount, depreciate, denigrate, or deny. Like the Bush 43 administration, citizens are prone in their everyday lives to fit the facts to their feelings. This is what we find in a series of experiments (reported in Chapters 4 and 5) exploring the impact of affect on political information processing. People find it difficult to override the spontaneously generated feelings triggered by their prior attitudes when evaluating political candidates, groups, and issues.

Forewarned Is Forearmed: General Expectations and Anticipated Objections

The simple act of evaluating is a human universal, "with survival depending on appropriately discriminating beneficial from harmful stimuli" (Ito and Cacioppo, 2005: 20). In our *John Q. Public* theory, as in Cacioppo, Gardner, and Berntson's (1997) *Evaluative Space Model* and Zajonc's (1980, 1984, 2000) *Primacy of Affect Model*, as well as the Marcus, Neuman, and MacKuen (2000) *Affective Intelligence Model*, evaluations are said to be generated by separate, somewhat independent positive and negative affective systems, each with unique activation functions that automatically adjust to fit the environmental context.

To the extent that *JQP* provides a reasonable account of the structures and processes of mental representations, most of our everyday life operates automatically (Bargh, 1997, 2007). The chapters that follow will document preconscious priming effects on political judgments, evaluations, and behavior, as well as even stronger effects of automatic affect when citizens are called upon to stop and think hard when evaluating political candidates, arguments, and policy recommendations. Virtually all the studies to be reported, and many more we will cite from the social and neuropsychological literatures, demonstrate the immediate or longer term consequences of unconsciously perceived affective events for sociopolitical evaluations and behavior. Before turning to the empirical tests of our theory, however, let us briefly list our major hypotheses and then anticipate concerns about the construct validity, reliability, and explanatory power of implicit measures of attitudes.

General Hypotheses. At the core of this book stand three basic expectations: *feelings drive thinking more than vice versa; conscious experience always follows and is a product of unconscious processing;* and *behavior is often propelled by feelings through processes we do not consciously control.* It is our claim that conventional models of political behavior have the causal order wrong. Conventional models fail to appreciate the significance of information processes that occur on a millisecond timescale. And conventional models err in seeing citizens as (imperfectly) rational actors who construct preferences through conscious deliberation about the attributes of political actors, groups, or ideas.

Stated more formally, the major hypotheses we test in this book are:

- The *hot cognition hypothesis,* that all political objects that have been thought about in the past are tagged to positive and/or negative feelings.
- The *automaticity hypothesis,* that significant information processes occur outside of conscious awareness with substantial effect on subsequent conscious thought and behavior.
- The *affect transfer hypothesis,* that current affective states or primes, whether intrinsic or irrelevant, can transfer positive and/or negative feelings to objects of current thought. This can happen when affect and objects are consciously experienced or when one or both are outside of awareness.
- The *affect contagion hypothesis,* that affective states or primes, whether intrinsic or irrelevant, can influence the retrieval of considerations from memory, favoring thoughts with congruent over incongruent valence. This can happen for both consciously experienced affective states or when operating below conscious awareness.
- The *motivated reasoning hypotheses,* that prior affect will bias attention to and processing of information in ways that favor acceptance of affectively congruent arguments or evidence and rejection of incongruent information. This can occur for both consciously and unconsciously experienced affect.

In addition, we will test a variety of subsidiary hypotheses that will examine related processes, moderators, and mediators. Among these will be a chapter extending the hot cognition hypothesis to group identifications and racial attitudes, several studies examining the "snowball" hypothesis that consciously thinking harder *increases* the impact of unconscious affect, and research showing that motivated biases are greatest for sophisticates and those who care the most about politics. Notably absent from the empirical work we will present are two of our seven postulates: We will not present tests of the somatic marker hypothesis and the online processing mechanism for affect updating. The former has been extensively tested by others, though not in a political context (but see Morris, Squires, Taber, and Lodge, 2003), while the latter is well-established in the social and political psychology literatures, including some of our own earlier work (Lodge, McGraw, and Stroh, 1989; Lodge, Steenbergen, and Brau, 1995).

We turn now to potential objections.

What are Implicit Attitudes and How Do They Relate to Explicit Attitudes? Much ink has been spilt over the past fifty years in arguments as to how, when, and why within-individual attitude measures fail to cohere, with correlations routinely in the .30 to .50 range. These explicit attitude measures, moreover, routinely account for just 10 to 15 percent of variance in observed behavior, casting doubt on one of the pillars of modern social psychology, the notion that attitudes cause behavior. Not much to show for fifty-plus years of empirical research! A similar concern pertains to the *relationships among implicit and explicit measures of attitudes* and their predictions of behavior. Some readers may wonder what implicit attitudes really are and how they relate both empirically and theoretically to the more familiar self-reported attitude.

Many of the same faults, findings, arguments, and explanations surrounding the instability of explicit measures and their inability to better predict attitude-relevant behaviors also characterize contemporary research looking at the relationships among different implicit measures, between implicit and explicit measures, and implicit versus explicit predictions of behavior (Petty, Fazio, and Briñol, 2009). We have already noted that latent variable structural models analyzing implicit and explicit measures of attitudes toward social objects demonstrate that a two-factor model, with implicit and explicit attitudes as separate factors, is superior to a single-factor specification (Nosek and Smyth, 2007).

Meta analyses comparing implicit to explicit relationships over a large number of separate studies report (here we go again) correlations dispersed around .30 (Blair, 2001; Dovidio, Kawakami, and Beach, 2001; Greenwald and Banaji, 1995; Hofmann, Gawronski, Gschwendner, Le and Schmitt, 2005; Nosek, Greenwald, and Banaji, 2005). For example, Greenwald, Poehlman, Uhlmann, and Banaji (2009) compared implicit to explicit measures drawn from 184 independent samples and 14,900 experimental subjects, finding that correlations vary widely (from .18 to .68), with the average correlation for attitudinal, judgmental, and behavioral measures just .274. In the Nosek and Smyth (2007) review of 126 studies comparing Implicit Association Test measures to explicit like-dislike measures across a broad range of attitudes, correlations ranged from a low of -0.05 for reactions to Male-Female body images to a high of .70 for Pro Choice-Pro Life attitudes. For Republican and Democratic Party identifications, they found a healthy .59 correlation, while for Liberal-Conservative attitudes the correlation was .56. It would seem that one can find empirical cause to believe that implicit and explicit attitudes are the same, are related, or are utterly different constructs, depending on the type of attitude, context, or measurement strategy. Clearly, reporting the average coefficients of implicit-explicit consistency across many studies as some have done does not capture the complexity of these findings. Rather, as is also true for the relationships among explicit attitude measures, the high variability in correlations suggests that moderator variables determine when correlations between implicit and explicit responses will be high, middling, or low.

As expected, given the motivation to control social impressions, the weakest correlations are uncovered when predicting explicit attitudes from implicit measures on such historically discriminatory attitudes as race, gender, and age, for such stigmatized people as the mentally and physically disabled, thin versus fat people, and those with AIDS, and for such risky behaviors as cigarette smoking, drug use, and unsafe sexual behavior. This finding suggests that implicit measures can sometimes reveal underlying attitudes that are not socially acceptable and therefore may not be revealed in overt surveys. In this sense, implicit measures may provide a "bona fide pipeline" to true attitudes (Fazio, Jackson, Dunton and Williams, 1995).

Before turning to a more detailed discussion of what are proving to be the most influential moderators of implicit-explicit relationships, let us note that *JQP*, as with virtually all modern-day models of evaluation in psychology, takes the "attitude-as-construction" perspective. When asked to think about why they prefer one object over another, respondents routinely construct their attitudinal responses on the fly, based on thoughts, feelings, and actions that are immediately accessible and easily verbalized (Wilson, Hodges, and LaFleur, 1995). People are found to construct their attitudes from:

- current thoughts and feelings (Chaiken and Yates, 1985; Judd and Lusk, 1984; Miller and Tesser, 1986; Wilson and Hodges, 1992);
- their present mood (Forgas, 1995; Petty, Schumann, Richman, and Strathman, 1993; Schwarz and Clore, 1983);
- their own behavior (Bem, 1967); and
- the immediate social context (Feldman and Lynch, 1988; McGuire, Padawer-Singer, 1976; Schuman and Presser, 1981).

The upshot of this view of attitudes-as-constructions is the expectation of attitude instability (which *JQP* shares with Zaller and Feldman's 1992 survey response model). The weak to moderate correlations that characterize the relationships among explicit measures, among implicit measures, between explicit and implicit measures, and between attitude measures and behavior, is an everyday consequence of the attitude construction process. That said, well-known factors moderate relationships among and between attitudes and their measures. Research on moderators of implicit-explicit (I-E) relationships focuses on interpersonal and intrapersonal contexts and measurement effects.

As we have implied, the historical impetus for development of implicit measures was initially concern with the biasing effect of *social desirability* on direct self-report measures of personally and socially sensitive issues, with much of the research in the United States focused on "impression management" in racial, religious, and gender stereotyping. By minimizing the opportunity for strategic responding, implicit measures reduce the opportunity for respondents to guide their responses. Nonetheless, self-presentation – that is, altering a response for personal or social purposes – does indeed moderate I-E correlations, almost always showing weaker correlations when social desirability is a concern for explicit measures.

Meta analyses find the *dimensionality of attitudes* to be an especially strong moderator of implicit and explicit measures of attitude consistency. Evaluations that conform to a simple, bipolar structure, in which liking for a concept (for example, pro-choice) implies disliking of a second concept (pro-life), tend to elicit stronger I-E correlations as well as increase the speed, consistency, and efficiency of processing – all hallmarks of automaticity.

A variety of internal factors tend to crystallize the evaluative dimension and increase I-E correlations. These include the number and quality of personal experiences in a particular domain (as is characteristic of political activists), identity-related comparisons (for example, male/female; American/foreigner; Republican/Democrat), and the frequency with which a response has been activated in the past. All of these factors promote the accessibility and consistency of attitudes toward a given object and consequently their automatic activation. A consistent finding across studies is that strong, well-defined attitudes elicit stronger I-E correlations than ones that are novel, unimportant, ambivalent, or infrequently thought about. Together, these intrapersonal factors account for a significant portion of variation in I-E correlations across domains, especially when the implicit and explicit attitudes are operationally measured by such simple affective ratings as good-bad, strong-weak, like-dislike, or warm-cold thermometer ratings (Hofmann, Gawronski, and Gschwendner, Le and Schmitt, 2005).

When individuals are *unable or unmotivated to search memory* or integrate additional information into an explicit evaluation, I-E correlations are typically stronger than when respondents are encouraged to deliberate before responding (Fazio, 1990). Three common ways of limiting cognitive processing is to encourage rapid responses, distract, or otherwise introduce additional cognitive demands so as to impede search and deliberation. There is a good deal of evidence showing that speeded responses and deliberative responses load on separate factors. Essentially, the richer the context, more complicated the format, or harder the questions, the more likely it is that *less-important* considerations will enter the evaluation. Here, we think the best course of action is to *not* follow Ben Franklin's dictum encouraging people to stop, think, and compute a preference, but rather to take the advice of Zen Master Chogyam Trungpa (1983): "First Thought. Best Thought."

Implicit-explicit consistency is also found to increase *when implicit and explicit attitudes are assessed similarly.* For example, following good measurement theory, modern explicit attitude measures often infer attitudes by aggregating levels of agreement across a variety of propositional statements, as does, for example, the Modern Racism Scale and the multiple item NES abortion scale. But the richness of these explicit measures may actually be a hindrance to observing strong I-E consistency because implicit measures are found to reflect relatively simple good-bad associative relations as in the association of racial groups with positivity or negativity rather than nuanced measures of support or disapproval. The more dimensions, propositions, or challenges to an explicit attitude beyond the basic good-bad, like-dislike association, the more likely it is that implicit and explicit representations will diverge. If we are right in believing that online tallies represent the experienced costs and benefits of earlier evaluations, then relying on this implicit response would be both a reasonable and efficient strategy.

Implicit measures are sensitive to many and perhaps many more of the same *contextual factors* that impact explicit measures (Deutsch and Strack, 2010; Gawronski and Srithanan, 2010; Petty and Briñol, 2010). Initial evidence for the influence of context on implicit-explicit consistency is seen in a study by Wittenbrink, Judd, and Park (2001). Before completing several explicit measures of racial attitudes and an implicit Black/White subliminal priming measure of racial stereotyping, participants viewed a video clip of African Americans either in a gang-related urban setting or at an outdoor, suburban barbecue. Positive I-E correlations emerged only for participants in the gang-related video condition. For these respondents, their implicit stereotypic negativity toward African Americans was momentarily deactivated in the positive context.

While meta analysis of I-E relations shows that implicit and explicit measures are generally related, a positive correlation is of course no guarantee that the relationship isn't spurious. Construct validity is judged by how well the measures predict and explain a relevant behavior. Where, when, and the extent to which the measures diverge is difficult to gauge in the abstract. Of special note here, we once again call your attention to the interdependence of implicit and explicit processes and emphasize that automatic cognitive and affective processes *always* precede explicit responses. Given that implicit attitudes directly influence explicit attitudes, it is no wonder that the correlation between measures is typically positive, unless for strategic reasons respondents censure their immediate response or – this we think common – a citizen may have an implicit but not an explicit attitude toward the object.

In general, attitudes that are strong, important, certain, univalent, and have been evaluated frequently in the past yield higher I-E consistency than do attitudes that are weak, unimportant, uncertain, multipolar, ambivalent, or ephemeral. This pattern of findings suggests that I-E consistency is a function of how attitude objects are structurally represented in memory, in particular the strength of node-link associations, which in turn is a function of one's prior experience with the attitude object (Fazio and Zanna, 1978a, 1978b). A reasonable theoretical shorthand: implicit measures tap automatic and direct associations (i.e., OL tags) while explicit measures tap an integration of multiple direct and secondary associations from memory. The more complex the explicit measures, the more various will be the considerations brought to bear and the less the response will correlate with direct automatic associations.

Are Priming Effects Short Lived? Research by psychologists measuring the persistence of priming as well as framing effects on memory and attitudes is typically restricted to one-session studies, with estimates thereby limited to mere minutes. Perhaps the strongest tests of unconscious long-term effects are brought together in Merikle and Daneman's (1998) meta-analysis of priming on patients under general anesthesia. Across multiple studies they find evidence of the persistence of priming effects upwards of 36 hours, and in some studies cannot rule out consequences lasting three weeks to four months. In our single-session lab studies, we routinely find subliminal priming effects on $t_1 - t_2$ attitude change upwards of fifty minutes. Obviously, much more research needs to be done on the impact of *both* implicit and explicit information processing on everyday functioning. Consumer research seems the ideal domain for such studies, as experimental manipulations, for example, price, the color of packaging, or an athlete's endorsement can be randomly assigned at different locations, and the number of products sold provides a clear, easily measured effect. Though much more still needs to be done before we have a satisfactory answer to this question, such experiments in consumer research do show strong effects of unnoticed factors on purchases minutes to hours later (Maison, Greenwald, and Bruin, 2004; Mast and Zaltman, 2005).

External Validity. One might, and we know many colleagues do, object that experimental findings demonstrating the spontaneous impact of unnoticed priming events on beliefs and attitudes in the lab may be nothing more than a clever parlor room trick that only works (presumably with small effects) in a contrived experimental setting devoid of any "real world" complexity. True enough, our research, like most social-psychological studies of information processing, is based largely on research conducted in well-controlled, distraction-free settings, tapping behaviors free of immediate, serious consequences to life and limb. As is the case for all experimental *and* survey research there is a tradeoff pitting internal against external validity and it is always the case in the social and behavioral sciences that betwixt the two is an abyss few of us have seen across. In our studies, we opt to maximize internal validity, because if the internal validity of a survey or experiment is compromised, questioning the external validity would be moot. Our basic argument for taking our lab results seriously is that the capacity for unconscious processing is hard wired in the brain and our lab results are demonstrations of an effect that operates in real, artificial, and virtual worlds.

That said, it is certainly the case that not nearly enough work has been done to establish the validity of *either* laboratory or survey research on the expression of beliefs and attitudes in real-world settings, but there are numerous studies that do address the challenge (Perugini, Richetin, and Zogmaister, 2010). One of the first field experiments on political behavior, Gosnell's 1927 classic *Getting Out the Vote*, showed that simply asking citizens whether they expected to vote increased voter turnout, this a "mere measurement" effect that has been replicated many times over (Greenwald et al., 1987). One of the earliest nonclinical studies we are aware of that looked at *un*conscious influences on attitudes was Razran's (1938) "luncheon technique" experiments, in which wall posters supporting different political causes were periodically displayed in a school cafeteria. Razran had people evaluate numerous political proposals before and after exposure to the posters, finding that although the participants were unable to discriminate those issues that had been exhibited on the lunchroom walls from those that had not, the proposals that had been displayed periodically at meal times gained significant approval. Razran, a student of Pavlov, interpreted this Type 2 cueing effect in terms of classical conditioning: food, a powerful unconditioned stimulus (the experiment was run at the height of the Great Depression), transferred affect to a paired object, here the unconsciously associated political issues.

Noticed but unappreciated effects are also at work in college classrooms where estimates of a teacher's height grow as a function of ascribed academic status (Wilson, 1968). And in the home, prerecorded laugh tracks on TV sitcoms, which most people say they dislike and claim have no effect, are shown to enhance the expressed enjoyment of shows (Fuller and Sheehy-Skeffington, 1974). More serious real-world social behaviors show even stronger effects, with a large literature showing a significant increase in suicides and suspicious single-driver vehicle fatalities following mass media reports of suicides, especially when the death is a celebrity of the same gender and age (Phillips, 1979; Gould and Schaffer, 1986). What is most striking about these real-world demonstrations of unconscious influences on behavior is that the priming effects appear stronger outside than inside the hallowed walls of the laboratory (Bushman and Anderson, 1998).

Much of the contemporary research on the external validity question is focused on the pursuit of goals, with many studies demonstrating that an intention to act can be as easily activated, as are semantic and affective associations (Bargh et al. 1996; Ferguson and Porter, 2010). The focus on goal behavior provides a compelling test of unconscious priming effects as the initiation and pursuit of goals is thought to be the epitome of volitional behavior (Chartrand and Bargh, 2002; Elliot and Fryer, 2007). Recall how the simple priming of the concept elderly led experimental participants to walk more slowly to the elevator and how the display of business paraphernalia promoted competitive behavior. In these studies not only were participants unaware that a goal had been primed but they also had no awareness of how or why they "consciously" decided to pursue the goal. Other research shows influences on goal-directed behavior generated by the mere passive activation of such relevant mental concepts as intelligence, politeness, power, cooperation, and achievement (Chen, Lee-Chai, and Bargh 2001).

Why Focus on Affect Rather Than Emotion? John.Q.Public is an affect-driven model and throughout we will have little to say about discrete or dimensional emotional responses, despite the fact that much recent research in political psychology focuses on its diffuse form, mood (Forgas, 2000), or on such specific expressions of emotion as anger, anxiety, fear, and hope (Brader, 2005, 2011; Huddy, Feldman, Taber, and Lahav, 2005; Just, Crigler, and Belt, 2007; Marcus, Neuman, and MacKuen, 2000; Marcus, MacKuen, and Neuman, 2011; Small and Lerner, 2008; Valentino, Hutchings, Banks, and Davis, 2008). In contrast, our approach focuses on the initial, more basic effects of positive and/or negative affect on the expression of beliefs, attitudes, and behavior. As we theorized above, valence affect is primary in setting the direction of response, in guiding subsequent appraisals of the situation, and in determining when and how citizens may or may not label their feelings as an emotion.

William James (1884) proposed what is still today one of the more compelling ideas on the psychology of emotion; to wit: each of the specific emotions is characterized by a unique pattern of somato-vascular changes, and it is the perception of these bodily changes that differentiates one emotion from another. Despite hundreds if not thousands of psycho-physiological studies testing this specificity of emotions hypothesis, it may come as a surprise to learn that while there are many studies showing specific patterns of autonomic nervous system (ANS) activity for one or more of the emotions (Ekman, 2003; Ito, 2010; Lerner and Keltner, 2000; Lerner, Small, and Loewenstein, 2004; Panksepp, 1998; Scherer, Shorr, and Johnstone, 2001), there is equal if not more disconfirming evidence (Barrett, 2006; Levenson, 2003; Russell, Bachorowski, and Fernández-Dols, 2003; Turner and Ortony, 1992). Although we often find some mean differences in such ANS responses as blood pressure, muscle tension, and sweat gland activity for a discrete emotion, most studies report modest to weak correlations, with still lower correlations across seemingly related situations (see the meta-analysis by Barrett, 2006). Heterogeneity trumps uniqueness (Zajonc and McIntosh, 1992).

Levenson (2003), in his overview in the *Handbook of Affective Sciences* on the psychophysiology of ANS patterns of discrete emotions, summarizes the current state of affairs:

Even if emotion elicitation tasks were usually successful in producing the desired emotion in most participants; even if the autonomic nervous system was inactive before and after being recruited in the service of emotion; even if emotion solicitations in the laboratory had the kind of sharp onset, close match to prototype, and high intensity that reliably produced full-blown emotional reactions; even if the autonomic concomitants of specific emotions were dramatically different; and even if effect sizes were huge, then it would still be critical to ensure that the autonomic physiology derived on a particular trial from a particular participant was in fact associated with the actual occurrence of the targeted emotion. In reality, none of these "ideal case" scenarios is likely to be true. Even the best of the available elicitation tasks often have unintended emotional outcomes; the autonomic nervous system is continually acting in the service of many masters other than emotion: laboratory-induced emotional elicitations are often pale comparisons of real-life ones; participants' emotional responses are often of low intensity and often include emotions other than the intended one; autonomic correlates of emotions are not unique but rather show complex patterns of overlap; and effect sizes are small.

What *can* be reliably differentiated by ANS measures is positive from negative affect (Lang et al., 1993; Ito and Cacioppo, 2005; Russell, 2003; Russell and Barrett, 1999).

Emotions, like beliefs and attitudes, but unlike valence affects, are constructed from what is accessible in memory, whether consciously perceived or not (Ruys and Stapel, 2008; Winkielman and Berridge, 2004), and in *JQP* the online tally representing the rewards and punishments of past evaluative experience anchors the construction process. A defining characteristic of emotional experience is its context, which triggers the reaction and gives feelings their shape, meaning, and functionality. The importance of the situational context for the labeling of an emotion is made apparent in studies that show how easy it is to manipulate how people categorize their emotions through subtle, even subliminal primes, or by varying contextual factors of which the person is unaware, hence the steep forgetting curve for source and contextual factors. You may remember having felt elated when your candidate scored a point in a debate or angry at the opposition's tactics, but you cannot reexperience the feeling itself (Niedenthal and Showers, 1991; Robinson and Clore, 2000). Except perhaps for strong, personally engaging experiences that were accompanied by heart-felt bodily responses (what Damasio, 2010, calls "body-loop" experiences), people have poor conscious access to such "objective" indicators of emotional experience as their heart rate, blood pressure, and other somatic changes, which could serve as important signals for labeling the emotional experience beyond good vs. bad and arousal (Cunningham and Van Bavel, 2009; Schachter and Singer, 1962; Strack, Martin, and Stepper, 1988). Note that somatic markers send simple signals of positivity-negativity and arousal that point out the direction of emotional response but cannot under everyday circumstances discriminate among the various negative or positive emotions.

The advent of brain imaging technologies has led many scientists to search for emotion specificity in the form of localization of discrete emotions. Two recent meta analyses of PET and MRI studies testing the hypothesis that fear, anger, sadness, disgust, and happiness have distinct neural circuits failed to find strong, consistent, or unambiguous evidence of localization in the brain for the specific emotions other than amygdala activation for fear (Murphy, Nimmo-Smith, and Lawrence, 2003; Phan, Wager, Taylor, and Liberzon, 2002). Moreover, thousands of connections to virtually every other brain module make it difficult to find a signature pattern for a specific emotion (Ito, 2010). Perhaps bigger and faster magnets with better spatial and temporal resolution will find localized emotions (Fowler and Schreiber, 2008; Ito, 2010; Westen, Blagov, Harenski, Kilts, and Hamann, 2006), but we are not there yet (van Veen, Krug, Schooler, and Carter, 2009).

Note that fMRI imaging cannot test the hot cognition, primacy of affect, or affective contagion postulates central to *JQP* because the fMRI brain-image "slices" are recorded in seconds while affect operates on a timescale of milliseconds. Electroencephalographic (EEG) recordings of brain wave activity from the scalp can be used to measure the activation of affect and is effects on cognitive connections, as in the Morris, Squires, Taber, and Lodge (2003) test of the hot cognition hypothesis, but cannot clearly identify spatial signature patterns.

Problems are apparent on the behavioral side as well where emotional responses are found to vary significantly by whether or not the experimental/survey setting allows the individual to express an appropriate coping strategy. For example, being angry may lead you to yell, stomp your feet, lash out, sit back seething, or walk away. The expression of anger is dependent in part on whether the antagonist is a powerful bully, your boss, an underling, a politician unreachable behind the TV screen, or something as uncontrollable as 9/11. Fear can be expressed behaviorally by vigilance, fleeing, or freezing like the poor soul in Edvard Monk's *Scream*. William James (1884) was right in believing that "thinking is for doing." Emotions evolved as behavioral triggers and coping mechanisms, yet most social science studies do not allow the individual to act out, to strike out, cower, vent their anger, or express any other "hot" emotion. This is a serious problem for political science research on emotion, where most of our studies look at very tempered responses of tepid emotions in inconsequential settings.

Parental Warning: Consider this "hot" example of the motivating power of arousal (and of the weak correspondence between survey response and real-world behavior). Ariely and Loewenstein (2006) asked how the sexual attitudes and behavioral intentions of rational, intelligent people (as a proxy, Berkeley male heterosexual undergraduates) change from a "cool" survey setting to when they are in an impassioned state. Twenty-nine questions were asked twice, the first time in a survey setting, the second time in the participant's dorm room, where alone with a copy of *Playboy* and a Saran-wrapped computer they recorded their "Yes"/"No" answers.

One series of questions asked the men to rate the attractiveness of different sexual prospects, among them (with first "cool" then "hot" Yes percentages in parentheses):

- "Can you imagine being attracted to a twelve-year-old girl?" ($23 \times 46\%$);
- "Can you imagine having sex with a sixty-year-old woman?" ($7 \times 23\%$);
- "If you were attracted to a woman and she proposed a threesome with a man would you do it?" ($19 \times 34\%$).

Other questions asked for the likelihood of engaging in such immoral acts as:

- "Would you keep trying to have sex after your date said no?" (20 × 45%);
- "Would you tell a woman that you loved her to increase the chance that she would have sex with you?" (30 × 51%);
- "Would you slip a woman a drug to increase the chance that she would have sex with you?" (5 × 26%).

In every case the young men's answers were dramatically different in their aroused state. Unaroused, they do not know what they think, like, or will likely do when in an ardent state. Self-protection, mainstream sexual conservatism, even morality were swept aside. Ariely (2008: 97) sums it up thus:

When the participants were in a cold, rational, superego-driven state, they respected women; they were not particularly attracted to the odd sexual activities we asked them about; they always took the moral high ground; and they expected that they would always use a condom. They thought they understood themselves, their preferences, and what actions they were capable of. But as it turned out, they completely underestimated their reactions.

True enough, for many of us the everyday life of conventional politics is not as arousing. But should we not assume that the emotional states of anger, jealousy, and excitement are similarly affected? Compared to the true colors of emotional experience, the recollected and prospective response is a bland, "as-if" experience, what Niedenthal and her colleagues (Niedenthal, Halberstadt, and Innes-Ker, 1999; Niedenthal, Halberstadt, and Setterlund, 1997) describe as a "hot-cold empathy gap." Predictions from emotion to behavior prove more reliable when the accompanying visceral response bolsters the attitudinal or behavioral response. The best chance for success in predicting public opinion and behavioral intentions are those experimental settings that manipulate emotions by exposing people to campaign ads, newscasts, or movie clips (Ansolabehere, Iyengar, Simon, and Valintino, 1994; Brader, 2006; Gilliam, Iyengar, Simon, and Wright, 1996; Valentino, Hutchings, and White, 2004), or challenge their beliefs and attitudes with real counterarguments and counterfactuals (Sniderman, Brody, and Tetlock, 1991; Taber and Lodge, 2006), or manipulate anxiety by having participants think about their own deaths and the rotting transformation of their bodies in the grave (Pyszczynski, Solomon, and Greenberg, 2003). Experiments that manipulate emotions grippingly appear better able to bridge the empathy gap by generating an experienced emotion rather than relying on an after-the-fact recollection.

Let us be clear: the question is *not* whether or not people have emotional experiences or whether they can read emotional expressions in themselves and in others. Surely they do, albeit not particulary well (Norris, Dumville, and Lacy, 2011). On this everyone is onboard. We all agree that great art, policy proposals, and politicians are more successful when they pull at the heart strings rather than appeal to the "brain" (Westen, 2008). What is problematic is when the attitude is measured cold while the predicted behavior is hot. The key question is whether people can reliably discern among and between their emotions, say anger from fear, and whether researchers can reliably discriminate them. The literature is clear: the answer is: "yes, "no," "sometimes," "to some degree or another" (Brader, 2011; Barrett, 2006; Ladd and Lenz, 2011; Marcus, MacKuen, and Neuman, 2011; Norris, Dumville, and Lacy, 2011; Rolls, 1999; Russell, 2003; Solomon, 2003). All that can be reliably discriminated from the correlate structure of neural, physiological, and subjective responses is the more basic good-bad affective response.

Moreover, it is typically the case that measured discrete emotions correlate so highly within the negative and positive domains (Barrett and Russell, 1998) that the specific emotions routinely fail to capture much unique variance (Feldman, 1995; Watson and Tellegen, 1985). The question emotion theorists need to answer is how much unexplained variance is left after controlling for valence? As we will show in the conclusion with NES data, not much.

Our view, shared with many appraisal theorists is that fundamental to all emotion responses is a common antecedent – positive and/or negative affect and arousal (see the overview by Forgas, 2003). Our focus on the primacy of affect fits comfortably within the affect-driven *primary appraisal stage* of appraisal theories of emotion in which an environmental situation is spontaneously perceived as positive, stressful, or irrelevant (Bower and Forgas, 2001; Clore, Schwarz, and Conway, 1994; Forgas, 2003; Niedenthal and Halberstadt, 2000). Generally, appraisal theory assumes that on exposure to an emotion-evoking stimulus, people *preconsciously* categorize their perception of the object as positive and/or negative. Critical here is that this immediate reaction occurs moments before a person is consciously aware of the stimulus, and may, *if* the individual is afforded the time and is sufficiently motivated, spur a conscious *secondary appraisal* seeking out reasons for "why I feel this way" (Robinson and Clore, 2002). The intensity of the affective response – presumably the degree of its sympathetic and parasympathetic activation – promotes a felt need to act in an affectively congruent manner, but the specific action taken depends on one's unconscious and conscious appraisals of the triggering event in context, which in turn depends on what coping strategies exist.

As we see it, in general agreement with the classic Schachter and Singer (1962) theory of emotion, appraisal of an emotion's cause produces the emotional label. Emotions are always about something; one cannot experience fear without being aware of the gun, be angry without seeing the opponent's sneer, be depressed without seeing the pictures of starving children. Appraisal of the cause of an affect is what produces an emotion. The secondary, subjective report of an emotional experience is the postappraisal labeling of one's affective response, which, if hot, is experienced viscerally, though perhaps not consciously (Lerner and Keltner, 2000). One may feel aroused, but the emotion itself requires a reason for the feeling. The actual label given the somatic ("gut") experience is context dependent and culturally-based, and will be strongly influenced by folkloric explanations for how people should respond in such situations (Robinson and Clore, 2000).

Again, we do not deny the existence of emotions or their demonstrable effects on animal and human behavior, but we are skeptical of our present-day skill as social scientists to reliably discriminate among like-valenced emotional responses (which routinely correlate in the .60–.80 range). There is incontrovertible evidence that a simple, good-bad, approach-avoidance response enters the decision stream spontaneously before an appraisal of the situation may guide the labeling of an emotion as anger, fear, anxiety, hope, or enthusiasm. Given the primacy of affect, once valence is controlled for there is precious little remaining unexplained variance for similarly valenced discrete emotional responses. The problem is exacerbated in the social sciences where our manipulations of emotions in experiments are typically weak. For example, we might induce sadness by having participants listen to a recording of the second movement of Schubert's *Death of a Maiden* while reading a news account of a candidate's policy proposals, or worse yet "manipulate" anxiety by informing respondents that a hypothetical candidate takes an issue position at odds with their own. At best such manipulations promote tepid, as-if emotional responses. The problem doesn't stop here: Few of our dependent variables capture an emotion as a coping mechanism by providing respondents the opportunity to strike out in anger, slump sadly, cringe, or actively seek out and cope with a threat.

Looking Ahead

The remainder of the book puts our key hypotheses to the test.

Chapter 3 will examine the *hot cognition hypothesis* with respect to political leaders, groups, and ideas. Chapter 4 will extend hot cognition to group and identity objects. In both chapters, we will seek to establish the *automaticity* of affective reactions to political stimuli. Chapter 5 will test the *affect transfer hypothesis* in the context of candidate evaluations, and will take a close look at our expectation that careful deliberation will increase the impact of unconscious processes. *Affect contagion* is the focus of Chapter 6, which will examine the degree to which the conscious generation of thoughts or considerations can be influenced by unnoticed affective primes, with downstream consequences for policy attitudes. Chapter 7 presents our empirical work on motivated reasoning about political policies. Our theory has been formalized as a computational model (*JQP*), and tests of the workings of this model are the subject of Chapter 8.

The seven postulates defining *JQP* place us squarely at odds with several of the most prominent models of public opinion, chief among them: (1) Zaller's (1992) "Receive-Accept-Sample" (RAS) model that informs his classic *The Nature and Origins of Mass Opinion* and the Zaller and Feldman (1992) application of the model to the survey response; (2) Marcus, Neuman, and

MacKuen's (2000) Affective Intelligence model; and (3) Lau and Redlawsk's (2006) models of heuristic decision making. These models are among the very best we political psychologists have developed to date and each makes a unique, positive contribution to our understanding of how citizens process information and inform their behavior. *JQP* shares much with each of these models at a general, descriptive level but differs significantly in theoretical process, in key predictions, in the manner of hypothesis testing, and in how we interpret the empirical results, both ours and theirs. We leave a discussion of the similarities and sharp differences between models to the conclusion in Chapter 9, when the reader will have the empirical tests of *JQP* in hand to make an informed evaluation of competing claims.

3

Experimental Tests of Automatic Hot Cognition

The central component of our dual-process model and force driving the rationalization of political beliefs and judgments is hot cognition (Postulate 2), which posits that all social concepts thought about and evaluated in the past become affectively charged – positively and/or negatively – and as depicted in Figure 2.1, this affective charge is linked directly to the concept in LTM. These positive and negative evaluative tags come automatically and inescapably to mind within milliseconds of exposure to the object (Postulate 1) – appreciably faster than do conscious appraisals of the object – thereupon signaling the object's affective coloration (Postulate 3). As with Clore and Isbell's (2001) "how-do-I-feel heuristic?" and Sniderman, Brody, and Tetlock's (1991) "likeability heuristic," this spontaneously evoked evaluative tally becomes immediately accessible information (Postulate 4), which infuses the judgment process from start to finish – from the encoding of information (Postulate 5), its retrieval and comprehension, to its expression as a preference or choice (Postulates 6 and 7). In this chapter we report on three experimental tests that show that many political concepts are hot cognitions whose affective tags are activated on mere exposure to the political leader, group, or issue. Later chapters will document the spontaneous biasing effects of these hot cognitions on what citizen's think and how they reason about the world of politics (Lodge and Taber, 2005; McGraw, Fischle, Stenner and Lodge, 1996; McGraw, Lodge, and Jones, 2002; Taber and Lodge, 2006; Taber, Lodge, and Glather, 2001).

Our focus in this chapter is on "snap judgments" – responses made quickly through the direct retrieval of online tallies, which automatically pop into working memory (WM) where they are "felt" to be good-enough responses in the situation, as when, for example, people tell you how well the president is handling his job without computing a response from recollected pros and cons. We will later turn to the impact of unnoticed affective processing on more

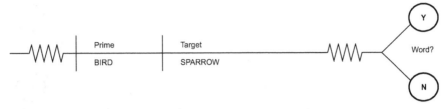

FIGURE 3.1. Lexical Decision Task

deliberative judgments and preferences, as when people are called upon to stop and think before responding.

Specific to the automaticity of affective snap judgments, we will demonstrate that:

- Citizens respond spontaneously to the affective components of a broad array of attitudinal objects (political leaders, groups, and issues), even when affective primes are presented below the threshold of conscious awareness;
- These automatic affective responses are strongest for those with the strongest prior attitudes and for the most sophisticated citizens; and
- These automatic responses are purely affective, so that even semantically and substantively unrelated affective cues reliably influence snap judgments about political leaders, groups, and issues.

The implication of these findings (to be replicated many times over in subsequent chapters) is that a simple good/bad affective tag is linked to many political objects in LTM, be they political leaders, groups, issues, abstract concepts, symbols, or events, and this affect is triggered automatically on mere exposure to the concept, even when the object is consciously unnoticed, and even when the object is politically irrelevant.

Experimental Paradigms for the Priming of Affect and Cognition

Several experimental methods have proven successful in demonstrating the influence of priming events on higher order mental processes: the *lexical decision task* is used extensively in cognitive psychology for determining the meanings of concepts and their semantic associations; the *sentence verification task* is also commonly used to test for semantic associations; and the *sequential attitude priming paradigm*, which tests for the association of feelings to concepts in memory.

In the classic *lexical decision task* pictured in Figure 3.1, an experimental participant is exposed to a "prime" word on a computer screen (here BIRD), followed quickly by a "target" stimulus, which is either a word (e.g., "sparrow") or a nonword foil (e.g., "praswor"). The task is to press "as quickly as possible without making too many mistakes" a button labeled "Yes," if

FIGURE 3.2. Sentence Verification Task

the target is believed to be a legal English word or a button labeled "No" if the target is not an English word. Referring back to the node-link spreading activation model of memory (Figure 2.1), the basic idea is that the closer the semantic association between the prime and target concepts in LTM the faster the reaction time (RT) to say the object is a word (with nonword trials typically dropped from analyses). For strongly associated concepts (e.g., bird: sparrow) we expect a facilitation effect, that is, relatively fast reaction times to verify the belief that "sparrow" is a word because of the close, well-learned semantic association between the two concepts in LTM. Where the prime and target are more distant (e.g., bird: penguin or bird: ostrich), we would predict a slower response time, at least among us city folk. When the prime and target are not associated (e.g., bird: armchair), we anticipate an inhibition effect, a still slower RT, and more errors. This paradigm can also be used to study conceptual relations in memory by targeting the characteristics of concepts, as for example, "wings," "beak," "eats worms" when primed with "bird." This cognitive priming paradigm produces robust effects demonstrating the associative nature of semantic memory (Collins and Loftus, 1975; Collins and Quillian, 1969).

The *sentence verification task* is also used to map semantic associations. Here again subjects are presented with a prompt, followed by a target word or phrase. Their task is to press "as quickly as possible without making too many errors" a key labeled "True" if the phrase is a true statement about the prompt or a key labeled "False" if it is not. The dependent variables are the T/F responses and the response latencies, which indicate the accessibility (and perhaps the strength) of the relevant belief. Figure 3.2 illustrates this procedure using a simple political example: Is Barack Obama an African-American? Note that the procedure can also be used for beliefs that are not "objectively true." For example, we could ask: Is Barack Obama a Patriot?

But what about affect? Are one's feelings also automatically activated when a concept is activated? That is the hot cognition question central to our *JQP* model of political judgment. To turn the hot cognition postulate from conjecture to a testable hypothesis, we turn to an experimental procedure known as the *sequential attitude priming paradigm* (Bargh, Chaiken, Govender, and Pratto, 1992; Fazio, Sanbonmatsu, Powell, and Kardes, 1986), which was designed to test experimentally whether positive or negative affect is directly

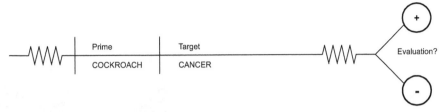

FIGURE 3.3. Sequential Attitude Priming

linked to a concept in memory and if so is it spontaneously activated on its mere exposure.

The logic of the design was that to the extent that presentation of the attitude object name activated the evaluation associated with the attitude object, this evaluation (good or bad) would then influence how quickly subjects could correctly classify the target adjective as positive or negative in meaning. If the adjective was of the same valence as the attitude object prime, responses should have been faster (i.e., facilitated) relative to a baseline response.... Conversely, if the adjective and prime were of opposite valence, responses should be slower (Bargh et al. 1992: 894).

As in the lexical decision task, this attitude priming procedure exposes subjects to a prime followed by a target concept, but now we are interested in the facilitation or inhibition of response time (RT) as a function of the affective congruence of the prime and target concepts. The subject's task is to press one button labeled "positive" or another labeled "negative," to indicate "as fast as possible without making too many errors" whether the target word, chosen for its *un*ambiguous positive or negative meaning (for example "delightful" or "cancer"), has a positive or negative connotation. The latency time from onset of target word to positive or negative button response is recorded.

If, as in Figure 3.3, "cockroach" were the prime and the target word "cancer," the hot cognition hypothesis predicts facilitation, a relatively fast RT because the prime and target are *affectively congruent*, though they are not semantically related. Conversely, if the prime were "cockroach" but the target word "sunshine," we would expect inhibition, a slower RT, to say sunshine is positive – because its relation to cockroach is *affectively incongruent*. Note that this is *a nonreactive task*: we never explicitly ask people to indicate whether the target word describes a cockroach or whether they feel positive or negatively toward cockroaches, but rather to simply indicate whether the target word carries a positive or negative meaning. Looking ahead, are politicians disgusting?

In an exploratory test of the hot cognition hypothesis, we had participants read a one page facsimile of a campaign brochure for a hypothetical Congressman William Lucas (Lodge and Taber 2000). In addition to the congressman's picture we provided a paragraph of information detailing his background

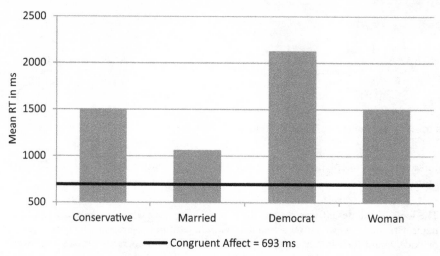

FIGURE 3.4. Comparison of Semantic and Affective RTs to the Prime "Lucas"

(for example, Lucas graduated from Syracuse University) and experience (for example, he is a two-term Republican representative), as well as a paragraph stating his strong position on gun control (manipulated so that he favored stricter controls for half the participants, opposition for the others). After reading the brochure, participants performed a variant of the sentence verification task in which they indicated by a True/False button response whether LUCAS was, for example, a Republican (Yes), a woman (No), pro (Yes) or anti (No) gun control (as in Figure 3.2).

We also engaged study participants in the attitude-priming task (Figure 3.3) where "Lucas" was used to prime such clear-cut positive trait and emotion target words taken from the National Election Survey (Kinder, 1986; Kinder et al., 1980) as "proud," "intelligent," "compassionate," "moral," and such negative targets as "angry," "afraid," "weak," and "dishonest." The subjects' task was to press a plus or minus computer key as quickly as possible to indicate whether the target word was positive or negative. The hot cognition hypothesis predicts an affect-congruence effect – faster reaction times for supporters of Congressman Lucas to the positive words, slower RTs to the negative words, and vice versa for participants who disliked Lucas because of his stand on gun control. We also predicted – given the primacy of affect hypothesis (Postulate 4) – that the affective responses to the trait words evaluated in the sequential priming task would be faster than the cognitive responses from the sentence verification task.

Figure 3.4 reports the reaction times for the belief-based True/False responses in this sentence verification task to the single-word targets "congressman," "married," "Democrat," and "woman," as well as the mean reaction time to the affectively congruent target words in the attitude priming task (the black horizontal line). The first two of these bars (congressman and married) report "Yes" responses; the last two (Democrat and woman) are "No" responses. The Y axis is response time (RT) with all response latencies measured in milliseconds (ms).

Because participants had previously indicated their feelings toward Lucas on a seven-point like-dislike scale, we can also test the hot cognition hypothesis by comparing the reaction times for affectively congruent prime-target pairings with reaction times for incongruent pairings: we would expect those subjects who dislike Lucas on seeing a negatively valenced target word (or those who like him on seeing a positively valenced target) to show a general pattern of facilitation – a faster than average response time as compared to the affectively incongruent associations where we anticipate inhibition. On average it did take participants significantly less time (M = 693 ms) to make an affectively congruent response than to make an affectively incongruent response (M = 759 ms) to Congressman Lucas. Moreover, in both cases the affective responses are about twice as fast as the time taken to verify the simplest of factual queries. We see this as tentative support for our "hot cognition" hypothesis and, what is more, as providing preliminary support for the "primacy of affect" hypothesis (Murphy and Zajonc, 1993; Zajonc, 1980, 2002) in showing that affect is responded to faster than are the cognitive associations that had been learned about a novel political object.

Noteworthy here is that both the cognitive verification and affective facilitation effects were created on only a one- to two-minute reading of the campaign brochure, with all the information except the candidate's position on gun control not especially interesting or arousing or personally involving to the participants. Yet, even under these minimalist laboratory conditions an evaluative reaction to the fictitious congressman was formed enabling a rapid affective response. An untested assumption here – evidence forthcoming – is that a summary impression of Lucas was formed online, in real time. As our participants read the facts and issue positions in the campaign brochure they were apparently able to spontaneously extract the evaluative implications of the information and then and there integrated this information into a summary evaluative tally of the congressman, which was then readily accessible to influence subsequent cognitive and evaluative processing.

Experimental Tests of the Automaticity of Affect for Political Leaders, Groups, and Issues

What the Lucas experiment did *not* do was demonstrate the *automaticity* of the evaluative responses. The affective responses were fast, significantly faster than the cognitive responses, but were they evoked without conscious appraisal of the congressman's traits and issue positions? To test for the automaticity of affect we need to employ the more powerful variant of the *sequential attitude priming paradigm* developed by Fazio and his colleagues (1986) and Bargh and his colleagues (1992). Critical here for demonstrating automaticity – as distinct from the simple associative strength effects found in our Lucas study – is to precisely manipulate the time from the onset of the prime to the onset of the target so that in the key experimental condition the prime appears too quickly for conscious considerations to inform the evaluation, while in long condition the prime is exposed long enough to allow conscious expectations to develop. The essential timing manipulation is called the stimulus onset asynchrony (SOA).

The time from the onset of the prime word to the onset of the target word is a critical feature of this priming paradigm as in the short condition it is too brief an interval for participants to develop an active expectancy or response strategy regarding the target adjective that follows; such conscious and flexible expectancies require at least 500 milliseconds to develop, and to influence responses in priming tasks (Neely, 1977; Posner and Snyder, 1975a, 1975b). Given an SOA of 300 milliseconds (the stimulus onset asynchrony, the interval from prime to target), then, if presentation of an attitude object prime influences response time to a target adjective, it can only be attributed to an automatic, unintended activation of the corresponding attitude (Bargh, Chaiken, Govender, and Pratto, 1992: 894).

Our hypothesis that hot cognitions arise *automatically* predicts that affective facilitation and inhibition effects should show up *only* in the short prime-to-target SOA condition when the prime is presented below the threshold of conscious expectations, and not at a long SOA when conscious expectancies about the target could be formed that will interfere with the response. While there are now hundreds of attitude priming studies in the literature (see Gawronski and Payne, 2010, and Wegner and Bargh, 1998, for broad surveys) and strong experimental support for the spontaneous processing of affective information (Bodenhausen and Todd, 2010; Ferguson and Bargh, 2003; Oskamp and Schultz, 2005), there have been few compelling tests of the automaticity of affect in the political domain for political leaders, political groups, and issues (Lodge, McGraw and Stroh, 1989; Morris, Squires, Taber, and Lodge, 2003), and still fewer explorations of the individual differences and situational constraints that are expected to condition the automaticity of affect on political evaluations.

Much of the experimental literature on automaticity focuses on how people form and update their impressions of other individuals (Amodio and Mendoza, 2010). The basic finding, dating back to the classic studies by Solomon Asch (1946), is that perceivers spontaneously infer traits, beliefs, attitudes, and motives of others that are thought to represent the dispositional characteristics of that person (Trawalter and Shapiro, 2010; Uleman, Newman, and Moskowitz, 1996). Seeking to understand why others act as they do, observers are prone to make online dispositional attributions as the information is being processed (Hastie and Park, 1896; Lichtenstein and Srull, 1987). While these initial inferences may subsequently be adjusted in light of new information, we seem predisposed to interpret the behavior of other people in terms of the target person's perceived underlying personality with little regard for situational factors. This effect is so strong it goes under the heading of the "fundamental attribution error" (Heider, 1958). In the political context, we expect that those citizens who have thought most about (and in so doing spontaneously evaluated) political figures will have developed a strong affective association linking the person to positive and/or negative feelings in LTM, which now on mere exposure to name or image will automatically activate the evaluation.

But what about group impressions? Can people form and keep a running tally of their moment by moment impressions of groups as spontaneously and efficiently as they manage their impressions of other individuals? The answer is it depends (Hamilton and Sherman, 1994), with a number of reputable scholars suggesting that the evaluation of political groups, and even more so of issues, may not be processed the same way as people are (see Bassili and Roy, 1998; Lavine, 2001; McGraw and Steenbergen, 1995).

Two arguments are advanced for why the evaluation of groups may differ from the evaluation of people: one is that the recognition and evaluation of other people, especially on seeing their facial appearance and posture, appears to be hard-wired in dedicated brain structures, hence easy and quick for us to make online evaluations of them. A second argument, specific to groups, is that because within-group variance, awkwardly called "entitativity" (Campbell, 1958), is typically greater than the perceived variance within individuals, people may not form affective associations spontaneously and may therefore rely on conscious considerations when evaluating groups (Hamilton and Sherman, 1996). Whereas impressions of individuals are primacy driven – first impressions count heavily and dominate the process – perhaps the assessment of groups is more memory-based, hence less reliant on retrieval of an evaluative tally.

The concern is even greater for issues where Zaller and Feldman (1992) make the case that when evaluating political issues, especially when the political parties take opposing positions (Zaller, 1992), citizens are apt to see two or more sides, and their awareness of the pros and cons may prevent them from being able to immediately form a crystallized evaluation, especially if they are themselves ambivalent about the issue. If this is the case, when called on to report a summary evaluation, perhaps citizens cannot spontaneously retrieve a good or bad affective tag from memory, but must rely on memory-based, piecemeal processing to sample whatever considerations are accessible in memory about the issue and only then construct an evaluation by integrating these conscious considerations into an evaluation (Fiske and Pavelchak, 1986; Tourangeau, Rips, and Rasinski, 2000; Zaller and Feldman, 1992).

To address these concerns we carried out a series of priming experiments designed to (1) test for the automaticity of affect by systematically employing the more powerful variant of the attitude priming paradigm which guarantees that processing operates at the unconscious level; (2) test for the generalizability of hot cognition across increasingly broad ranges of political leaders, groups,

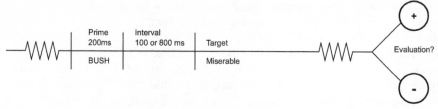

FIGURE 3.5. Political Hot Cognition Experiments

issues, and abstract concepts; and (3) test for individual moderators of the automaticity of facilitation and inhibition effects.

Because these studies are similar in design, differing primarily in the breadth of political primes, an expanded set of targets, and the treatment of SOA, let us discuss them together.

Experimental Procedures. Undergraduate students in introductory political science courses at Stony Brook University received extra credit for their participation: Study 1, N = 80; Study 2, N = 162; Study 3, N = 95. All studies were conducted in our Laboratory for Experimental Research in Political Behavior, with study participants carrying out the tasks individually on personal computers in separate experimental rooms.

The experiments proceeded in stages: first, participants were instructed in and given practice using a button response on a computer keyboard to indicate "as quickly as possible without making too many errors" whether the connotation of a target word was "positive/good" or "negative/bad," as depicted in Figure 3.5. In all experimental trials, a prime word (for example BUSH) appeared in upper case and remained in the center of the screen for 200 milliseconds, followed by either by a 100 milliseconds blank screen for a short SOA totaling 300 milliseconds or by an 800-millisecond blank screen for a long SOA of 1000 milliseconds. A target word (for example, "miserable") then appeared center-screen in lower case and remained on screen until the participants' "Good" or "Bad" button responded to the target word. Trials were separated by a two-second pause.

Following this attitude-priming task, participants completed a computer-based survey to collect explicitly: (1) each participant's good-bad ratings of the target words; (2) their Likert ratings of the positivity of the prime words and separately their negativity ratings of the prime words, which allows us to measure both the valence and level of ambivalence of the primes; (3) Likert ratings of their strength of attitude toward the political leaders, groups, and issues; (4) basic demographics; and (5) general political knowledge questions and questions about the current or most recent office held by each of the political figures among the primes. Table 3.1 lists the primes and targets used in each of the three studies.

Primes and Targets. In choosing primes for our studies we wanted a fairly broad range of political objects (persons, groups, and issues), a close-to-even

TABLE 3.1. *Primes and Targets for Hot Cognition Experiments*

Person Primes	Group Primes	Issue Primes	Positive Targets	Negative Targets
		Study 1		
Clinton	Democrat	Anti Abortion	appealing	awful
Gore	Politician	Death Penalty	beautiful	horrible
Guiliani	Republican	Peace	delightful	miserable
Hitler		Taxes	magnificent	painful
Lincoln			marvelous	repulsive
Pataki				
		Study 2		
Bush	Democrats	Guns	comedy	cancer
Gore	Politician	Peace	rainbow	funeral
Hillary	Republicans	Taxes	miracle	mutilate
Hitler			love	toothache
Lincoln			joy	death
Rudy			laughter	rape
		Study 3		
Colin Powell	African-	Affirmative Action	gift	death
George W. Bush	Americans	Counter-Terrorism	hug	demon
Giuliani	Americans	Death Penalty	joy	grief
Hillary	Arabs	Free Speech	laughter	pain
Hitler	Democrats	Gun Control	rainbow	rabies
Kennedy	Jews	Pro-Choice		
Lincoln	NAACP	Pro-Life		
Mark Green	NRA	Taxes		
Mike Bloomberg	Politicians	Welfare		
Osama bin Laden	Republicans			
Pataki	Terrorists			

split for our study participants between positive and negative primes, and some primes expected to stir up ambivalence. Target words were selected from a list of concepts compiled and nationally normed by Bradley and Lang (1999). The most important criterion for target words was that each must have a clearly univalent and widely accepted evaluative implication, half of them positive and half negative.

Measures and Data Manipulations. The valence of each prime was measured as the difference between the positive and negative evaluations of the object for each participant dichotomized so that any difference greater than zero is coded positive, any difference less than zero is coded negative, and any difference equal to zero is set to missing. The nine-point measure of prime strength was dichotomized around the scale midpoint to differentiate weak from strong evaluations. Prime ambivalence was computed using the Griffin formula, which averages the positive and negative ratings and subtracts the absolute value of the difference between positive and negative ratings (Lavine, 2001; Meffert, Guge, and Lodge, 2004; Thompson, Zanna, and Griffin, 1995) and then splits at the scale midpoint to discriminate low from high ambivalence. Sophistication was measured as the number of correct responses on the political knowledge test (seventeen possible), subjected to a median split to differentiate unsophisticates from sophisticates.

By their nature, reaction time data are positively skewed as there is a lower limit in one's response time, and this skewness can affect group means in the analysis of variance. To correct for positive skewness, we converted the raw reaction time data to natural logs. All statistical results we report are computed on these log transformed reaction time data (the overall pattern of results emerges with or without this transformation). In addition, as is common practice, we eliminated trials involving targets that had been incorrectly rated in the survey (for example, someone might say that "repulsive" was a good thing, in which case we excluded the trials for that subject for that target; this procedure eliminated .04 percent of trials across the three studies), and we also dropped trials in which there was an incorrect response to the target on the RT (for example gift/bad; .05 percent of trials across the three studies).

Hypotheses and Design. Studies 1 and 2 were mixed model designs with repeated measures on prime and target valence: we manipulated the interval between prime and target presentation so that half of our participants received a long interval and half received a short interval (long versus short SOA), the valence of the political prime word (positive versus negative), and the valence of the non-political target word. Study 3 differed in that SOA was manipulated within subjects so that the same subjects sometimes received long and sometimes short intervals.

In each of the studies, we expect that response times will be faster for affectively congruent prime-target concepts (pos/pos and neg/neg) than for incongruent pairs (neg/pos and pos/neg), which is the basic hot cognition hypothesis. If, as predicted, evaluations arise automatically rather than deliberatively, we also expect that the predicted facilitation and inhibition effects will show up *only* in the short SOA condition and not in the long SOA condition when conscious expectancies will impede the spontaneous activation of hot cognitions. Operationally, these expectations are represented by the three-way interaction, SOA × prime valence × target valence. In order to explore potential moderating factors, we will break down these results by sophistication (between participant correlate) and attitude strength (within participant). In general, we predict that political sophisticates and those with strong attitudes would be most likely to have formed online affective links for the political leaders, groups, and issues, and so we expect stronger results for sophisticates than for unsophisticates and for objects that evoke strong rather than weak attitudes.

Finally, the expectation of some that groups and issues will be less linked than persons to evaluative affect is fundamentally based on the argument that

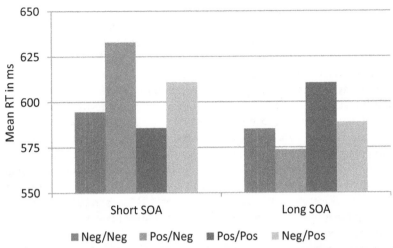

FIGURE 3.6. Average Reaction Times for Congruent and Incongruent Trials, Study 1

attitudes toward these less "unitary" objects require a conscious assessment of sampled pro and con considerations and consequently should not evoke an automatic facilitation effect. Therefore, in addition to testing the hot cognition hypothesis for the three types of primes (persons, groups, issues), we will directly test the underlying contention that hot cognition should be weaker for ambivalent primes.

Results. To examine whether evaluatively congruent prime-target pairs will elicit faster reaction times (RT) than incongruently paired concepts in the short SOA condition but not the long SOA condition, we performed a 2 (SOA) × 2 (prime valence) × 2 (target valence) mixed effects analysis of variance with repeated measures on the second and third factors on the log transformed reaction time data from experiments 1 and 2. For experiment 3, SOA was manipulated within subjects and so is treated as a repeated measure in the analyses. We are also interested in seeing if this basic interaction is conditioned on prime type (whether person, group, or issue), on the sophistication of respondents, on one's strength of attitude toward the prime, and on ambivalence toward the prime, all of which entail higher order interaction analyses.

Following a presentation format in Figure 3.6 that we use for reaction time data throughout this book, results are depicted as bar graphs in sets of four bars, each representing the RT mean for each of the basic groups defined by the prime-by-target valence interaction. Congruent pairings are shown in columns 1 and 3 (negative primes/negative targets, positive primes/positive targets), with incongruent pairings in columns 2 and 4 (positive primes/negative targets, and negative primes/positive targets). To ease interpretation, all bar charts depict raw reaction times, but because of positive skewness, statistical analyses are computed on log normal transformed RTs. The hot cognition hypothesis posits that the response times to the attitudinally congruent concepts will be faster (shorter bars, signaling facilitation) than RTs to attitudinally incongruent pairs (longer bars, indicating inhibition). The most informative comparison is between the first and second bars (for negative targets) and between the third and fourth bars (for positive targets).

Looking first at the basic hot cognition prediction for Study 1 (for all political primes combined), we find strong support for the hypothesized three way interaction of SOA, prime, and target, $F(1, 78) = 14.29$, $p < .001$, with no significant main effects. This result is illustrated in Figure 3.6, which contrasts the basic expected pattern of pronounced facilitation and inhibition effects at short SOA, but with no statistically discernable facilitation or inhibition effects at long SOA across all political leaders, groups, and issues combined. Follow-up contrasts confirm the apparent pattern: under short SOA, responses to negative targets are significantly faster when preceded by negative primes, $t(45) = 2.02$, $p = .025$ (one-tailed), while positive targets elicit faster response times when paired with positive primes, $t(44) = 2.26$, $p = .02$. As called for by theory, similar contrasts for the condition in which participants had sufficient time to prepare a conscious response failed to reach significance. The remaining figures will focus only on the theoretically important short SOA condition which signals the automaticity of responses.

Study 1 provides initial support for the hot cognition hypothesis: affect it seems *is* triggered automatically on mere presentation of a political attitude object and has discernible effects on the affective ratings of target words. It is still possible, however, that this priming effect represents a *semantic* rather than *evaluative* association in memory for our participants. That is, perhaps the trait adjectives used in Study 1 (appealing, delightful, awful, repulsive) were somehow semantically associated with some of the leaders, groups, or issues used as primes, whereupon a cognitive association could generate the priming effect we attribute to affect. People are prone to make trait inferences spontaneously based on little direct evidence (Park, 1989; Rahn, Aldrich, and Borgida, 1994; Rapport, Metcalf, and Hartman, 1989; Uleman and Bargh, 1989), so perhaps their affective responses are being cognitively mediated, i.e., it's conceivable that something the Democrats did led our participants to infer that they are "horrible" or something Clinton did was "marvelous." This is in fact the implication of the classic affect-free semantic network model that began the cognitive revolution (Lindsay and Norman, 1977): people store their trait inferences with the concept node in LTM and only later compute an evaluation from the considerations that come to mind. Accordingly, the prime "Giuliani" would activate the network of associations linked to him (mayor, tough) and, spreading activation, energize a connection to something he said or did that was interpreted as "magnificent" (reduced crime in NYC) and consequently the target word is now responded to more quickly. While it is even more of a stretch to see how the trait concepts would be linked to such issues as "peace" and "taxes," it is conceivable that groups and policies may be metonymically "personalized" with trait attributes (Lakoff, 1991, 2001).

We believe that our alternative hypothesis, the hot cognition and primacy of affect interpretation of these results, is more plausible (Zajonc, 1980; 2000; Murphy and Zajonc, 1993). In this view, the cognitive and affective systems follow separate, albeit interdependent pathways in the brain, with feelings following a quick and dirty route (LeDoux, 1996) that "prepares" a behavioral response *before* one's cognitive associations can traverse the neo cortex to reach conscious awareness. A strong test of this hypothesis within the attitude-priming paradigm would be to break any cognitive connection between the attitudinal prime and the target concepts. This is what we do in Studies 2 and 3.

Referring back to Table 3.1 for the full set of primes and targets across Studies 2 and 3, the attitudinal primes are here again political persons, groups, and issues, but now the affective target words are nouns selected from Bradley and Lang's (1999) *Affective Norms for English Words*, chosen by us to be affectively *un*ambiguous *and* semantically *un*related to the leaders, groups, or issues (for example, comedy, miracle, rainbow, toothache, cancer, rape). If we find facilitation effects for these semantically unrelated but affectively congruent prime-target pairings and inhibition for semantically unrelated but affectively incongruent pairings, we will have a compelling demonstration of the automaticity of affect for political objects as well as evidence that the affective tag linked to well-formed attitudes can be activated *independently* of the cognitive considerations that originally led to the affective evaluation. In addition, Study 3 introduces a within subjects manipulation on SOA (the same subjects do half their trials with a long and half with a short interval between presentation of the prime and target words) so as to increase statistical power. And more importantly, Study 3 introduces a much expanded set of less familiar leader, group, and issue primes to allow us to better test for attitude strength, ambivalence, and sophistication effects.

Figure 3.7 presents the results at short SOA for Studies 2 and 3 for all political primes combined. Again, as predicted, the three-way interaction for SOA, prime valence, and target valence was highly significant in both studies (computed on log transformed data): Study 2: $F(1, 160) = 20.26$, $p < .001$; Study 3: $F(1, 94) = 20.40$, $p < .001$. All main effects were insignificant. Planned follow-up contrasts confirm the expected pattern, with means shown in Figure 3.7: in the short SOA condition, when responses can only be attributed to automatic processing – positive and negative congruent pairs were significantly faster than incongruent pairs (Study 2: for positive targets, $t(82) = 5.19$, $p < .001$ (all one-tailed tests); negative targets, $t(81) = 4.08$, $p < .001$; Study 3: positive primes, $t(100) = 2.43$, $p < .01$; negative primes, $t(100) = 4.21$, $p < .001$). Again, no contrasts were significant at long SOA.

Taken together, the support for hot cognition across these three studies and a broad array of political concepts is striking, showing clear evidence of an automatically accessible, readily-retrieved connection in memory between positive or negative affect and political leaders, groups, and issues. Moreover, the purely affective target words in Studies 2 and 3 eliminate any semantic

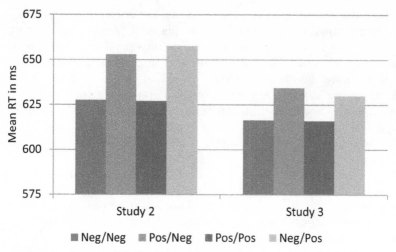

FIGURE 3.7. Average RTs for Congruent and Incongruent Trials, Studies 2 and 3

interpretation of these facilitation and inhibition effects. Evidently, simple positive or negative evaluative tags are directly attached to many familiar political concepts in LTM and this "hot" affect-to-cognition connection is evoked without the individual having to tally up any semantic considerations that conventional models say drive affective evaluation. "Giuliani" is good or bad (facilitating "rainbow" or "rabies") before you conger up that he is a Republican, mayor, crime stopper, or adulterer.

What about our contingent hypotheses predicting hot cognition not only for persons, but also for political groups and issues? Are groups and issues less prone than persons to promote automatic evaluative feelings as some have argued, or is it as we contend that *any* political object that has been evaluated in the past becomes tagged to feelings and thereupon will show automatic affective facilitation and inhibition effects on mere exposure? Pushing the logic of our claims one step further, are political sophisticates, because of their greater interest in and we suppose their more frequent evaluation of political objects, more prone to the effects of automatic affect on political attitudes than unsophisticates?

Because of the relatively small sample size in Study 1, we need to focus on Study 2 (N = 162) and Study 3 (N = 95). Figure 3.8, Panel a, breaks down the basic interactions for Study 2 at short SOA. When participants are not given time to form conscious expectancies, congruent primes for political leaders, groups, and issues elicit faster response times than incongruent pairings. That is, we find support for the automatic activation of positive or negative feelings for the expanded range of political leaders, groups, and issues *without the mediation of cognitive considerations.*

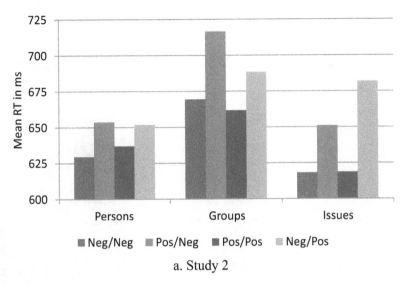

a. Study 2

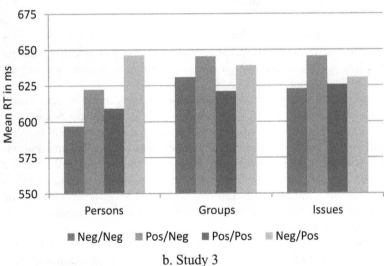

b. Study 3

FIGURE 3.8. Hot Cognition for Persons, Groups, and Issues

Figure 3.8, panel b displays the results for Study 3, which tests a broader set of familiar and less familiar political objects for a political sophistication effect. In addition to the leaders used as primes in Studies 1 and 2, we added Colin Powell, Kennedy, Mike Bloomberg (the then newly elected mayor of New York City), Mark Green (Bloomberg's Democratic opponent), and Osama bin Laden; to groups we added African-Americans, Americans, Arabs, Jews, NAACP, NRA, and terrorists; and to issues we added Affirmative Action,

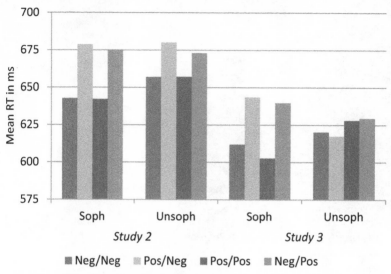

FIGURE 3.9. Hot Cognition by Sophistication

Counter-Terrorism, Free Speech, Pro-Life, Pro-Choice, and Welfare. Analyses of the key three-way interactions confirm the automaticity of affect for leaders and groups, but *not* for issues, which point in the expected direction but do not reach statistical significance.

We also predicted that automatic facilitation and inhibition effects would be contingent on a citizen's political knowledge. Political sophisticates, we reason, have thought about and repeatedly evaluated most of the political leaders, groups, and issues, while those citizens whose political interest and knowledge falls below the sample median are less likely to have formed affective associations in memory, and therefore should not display the pattern of facilitation and inhibition that indicates automatic affect. This difference should be most pronounced for Study 3 because this study included less mainstream and well-known political primes.

The pattern of sophistication effects depicted in Figure 3.9 shows an intriguing difference across studies. Whereas in Study 2 we find facilitation and inhibition effects, indicating hot cognition, regardless of sophistication, in Study 3 we find pronounced sophistication differences – low-knowledge subjects do not display automatic affect toward the broader and less familiar set of primes or for each prime type taken separately.

This overall pattern lends credence to the theoretical expectations underlying the formation of OL tallies in suggesting that sophisticates, because of their interest in politics, have developed attitudes for a broad range of political objects. Recall that the person and group primes selected for Study 2 were more mainstream, "easier" (Cobb and Kuklinski, 1997), and more likely to have been thought about and evaluated by our study participants than were many of the primes in Study 3. Virtually all New Yorkers in the aftermath of the 2000 election, regardless of level of sophistication, would presumably have given some thought to Bush, Gore, Hillary, and Rudy. Similarly, most everyone would have formed an attitude about such mainstream groups as Democrats and Republicans. By contrast, consider now the broader sample of issue primes selected for Study 3. We assume (knowing all-too-well the low level of political sophistication of many of our undergraduates) that these "harder" concepts, especially the issue primes, would require more thought than unsophisticates had likely given them and would consequently yield weaker or nil automatic attitude effects. Moreover, we suspect that these issues would more likely induce ambivalence among sophisticates.

One of the more interesting theoretical arguments made about the automaticity of feelings is the contention that ambivalent attitudes may require a different processing mechanism and a different pattern of linkages in LTM than simpler univalent attitudes (Bassili and Roy, 1998; McGraw and Steenbergen, 1995; Lavine, 2001). Referring back to our associative network model as shown in Figure 2.1, ambivalent attitudes are captured as objects with links to *both* positive and negative evaluations, and the stronger the respective affective links the greater the ambivalence. In theory, priming an ambivalent attitude object should simultaneously pass activation to both positivity and negativity, and this dual activation should generate competitive facilitation and inhibition effects that would suppress the spontaneous response in our priming studies.

Both Studies 2 and 3 confirm the existence of well-formed, accessible, univalent attitudes toward many political primes. But when we test hot cognition for political persons, groups, and issues about which our respondents are ambivalent, the effect disappears. Figure 3.10 shows the automatic activation of affect for both univalent and strong primes, but neither ambivalent nor weak primes elicit significant facilitation/inhibition effects in the short SOA condition that would indicate automatic hot cognition. In both studies, the four way interactions among SOA, prime valence, target valence, and ambivalence (as measured using the Griffin formula) were statistically significant, as were the four-way interactions among SOA, prime valence, target valence, and attitude strength. In short, McGraw and Steenbergen (1995) and Lavine (2001) were right: univalent and strong primes promote the expected pattern of facilitation for affectively consistent targets and inhibition for affectively inconsistent targets, while ambivalent and weak primes showed no discernable evidence of automatic hot cognition. Note that in our theory citizens who are ambivalent about a given person, group, or issue have *conflicting* hot cognitions that interfere with the facilitation effects we observe for univalent primes, while those with weak or non-attitudes simply lack hot cognitions toward those objects.

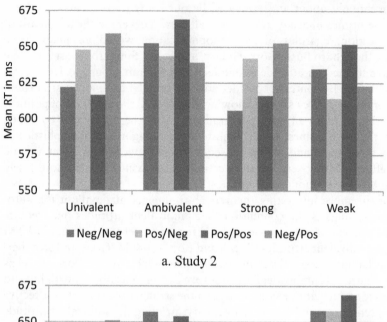

a. Study 2

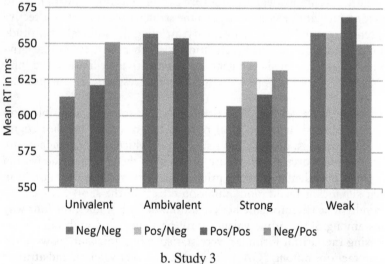

b. Study 3

FIGURE 3.10. Hot Cognition by Ambivalence and Attitude Strength

Discussion

Complementing research in psychology on the automaticity of nonpolitical attitudes (Bargh et al., 1992; Fazio, 1992; Greenwald and Banaji, 1995; Nosek et al., 2010), we found robust facilitation and inhibition effects in the spontaneous evaluation of political leaders, groups, and issues (especially for strong univalent attitudes, and for sophisticates in the evaluation of "hard" political issues). More intriguing still from our perspective is the finding that the predicted prime valence by target valence interactions still hold when the targets are *semantically unrelated* to the primes. Even when there is no discernable semantic link between, say, Bush and toothache, or Gore and joy, the responses are speeded up significantly when the prime and target concepts are affectively congruent and slowed down when attitudinally incongruent. These results offer strong support for the prevalence of hot cognition in political information processing which cannot be explained by purely cognitive models. Moreover, these effects are clearly outside the conscious control of citizens, and so provide the first step in the cascade of automatic affective processes that we claim drive motivated reasoning and the rationalizing voter.

4

Implicit Identifications in Political Information Processing

In Chapter 3, we documented the automaticity of affect toward political candidates, groups, and issues. We turn now to the question of political and social identifications and the implications of automatic intergroup feelings and stereotypes for political information processing. Ethnocentrism and group-based prejudice have long been thought to originate in fundamental categorization processes. More generally, we expect that our basic political attitudes and beliefs will be influenced by unconscious group categorization and identification processes. That so, we expect automatic group identifications to exert a strong pull on support for parties, candidates, and political issues outside of a citizen's awareness.

This chapter reports multiple experimental tests of the hot cognition hypothesis for ideological, partisan, in-group, and out-group identifications. Our expectation, in line with the symbolic politics perspective of Kinder and Sears (1981; Sears, 2001; Sears and Henry, 2003), and our own emphasis on the primacy of affect in political judgment, is that the "simple" act of categorizing oneself or others as a member of this or that group is not so simple after all, as it engages both cognitive and affective processes that prove to be impossible to disentangle. From our hot cognition perspective, the labeling of one's self or others as a Democrat, Independent, or Republican, man or woman, black, white, or Asian is affectively charged, spontaneously triggering a positive self-to-in-group labeling effect and typically a less-than-positive or even negative affective evaluation of the out-group.

To push the argument further, in one experiment we will use the most generic of group labels – "we," "they," "us," "them" – to see whether even these most basic of group identifications will activate affectively charged judgments, and if so whether, as predicted, these evaluations are influenced in a prime-congruent direction. If it proves to be the case that the affective component of the categorization process is primary in the sense that the affective tag attached to one's self, in-groups, and out-groups comes to mind spontaneously (Postulate 4), then the way we political scientists think about, analyze, and *make normative prescriptions for control of stereotyping* is in need of fundamental revision.

Categorization is among the most basic acts of human information processing (Barsalou, 1992; Eysenck and Keane, 2005; Lachman, Lachman, and Butterfield, 1979; Neely, 1976; 1977; Rosch, 1975; 1978). The labeling of oneself, another person, object, or event as a member or instance of a group, be it a robin is a bird, or a politician is a Democrat, is critical to how we think and reason, as the categorized group member spontaneously inherits many of the prototypical characteristics of the group label (Trawalter and Shapiro, 2010; Uleman, 1999). While categorization can and does serve important beneficial functions (we could not function intelligently without categorizing and classifying), when applied to people it has its well-documented downside in the rapid and spontaneous creation of in-groups and out-groups and the subsequent tendency to favor "us" at the expense of "them." People tend to see members of in-groups as more similar to themselves, while viewing out-group members as less similar and less individually variable (Perdue, Dovidio, Gurtman, and Tyler, 1990). The simple act of categorization can promote discriminatory attitudes and behavior even when there are no objective differences between the groupings (Piliavin, Dovidio, Gaertner, and Clark, 1986; Tajfel, 1981).

Categorization may occur consciously, as when one explicitly labels "us" versus "them," or unconsciously, as when one responds automatically to an individual in terms of some group characteristics (Perdue et al., 1990; Taylor, 1981, 1982). Calling an act of group categorization "automatic" reflects the now-established finding that feelings and beliefs about in-groups and out-groups can be sparked in milliseconds on mere exposure to a group member or symbol, with little or no effort, intention, awareness, or conscious control (Bargh, 1994, 1997, 2007). Further, it is now clear that social categories are "hot," that is, most if not all social and political objects are affectively charged (Bargh et al., 1992; Fazio, 1992; Fazio, Sanbonmatsu, Powell, and Kardes, 1986; Lodge and Taber, 2000, 2005; Morris, Squires, Taber, and Lodge, 2003). In short, cognitive and affective processes conspire to provide both stereotype information and strong feelings about group identifications that are difficult to suppress and impossible to disentangle (Amodio and Mendoza, 2010). From this "hot identifications" perspective the categorization of self, in-groups, and out-groups is an affectively charged process.

We turn first in this chapter to a test of the automaticity of political identifications under minimalist, context-free conditions. We are particularly interested in the implicit influence of political identifications on other political identifications, on basic political attitudes, and on support for political candidates and issues. Following this logic, our first experiment examines the momentary, unconscious impact of self, in-group, and out-group identifications on political beliefs and attitudes. In the later sections of this chapter, we will describe some of our experimental work on the role of group stereotypes and ideological beliefs in driving political attitudes toward group-target policies like affirmative action or welfare.

An Experimental Test of Implicit Identifications

Political and social identifications have long been thought to provide powerful orienting forces for political attitudes and beliefs (Brewer and Brown, 1998; Converse, 1964; Deaux, Reid, Mizrahi, and Ethier, 1995; Fiske, 1998; Kinder, 1998; Taber, 2003). One of the most firmly established findings in this literature, for example, is that black and white Americans differ in their positions on many political issues, sometimes quite markedly. Important debates remain concerning the degree to which racial prejudice has declined in recent decades, the theoretical interpretation of "modern racism" (Kinder, 1986; Sniderman and Tetlock, 1986a, 1986b), and the role of "realistic group conflict" in explaining discrimination (Bobo, 1988; Coser, 1956; Duckitt, 1992), but race clearly remains a potent orienting force for many Americans (Black and Black, 1987; Bobo and Kluegel, 1993; Dawson, 1994; Dijksterhuis, Albers, and Bongers, 2009; Kinder and Mendelberg, 1995; Kinder and Sanders, 1996). Similarly, attitudes on welfare (Gilens, 1995), immigration (Pettigrew and Meertens, 1995), and AIDs policy (Price and Hsu, 1992) all turn on hostility toward an out-group, just as beliefs and attitudes about party, gender, class, nationality, and religion orient citizens on many political issues.

Hypotheses. We expect that political and social identifications vary in their chronic accessibility, with more "basic" or practiced identifications coming more quickly and easily to mind than less practiced ones. As set forth in Chapter 2, accessibility is a function of either repeated or momentary activation. Our *accessibility of identifications hypothesis* predicts that automatic identifications will vary in chronic accessibility and this variance will be related to the prevalence of the given group in one's political and social information processing, that is with the group's salience to the citizen. This latter expectation allows us to make specific predictions that more "natural," perhaps biologically derived categories will be more chronically accessible than more socially or politically defined categories. Specifically, we expect that race and gender identifications will be the most chronically accessible, with partisan and ideological identifications the least chronically accessible. Most citizens think about race and gender identifications more frequently than partisanship or ideology in their daily lives, and these more frequently used categories will be more chronically accessible.

We conceive of identifications as associative knowledge structures in long-term memory with varying chronic and momentary accessibility, and we predict that the accessibility of one's own identifications will be influenced by the momentary accessibility of other identifications. In particular, we hypothesize a *congruent identifications effect* such that priming an in-group will increase the accessibility of all in-group identifications and inhibit out-group identifications, while priming an out-group will facilitate the accessibility of all out-group identifications and reduce the accessibility of in-group identifications. Operationally, we expect that people will be faster to say they are members of an in-group when primed with another of their in-group identifications and faster to say they are not members of an out-group when primed with another out-group identification. It is worth noting that because group identifications are hot (and affect is generally more positive toward in-groups than out-groups), any congruency effect we observe could be due to affective congruence as was the effect of the purely affective primes sunshine and cancer used in the last chapter. At the moment, let us look at this hypothesis in terms of in-group/out-group congruency rather than pure affective congruency. We expect these congruency effects to be strong enough to overcome purely cognitive associations in memory that will also exist for some of our prime-target pairings. For example, many participants may associate African Americans with the Democratic Party or rich people with Republicans. These cognitive associations will sometimes work in tandem with the pull of identifications, but sometimes cognitive associations will work against the congruent identifications effect. For example, when a white Democrat is primed by the out-group identification Black and responds to the in-group target Democrats, the likely cognitive association between Black and Democrats will tend to facilitate the response and counter the inhibition we expect from an out-group prime on an in-group target.

We expect that the most general, and minimal, of identification words, the personal and group pronoun primes ("me" vs. "you" and "we" vs. "they") will show the same congruency effects as do the political identification primes: me/we should facilitate in-group targets and inhibit out-group targets, while you/they should have the opposite effects. Beyond this *minimal congruent identifications effect*, we also predict that the group pronouns (we/they) will show even stronger facilitation and inhibition effects than will the personal pronouns (me/you). Perdue, Dovidio, Gurtman, and Tyler (1990) found that nonsense syllables repeatedly paired subliminally with in-group designating pronouns (us, we, ours) were later rated by experimental participants as more pleasant than nonsense syllables paired with out-group pronouns (they, them, theirs), even under these minimal conditions outside of a social context and even though the participants were consciously unaware of the primes. They also found that experimental participants were able to make decisions concerning positive traits in a trait-rating task significantly faster after exposure to the in-group designators than after exposure to out-group pronouns.

Beyond the effects of identification primes on the accessibility of other identifications, political and social identifications should also have measurable effects on support for political candidates and issue statements. To test this, we will vary the accessibility of identifications through a priming task and observe variations in support for known political candidates and issues. Here, we predict an *identity support effect*, such that in-group primes will lead to faster positive responses for supported candidates and issue targets and slower negative responses for unsupported candidate and issues, while out-group primes will have the opposite effect. That is, when primed with an in-group label, we expect faster times to say one favors a supported political candidate or issue. Note that, as with the congruent identifications hypothesis, these effects will sometimes have to overcome semantic associations between a prime and a target while at other times these semantic associations will work in tandem with the congruency support effect.

In a *minimal identity support effect*, we predict that the personal and group pronouns will also show this identifications effect on candidate and issue support, such that self or in-group pronouns will facilitate responses to liked candidates and issues while inhibiting responses to disliked candidates and issues, with the opposite pattern for other or out-group pronouns.

Experimental Procedures. Undergraduate students in introductory political science courses at Stony Brook University received extra credit for their participation ($N = 224$; 92 female; 114 nonwhite; 112 Democrat, 51 Republican). The study was conducted in the fall of 2002 ($N = 106$) and the spring of 2003 ($N = 118$).

This experiment presents subjects with two sentence verification tasks (for a general description of this procedure, see Figure 3.1). In the first, which we call the "I AM" task, we test how quickly participants can categorize themselves as belonging or not belonging to basic social/political groups. We are interested both in the relative accessibility of these categories and in the degree to which one's basic categorizations can be influenced by Type 1 (subliminal) primes. In the second task, which we call the "I SUPPORT" task, we are interested in the impact that the subliminal priming of such basic identifications will have on the evaluations of political persons and issues.

As we have already shown, the case for the automaticity of social beliefs, attitudes, and behaviors has been strengthened considerably in the last decade by reducing the prime exposure time (the stimulus onset asynchrony, or SOA) in priming studies to subliminal speeds as brief as 15 milliseconds (Murphy and Zajonc, 1993). At exposure times of 200–300 milliseconds, most participants in priming studies are somewhat aware that a word or picture flashed onscreen before the target word, although they cannot establish conscious expectancies to guide their responses. By reducing the prime exposure time below 50 milliseconds the word or picture primes appear as no more than a flicker on the computer screen and extensive debriefing reveals no awareness among respondents of having been primed. (See reviews of subliminal priming in Bargh, 1989, 1994, 1997; Greenwald and Banaji, 1995; Higgins, 1989; Smith, 1994; Wyer and Srull, 1989, with many studies directly comparing explicit to implicit measures.)

This study was conducted in our Laboratory for Experimental Research in Political Behavior on Windows-based personal computers using EPrime, an experimental software package developed by Psychology Software Tools, Inc.

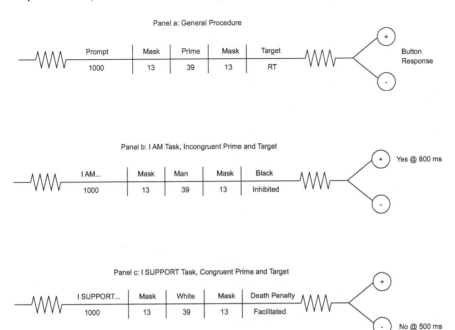

FIGURE 4.1. Procedure on Each Experimental Trial

Subjects completed the experimental tasks singly in separate rooms. They received verbal and on-screen instructions and practice in using two buttons on a computer keyboard to indicate their responses "as quickly as possible without making too many errors." Figure 4.1a illustrates the basic procedure: each trial begins when a prompt appears for 1 second in the center of the screen. This prompt – "I AM..." for the first set of trials and "I SUPPORT..." for the second set – serves both to prepare the subject for their response to the target word and to orient their visual focus to the exact center of the screen. A forward mask follows for 13 milliseconds, followed by the prime word for 39 milliseconds and a backward mask for 13 milliseconds. It is very important, given our interest in automaticity, to understand that each part of this sequence occurs too quickly to be consciously perceived, so that any effects of the prime on subsequent processing must be outside of awareness. The masks, which consist of jumbled strings of letters, serve to replace the contents of visual sensory memory (ensuring that an afterimage of the prime does not remain in sensory memory even after it has disappeared from the screen). Finally, the target word appears and remains on the screen until the subject presses one of two keys to indicate their response to the target (group membership for the I AM task or candidate/issue evaluations for the I SUPPORT task). Each subject completed 170 I AM trials followed by 212 I SUPPORT trials (not counting practice).

TABLE 4.1. *Primes and Targets for Hot Identifications Experiment*

I AM Task				
Primes			Targets	
Political Groups	Pronouns	Affect	Political Groups	
Black	Me	Cancer	Black	
White	You	Sunshine	White	
Woman	We		Woman	
Man	They		Man	
Poor			Poor	
Rich			Rich	
Democrat			Democrat	
Republican			Republican	
Liberal			Liberal	
Conservative			Conservative	

I SUPPORT Task				
Primes			Targets	
Political Groups	Pronouns	Affect	Persons	Issues
Black	Me	Cancer	Al Gore	Abortion Rights
White	You	Sunshine	George W. Bush	Affirmative Action
Woman	We		Hillary	Death Penalty
Man	They		Pataki	Green Party
Poor				Gun Control
Rich				Welfare
Democrat				
Republican				
Liberal				
Conservative				

Figure 4.1b illustrates the I AM task in the case of an *in*congruent prime-target pair. Our subject, who is African American in this example, is expected to be slower to press the button indicating that she is black because of the inhibiting influence of the incongruent identification prime word, Man. By contrast, we see facilitation illustrated in panel 4.1c for the I SUPPORT task: our subject is faster to respond that she opposes the death penalty because she was primed with an out-group label (White).

Table 4.1 lists the primes and targets used in this study. For targets in the I AM task, we chose basic political groups known to be important in orienting citizens in American politics: race, gender, class, party, and ideological labels. As we will see, these categories are all chronically accessible, though variably so – subjects generally have no trouble placing themselves in or out of these groups, though their speed does vary systematically. For this task, we

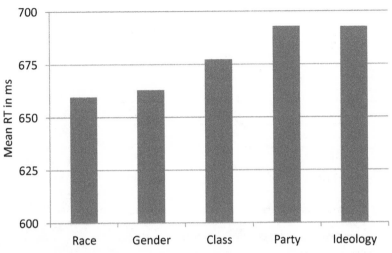

FIGURE 4.2. Accessibility of Group Identifications

used three types of primes: political identification primes (the same set used as targets), general pronouns (two personal, two group), and pure affect words (semantically unrelated to the target). This allows us to examine the impact on responses to the targets, if any, of pure affect primes (e.g., "sunshine"), the most minimal of group primes that have been found to evoke self, singular other, in-group, and out-group orientations (e.g., "we" or "they"; Perdue et al., 1990), and political group primes thought to be most relevant in American electoral politics (e.g., "Republican"). Each prime was paired once with each target, excluding same prime-target pairs (black was never paired with black, for example). For the I SUPPORT task, targets were selected to represent political persons and issues that were well-known in the news at the time of the study.

Following the two priming tasks, we collected basic demographics and responses to an open-ended political knowledge test.

Results. We hypothesized that political and social identifications will vary in their chronic accessibility, in particular that the more practiced biological categories of race and gender would be more accessible than the socially or politically defined categories of class, ideology, or partisanship. To test this *accessibility of identifications hypothesis* we can examine the speed with which people identified themselves as belonging to a given group category in the I AM task, averaging across all trials for the relevant category target. Figure 4.2 presents these response times for race (black/white), gender (man/woman), class (rich/poor), political party (Democrat/Republican), and ideology (liberal/conservative) targets, averaged across all priming trials in which the given identification was a target.

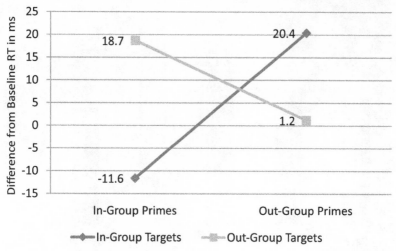

FIGURE 4.3. Congruent Identifications Effect

These results clearly support the varying accessibilities of sociopolitical identifications. A repeated measures ANOVA on RTs in the I AM task showing
a highly significant main effect for target group: $F(228,4) = 95.97$, $p < .001$.
Black, white, male, and female were the most accessible group identifications
among all our targets. Contrasts found race and gender to be significantly faster
than class, which was significantly faster than party ID and ideology; there was
no significant difference between party and ideology, and race and gender were
only marginally different from each other.

We also predicted a *congruent identifications effect*: group identifications,
we hypothesize, are organized in long-term memory such that groups with
which one identifies are linked to self as in-group identifications, while groups
with which one does not identify are linked together as out-group identifications (Schnabel and Asendorph, 2010). In our theory, it is this organization of
memory objects along with associated automatic affective tags that kick-starts
in-group/out-group and stereotyping effects. To test this hypothesis, we can see
whether in-group (out-group) identifications in the I AM task are facilitated
by in-group (out-group) primes and inhibited by out-group (in-group) primes.
Because these primes appear at subliminal speeds any effect we observe must
be unconscious.

In Figure 4.3 we see the expected interaction between primes and targets. In
order to determine whether the effects of a prime facilitate or inhibit RT to a
target, we compute our dependent variable as the difference between the RT
to a target when preceded by an in-group or out-group prime and the RT to
the same target when preceded by a semantically meaningless baseline prime
(NNN, BBBBBB). Negative differences indicate facilitation while positive differences show inhibition relative to an "unprimed" baseline response to the

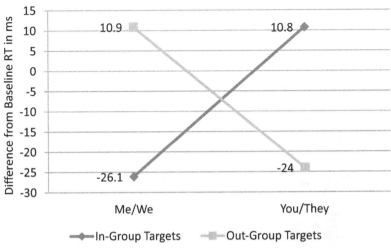

FIGURE 4.4. Congruent Identifications for Pronoun Primes

same target. Figure 4.3 shows that in-group primes increase the accessibility of in-group targets and decrease the accessibility of out-group targets, while out-group primes decrease the accessibility of in-group targets, all relative to the "unprimed" accessibilities of the targets. A repeated measures ANOVA on the difference between baseline and primed RTs for trials grouped by in- and out-group primes and targets showed a highly significant interaction, $F = 69.32$, $p < .001$. Follow up contrasts confirm that in-group primes significantly facilitated in-group targets in the I AM task and significantly inhibited out-group targets; out-group primes significantly inhibited in-group targets but did not facilitate out-group targets.

For example, when a white female Democrat encounters the in-group prime white, even incidentally and outside of awareness, she will on average identify more rapidly as a woman and as a Democrat. But will a similar congruency effect be found for the minimal identifications represented by in- and out-group pronouns? That is, would cueing the word "they" outside of awareness for a white Republican slow her down in identifying herself as a Republican and speed her up in saying she is not a Democrat? The answer appears to be yes.

Figure 4.4 shows the expected pattern of congruency effects for the pronoun primes when paired with group identification targets. A repeated measures ANOVA found this interaction between pronoun primes and political targets to be highly significant, $F = 94.93$, $p < .001$. Follow-up contrasts support the expected pattern, with all inhibitions and facilitations significantly different from baseline RTs. In short, even the most basic of self-identification primes influence how one identifies with sociopolitical groups, with the pronouns me and we strengthening in-group and weakening out-group identifications, and the pronouns you and they having the exact opposite effects on group

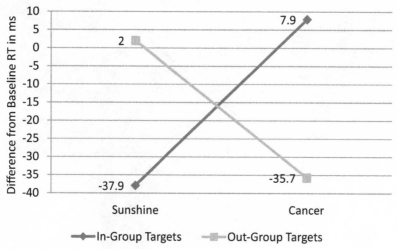

FIGURE 4.5. The Hot Identifications Hypothesis

identifications. These data provide strong evidence that group identities are triggered automatically and tightly linked within our long-term memories.

As demonstrated in Chapter 3, positive and negative feelings associated with most if not all political objects are automatically invoked on mere exposure to the object. Such hot cognitions, we have argued, influence political information processing about political persons, issues, and also groups. The group identifications in the current study undoubtedly carry affective as well as cognitive associations, and it is possible that the congruency effects for identifications just described are to some degree driven by automatic affect. To test this possibility, we included among our primes in the I AM task two simple affect primes, cancer and sunshine, with the expectation that sunshine would facilitate in-group identifications and inhibit out-group identifications while cancer would have the opposite effects.

In support of this *hot identifications hypothesis* we found in a repeated measures ANOVA a highly significant interaction between the pure affect primes and political identification targets, $F = 53.43$, $p < .001$. In-group and out-group targets are facilitated by both positive (sunshine) and negative (cancer) affect prime words respectively (Figure 4.5). The inhibition of in-group targets when preceded by cancer was marginally significant ($p < .1$), though there was no significant inhibition for out-group targets when primed by sunshine. Unlike the group primes, these affect primes have no semantic association in memory with the political group targets, so these facilitation effects can only be attributed to affective congruence with the targets. That we achieve such strong results for facilitation by affectively congruent primes at the subliminal presentation speed of 39 milliseconds makes very clear the automatic nature of hot group identifications.

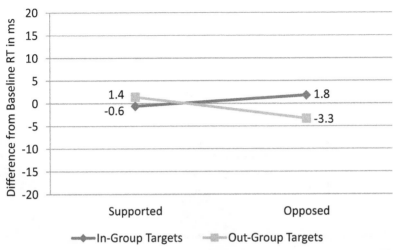

FIGURE 4.6. The Congruent Support Hypothesis for Political Candidate Targets

Finally, we predicted an *identity support effect* in which in-group primes would increase support for liked political candidates and issues and inhibit support for disliked candidates and issues, while out-group primes would have the opposite pattern of effects. The I SUPPORT task in our study was designed to test this hypothesis, using the RT to indicate one supports or opposes a candidate or issue as the key dependent variable. Participants indicated by rapid Yes or No button press whether they support a candidate or issue target. The research question is whether subliminally presented group primes will influence the speed with which they make this judgment.

Although the means are weakly in the right direction, in Figure 4.6 we see that group identification primes have no significant effect on activation or inhibition of support for political candidates relative to evaluation times for the same candidates when they are not primed. A closer look at the data reveals that the expected pattern is marginally obtained for the *less* sophisticated respondents in our sample (by median split, where the median was 11/17 questions correct on the knowledge measure), which suggests that unsophisticated citizens may be more influenced by their group identifications than sophisticated citizens.

By contrast with the weak and contingent congruency effects of group primes on political candidates, we do find a strong and significant interaction between group ID primes and issue targets ($F = 35.2$, $p < .001$). That is, support or opposition for political issues is very strongly influenced by group identification primes. Figure 4.7 shows that in-group primes significantly facilitate the expression of support for favored issues and inhibit disfavored issues, while out-group primes strengthen opposed issues, and weaken supported issues.

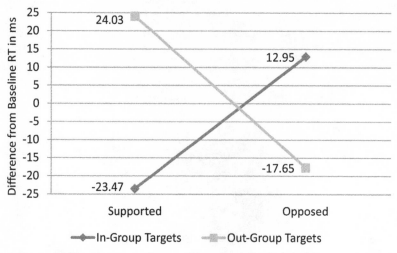

FIGURE 4.7. The Congruent Support Hypothesis for Political Issue Targets

Interestingly, the minimal identification pronoun primes (me/we, you/they) strongly influenced the accessibilities of supported and opposed candidates and issues in the expected directions. That is, me and we strengthened support for liked candidates and issues, while you and they strengthened opposition to disliked candidates and issues. The interaction of pronoun primes and political targets was highly significant for both candidate ($F = 43.32$, $p < .001$) and issue targets ($F = 19.95$, $p < .001$). This was true for both singular (me/you) and group (we/they) pronouns, though the group pronouns had a somewhat larger effect.

Finally, we replicated with a different design the hot cognition hypotheses discussed in Chapter 3 by pairing pure affect primes with candidate and issue targets, again finding the expected interaction effect between purely affective primes (cancer and sunshine) and candidate and issue targets (candidates: $F = 22.9$, $p < .001$; issues: $F = 10.28$, $p < .01$, respectively). Follow-up contrasts support our congruency hypothesis for all combinations of target and prime except the expected facilitation of supported candidates and issues by the positive prime sunshine, which is in the right direction but fails to achieve significance.

Discussion. While these results indicate that an automatic process is triggered when in-group and out-group cues are encountered (even subliminally) and that this process largely follows a congruency pattern, it is not entirely clear what this process entails. One strong possibility is that pure affect is driving these results and that we have simply extended our earlier findings on hot cognition in political information processing to the case of group identifications. The fact that sunshine and cancer are able to activate group identifications for both candidates and issues according to one's group membership suggests that group identifications have a strong automatic affective component that is activated spontaneously on mere exposure. Accordingly, one explanation for our results is that the group identification primes transmit positive and negative feelings as do sunshine and cancer. In this explanation, in-group primes automatically evoke a positive feeling that then primes pathways to affectively congruent positive associations, while out-group primes do the opposite.

Perhaps our results are better explained by the chronic accessibility of basic group identifications. That is, automatic affect may matter less than the fact that the prime is automatically recognized as an "in-group" and this may ready a response to other in-groups. If this is true, then we might expect the effects of these identifications as primes to depend on their accessibility, which we already know varies.

Another possibility is that the semantic relationships that exist among concepts in memory may sometimes override the affective or identification components. For example, a rich Democrat may have positive affect toward the wealthy, but associate them semantically with the Republican party, in which case the prime "rich" would have countervailing tendencies to facilitate a semantic association and inhibit (via both affective and identification incongruence) responses to the out-group target "Republican."

As a first test of this notion, we examined all prime-target pairings in the I AM task, searching inductively for any significant semantic associations in our sample. That is, if rich is associated with Republican, black with Democrat, and so on, these associations should emerge in significant facilitation effects for those pairings regardless of the group memberships of the individual subjects. Surprisingly perhaps, only one such pairing reached conventional levels of significance: participants primed with "Republican" were faster to respond that yes they were or no they were not "conservative" ($t = -2.83$, $p < .01$). Two marginally significant pairings surfaced, both of which we might expect to be semantically related: "conservative" activated "rich" and "woman" activated "man." Any additional semantic effects were washed out by the much stronger congruency effects based on affect and individual group identifications. Indirect support for this mechanism also comes from the fact that the pronoun primes, which we might expect to have the weakest semantic associations with the targeted candidates and issues, had in fact the strongest facilitation and inhibition patterns. These primes exert influence almost entirely through affective or identification congruence, unmuddied by strong semantic associations.

We have reported strong congruency effects for the influence of subliminally presented group, pronoun, and affect primes on group identification targets and on support for political candidates and issues. Though we cannot be sure of the primary mechanisms that underlie our results, we strongly suspect that the combination of affective congruence and the automatic in-group/out-group identifications offers the best explanation. We might speculate, in keeping with current theory in cognitive neuroscience, that affective systems are designed by evolutionary processes to provide rapid responses to environmental stimuli (Hofmann and Wilson, 2010). From this perspective group categorizations are likely designed by evolutionary processes to quickly identify friend and foe, in-group and out-group. These processes and systems are likely not identical, but they are almost certainly interrelated. The evidence we have presented suggests that affect and self-identifications both enter the processing stream at an early and preconscious stage and strongly influence subsequent political information processing.

An Experimental Test of the Influence of Racial Stereotypes on Policy Support

Since the 1960s, opinion polls reveal remarkably little racism in the American public. Racial stereotypes and labels once accepted as reality are now said by most Americans to be offensive and inappropriate, and political policies of segregation and discrimination find little overt support (McConahay, 1986). This apparent shift in racial relations has led some scholars to suppose that racism is "dead" (Roth, 1994; D'Souza, 1995) and others to argue that race is no longer the driving force it once was in American public opinion (Hagen, 1995; Sniderman and Piazza, 1993).

Experimental work, by contrast, has shown that racial stereotypes continue to exert significant influence over social and political cognition (Bargh, Chen, and Burrows, 1996; Devine, 1989; Fazio, Jackson, Dunton, and Williams, 1995; Mendelberg, 2001). Certainly opposition to race-targeted policies like affirmative action and President Obama's heath care plan remains potent among many white Americans (Knowles, Lowery, and Schaumberg, 2010), but the question remains whether such opposition is driven by stereotypes and antiblack feelings, by conservative ideological beliefs, or by some mix of racial attitudes and conservatism.

Burdein and Taber (Burdein, 2007; Burdein and Taber, 2004) conducted a series of experiments designed to test the relative potency of African American stereotypes and individualist or egalitarian beliefs in driving opposition to race-target political policies.

Hypotheses. What do people think about when they consider racial policies? Do they think about the principles these policies represent or challenge, or do they think about the groups these policies affect?

One possibility is that ideological considerations stand behind most opposition by political conservatives to race-target policies. In particular, the Protestant work ethic and the more general principle of individualism may drive such opposition. In short, *principled conservatism* predicts that conservative opponents will habitually associate principles more than racial stereotypes with race-target policies, while liberals will associate race more. This position is usually linked to Paul Sniderman and colleagues (Sniderman and Carmines, 1993, 1997; Sniderman and Piazza, 1993; Sniderman, Piazza, Tetlock, and Kendrick, 1991; Sniderman and Tetlock, 1986), though the term "principled conservatism" was coined by Sidanius, Pratto, and Bobo (1996) in a critique of that position. Whatever the origins of the label, there is no doubt that principled conservatism has been a contested position in the public opinion and political psychology literatures.

By contrast, Sears, Kinder and colleagues (Kinder and Sears, 1981) argue that when liberals or conservatives alike are faced with a racial policy they perceive it primarily in terms of race, and only secondarily in terms of ideological principle. *Modern racism* asserts that racial stereotypes will be strongly associated with racial policies for most Americans, liberal or conservative, with ideological principles less associated. Our own theory and the evidence presented earlier in this chapter on the potency of group identifications suggest that group stereotypes will be strongly and automatically associated with issues that implicate those groups, and that the feelings and cognitions represented in these stereotypes will be among the earliest and strongest considerations retrieved in the stream of processing upon encountering an appropriate issue stimulus. Our theory is less clear on the role of ideological principles in guiding thinking about race-target policies.

Experimental Procedures. Undergraduate students in introductory political science courses at Stony Brook University received extra credit for their participation ($N = 163$; 66 female; 38 nonwhite; 25 conservative, 43 liberal).

To avoid social desirability biases and because people may not be aware of their own racial beliefs and attitudes, we used an implicit method – the lexical decision task (fully described in Chapter 3) – to gauge what comes to mind when people are exposed to race-target policies. In the lexical decision task, recall that participants are asked to press "as quickly as possible" a given key to indicate that a letter string presented on a computer screen is a word and a different key if it is not a legal English word. To ensure that subjects cannot develop expectancies about the frequencies of words and nonwords, half of all trials are nonword foils. For example, if a subject sees "diamonds" she should indicate this is a word by pressing the "yes" key; by contrast the pronounceable nonword "mondasdi" should elicit a press of the "no" key. The basic logic of this task is that people will be faster in indicating "yes" when the word they see is more accessible in memory, either because it is chronically accessible or, as in our study, because it has been primed. Hence, reaction time (RT) reflects the momentary accessibility of concepts and, in priming studies, it measures the association between a target concept and a prime concept. If a person were primed with the word "jewelry," for example, he would be quicker to recognize "diamond" as a word than "football." Although the actual task of reading the word is explicit, or conscious, the task is implicit in the sense that the subject is unaware that the prime has influenced his response. And if the prime is presented subliminally, as here, any impact of the prime on the accessibility of the target word must be unconscious.

To test associations in memory between race-target issues and either African American stereotypes or ideological principles, we presented trials that paired issue primes with race or principle targets in a lexical decision task. It is important to recognize that any associations we may find will reveal histories of coactivation of concepts that go far beyond the simple facilitation we see in the lab. In fact, these associations reveal the habitual patterns of thought that derive from how our participants routinely think about these issues. This is a strong test of what people think about when presented with racial policies, and because the primes are presented subliminally the associations we find represent uncontrolled responses.

The present study used three issue primes: "affirmative action," progressive taxation (presented as "tax the rich"), and "welfare." These issues vary in the degree to which they target racial groups, but all three issues theoretically should elicit similar ideological considerations. Particularly, affirmative action and welfare have been long associated with both race and ideology, while progressive taxation is more clearly associated with ideology alone. We will focus our discussion on the results for the affirmative action primes, presenting the taxation and welfare findings only briefly.

Thirty-seven target words were used in the study, one-third of which relate to race and two-thirds to principle. For the race words we chose words used in previous research on African American stereotypes: rhythm, rap, hip-hop, basketball, Afro, hostile, aggressive, gang, and nigger. We avoided words that would be directly associated with the concept category African Americans. That is, words like "black" and "African" were not included, because presumably "affirmative action" will elicit "black," "women," "minority," etc. simply because these concepts are likely part of the definition of the issue itself. If a person opposes affirmative action on the grounds that it is not fair, words that are stereotypic or derogatory toward blacks should not be activated (though the concept "black" may well be), and words representing conservative concepts like individualism should be activated. On the other hand, if stereotype words are activated while ideological words are not, this suggests that affirmative action is largely perceived as a race issue. In short, the target words were chosen for their close ties to considerations about racial stereotypes and absence of ties to other possible considerations that one might expect to be linked directly to the three policies used as primes.

To measure associations to principles, one third of the target words were chosen to indicate individualism and one third to represent egalitarianism. The individualism words were self-reliance, individualism, earn, freedom, work ethic, merit, hand-outs, hard work, undeserved; for egalitarianism: equality, opportunity, help, sympathy, prejudice, oppression, need, disadvantage, and mistreated. Target words were also chosen to provide a mix of positive and negative feelings so we could control for affective congruency effects (hot cognition) examined in Chapters 3 and 4 and so we could test for actual negativity in the association of race words with race issues, which might suggest that thoughts on race were predominately negative and perhaps genuinely "racist." To determine positivity and negativity, participants were asked to explicitly evaluate all targets after they completed the lexical decision task.

FIGURE 4.8. Procedure on Each Lexical Decision Trial

For each target word used in the lexical decision task, there was a nonword that contained a pronounceable reordering of the same letters. Each subject was instructed to simply indicate whether the string they saw was a word (which happened 50 percent of the time) or a nonword. Each subject was given a short practice trial before the targets of interest were shown. The actual implicit task involved a sequence of four different stimuli, as shown in Figure 4.8. After a 4 milliseconds forward mask (a string of jumbled letters to standardize the contents of visual memory), the primes came on the screen for 40 milliseconds, too fast for conscious awareness. A 4-millisecond backward mask immediately followed (to insure that afterimage of the prime word was erased from the visual buffer). The first thing the subject *consciously* saw was one of the target words or its respective nonword. Each target word was paired once with each of the three issue primes. Both the target words and the prime words were randomized for each subject to control for response effects. In addition to the three issue primes, there was a baseline prime (a string of letters with no semantic meaning – i.e., BBBB) that preceded each of the targets. The baseline reaction time to each target was later subtracted from all other reaction times to the same target, to control for the possibility that some words are simply more accessible than others, and also for the differences in general response time across people. Hence, the response times that were analyzed depict facilitation or inhibition of targets relative to each respondent's individual baseline response time for the target.

Given this procedure, the basic hypotheses can be operationalized thus: the principled conservatism hypothesis predicts that all three primes (affirmative action, welfare, tax the rich) will facilitate individualism targets much more than race stereotype targets for conservative opponents of the policy; the modern racism hypothesis expects that the more a policy targets race, the more it will facilitate race stereotype words for opponents of the policy, with relatively less facilitation of individualism (that is, affirmative action should show the strongest race associations and weakest principle associations, followed by welfare, and taxation should show the weakest race associations).

Results. So what comes to mind for our participants when subliminally primed with a race-target policy in the lexical task? As depicted in Figure 4.9, affirmative action significantly facilitated African American stereotype words but not ideology words for analyses pooling across all subjects. When broken down by policy position, however, one group clearly *was* thinking

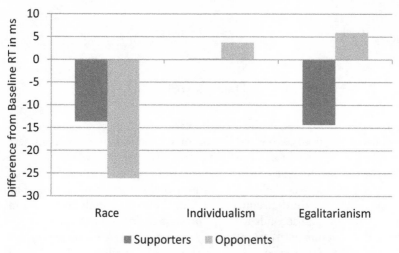

FIGURE 4.9. Accessibility of Race and Principle by Affirmative Action Stance

ideologically, but this was the supporters ($N = 62$) rather than opponents ($N = 60$) of affirmative action. In fact, for opponents of affirmative action, ideology was significantly inhibited (positive bars indicate slower than baseline RTs). In other words, opponents of affirmative action were slower to recognize words like "merit" and "work ethic" then they normally would be. For them, stereotype words like "afro" and "gang" were the *only* type of words activated by the affirmative action prime. By contrast, supporters of affirmative action were significantly faster than baseline in identifying both race and egalitarian targets, showing that for the liberals in our sample affirmative action is a mix of racial and egalitarian policy associations.

But perhaps it is only the sophisticated opponents of affirmative action who are principled. We did find an activation of principle targets (23 milliseconds faster than baseline on average) among sophisticated opponents, but this is too small a difference to reach statistical significance. Note, however, that even sophisticated opponents think along racial lines when prompted with affirmative action, and this effect *was* large enough to reach marginal significance, despite the small sample ($M = -52$ ms, $t = 1.56$, $p < .1$). Moreover, a much larger study ($N = 1082$) using adult participants from five U.S. cities found that sophisticated conservatives showed no implicit association of affirmative action to principles, but did show strong facilitation effects for black and female stereotype words (Taber, 2011).

Figure 4.10 provides our results for the welfare and progressive taxation primes, broken down by supporters and opponents of each issue. First, all groups of subjects associate both welfare and progressive taxation with the underlying principle of egalitarianism. Equality and fairness seem inseparable from these policy issues for supporters and opponents alike, which is an

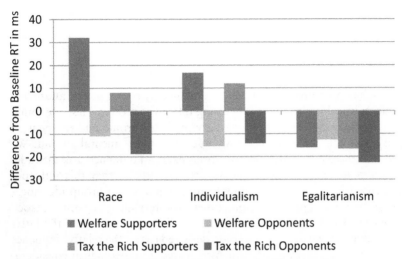

FIGURE 4.10. Accessibility of Targets by Progressive Taxation Stance

interesting contrast with affirmative action, which was only associated with egalitarianism for supporters. Second, race stereotypes are activated by both welfare and "tax the rich" for opponents, but not for supporters. Most likely, opponents on both issues see African Americans to be beneficiaries of welfare and wealth redistribution just as they benefit from affirmative action, and opposition is at least partly due to resentment. Finally, the principle of individualism is clearly related to both issues by opponents, but not supporters. In our data, opposition to welfare and progressive taxation involves a mix of racial resentment and principles, while opposition to affirmative action turns on race and not principle. It is worth noting that the fact that individualism is related to welfare and progressive taxation defuses the potential criticism that we have not captured the concept of individualism with the set of target words we have chosen. Overall, these results provide clear support for modern racism and undermine principled conservatism.

The automatic associations of affirmative action, welfare, and progressive taxation with race for opponents reveal longstanding habits of thought in which racial stereotypes come to mind spontaneously when thinking about the issues. In contrast to the expectations of principled conservatism, supporters of affirmative action reveal both ideological and racial components in their spontaneous thoughts, while opponents think largely about race. In a more general sense, these results fit our *JQP* theory and a great deal of accumulating evidence from psychology in showing that stereotype activation is largely unavoidable and occurs very early in the processing stream. These findings also illustrate the general point that what people say is not always what they think. Conservatives and liberals alike rationalize their responses in order to make sensible and defensible explanations of behaviors whose origins lie outside of their awareness.

General Discussion

This chapter has presented experimental evidence of two types of automatic influence on political information processing related to groups. First, we found that political and social identifications vary in their chronic and momentary accessibility and can therefore be easily cued by environmental stimuli. We also found that these automatic identifications exert an influence over attitudes toward both political candidates and issues. We argued that this influence is largely caused by affective reactions to in-group and out-group identifications and sometimes supportive, sometimes countervailing semantic associations between identifications and political candidates or issues. In the latter stages of the chapter, we described a study designed to test the relative influence of a group stereotype (toward African Americans) and ideological considerations on support for three political issues that varied in the directness of their connection to racial minorities. Our specific question was which type of consideration – race stereotype or ideological principle – came automatically to mind for opponents and supporters of the issues, and we found that race pervaded automatic thought on the most racially charged issue, affirmative action, to the exclusion of ideology for opponents but alongside a concern for egalitarianism for supporters. For less racially charged issues, opposition was linked to both race and ideology.

5

Affect Transfer and the Evaluation
of Political Candidates

Previous chapters have documented uncontrolled and momentary effects of positive and negative feelings and group cues on the expression of snap judgments for a variety of political objects, including candidates, parties and groups, ideas, and issues. We now turn to a somewhat different question concerning the "downstream" effects of implicit cues on political information processing. Much of the import of our theory derives from the contention that early influences, even small and substantively irrelevant ones, will propagate through subsequent information processing by providing motivation, setting direction, and altering the accessibility of considerations in memory for downstream thought processes.

In this chapter we focus on how information presented both implicitly and explicitly influences how people form and update their impressions of political candidates. In two studies, we experimentally manipulate the similarity between a participant and a fictional politician by matching the participant's responses from a preexperimental questionnaire to the positions the candidate takes in a news article (one version reprinted in Appendix 5A at the end of this chapter). Because similarity is both a strong and uncontroversial predictor of candidate preference and voting behavior – indeed, it is the driving force behind spatial and directional models of electoral competition – we fully expect similarity to foster positive candidate evaluations while dissimilarity should promote more negative evaluations.

Nothing new there, but now, two experimental procedures are introduced to measure the effect, if any, of positive and negative primes on candidate evaluation, asking whether subliminally delivered affective prime words (including some of the same used in the snap judgment studies) will modify the evaluations of similar and dissimilar politicians in a prime-congruent direction. That is, we will now test the *affect transfer hypothesis*, introduced in Chapters 1 and 2 and represented by arrow d in Figure 1.3.

TABLE 5.1. *Affective Words Used as Subliminal Primes in Both Studies*

Positive Prime Words		Negative Prime Words	
triumphant	excellence	suicide	death
paradise	friendly	vomit	sad
love	fun	funeral	infection
laughter	terrific	cancer	syphilis
orgasm	success	rejected	grief
joy	romantic	murderer	terrified
humor	pleasure	torture	disaster
miracle	graduate	suffocate	rabies
happy	rainbow	unhappy	ulcer
kiss	sweetheart	loneliness	mutilate

Experimental Tests of Affect Transfer for Political Candidate Evaluations

It may be useful to start with the affective primes used in these studies, listed in Table 5.1. Selected from Bradley and Lang's (1999) *Affective Norms for English Words* (ANEW), these primes are consensually rated by several national samples as pleasant or unpleasant and screened by us to be unrelated to the candidate's character or issue positions. The question at hand: will such positive primes as "love," "joy," and "kiss" promote an even more favorable evaluation of the candidate in the candidate-similar condition and weaken the negative evaluation when he voices policy positions contrary to participants', and will such negative primes as "sad," "grief," and "rabies" do the opposite? Such a pattern of findings would provide support for the affect transfer hypothesis and lend credence to our contention that momentary and unnoticed cues have politically relevant downstream effects.

Because we are interested in the nature of the processes that underlie affect transfer, we introduce a depth of information processing manipulation in Study 2. This second experiment will replicate the candidate similarity and positive and negative priming conditions from Study 1, but we will also cross these factors with a deliberations manipulation in which one-third of the participants are asked to stop and think about the candidate's issue positions, one-third are instructed to proceed at their own pace, and one-third are given a distracter task, which we expect to interfere with their ability to deliberate about the candidate's positions.

The question now turns to who we should expect to be affected by the primes. The node-link associative network structure built into *JQP* presupposes that political sophisticates differ from unsophisticates in having more politics-related nodes in LTM, stronger affectively charged links between concept nodes, and a more hierarchical memory structure. Add to this the built-in hot cognition postulate that all nodes and links are affectively charged, and it follows that political sophisticates should be more not less affected by the priming of positive and negative feelings as compared to the less politically sophisticated. In addition, sophisticates should be more capable of processing new political information. If this proves to be the case, more knowledgeable citizens should experience greater affect transfer, and because more affective-laden information is accessible to sophisticates when forming and updating their evaluations there should be a greater likelihood for their feelings to bias the retrieval of information from LTM.

This expectation clearly violates conventional views of candidate evaluation, which assume that the least politically knowledgeable will be most susceptible to affectively charged incidental information (but see Huddy and Gunnthors-dottir, 2000; Huber and Lapinski, 2006). *JQP* predicts the opposite based on the fact that the most politically sophisticated have the richest number of affectively charged associations in LTM; thus, the richer the knowledge structure the greater the opportunity for priming events to deposit prime-congruent evidence into the decision stream.

In another departure from conventional expectations, we predict that those who are encouraged to think more deeply about the candidate and his issue positions will also be more strongly affected in a prime-congruent direction than will those paying cursory attention. The rationale here is similar to that given for our expectations about sophisticates: assuming that more thought will bring more associations to mind, the greater the number of affectively charged considerations that enter the processing stream, the greater the opportunity for affect transfer to influence candidate evaluations.

To test these hypotheses four key variables will be experimentally manipulated or measured: (1) the similarity between the participant and the candidate will be consciously manipulated, (2) the valence of the prime will be unconsciously manipulated, (3) the sophistication of participants will be measured, and (4) the extent of cognitive deliberation that participants engage in will be manipulated through instruction and task. These four variables lead to four experimental hypotheses: *The similarity hypothesis* expects that participants will evaluate candidates who profess issue positions similar to their own positions more positively than candidates who profess dissimilar issue positions. Over and above the predicted similarity effect, *the affect transfer hypothesis* predicts that participants will evaluate candidates who are paired with positive subliminal primes more positively than they will evaluate candidates paired with negative subliminal primes.

Because political sophisticates have a larger storehouse of political concepts and relevant linkages, we expect that their evaluations will be more influenced by both candidate similarity and the congruence of the primes when compared with non-sophisticates, which is *the sophistication hypothesis*. And we expect that the more carefully a participant thinks about the candidate and the issue positions he is evaluating, either because he is politically sophisticated or because he is induced to think carefully about the candidate, the greater effect the subliminal prime will have on his subsequent evaluations, which we call *the deliberation hypothesis*.

Study 1

Our first experiment will test the similarity and affect transfer hypotheses, as well as their moderation by sophistication, by manipulating candidate-participant similarity and subliminal exposure to positive or negative prime words, measuring political knowledge, and examining their relative effects on candidate evaluations.

Participants. One-hundred-sixty-five participants were recruited for Study 1 from political science classes at Stony Brook University in the spring semester of 2006 in exchange for extra class credit. Because English words served as subliminal primes, participants were excluded if English was not their first language, resulting in 56 participants being excluded. Of the 109 remaining participants in the study, 62 were male; and 62 identified as white, 12 as black, 9 as Hispanic/Latino, 24 as Asian, and 2 as Pacific Islander. When asked the standard NES partisan and ideological identification questions, 51 participants identified with the Democratic Party, 30 as Independents, and 23 with the Republicans; 50 participants identified as liberals, 31 as moderates, and 19 as conservatives. As is typical for Stony Brook undergraduate samples, there is a noticeable liberal and Democratic bias, but this will not affect our results as we manipulated similarity without presenting prototypically liberal or conservative candidates: liberal and conservative participants were equally likely to see a similar or a dissimilar candidate based on their particular policy positions. Political sophistication was measured using ten factually based civics-type knowledge items, with a median split that produced fifty-five political sophisticates, and fifty-four unsophisticates.

Experimental Design. The experimental session was administered on PCs in Stony Brook's Laboratory for Experimental Research in Political Behavior. A general outline of the experimental tasks is depicted in Figure 5.1. After obtaining consent, participants completed a political attitudes questionnaire to determine their positions on several key issues. The focal issues for the similarity manipulation in Experiment 1 were *affirmative action*, measured by the "racial resentment scale" with one additional direct affirmative action item taken from Kinder and Sanders (1996), and attitudes toward the Iraq War, measured by the "attitudes toward war scale" (Stagner, 1942), with an additional item focused specifically on the war in Iraq. On completing the political attitudes questionnaire, participants read a fictional newspaper article about a hypothetical Congressional Candidate William Lucas, who was running to fill an empty seat (one version of the Iraq War article, broken into two parts by manipulation, comprises Appendixes 5A and 5B). To facilitate the

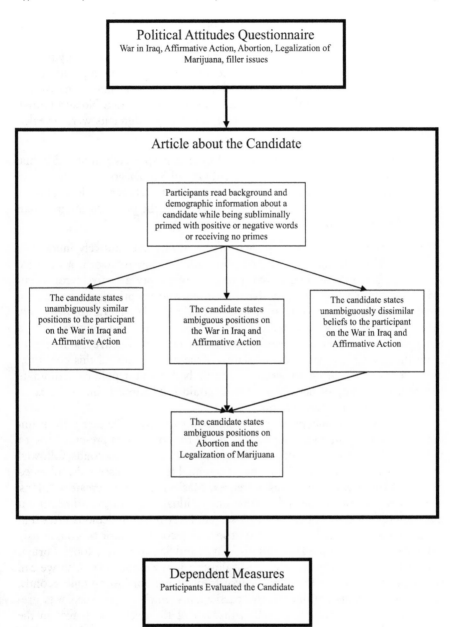

FIGURE 5.1. Participant Timeline for Experiment 1

construction of a candidate evaluation, a picture of Candidate Lucas remained on the screen while participants read the article.

The news article was presented in three sections so we could cleanly manipulate our two factors. To administer the affective priming manipulation, the first section of the article was presented one sentence at a time, using twenty general statements about the candidate, campaign, or district. No substantive issue positions that might influence policy similarity judgments were revealed in these sentences. For example,

- "The Eastern portion of this electoral district is sparsely populated, while the western portion includes several suburbs of San Diego."
- "The electoral race is predicted to be one of the closest races in the country."
- "Lucas made the decision to run for office, after the previous congressman had decided not to seek reelection."

Immediately prior to reading each of the twenty substantively innocuous sentences, participants were primed with either a positive word, a negative word, or no word, yielding a total exposure of twenty affectively consistent primes in the positive and negative conditions and no primes in the control condition. The prime words are listed in Table 5.1. We chose to affectively prime a set of nonissue statements before participants saw any of Lucas's issue positions, so we could cleanly separate the implicit affective manipulation from the explicit similarity manipulation. One might think of this condition as analogous to hearing something good or bad about a political candidate before learning any of her policy stands (could it be Sarah Palin at the 2008 Republican National Convention?).

As with the subliminal priming paradigms introduced in Chapter 3, the priming procedure began with a forward mask of random letters presented for 13 milliseconds, followed by a prime word presented for 39 milliseconds, followed by a backward mask of random letters presented for 13 milliseconds, followed by one of the twenty innocuous sentences. Masks are used to create a "blank visual slate" for the prime and to erase any residual image of the prime after it has been removed from the computer screen. Prior research demonstrates that prime words presented for less than 100 milliseconds cannot be consciously perceived (Devine, 1989; Dijksterhuis, Aarts, and Smith, 2005; Moors, Spruyt, and DeHouwer, 2010; Murphy and Zajonc, 1993; Zajonc, 1980), so we can be confident that our masked prime words, presented for just 39 milliseconds, were not consciously visible to the participants. Each prime word was presented once and randomly paired with each of the twenty sentences in the first section of the article, and participants were never primed while reading the candidate's substantive issue positions. In the no-prime control condition, forward and backward masks were presented for 13 milliseconds each, with a 39-millisecond blank screen between.

In the second section of the news article, participants read a paragraph describing the candidate's policy positions toward the Iraq War and Affirmative

Action, each manipulated to be either similar or dissimilar to the participants' positions. We programmed our experiment to attribute to candidate Lucas the same or the opposite positions on these issues as were taken by the given participant in the preexperiment questionnaire. Subjects were assigned to either the similar condition, in which case Lucas took their positions on both issues, the dissimilar condition, in which case Lucas took the opposite position on both issues, or an ambiguous candidate condition, in which case Lucas did not take a clear position on either the Iraq or Affirmative Action issues. We expect participants to like Lucas best when he is similar to them, least when he is dissimilar, and in between when he is ambiguous.

The final section of the news story reported on the candidate's fundraising capabilities and advertising expenses, which we do not analyze here. This unreported manipulation did not interact with or influence the similarity or priming manipulations in determining candidate evaluations.

After participants finished reading the article, we collected two dependent variables: first, we asked whether the participant would vote for the candidate; and second, we asked participants to rate how much they liked the candidate. Both variables were assessed on six point Likert scales. Finally, at the end of the experiment, we collected demographic information and answers to the ten political knowledge questions that measured political sophistication.

To recap, participants responded to a political attitudes survey, and were then randomly assigned to be subliminally primed with twenty positive words, twenty negative words, or no words while reading nonissue statements about the candidate, district, or race (to test for implicit affect transfer). They then read an issue paragraph on the Iraq War and one on Affirmative Action, manipulated to be similar, dissimilar, or ambiguous with respect to each participant's positions on these issues (to test the explicit similarity hypothesis). We then collected their vote intentions, candidate evaluations, demographics, and political knowledge.

Results. The data for the evaluation of the candidate were initially analyzed using an omnibus 3 (subliminal prime: positive, none, or negative) × 3 (candidate similarity: similar, ambiguous, or dissimilar) × 2 (sophistication: high vs low) Analysis of Variance (ANOVA). The ANOVA revealed significant main effects for explicit candidate similarity, $F(2, 91) = 9.88$, $p < .05$, and implicit prime valence, $F(2, 91) = 3.62$, $p < .05$. These main effects were qualified by a significant three-way interaction between prime valence, candidate similarity, and political sophistication, $F(4, 91) = 2.79$, $p < .05$. No other significant effects were observed. We followed up the omnibus analysis with more targeted hypothesis tests.

First, we carried out a linear trend analysis for both the prime and similarity manipulations. The trend analysis constrains the manipulated variables to conform to a previously specified linear pattern: positive primes should promote a more positive evaluation than no primes, which in turn should be more positive than negative primes. It should also be the case that a similar candidate should be evaluated more positively than an ambiguous candidate, who in turn should be evaluated more positively than a dissimilar candidate. The three-way ANOVA revealed a significant main effect for candidate similarity $F(1, 101) = 25.44$, $p < .05$, and a significant main effect of the subliminal prime, $F(1, 101) = 7.54$, $p < .05$. These main effects were again qualified by a significant three-way interaction between candidate similarity, the subliminal prime, and political sophistication, $F(1, 100) = 9.12$, $p < .05$, with no other effects reaching significance.

To further explore the three-way interaction, we examined the model for the two levels of sophistication, by analyzing two sets of parallel ANOVAs. A graphical depiction of the results is reported in Figure 5.2. Unsurprisingly, both sophisticates and unsophisticates are influenced by candidate similarity, $F_{high soph}(1, 51) = 11.71$, $p < .01$, $F_{low soph}(1, 50) = 13.79$, $p < .001$. This main effect confirms the similarity hypothesis, in that similar candidates are evaluated more positively than dissimilar candidates.

What is striking here is that high sophisticates, as predicted by *JQP*, are indeed influenced by the subliminal primes, while the low sophisticates are not, $F_{high soph}(1, 51) = 9.59$, $p < .01$, $F_{low soph}(1, 50) = 0.50$, $p > .10$. The main effect of the subliminal primes for those above the median on our political knowledge scale is significant and confirms the hypothesis that sophistication will moderate the influence of implicit primes. For the politically unsophisticated, the primes have no discernable effects. These main effects were qualified by a significant interaction for the high sophisticates between our similarity and priming manipulations, $F(1, 51) = 9.21$, $p < .01$, with no such interaction for the low sophisticates, $F(1, 50) = 1.63$, *ns*. This interaction for the high sophisticates is driven primarily by the much greater influence of negative primes, which made participants in the dissimilar condition much more negative than did positive primes make the similar candidate more positive. This pattern of means for the high sophisticates is consistent with the positivity offset and negativity bias whereby negative information carries more weight (Cacioppo and Berntson, 1994; Cacioppo, Gardner, and Berntson, 1997; Ito and Cacioppo, 2005; Lau, 1985; Lau, Sigelman, and Rovner, 2007).

Discussion. The results of Study 1 support our first three hypotheses. In line with the similarity hypothesis, issue similarity between the candidate and the participants led to more positive evaluations of the candidate. Based on the massive literature on issue-proximity in political science and the similarity-liking hypothesis in psychology (Berleson, Lazarsfeld, and McPhee, 1954; Black, 1948; Byrne, London, and Reeves, 1968; Downs, 1957; Granberg and Holmberg, 1986; Lau and Redlawsk, 1997), this is not a surprising result. Conversely, support for implicit affect transfer, especially for sophisticated participants is, we believe, unanticipated by conventional political science models. Clearly, political sophisticates evaluate the candidate differently when they are implicitly primed with positive or negative information. The important conclusion we draw from this finding is that people's candidate evaluations are the product of

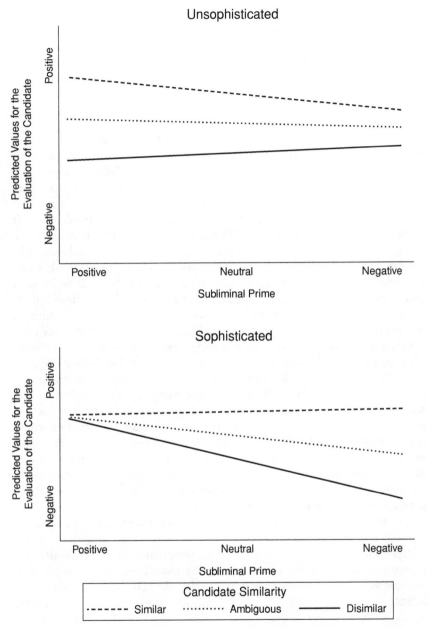

FIGURE 5.2. Similarity and Affect Transfer, Moderated by Sophistication, Study 1

far more than they are consciously aware of. What we see as remarkable about these finding is that the subliminally delivered affective primes significantly influence the classic effects of similarity on evaluation, even though the primes were not linked to any of the candidate's issue positions, but for reasons soon to be explored, are largely limited to the politically sophisticated.

Study 2

The expectation informing many contemporary models of candidate evaluation and vote choice in political science is that citizens somehow match their most important issue preferences to the policy stands of the candidates and in some way or another compute a difference score and vote for the most proximate candidate. Ostensibly, the more deeply one thinks about one's own and the candidates' positions, the better (dare we say more "rational"?) the decision. It is widely assumed that the greater the deliberation the better the chance to bring additional considerations to mind and keep one's focus on what is substantively important. The clear expectation is that the more carefully people think about the candidates and their issue stands, the less influenced they will be by such "extraneous" factors as, say, the physical attractiveness of the candidate or such seemingly inconsequential influences as ballot position (all of which, if made conscious, would be explicitly rejected as irrelevant considerations).

Contrary to this commonsense notion, contemporary research in psychology shows that encouraging decision makers to stop and think before deciding can actually reduce the quality of the decision vis-à-vis their first impression (Dijksterhuis, 2004; Dijksterhuis et al. 2006; Forgas, 1995; Hofmann and Wilson, 2010; Wilson and Schooler, 1991). Interestingly, individuals motivated to be accurate – which encourages a deeper memory search – are often found to be even more biased by their prior attitude than those relying on their first impression (Kunda, 1990; Taber and Lodge, 2006). Worse yet, there is strong empirical evidence showing that one's seat-of-the-pants impression often proves to be a better predictor of long-term satisfaction with the choice (Acker, 2008; Gigerenzer, 2007; Wilson and Schooler, 1991).

In *JQP* the very act of deliberation influences the accessibility of considerations in memory and will necessarily impact the evaluation respondents make. The deeper the thought given an evaluation, the greater the effect of affective congruence on the sampling of considerations from long-term memory and, consequently, the stronger the bias in evaluation. In *JQP*, as in life, OL-based preferences can be deflected by the amplification of affect-congruence effects in the augmented sample of considerations brought to mind by the motivated search for considerations. And were we to affectively prime respondents as they think about the candidate's issue positions (as we will do in Chapter 6), we would expect unconscious priming events to be even more influential, because the affect triggered by the primes promotes the retrieval of supportive considerations from which an evaluation is updated.

Given the postulates underlying *JQP*, two separate effects are predicted: (1) Asking those who initially like a candidate because they have been positively primed to stop and think will lead them to like the candidate even more, with the reverse true for negative priming. As the number of positive or negative thoughts entering working memory increases, the voter's evaluation of the candidate will adjust accordingly to track the congruence-biased sample of associations (MacLeod and Campbell, 1992; Tversky and Kahneman, 1973; Kahneman and Tversky, 1974). And (2) if the individual is simultaneously primed when searching memory, the number of congruent considerations will also be increased.

To test these hypotheses, in Experiment 2 we allow half of the participants to read the article at their own pace and respond when ready without encouraging them to stop and think. The expectancy here is that the attitude-priming effect will hold. The other half of the participants were asked to think carefully about the candidates and write down their thoughts before responding. If the conventional wisdom is correct, thinking carefully about the candidates will override the effect of the subliminal primes. Our prediction is contrary – in *JQP* thinking deeply brings more affectively consistent thoughts to mind, and consequently participants will be more influenced by the incidental primes than those reporting their top-of-the-head, OL impression.

The second issue that the first study did not address was whether the results could be driven by a mood rather than a priming effect. The effect of incidental mood on evaluations is well documented (Bower, 1981; Forgas, 1995; Schwarz and Clore, 1983). We, however, in line with Petty and colleagues (2006), do not see the participant's mood as the mechanism driving the evaluative differences we find for priming. This question is, of course, an empirical one. To test experimentally whether the effects we observe are due to mood or due to priming, in Experiment 2 we include two candidates, one paired consistently with positive primes, the other with an equal number of negative primes. If the differences in evaluation are due to priming, we should observe priming effects for both candidates as in Study 1 as the evaluations of the two candidates are driven in opposite directions. If, however, the differences in evaluation are due to mood, we should not observe this priming effect at all, but a moderating of evaluations as the positive and negative primes cancel one another out.

Participants. One-hundred-ninety-six participants were recruited from political science classes at Stony Brook University in exchange for class credit. Again, English words were used as subliminal primes, which resulted in thirty-one nonnative speakers being excluded from all analyses. Of the remaining 165 participants, 70 were female; 88 identified as white, 7 as black, 11 as Hispanic/Latino, 51 as Asian, and 8 identified as other. In answer to the standard party ID question, 92 participants identified with the Democratic Party, 33 as Independents, and 34 as Republicans. On ideological self-placement, 67 participants identified as liberals, 81 as moderates, and 17 as conservatives. Again, ten knowledge items were used to assess political sophistication. A median split categorized 88 participants as politically sophisticated and 77 as politically unsophisticated.

Experimental Design. The basic design for the second study followed the design of the first, with three major changes as depicted in Figure 5.3. As in Experiment 1, participants first completed a political attitudes survey, were then primed on reading banal statements about two candidates, then read a fictitious newspaper article describing the candidates vying for a seat in Congress, and finally responded to a battery of questions assessing their evaluations of the candidate and their perceptions of his issue positions.

The first change to the design was to include a deliberation manipulation, where one-third of the participants were induced to explicitly deliberate about the candidates, one-third of the participants were left to their natural pace, and the remaining participants were distracted by audio clips while they read the information about the candidates. To induce deliberation, after every issue statement participants were asked two open-ended questions: (1) what do you think about the candidate's position, and (2) what would you change about the candidate's position to make him more attractive to you? We opted to not ask the standard NES open-ended likes and dislikes question as our goal was to induce participants to think carefully about the candidates and not explicitly encourage them to evaluate the candidates. Content coding of the responses was carried out for the subset of participants in the cognitive deliberation condition. Analyses show that despite our effort, (but as *JQP*'s hot cognition and OL postulates would predict), most participants made affective evaluations even though they were not explicitly asked to do so. Approximately one-third of the participants' thoughts were purely affective (e.g., I like candidate A), another third were a mixture of affect and substance (e.g., I like candidate A's position on immigration), and the final third essentially stated the candidate's position (e.g., Candidate A is pro-choice). The open-ended responses suggest that participants in the deliberation condition did indeed think more deeply about the candidates than they otherwise would have.

In the experimental condition in which participants proceeded at their own pace, after being primed along with innocuous information they simply read the news article and then answered the postarticle questionnaire without being asked to stop, think, and write down any thoughts. A third condition introduced a cognitive load manipulation in which audio weather reports played as participants read the news article. This background information made it more difficult for the participants to process the message, thus creating an additional load on the participant's cognitive resources and making it more difficult for these participants to form impressions of the candidates. However, this task proved to be more distracting than we wished as it essentially reduced both candidate similarity and priming effects to insignificance. This condition is dropped from the forthcoming analyses.

The second change to the design was to have participants read about and evaluate two candidates rather than only one. This more closely mimics the way

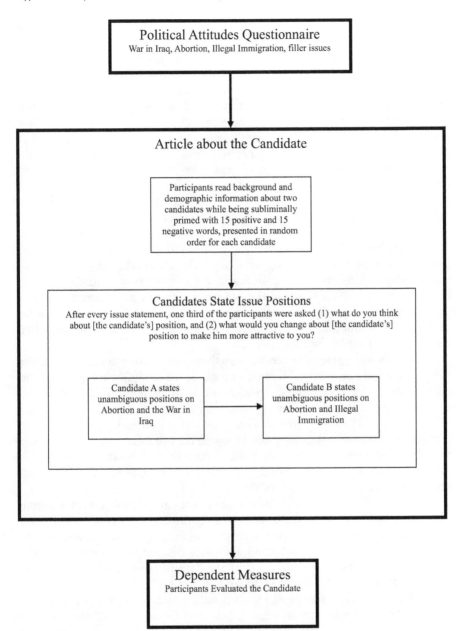

FIGURE 5.3. Participant Timeline for Study 2

newspaper articles present election-eve information about candidates. More importantly, the two-candidate design allows us to rule out a mood explanation for our results. The additional political candidate, however, increases the cognitive demands on the participants in all conditions, requiring them to form and update two evaluations rather than one. As in the first study, participants read thirty-five statements: five neutral introductory statements devoid of any issue or character trait content and fifteen pieces of demographic information about each candidate. For half the participants, the nonsubstantive information about candidate A was paired with positive primes, while for candidate B they were paired with negative primes; for the other half of the participants, the reverse. The masking procedure was identical to Study 1. Therefore, every participant received fifteen positive primes for one candidate *and* fifteen negative primes for the other, all outside of conscious awareness. Because they received the same number of positive and negative primes, any resulting mood should be neutral. To further ensure that the primes did not create a mood state, participants were randomly assigned to read about candidate A or B first and each candidate was randomly paired with either positive or negative primes. In addition, we included a condition where the primes were interspersed, so that the participants did not receive fifteen consecutive positive or negative primes. In this condition, a participant was presented with no more than five consecutive primes of the same valence.

Results. Before presenting the main analyses, we examined the order effect of the candidates and the subliminal primes. In the analyses, we included the order of the candidates and the primes as a main and conditional effect. In no situation did either order effect approach significance. Given this, we exclude order effects in the rest of the models. The lack of an order effect provides tentative evidence that the effect of priming on the candidate evaluations is due to a direct priming effect and not a mood state created by the primes. For a more definitive demonstration of this we will now turn to the effects of priming on the participants' evaluations of the candidates.

To analyze the participants' evaluations of the candidates, we will examine each candidate separately and analyze the results conditional on which level of the deliberation manipulation the participant was randomly assigned to. As in Study 1, evaluations of each candidate were computed as the mean of the participant's willingness to vote for the candidate and their level of (dis)liking. These evaluations were analyzed separately for each candidate using three parallel 2 (similarity: similar versus dissimilar) × 2 (prime: positive versus negative) × 2 (sophistication: high versus low) factorial ANOVAs for each level of the cognitive deliberation manipulation. Because the effect of candidate similarity is as in Study 1 strong and pervasive, to simplify the presentation of the results, in Figure 5.4 we present the simple main effects of the affective subliminal primes on evaluations of candidate A at each level of cognitive effort for political sophisticates. Similarity does not moderate the effect of subliminal priming on candidate evaluations.

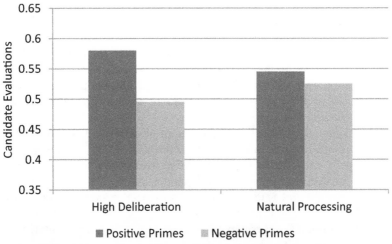

FIGURE 5.4. Effect of Primes on Evaluations of Candidate A

On analyzing the evaluations of candidate A, we see the familiar pattern observed in Study 1: when examining the politically sophisticated participants, the subliminal primes exert the expected effect; however, this effect is only statistically significant for the participants in the deliberation condition, $F(1, 46) = 4.30, p < .05$, and did not have a significant impact on the evaluations of the participants in the natural-pace condition, $F(1, 34) = 0.14, p > .10$. When a candidate is paired with positive subliminal primes, the primes strengthen the association between the candidate and general positivity. So, when the participants are asked to think carefully about the candidates, their thoughts reinforce these associations, subsequently leading to more positive candidate evaluations. None of the priming effects were significantly moderated by candidate similarity.

Again, as hypothesized, there was also a highly significant main effect of candidate similarity for sophisticates, $F(1, 111) = 20.59, p < .05$. This effect was especially pronounced in the cognitive deliberation condition, $F(1, 46) = 12.24, p < .05$, and less pronounced but statistically significant in the proceed-at-one's-own-pace condition, $F(1, 38) = 3.48, p = .05$. In sum, the more that sophisticated participants thought about the candidate, the stronger their evaluations corresponded with their issue preferences, which is exactly what would be predicted by conventional proximity models of candidate evaluation. Finally, the interaction between the subliminal prime and candidate similarity was not significant in any of the models.

The analysis of candidate B was conducted in the same manner as for candidate A. Again, evaluations of candidate B were analyzed using three parallel 2 (similarity: similar vs dissimilar) × 2 (prime: positive vs negative) × 2 (sophistication: high vs low) factorial ANOVAs for each level of the cognitive deliberation manipulation. The only participants whose evaluations of the candidates were significantly influenced by the subliminal primes were political sophisticates in the deliberation condition, $F(1, 46) = 5.86$, $p < .05$. In the natural deliberation condition, the effect of the prime is in the right direction, but marginal $F(1, 34) = 1.64$, $p > .10$. These effects again demonstrate that the subliminal primes altered the way that participants evaluated the candidates: positive primes lead participants to like the candidate more and negative primes lead them to dislike the candidate.

As with candidate A, political sophisticates in general evaluated a similar candidate B more positively than a dissimilar candidate B, $F(1, 111) = 5.256$, $p < .05$. And again, this effect is driven by the participants who were encouraged to think more deeply about the candidate, $F(1, 46) = 5.43$, $p < .05$, while candidate similarity did not lead those in the self-paced condition to reliably alter their evaluations of the candidate ($F(1, 34) = 1.90$, $p > .10$). As for the low sophisticates, no significant results emerge for either candidate similarity or for a subliminal priming effect for candidate B. Apparently, in this more complex two-candidate scenario, the less politically sophisticated participants were unable to form an evaluation of the candidate. It appears as if the additional information simply overwhelmed them.

From these results it is clear that the more sophisticated participants thought about the candidates, the more the subliminal primes affected their evaluations of the candidates in a prime-congruent direction.

Discussion. Study 2 replicates and extends the findings of Study 1 in showing that unnoticed Type 1 priming effects emerged for sophisticated participants who thought more carefully about the candidates' issue positions. When primed subliminally with affectively congruent positive words, candidates were evaluated more positively then were candidates who had been primed negatively. This unconscious priming effect was consistent across two candidates and emerged most strongly when the politically sophisticated participants were encouraged to think about the candidate's policy positions before responding. This effect held even when evaluating candidates taking an ambiguous position on the Iraq War and affirmative action. In short, support for all three hypotheses from Study 1 was replicated in Study 2.

The major extension of Study 2 was the inclusion of the deliberation condition. Here we encouraged some participants to think more systematically about the candidates' position on the issues. From a normative standpoint, subliminal primes should not have a greater effect on the participants' evaluations of candidates when they think carefully about and evaluate the candidates' policy proposals. But this is what we found: when sophisticates were induced to deliberate about the candidates, positive subliminal primes led them to evaluate the candidates *more* positively and negative subliminal primes led to *more* negative candidate evaluations. Thinking can be dangerous!

Participants who proceeded at their own pace did not show this pattern of effects. Keep in mind that in Study 2, the addition of a second candidate doubled the amount of information participants were exposed to, thus increasing the cognitive resources that would be required to process the information. As such, even the sophisticated participants did not show the priming effect *unless* they were asked to think about the information carefully and required to list their thoughts.

Finally, it is also clear that the effects are not due to the subliminal primes inducing a mood state in the participants. Because participants in Experiment 2 were exposed to an equal number of positive and negative primes across the two candidates, the resulting mood would be neutral. However, the same predicted priming effect emerged for both candidates in Study 2 as emerged for the single candidate in Study 1. When one of the candidates was paired with a positive prime and the other was paired with a negative prime, the positive prime consistently led to more positive evaluations (and the opposite for the negative prime) regardless of which candidate was paired with which prime. If this was truly a mood effect, the subliminal primes would have cancelled out. One oddity: some might argue that given the well-documented negativity bias in judgments the effect of the negative primes should be stronger than the positive primes (Cacioppo and Berntson, 1994; Ito and Cacioppo, 2005; Kahneman and Tversky, 1974). We too expected, but did not find, a pronounced negativity bias in this study.

General Discussion

These two experiments demonstrate that information presented outside of conscious awareness influences the way people evaluate political candidates. It is a staple of the existing candidate evaluation literature that people favor candidates who share their political attitudes. In these experiments, we explicitly incorporated the participant's prior attitudes toward the candidates (via the similarity manipulation) and crafted candidates that participants would either like or dislike. Importantly, issue proximity proves to be a strong predictor of how people form their evaluations of political candidates, as most prior research has suggested. True enough, but the current studies demonstrate that more goes into candidate evaluations than issue proximity: people are also influenced by the information that they are exposed to outside their conscious awareness, and this information systematically impacts their candidate evaluations.

What we see as an important addition to this literature on candidate evaluation is the finding across both studies that the politically sophisticated are more strongly influenced by incidental information than are the less politically knowledgeable. And, contrary to conventional wisdom and volumes of philosophical advice, the more that sophisticates thought about the candidates, the more these unnoticed priming events influenced their evaluations of the candidates. This finding is predicted by *JQP* and consistent with previous findings (Lodge and Taber, 2005; Taber and Lodge, 2006). Normatively, it is the most knowledgeable among us who should be best able to resist incidental influences, but empirically, these are the very citizens – people like ourselves – who are most affected.

A core presumption of *JQP* in need of extensive study is that in-depth processing will systematically bias the retrieval of associations in favor of one's prior attitude and deposit in working memory an ever-more-biased sample of considerations from which explicit evaluations will be constructed. If so, attitude polarization is the expected result when the prior attitude or prime share a common valence, but moderation when prior and prime are affectively incongruent.

But note that this mediation model of affective contagion, in which prime-activated thoughts enter the decision stream to push an updated evaluation in a prime-congruent direction, was *not* directly tested in the experiments reported in this chapter. Here, our interest was in affect transfer in which primes presented minutes *before* the candidates voiced their issue stands transfer their affect directly onto the candidates. The upcoming chapter will directly test affective contagion and the mediation model.

Appendix 5.A. Article for Study 1

Nonissue Priming Paragraph

Participants read this paragraph one sentence at a time. Before reading each sentence they were presented subliminally with either a positive or negative word or no prime.

William Lucas is running for U.S. Congress for California's 34th electoral district, which covers the Eastern portion of San Diego County. The eastern portion of this electoral district is sparsely populated, while the western portion includes several suburbs of San Diego. The electoral race in this district is predicted to be one of the closest races in the country. One of Lucas's closest aides told *The Daily Transcript* that, in all the years that he has worked for politicians, he has never thought that the race was as evenly matched. Lucas made the decision to run for office after the previous congressman had decided not to seek reelection. Lucas says that he has always wanted to pursue a life of public service and that when the house seat in his district opened up he saw the opportunity to pursue his goal of becoming a member of congress. Until now, Lucas has been a hospital administrator at a local hospital, where he has worked for the last fourteen years. Lucas is a forty-six-year-old San Diego resident. His family has been living in San Diego for three generations. His grandfather moved the family to San Diego from Ohio in 1932 to find work. After finding a job at a local lumber mill, and meeting Lucas's grandmother, his grandfather decided to stay in San Diego. His father was a salesman at a local store in the north end of San Diego County. Lucas has a brother and a sister, who also both live in San Diego. Lucas went to Mt. Carmel High School, in the northeast portion of the county. He also went to college in San Diego at the University of California. While at UCSD, Lucas met his wife Janet, who was in one of his classes. Janet is a teacher at a local elementary school, and she plans to keep her job if Lucas is elected. They now have two children, a boy and a girl, who are fourteen and eleven, respectively. The public's eye has been focused on several campaign issues: affirmative action, tax policy, the legalization of marijuana, the war in Iraq, the death penalty, and abortion. Both candidates have spoken about the issues at great length.

Appendix 5.B. War Paragraph

Participants read one of the following paragraphs that was either similar or dissimilar to their previously stated beliefs

Lucas was a strong advocate against the Iraq War. He argues that the public no longer supports the war, and that the insurgents are not going away. "The war in Iraq has increased the probability of another terrorist attack on US soil." Lucas also stated that "The number of casualties in Iraq is too high. It is time to leave the Iraqi people to solve their own problems." Even more important to Lucas is his repeated suggestion that the war is making the United States less credible with the Arab world, and that it has strained relations with strong U.S. allies like Germany and Canada.

Lucas was initially opposed to the war in Iraq, but over time he became an advocate for the war. He suggests that, "Contrary to what is being reported in the media, real progress is being made in Iraq. The debate over whether or not America should have gone to war in the Persian Gulf is over. The debate must turn to ways of helping the Iraqi people." However, Lucas has repeatedly suggested that the war is making the United States less credible with the Arab world, and that it has strained relations with strong U.S. allies like Germany and Canada.

Lucas was a strong advocate for the Iraq war. He suggests that, "Contrary to what is being reported in the media, real progress is being made in Iraq. We must stay the course. The debate over whether or not America should have gone to war in the Persian Gulf is over. The debate must turn to ways of helping the Iraqi people." In another speech he said, "Saddam was an evil man. Removing him was the best possible option." He has suggested that the United States should promote democracy throughout the world, and that is what he believes the Iraq War is about.

6

Affective Contagion and Political Thinking

There are now hundreds of attitude priming studies in the literature (Petty, Fazio, and Briñol, 2009; Wegner and Bargh, 1998), and as seen in earlier chapters we have found strong experimental support for the spontaneous processing of affective information, but to our knowledge there are no experimental analyses of the effects of preconscious feelings on people when they stop to think and reason about political issues (Nosek, Graham, and Hawkins, 2010). What is more, there is good reason to believe that the way citizens evaluate public policy issues may be different from the way they think about and evaluate political persons. Zaller and Feldman (1992) make the case that when evaluating political issues, especially when the political parties take opposing positions (Zaller, 1992), citizens are apt to see two or more sides, and their awareness of the pros and cons may prevent them from forming a crystallized evaluation, especially if they are ambivalent about the issue (Basinger and Lavine, 2005; Lavine, Steenbergen, and Johnston, forthcoming). If this is the case, when called on to form or report a summary evaluation for an issue, citizens may not possess a readily available positive or negative affective tag to retrieve from memory, but rather may rely on memory-based piecemeal processing to sample whatever considerations are accessible in memory and only then construct an evaluation by integrating these *conscious* recollections into an evaluation (Fiske and Pavelchak, 1986; Tourangeau, Rips, and Rasinski, 2000; Zaller and Feldman, 1992).

Our *JQP* account of how political judgments are formed and expressed claims that the feelings aroused in the initial stages of processing sociopolitical concepts, including candidates, groups, and political ideas or issues, inevitably color *all* phases of the evaluation process. When a citizen is called upon to make a judgment, given sufficient time to think and motivation to query memory, the sample of considerations that enters consciousness will be biased by the valence of initial affect. That is, our theory posits that considered thought will be the joint product of memory-based processing and initial feelings, which are routinely triggered by affective tallies formed through online processes as well as affect aroused by contextual events and mood. We will show in upcoming analyses that what comes to mind when citizens voice an opinion, as when they respond to the NES open-ended question asking for reasons why they like or oppose a policy proposal, will reflect what information is currently accessible in memory, and this accessibility is biased by *affective contagion* – the facilitation of considerations from memory that are affectively congruent with initial feelings and the inhibition of incongruent considerations.

In short, the thoughts that come consciously to mind for citizens are *un*likely to be a balanced sample of pro and con associations, but rather will be biased systematically by the feelings aroused in the first few milliseconds of processing. Sometimes these initial feelings result from the arousal of *intrinsic affect* (affect or attitudes directly associated with the objects of thought), but they may also be triggered by *incidental affect* (feelings aroused by substantively unrelated environmental stimuli or prior mood). Whatever their source, positively valenced feelings facilitate the activation of positive considerations in memory and inhibit negative thoughts, while negative feelings inhibit positive and facilitate negative thoughts. In *JQP*, this underlying affective bias in processing drives motivated reasoning and rationalization in political thinking (Kim, Taber, and Lodge, 2010; Taber and Lodge, 2006).

Earlier chapters have already discussed how "snap judgments" about a variety of social and political objects are strongly influenced by Type 1 and Type 2 cues. These studies focus on the immediate and direct effects of unnoticed stimuli on judgments, attitudes, or simple behaviors through *affect transfer*. Recall, for example, Todorov and colleagues (2005) found that competence judgments of real but unknown political candidates whose faces had been presented for a mere second predicted the outcomes and margins of victory of actual U.S. elections, a result that we explain as the product of the direct transfer of initial feelings triggered by attractiveness and age (Verhulst, Lodge, and Lavine, 2010). In this chapter, we will go beyond the effect of affect transfer on snap judgments to test the influence of unnoticed affective stimuli on the generation of thoughts when people consciously deliberate about political issues and will track the downstream effects on a longer timescale. That is, we will put our *affect contagion hypothesis* to direct test in the context of conscious, deliberative thinking. The affective balance of considerations and thoughts, we expect, will be shaped by prior feelings, even when these feelings are completely incidental to the object of thought. In short, we hope to demonstrate that unnoticed affective stimuli influence the course of conscious deliberation about political policies and ultimately drive attitudes toward these policies expressed a significant span of time after the direct memory effects of the stimuli have decayed.

Two Experiments on Affective Contagion in Political Reasoning

We theorize that initial affect, triggered by both intrinsic and irrelevant sources, will bias conscious thinking about political issues. In line with conventional models, we expect that when experimental participants are asked to stop and think about a political issue or policy proposal, their prior attitudes toward the issue will systematically impact what thoughts and feelings enter the decision stream. More surprising from the point of view of conventional models of political reasoning, we also predict that completely incidental and substantively irrelevant affective stimuli presented outside the awareness of experimental participants will bias the affective balance of their thoughts. Conscious thoughts that come to mind for our experimental participants will be influenced by both prior attitudes and unnoticed affective stimuli. Moreover, this affect contagion will be subjectively experienced as valid and relevant regardless of the source, leading to changes in the subsequent expression of attitudes on the issue. When affective priors trigger this process, it drives motivated reasoning, attitude perseverance, and polarization (Taber and Lodge, 2005; see Chapter 7); when irrelevant and unnoticed stimuli promote affect contagion, it can promote either pro- or counterattitudinal rationalizations, depending on the valence of the unnoticed stimuli, and may provide an opportunity for the manipulation of attitudes by media or elites. Both forms of bias raise important normative concerns (to be addressed in the conclusion). In this chapter, we focus on the affective contagion of irrelevant, subliminally presented primes on the thoughts and feelings coming to mind when people think and reason about political policies. The next chapter will trace the processes promoting motivated reasoning and the rationalization of beliefs and attitudes.

Hypotheses. Stimuli encountered early in the processing stream can influence subsequent conscious thinking and reasoning, even when they are not consciously perceived and even when they are semantically unrelated to the objects of conscious thought. Retrieval of thoughts and considerations when thinking about political issues can be biased by affectively charged events occurring outside of conscious awareness.

Hypothesis 1: An *affective contagion effect*, such that an unnoticed positive prime promotes positive thoughts and inhibits negative thoughts, while an unnoticed negative prime promotes negative and inhibits positive thoughts.

In line with our theory of affect-driven information processing, we expect that implicit affective primes will also influence reported attitudes and policy preferences on the political issues that people are asked to think about, as mediated by their thoughts. That is, the expectation here is that the incidental priming of feelings will shape not only the sample of considerations that come to mind while thinking about a political issue, but also change subsequently reported attitudes and policy preferences on the issue, as mediated through the unbalanced set of thoughts produced as subjects think about the issues after having been subliminally primed with positive or negative stimuli.

Hypothesis 2: An *affective mediation effect*, such that affectively biased thoughts enter into the construction of reported evaluations and promote prime-congruent policy preferences and attitude change.

Note that we do *not* expect direct affect transfer from our primes to subsequent attitudes. The activation triggered by the positive and negative primes will have long since dissipated by the time attitudes are reported at the end of our studies. A great deal of research, beginning with Neely's classic 1977 study of the influence of primes on memory accessibility, demonstrates that *direct* priming effects decay within seconds, while the primes in our studies are presented at least thirty minutes before the recording of attitudes.

To reiterate, these experiments go beyond what has been reported in the political or social psychological literatures. Unlike research on the direct effects of primes on snap judgments, we now ask whether unconscious feelings influence the stream of information processing that underlies how people think and reason when called on to deliberate. We predict that unnoticed, irrelevant events will shape political preferences *even when people think deeply* about an issue. This result would be the strongest evidence to date that conscious political thinking may not provide a solid footing for rational political action, as is historically and conventionally believed.

Study 1 procedures. Study 1 was designed to test our affective contagion hypothesis. It was conducted in the Laboratory for Experimental Research in Political Behavior at Stony Brook University. Participants were undergraduate students in Political Science courses ($N = 224$; 48% male; 43% white; 50% greater than twenty-one years of age; 55% Democrat, 18% Republican, and 27% Independent).

Following consent procedures, participants were seated in front of personal computers in individual experimental rooms. Their first task was to report attitudes on a number of political issues including the target issues of illegal immigration and energy security (Figure 6.1). This pretest questionnaire asked for evaluations of illegal immigration and energy security as well as the attitude strength dimensions of certainty, extremity, importance, knowledge, and relevance (Krosnick and Petty, 1995; Wegener, Downing, Krosnick, and Petty, 1995). Theoretically, we view a general attitude on an issue as a multiplicative function of position and strength (Fishbein and Ajzen, 1975), so we compute our general *prior and posterior attitude measures* as the product of attitude position and strength, yielding continuous variables ranging from -3 to $+3$ with a neutral attitude position of 0. Both the seven-item attitude position scales and the five-item attitude strength scales were reliable. The composite attitude measure ranges from -3 to $+3$ with a true neutral midpoint at 0.

To show the influence of incidental, affective primes on the retrieval of considerations about these political issues, we engaged subjects in a primed

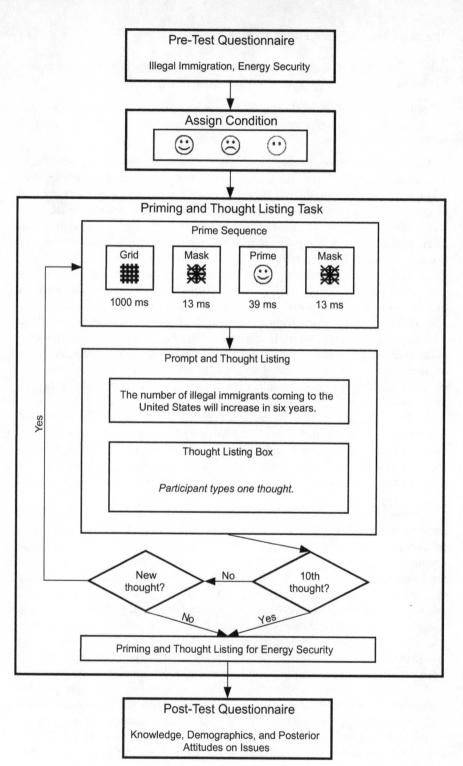

FIGURE 6.1. Experimental Design for Study 1

thought-listing procedure (Petty and Cacioppo, 1981; Gamson, 1992; Lane, 1969; Zaller and Feldman, 1992), where the primes were simple cartoon faces, either a smiling face, a frowning face, or a neutral face (no mouth) presented for just 39 milliseconds. Primes were masked before and after to erase the contents of visual memory and impose strict control on prime exposure. Immediately following subliminal exposure to a prime, a general issue statement appeared along with an empty response box, and participants were asked to type a single response thought to the political prompt. For illegal immigration the prompt was "The number of illegal immigrants coming to the United States will drastically increase in six years," while for energy security it was "The extent of energy consumption and the need for energy resources in the United States will drastically increase in the next decade." Upon completing a thought response to one of these prompts, another prime exposure and thought listing sequence was presented, up to a maximum of ten thoughts per issue. This procedure was followed first for illegal immigration and then for energy security policy, using the same smiling, neutral, or frowning face prime before each thought. In total, participants were exposed to between two and twenty presentations of the same prime and they typed zero to twenty thoughts; the number of prime exposures in Study 1 was determined by the number of thoughts a participant wished to type.

There were three randomly assigned experimental groups: approximately one-third of the sample consistently received negative affective primes (the frowning cartoon face), one-third received positive affective primes (the smiling cartoon face), and one-third received neutral primes (the expressionless cartoon face).

Participants then answered political knowledge and demographic questions, followed by a second administration of the attitude battery. Finally, they were debriefed and asked questions to verify that they were not consciously aware of the primes and could not guess the study purposes. None of the participants reported awareness of the affective primes and none reported any suspicion of our aims.

Two judges, who were blind to the experimental conditions and unaware of our research hypotheses, coded the listed thoughts for affective valence, providing measures of the number of positive and negative thoughts offered by each participant. For example, the thought "they can come here and make good money" was coded positive, while "we need stricter laws and regulations to keep illegal immigrants from entering our country" was coded negative. Intercoder reliability was very strong, and the few disagreements were resolved by discussion.

Study 1, designed to test affective contagion, manipulates exposure to positive, negative, or neutral incidental primes and measures general attitudes toward illegal immigration and energy security. These are the critical independent variables for testing affective contagion. To be predicted in this analysis are the numbers of positive and negative thoughts listed for each issue.

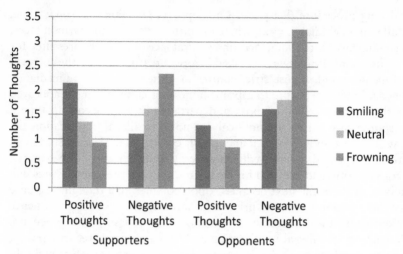

FIGURE 6.2. Affective Contagion of Incidental Affective Primes on Immigration Thoughts

Study 1 results for affective contagion. We predict that the incidental affective primes, presented preconsciously, will influence retrieval and construction of thoughts in response to the general prompts on illegal immigration and energy security, and this bias will be in the direction of prime valence. We also expect that the valence of thoughts will be strongly influenced by prior attitudes on the issue.

Do affective primes influence the valence of thoughts that come to mind for illegal immigration? Figure 6.2 shows the numbers of negative and positive thoughts elicited by the general statement on illegal immigration in Study 1, broken down by prior attitude and experimental condition. An analysis of variance (ANOVA) on the number of negative thoughts revealed main effects for prior attitude, $F(2, 182) = 2.92, p < .06$, and priming condition, $F(2, 182) = 8.97, p < .001$, with no significant interaction. Positive thoughts showed the same pattern: main effects for prior attitude, $F(2, 182) = 3.57, p < .05$, and priming condition, $F(2, 182) = 8.89, p < .001$, and no interaction. The expected linear pattern of means for both prime manipulation and prior attitudes is apparent in Figure 6.2, and follow up contrasts verified that positive primes elicited significantly more positive and fewer negative thoughts and negative primes drove more negative and fewer positive thoughts, with neutral primes between the positive and negative primes for both types of thoughts. In short, we found both the conventional influence of prior attitudes on the generation of thoughts as well as evidence of affective contagion from the incidental primes.

Our theory predicts that *both* prior attitudes and incidental affective primes influence the generation of thoughts and that is what we found, but how sizable are these effects? In both ANOVA models, the effect size of the prime

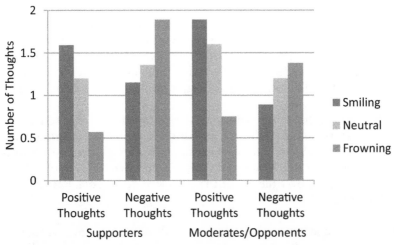

FIGURE 6.3. Affective Contagion of Incidental Affective Primes on Energy Security Thoughts

manipulation was medium-to-large (Cohen's $f = .31$), while the effect size for prior attitudes was small (.20 for positive thoughts and .18 for negative thoughts). It turns out that for illegal immigration, affective contagion from unnoticed, incidental primes had a *greater* impact on the generation of thoughts than did prior attitudes.

We find much the same thing for energy security, though with weaker and less consistent effects for prior attitudes (Figure 6.3). The affective priming manipulation strongly influenced the valence of thoughts recalled in response to the general energy security prompt, with again roughly twice as many congruent as incongruent thoughts. The ANOVA for negative thoughts found a significant main effect for prime condition, $F(2, 190) = 5.09, p < .01$, but interestingly not for prior attitude. For positive thoughts, we found main effects for both prior attitude, $F(1, 190) = 3.70, p < .06$, and prime condition, $F(2, 190) = 22.40, p < .001$. Again, there were no significant interactions in either analysis. As for immigration, planned follow up contrasts showed that these effects fall into the expected linear pattern of means. Moreover, the effect size (Cohen's f) of the affective prime manipulation for these ANOVA models was on average .36, a large effect, while the average effect size for prior attitudes was just .12. Once again, not only was there significant affective contagion from an incidental affective prime, it was of *greater magnitude* than the more conventional prior attitude effect.

In short, Study 1 strongly supports our affective contagion hypothesis for both issues. Regardless of one's prior attitude, in comparison with the control group, negative primes promote negative thoughts and inhibit positive thoughts, while positive primes trigger positive and inhibit negative thoughts.

Simple cartoon faces flashed outside the conscious awareness of experimental subjects significantly and consistently altered their thoughts and considerations on a political issue, with effects greater in size to those of prior attitudes on the issue. In support of the substantive power of affective congruence, participants in Study 1 listed on the order of *twice* as many thoughts that were congruent with the prime as those that were incongruent, regardless of their prior attitude on the issue.

Study 2 procedures. Study 2 was designed to replicate the affective contagion results while also testing the affective mediation hypothesis. Undergraduate participants completed Study 2 in our Laboratory for Experimental Research in Political Behavior, for which they received subject pool credit ($N = 125$; 60% male; 42% white; 50% over the age of 21; 52% Democrat, 20% Republican, and 28% Independent).

General procedures were similar to Study 1: after informed consent, participants were seated at personal computers in individual experimental rooms. Attitudes on a number of political issues, including the target issue of illegal immigration, were collected before and after an experimental procedure that collected primed thoughts on illegal immigration (Figure 6.4).

There were two key differences from Study 1, however: Study 2 exposed all participants to a fixed rather than variable number of primes, and Study 2 used six specific policy statements on illegal immigration rather than a single general issue statement to prompt thoughts. As in Study 1, each priming trial involved a sequence of a one-second attention grid, a 13-millisecond forward mask, a 39-millisecond affective prime, and a 13-millisecond backward mask, followed by the prompt and thought listing box.

All participants completed seven prime/thought listing trials for each of six different policy prompts on illegal immigration, though they could choose not to enter a new thought before proceeding to the next thought listing box. This procedure resulted in a fixed total of forty-two prime presentations and the collection of zero to forty-two thoughts on illegal immigration, with no second issue.

There were three antiillegal immigrant prompts:

- "All illegal immigrants should be deported,"
- "The Minutemen group should be supported by the government," and
- "Illegal immigrants should be stopped from entering the United States by building more fences";

and three proillegal immigrant prompts:

- "Illegal immigrants in the United States should be allowed citizenship if they learn English, have a job and pay taxes,"
- "Temporary visas should be granted to immigrants not in the United States so they can do seasonal/temporary work and return to home countries," and
- "Illegal immigrants already here should be allowed to stay permanently";

and these prompts were presented in random order.

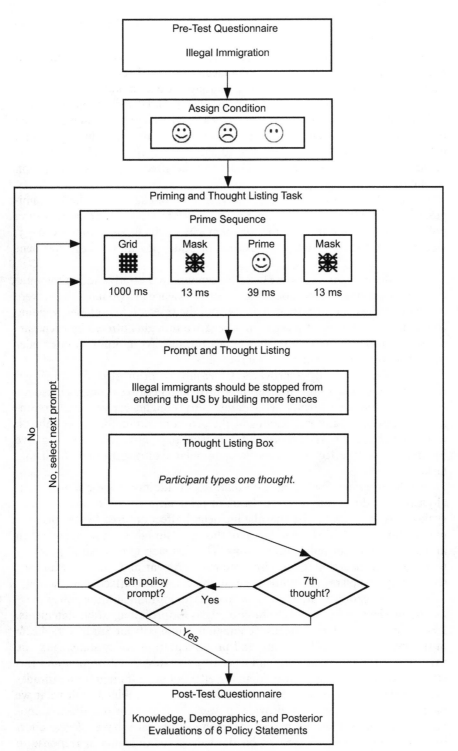

FIGURE 6.4. Experimental Design for Study 2

Participants were randomly assigned to three experimental groups: negative affective primes (frowning cartoon face), positive affective primes (smiling cartoon face), and neutral primes (expressionless cartoon face).

Participants then answered political knowledge and demographic questions, followed by collection of their evaluations of all six policy statements used to prompt thoughts. Finally, the pretest attitude battery, including general questions on illegal immigration, was administered again. As in Study 1, none of the participants reported any awareness of the affective primes or suspicion of our aims.

Because there was considerable ambivalence in our sample on the six immigration policy statements, we constructed separate anti- and proimmigration policy evaluation variables. Both three-item scales, which range from -3 to $+3$, were reliable, and these two policy evaluation scales provide our key dependent variables for the affective mediation analyses.

Again, the thoughts that were listed in response to the anti- and proimmigration policy statements were coded for affective valence by two judges who were unaware of the experimental conditions and the research hypotheses, yielding counts for the number of positive and negative thoughts offered by each participant in response to each type of policy prompt. As in Study 1, intercoder reliability was very strong across all thoughts.

To summarize, Study 2 provides a measure of prior attitudes on illegal immigration, counts of the number of positive and negative thoughts listed for each policy statement, which we separate into thoughts for pro- and antiimmigration policies, and evaluations of the pro- and antiimmigration policies, collected at the end of the experiment. Exposure to positive (coded 1), negative (0), or neutral (.5) affective primes was manipulated during the thoughts listing task.

Study 2 results for affective mediation. In addition to the conventionally expected direct and indirect effects of prior attitudes on posterior policy evaluations, we hypothesize that the incidental affect aroused by our priming manipulation will bias the generation of thoughts, and these thoughts will then influence subsequent policy evaluations. The first step in this causal pathway replicates affective contagion with a new experiment and sample, while the second step completes the indirect causal process we call affective mediation.

Figure 6.5 reports a path regression analysis for antiimmigration policy statements, and Figure 6.6 shows the same analysis for proimmigration statements. First, it is clear that the affective contagion findings from Study 1 replicate in this experiment. For both anti- and proimmigration policy statements, the valence of thoughts is strongly influenced by the subliminal primes, and this effect is two to three times larger than the effect of prior immigration attitudes on the valence of thoughts. This astonishing result, combined with what we have reported from Study 1, provides powerful support for the affective contagion hypothesis. Fleeting images of cartoon smiley faces have a *larger* effect than prior immigration attitudes on the valence of thoughts in response to

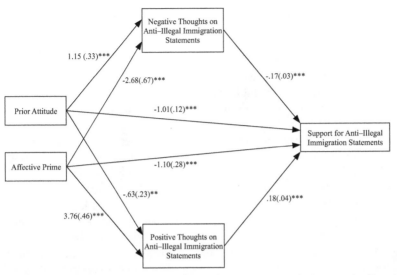

FIGURE 6.5. Effects of Prior Attitudes and Prime Manipulation on Antiimmigration Policy Evaluations

illegal immigration policy prompts. But does this immediate effect on thoughts influence downstream evaluations of these policies collected up to forty-five minutes later?

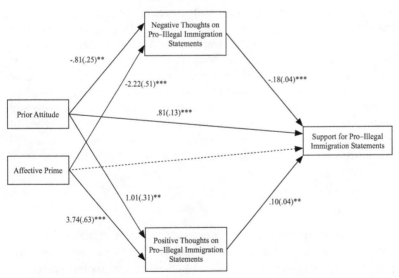

FIGURE 6.6. Effects of Prior Attitudes and Prime Manipulation on Proimmigration Policy Evaluations

The answer is clear and even more astonishing. Both analyses show strong support for the affective mediation hypothesis. Negative thoughts about a policy, whether they come from intrinsic political attitudes or incidental affective primes, reduce support for that policy, while positive thoughts increase support. For antiimmigration policies (Figure 6.5), the total indirect effect of the affective prime on support through the generation of positive and negative thoughts is 1.13, which is more than three times the indirect effect of prior attitudes.

Interestingly, though we did not hypothesize a direct effect of the primes on policy evaluations collected three quarters of an hour later, we do find such an effect for anti-illegal immigration policies. Subliminal exposure to smiley (frowny) faces significantly reduces (increases) subsequent support for building walls or deporting illegal immigrants. Given what is known in cognitive psychology about the fleeting duration of concept activation (Barsalou, 1992; Eysenck and Keane, 2010; Neely, 1977), this result must be interpreted as a mood effect. That is, participants in the positive prime condition enter into a positive frame of mind through their subliminal exposure to forty-two smiling faces, while those in the negative condition develop a negative mood, and this occurs in much the same way as the sunny day effect on reported life satisfaction. In this study it appears that the positive mood reduces subjects' support for "nasty" immigration policies, while those in a negative mood are more inclined to punish illegal immigrants. Interestingly, we find this mood effect *only* for participants below the median in political knowledge, with more sophisticated participants showing no significant direct effect of prime on evaluations of antiimmigration policies, and we do not find it at all for proimmigration policy evaluations, even among less-sophisticated respondents.

Figure 6.6 shows exactly the same overall pattern of results that we found for antiimmigration policies. Negative thoughts about a policy reduce support for that policy; positive thoughts about a policy increase support, and because these thoughts are driven by prior attitudes and even more strongly by incidental affective primes, we find significant and sizable indirect effects of prior and prime on posterior policy evaluations. And in this case the indirect effect of the primes was more than four times the size of the indirect effect of prior attitudes. Taken together, these analyses strongly support our affective mediation hypothesis.

General Discussion

The research reported in this chapter suggests a conclusion different from the conventional emphasis on the power of deliberation. Unnoticed affective cues, even when they are semantically unrelated and irrelevant to the objects of thought, influence what we remember and how we think about political issues and public policies. Two studies reported in this chapter strongly point to the same conclusion that incidental, out-of-awareness primes can alter the course of political thinking and reasoning. These affective primes, in our studies chosen to be politically irrelevant and semantically unrelated, cause valence-congruent considerations to be disproportionately retrieved or constructed in the course of thinking about a political issue on which our respondents had preexisting attitudes. The balance of thoughts in turn has a large and robust effect on evaluations of specific policy recommendations. It seems hard to escape the conclusion that much of the conscious political thinking and deliberation that we conventionally treat as causally prior to our attitudes and policy positions, in fact rationalizes the joint effect of these attitudes and any environmental affective primes on our thinking, all outside of our awareness.

A natural and reasonable objection to much of our research is that the processes we study often operate on a time scale that seems irrelevant to the forces and machinations believed to drive political behavior. Who cares what happens at 39 milliseconds? An important answer to this question comes out of the two experiments reported in this chapter: we must care what happens at 39 milliseconds because influences on cognition at this scale propagate through subsequent thought processes and drive evaluations that occur far down the stream of information processing.

These findings bring us a step closer to understanding such real world phenomena as place-of-voting and ballot order effects, candidate appearance and trait attributions, the impact of symbols or emotive music in campaign advertising, the shadow of race or gender on political action, and motivated bias in counterarguing uncomfortable arguments or evidence. All of these are explained in our theory as the result of unnoticed influences of early political or contextual cues on the stream of political information processing. Affective cues, whether incidental or deliberately embedded in political messages, produce strong contagion on the generation or retrieval of thoughts. The most effective political symbols, slogans, and events, however, will be those that trigger *both* feelings and concepts in mutually reinforcing ways, and our *JQP* theory provides an explanation for why this is so. A politician announcing her candidacy with the Statue of Liberty as backdrop gains the advantage of positive feelings through direct affect transfer and the indirect influence of affective contagion, and these inclinations are reinforced by the conceptual activation of concepts like "freedom," "liberty," "egalitarianism," and other semantic associates of Lady Liberty. Of course, we would anticipate that citizens from the opposing party would view the event as "transparently strategic" and experience the countervailing force of a negative prior attitude effect and motivated bias in the construction of considerations.

These findings support several heretofore untested hypotheses that emerge from our theory. Our theory claims – and our empirical studies show – that the feelings aroused in the initial stages of processing color *all* phases of political thinking. When a citizen is called on to express a judgment, the considerations that enter into consciousness will be influenced by the valence of initial affect, whether that affect is intrinsic (e.g., prior attitudes) or extrinsic (e.g., smiley faces) to the process. *Affective contagion* is the underlying process that drives motivated reasoning and rationalization in political thinking. The next chapter will consider the role of intrinsic affect in the form of prior political attitudes in driving motivated reasoning.

7

Motivated Political Reasoning

Citizens are rarely, we believe never, dispassionate when thinking about politics. Feelings as well as thoughts are triggered spontaneously by the people, groups, symbols, and ideas they see, hear, and ruminate about. Some of these feelings are incidental to the objects of thought, as when one's mood or some irrelevant environmental stimulus cues feelings that influence subsequent thoughts and behaviors. As demonstrated in Chapter 6, we may experience incidental feelings as relevant information about political objects, misattribute such feelings to political causes, and then rationalize these extrinsic feelings through the recollection of congruent considerations. Of course, our prior attitudes and beliefs about political objects also direct the course of information processing and serve as powerful anchors on subsequent thought. These intrinsic feelings and the affective contagion they arouse promote persistence of attitudes and motivated biases in the treatment of political arguments and evidence. "A fact is not a truth until you love it," wrote the English poet John Keats. Showing similar intuition, the Irishman William Butler Yeats put it this way: "We taste and feel and see the truth. We do not reason ourselves into it." Citizens are inclined to think what they feel, and defend these feelings through motivated reasoning processes, whether the feelings arise from political causes or unrelated cues. Chapter 6 explored the effects of incidental feelings on political information processing and attitude change; here we will focus on intrinsic affect about political objects and how these prior feelings can drive political information processing in the service of attitude perseverance and polarization.

Rather than treating information about political parties, candidates, or issues evenhandedly, as normative models of rational decision making prescribe, citizens are prone to accept those facts and arguments they agree with and discount or actively counterargue those that challenge their preconvictions, where agreement or disagreement is marked by the *feelings* that are automatically triggered in the earliest stages of thinking about the issues. In short, citizens are often *partisan* in their political information processing, motivated more by their desire to maintain prior beliefs and feelings than by their desire to make "accurate" or otherwise optimal decisions. In the marketplace of ideas, citizens are confronted daily with arguments designed to bolster their opinions or challenge their beliefs and attitudes (Gamson, 1992). Ideally, one's prior beliefs and attitudes should "anchor" the evaluation of new information and then, depending on how credible the evidence or strong the argument, impressions should be adjusted upward or downward (Anderson, 1981). The informal Bayesian updating rule would be to increment the overall evaluation if the evidence is positive, decrement if negative. Assuming a well-grounded initial belief (attitude or hypothesis), normative models of human decision making posit a two-step updating process, starting with the collection of belief-relevant evidence, followed by the integration of new information into the prior to produce an updated judgment. But normative models require that the collection, evaluation, and integration of new information be at least somewhat independent of one's prior impressions (see Evans and Over, 1996).

In this chapter we report the results of a series of experiments investigating whether, and if so to what extent, citizens overly value supportive evidence while finding reasons to dismiss out of hand evidence that challenges their prior attitudes. Our starting premise (following Kunda, 1987, 1990) is that *all reasoning is motivated*. From this perspective, citizens do experience motivation to be accurate, but they are typically unable to control their preconceptions, even when encouraged to be objective. This competitive tension between the drive for accuracy and belief perseverance underlies all human reasoning. From this perspective, citizens' motives can be seen as falling into two broad categories: *accuracy goals*, which motivate them to seek out and carefully consider relevant evidence so as to reach a correct or otherwise good-enough conclusion (Baumeister and Newman, 1994; Fiske and Taylor, 1991), and *partisan goals*, which motivate them to apply their reasoning powers in defense of a prior, specific conclusion (Kruglanski and Webster, 1996).

In *JQP*, partisan goals and subsequent selective information processing are driven by automatic affective processes that establish the direction and strength of biases (Lodge and Taber, 2005). Earlier chapters have shown that for most people most socio-political concepts are "hot," and associated attitudes come automatically to mind along with, if not prior to, the retrieval of explicit semantic information. One's likes or dislikes for Barack Obama, for example, are aroused even before conscious awareness of his identity and other semantic associations enter working memory — that he is a man, a Democrat, or a president (Morris, Squires, Taber, and Lodge, 2003). These "hot cognitions," within *JQP*, motivate partisan goals that will predictably bias subsequent conscious reasoning through selective exposure, attention, and judgment processes.

Selective information processes are particularly important because they impact the development, updating, and expression of attitudes and behaviors and because of their implications for the distribution of aggregate public opinion (Zaller, 1992). Selective attention and exposure drive *attitude persistence* and *attitude polarization*: those holding strong prior attitudes defend those attitudes against challenging information and may become attitudinally more extreme on reading pro and con arguments because they assimilate congruent evidence uncritically but vigorously counterargue incongruent evidence (Ditto and Lopez, 1992; Rucker and Petty, 2004). Oddly, the empirical evidence for this classic expectation is not well-established in the social-psychological literature (Sears and Freedman, 1967; Sears, Freedman, and O'Connor, 1964). The most cited support for attitude polarization comes from the 1979 Lord, Ross, and Lepper study of attitudes toward the death penalty, but even this study is not particularly convincing because it is based on a subjective rather than direct measure of polarization. Rather than addressing actual attitude change, as measured by a t_2 minus t_1 comparison, Lord and colleagues asked subjects to report subjectively whether their attitudes had become more or less extreme after evaluating pro and con arguments on capital punishment as a deterrent to crime. Numerous attempts to replicate polarization using direct t_1 and t_2 measures of social and political attitudes have failed (e.g., Kuhn and Lao, 1996; Miller, et al., 1993; Pomerantz, Chaiken, and Tordesillas, 1995).

Attitude polarization has been elusive in psychological research for at least two reasons. First, the arguments and evidence used in many psychological studies are rather tepid, and they may not arouse sufficient partisan motivation to trigger vigorous processing. Some research, for example, relies on syllogistic arguments that pose no obvious challenge to one's prior beliefs or attitudes (e.g., Oakhill and Johnson-Laird, 1985); other research used oversimplified policy statements composed of a single, stylized premise and conclusion (Edwards and Smith, 1996). In *JQP* selective biases and polarization are hypothesized to be triggered by an initial (and uncontrolled) affective response; by contrast, most of the work on selectivity and polarization in social psychology used bloodless, affect-free arguments and relied on theories of *cold* cognition. For this reason, our motivated reasoning experiments will use statements and arguments taken directly from political interest groups, which are far more contentious and emotive than those used in psychological research (Ailes and Kraushar, 1989; Ansolabehere and Iyengar, 1995). Such statements should generate stronger affective responses among engaged citizens.

A second issue for those testing for genuine t_1 to t_2 attitude polarization concerns the measurement of attitude change and the problem of scale constraints. Researchers have typically (e.g., Edwards and Smith, 1996) relied on a single item, presented pre- and posttask, to measure attitude position and change. The problem, of course, in addition to the weak reliability of a single item, is that our theory predicts that those with the most extreme attitudes to begin with will be most prone to polarize, but detecting any such change is thwarted by the upper and lower bounds of the scale and by regression to the mean. We will employ a multiitem additive scale to measure attitudes at t_1 and t_2, which improves measurement reliability and reduces the number of respondents at or near the far reaches of scale limits at t_1.

Experiments on the Mechanisms of Motivated Reasoning

We report three experimental tests of the following motivated reasoning hypotheses derived from our *JQP* theory.

Hypothesis 1: A *prior attitude effect*, whereby people who feel strongly about an issue, even when encouraged to be objective and leave their preferences aside, will evaluate supportive arguments as stronger and more compelling than opposing arguments;

Hypothesis 2: A *disconfirmation bias*, such that people will spend more time and cognitive resources thinking about and challenging attitudinally incongruent than congruent arguments; and

Hypothesis 3: A *confirmation bias*, such that when free to choose what evidence to look at and evaluate people will seek out confirming over disconfirming arguments.

Because each of these mechanisms deposits more supporting than repudiating evidence in mind, we predict:

Hypothesis 4: *Attitude polarization*, whereby t_2 attitudes will become more extreme than the t_1 attitude even when participants have been exposed to a balanced set of pro and con arguments.

A cautionary note: our theory, at first glance, might suggest we are arguing that people are entirely closed-minded, consciously deceiving themselves to preserve their prior beliefs. On the contrary, our key argument is that people are largely unaware of the power of their priors in their search for and evaluation of information. It is not that they openly lie to themselves. Rather, they want to get it straight. They try hard to be fair-minded or at least preserve the "illusion of objectivity" (Pyszczynski and Greenberg, 1987), but are unable to do so. On the other hand, as the persuasion literature clearly shows (Petty and Wegener, 1998) and as attested to in studies of voting behavior (Aldrich, Sullivan, and Borgida, 1989; Rabinowitz and MacDonald, 1989), even those committed to their positions can be persuaded by strong and credible counterevidence (Festinger, 1957). But the research we report suggests that, once attitudes have become crystallized, persuasion is difficult. Asymmetrical skepticism – being hypercritical of contrary evidence, as would be reflected in the type of thoughts that come to mind as we read pro and con arguments – deposits in mind all the self-generated evidence needed to justify and bolster our priors with a clear conscience (Ditto, Scepansky, Munro, Apanovitch, and Lockhart, 1998).

We expect that hypotheses 1–4 predicting motivated reasoning will be conditional on the strength of one's prior attitude (motive) and on one's level of political sophistication (opportunity) (Lavine, Borgida, and Sullivan, 2000;

Pomerantz, Chaiken, and Tordesillas, 1995), which lead to the following conditional hypotheses.

Hypothesis 5: An *attitude strength effect*, such that those citizens voicing the strongest policy attitudes will be most prone to motivated skepticism; and

Hypothesis 6: A *sophistication effect*, such that the politically knowledgeable, because they possess greater "ammunition" to counterargue incongruent facts, figures, and arguments, will be more susceptible to motivated bias than will unsophisticates.

Procedures and Participants, Studies 1 and 2. Experimental subjects were recruited from introductory political science courses at Stony Brook University. Their participation, for which they received course credit, consisted of a single session lasting less than one hour (Study 1: N = 126, 47% male, 56% white, 51% Democrat, 27% Republican; Study 2: N = 136, 50% male, 47% white, 45% Democrat, 15% Republican). Because the two experiments share the same basic design, differing in but one important manipulation, we will describe them together (Figure 7.1).

On entering the laboratory, participants were seated individually at computers in separate experimental rooms and instructed that they would take part in a study of public opinion. Their first task was to evaluate twenty contemporary political issues, among them a battery of items tapping their attitudes on either affirmative action *or* gun control (with the sample randomly split into two conditions). The attitude measures included four items designed to measure *attitude strength* (recorded on 100-point sliding response scales) and six items that measure *attitude position* or extremity (9 pt. agree/disagree Likert items). Additive scales were constructed for both variables and rescaled to [0,1] with a neutral midpoint at 0.5. Consistent with prior research (for an overview, see Petty and Krosnick, 1995), strength and position are independent attitudinal dimensions such that respondents may take extreme positions on an issue without feeling strongly about their stand, and some moderates ride the fence with conviction. Correlations between (folded) extremity and strength did not exceed .20, demonstrating their independence. Both scales were reliable, with alphas ranging from .72 to .93. Responses were skewed slightly toward support for affirmative action (median extremity score: .56) and strongly toward support for gun control (median extremity score: .67).

After completing the attitude battery, participants practiced using an information board designed to track their search for pro or con information about affirmative action (or gun control in the other condition). They were instructed to view the information in "an even-handed way" and that they would be called on at the end of the experiment to explain the issue to other students (these instructions reliably enhance accuracy motivation and mitigate partisan motivation, thereby creating a conservative test of motivated biases). The information board contained a matrix of sixteen hidden policy arguments with rows and columns randomized, which participants could only view by clicking

FIGURE 7.1. Experimental Design for Motivated Reasoning Studies

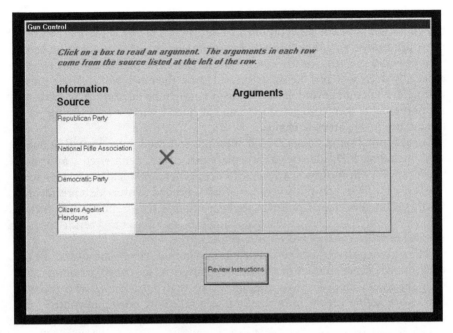

(a) Information Board

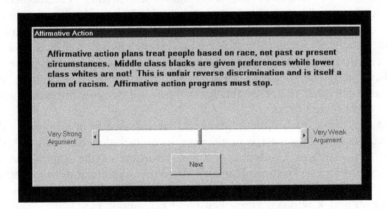

(b) Argument Strength Rating Box

FIGURE 7.2. The Primary Experimental Tasks

a button in the matrix (see Figure 7.2a). Rows of arguments were labeled with a known source, so that participants could easily infer which hidden arguments would favor and which would oppose the issue; moreover, participants were explicitly told each group's general position on the issue as part of their instructions and were subsequently tested to make sure they understood who would likely say what. Participants viewed eight arguments with no time limit, but could not view the same argument a second time. The computer recorded the order and viewing time for each argument selected. This information board task provides our test for the *confirmation bias* – the prediction that people, especially those who feel the strongest and know the most, will seek out confirmatory evidence and avoid what they suspect might be disconfirming evidence. All participants then completed the same attitude battery a second time so as to measure $t_1 \to t_2$ attitude change.

A substantial set of demographic questions followed the information board task, including PID, ideological self-placement, race, gender, etc., and most important for our purposes, a seventeen-item general political knowledge scale (asking, e.g., "What proportion of Congress is needed to override a presidential veto?"). Our measure of political sophistication is the proportion of correct responses, which for many subsequent analyses we subject to a tertile split (so we may contrast the top and bottom thirds of the sample).

The second part of the experiments, testing for a *disconfirmation bias*, began with a third administration of the attitude battery as described previously, but with the issues flipped across conditions, so that participants who received affirmative action for the information board task now rated gun control, and vice versa. Participants were then asked to rate the strength of eight arguments, four pro and four con (presented sequentially in random order; see Figure 7.2b for a sample strength rating box). Again, participants were instructed to be "even-handed," to "leave their feelings aside," and told that they would be asked to explain the controversy to other students (again to encourage accuracy goals). This argument strength rating task was followed by the posttest attitude battery and a recognition memory test. In addition, and this is the only significant difference between Studies 1 and 2, participants in Study 2 were asked to write down their thoughts for two pro and two con affirmative action or gun control arguments.

The arguments used in our experiments were drawn from print and online publications of real issue-relevant interest groups (including the NRA, NAACP, Brady Anti-Handgun Coalition, and the platforms of the Republican and Democratic Parties). To control for such alternative explanations for processing bias as the "argument length = strength" or "complexity = strength" heuristics (Cobb and Kuklinski, 1997; Petty and Cacioppo, 1981), the arguments were edited such that they had similar complexities (length of sentence, average number of syllables, words per sentence, sentences per argument, reading level, and so forth) and were pretested on student samples.

Results for prior attitude effect. Our first hypothesis points to the difficulty people have in putting aside their prior feelings when evaluating evidence and information, even when pro and con arguments have been presented to them in a balanced manner, and even when, as here, participants are instructed repeatedly to "set their feelings aside," to "rate the arguments fairly," and to be as "objective as possible."

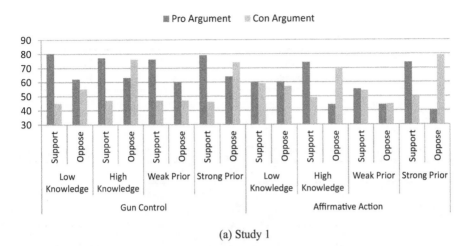

(a) Study 1

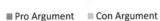

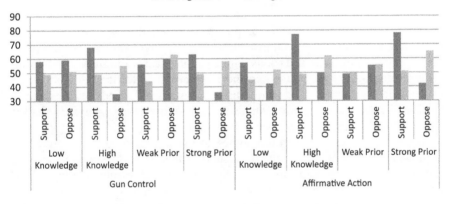

(b) Study 2

FIGURE 7.3. Argument Strength Ratings, by Sophistication and Strength of Prior

As an initial test of the prior attitude effect, we compare the average strength ratings for proattitudinal and counterattitudinal arguments, expecting participants to rate the congruent stronger than the incongruent arguments. Arguments were rated on a [0,100] scale, with larger values denoting stronger ratings.

Figure 7.3 displays the results in sets of four bars, broken down by study, issue, sophistication, and strength of prior attitudes. Dark bars represent average strength ratings for pro arguments on the issue, light bars con arguments. In all the data graphs the first pair of bars shows the responses of proponents of the issue and the second pair shows responses of opponents. The prior attitude bias is present wherever we see higher ratings for congruent than incongruent

TABLE 7.1. *Test of Prior Attitude Effect: Regressions of Argument Strength Ratings on Prior Attitudes*

	All Participants	Least Sophisticated	Most Sophisticated	Weak Priors	Strong Priors
			Study 1		
Affirmative Action	.415 (.102)***	−.234 (.212)	.667 (.135)***	.078 (.250)	.646 (.164)***
Gun Control	.471 (.093)***	.691 (.204)**	.632 (.143)***	.479 (.154)**	.537 (.161)**
			Study 2		
Affirmative Action	.381 (.075)***	.257 (.172)	.513 (.114)***	.047 (.117)	.494 (.104)***
Gun Control	.331 (.083)***	.103 (.143)	.477 (.151)**	.261 (.199)	.289 (.116)*

Cells report unstandardized coefficients and standard errors. *** $p < 0.001$; ** $p < 0.01$; * $p < 0.05$.

arguments. Across these and prior pretest samples, the eight arguments for each issue have statistically equivalent average strength ratings, yet the prior belief effect is systematic and robust among sophisticates and those with strong feelings, despite our best efforts to motivate even-handedness. In contrast to the most knowledgeable and attitudinally "crystallized" thirds of our sample, the least sophisticated respondents and those with weaker prior attitudes on these issues show little or no prior belief effect.

Table 7.1 reports regression analyses of the impact of prior attitudes on argument strength ratings, with contrasts for the least and most sophisticated thirds of our samples and those with the weakest and strongest priors. Each participant's overall rating of the strength of arguments (our dependent variable) was computed as the summed ratings of the pro arguments minus the summed ratings of the con arguments, recoded to [0,1]. To test for a prior attitude bias, we regressed these argument strength ratings on pre-test attitude extremity as measured by the six-item scale described previously, recoded to [0,1]. Significant, positive coefficients support the hypothesis: participants who favored gun control or affirmative action rated congruent arguments as stronger than incongruent arguments, while those opposed saw the con arguments as stronger. Table 7.1 shows a strong prior attitude effect in the predicted direction for sophisticates and for those with strong attitudes, while nonsophisticates and those with weak priors did not consistently show the effect.

Results for the disconfirmation bias. In addition to the prior belief effect, *JQP* predicts a disconfirmation bias: people too readily accept confirmatory arguments at face value but subject incongruent information to *active counterarguing*. That is, they recruit whatever considerations or evidence they

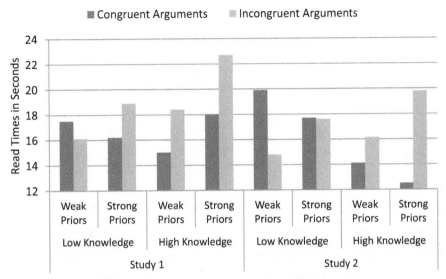

FIGURE 7.4. Processing Times for Argument Strength Ratings

hold in prior knowledge to discredit or undermine new information that is incongruent with their prior attitudes. This bias should also vary with sophistication and strength of prior attitude, especially since successful counterarguing may require the retrieval and application of considerable prior knowledge. Our experimental design allows several tests of these predictions. If indeed people actively challenge attitudinally incongruent arguments, we would expect them to take more time processing counterattitudinal arguments than proattitudinal arguments, and to spend the extra time denigrating, deprecating, and counterarguing the incongruent information.

As participants read and rated the eight arguments, the computer collected the time that elapsed from when they clicked open an argument box until they made their strength rating. This processing time variable provides an initial test of the disconfirmation bias. Because the pattern of results is the same for both affirmative action and gun control, we combine the issues in Figure 7.4, and break them down by study to underscore the robustness of the results across the two experiments. For simplicity, and because each study shows virtually the same pattern when taken separately, we report ANOVA analyses for both studies combined. Participants in both studies across both issues did take significantly longer to read and process attitudinally challenging arguments, $F(1,107) = 3.39$, $p = .068$. When averaged across all participants this difference was fairly small (on the order of 1–2 seconds), but the contrast is much more pronounced for sophisticates and those with stronger prior attitudes (4–7 seconds, a 25–50 percent increase). Indeed, though there were no significant main effects on processing time for sophistication and attitude strength, the

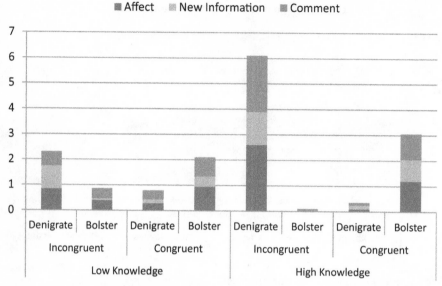

FIGURE 7.5. Mean Number of Thoughts for Congruent and Incongruent Arguments

interactions of sophistication and strength with argument congruence were highly significant: congruence by sophistication, $F(1,107) = 9.96$, $p = .002$; congruence by attitude strength, $F(1,107) = 4.41$, $p = .038$. Finally, we note that unsophisticated participants with weak prior attitudes actually spent more time processing congruent arguments, which implies a confirmatory bias for those participants who lack the issue-domain knowledge and motivation to disconfirm challenging arguments.

To explore the question of what considerations came to mind on their rating of the arguments, we had participants in Study 2 list their thoughts for four of the eight arguments they rated, two pro and two con. Our theoretical expectation is that whereas most participants quickly (and apparently effortlessly) assimilate supporting arguments, they become more actively engaged when processing contrary arguments, generating thoughts to denigrate or counter these arguments. This is a more direct test of the disconfirmation hypothesis than the rating time data since we now examine the actual content of the thoughts participants listed in response to two pro and two con arguments for each issue. We coded each thought into three basic response types: positive or negative *affect*, including general affect for the argument, for the evidence, or for the conclusion; *new information*, including a new fact not present in the argument or a new argument; and *comments* about the evidence or about the source. And of course each thought was coded as either denigrating or bolstering the presented argument.

Figure 7.5 depicts these data graphically for both issues combined, breaking down the mean number of thoughts by congruence and sophistication.

On average, participants listed two and a half comments per argument (for a total of ten thoughts across the four arguments), but there were considerable differences across participants. Not surprisingly, sophisticated participants produced more thoughts overall than did their less knowledgeable peers. More interesting, as predicted, incongruent arguments elicited far more thoughts than did congruent ones and these thoughts were almost entirely denigrating. Both sophisticated and unsophisticated participants showed this basic pattern of bolstering congruent arguments while denigrating incongruent ones, though sophisticates were clearly more biased. Finally, although we had asked participants to leave their feelings aside and to concentrate on what made the arguments weak or strong, we see clear evidence of primacy of affect in that a goodly number of participants made simple, content free affective statements (the darkest portion of each bar), to the effect "I like (don't like) this argument or conclusion," or simply acknowledged that they liked or disliked the facts or figures supporting an argument. A more cognitively demanding type of response would be the introduction of a new fact or an original argument (light gray bar) or a comment on the source or quality of the evidence (medium gray). In both instances the new evidence brought to mind was overwhelmingly supportive of their prior attitudes. Overall, this pattern nicely conforms to our expectations of active disconfirmation in the evaluation of arguments.

A mixed-model ANOVA on the number of thoughts generated, with sophistication as a between-subjects variable and argument type (congruent or not) and response type (bolster or denigrate) as within subjects variables, strongly confirms the pattern reported above, with significant main effects for sophistication, $F(1,89) = 6.37$, $p = .013$, and argument congruency, $F(1,88) = 4.57$, $p = .045$. Moreover, there was a highly significant two-way interaction between argument congruency and type of response, $F(1,88) = 10.05$, $p = .002$, and a significant three-way interaction between congruency, response type, and sophistication, $F(1,88) = 4.07$, $p = .047$, such that sophisticates even more than unsophisticates had the knowledge and motivation to denigrate incongruent arguments and bolster congruent ones.

Results for the confirmation bias. Both experiments also tested the hypothesis that, when given control over what information to view, people will generally try to limit their exposure to challenging and seek out congenial information. This selective exposure hypothesis has a long history in psychology, mostly coming from the cognitive dissonance tradition, though there has been controversy about the empirical validity of selective exposure (Eagly and Chaiken, 1993, 1998; Freedman and Sears, 1965; Frey, 1986). Both in the "real world," where conservatives tune in to Rush Limbaugh and liberals prefer "The Daily Show," and in laboratory experiments using an information board (Figure 7.2a), citizens can oftentimes choose to look or not look at information from the opposing side. In our theory, the motivation for selective exposure comes from spontaneously generated affect toward political objects, and we believe that the past failure to clearly confirm this classic expectation of the cognitive

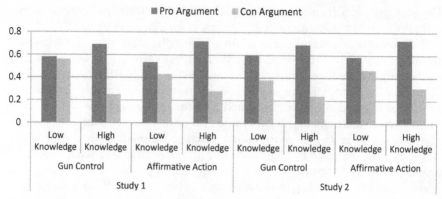

FIGURE 7.6. Proportion of Proattitudinal Hits in Free Search

dissonance tradition is at least partly due to the affectively tepid issues and arguments that had been used to test it, which provide insufficient motivation to engage in selective exposure (Edwards and Smith, 1996). We expect to find evidence of the confirmation bias with the more contentious and challenging political issues and arguments culled from real-world politics. Part 1 of both experiments presented participants with a computerized information board, a four-by-four matrix of policy arguments where each row was labeled with a well-known opinion source on either affirmative action (the Republican Party, Democratic Party, NAACP, and Committee to End Preferences) or gun control (the Republican Party, Democratic Party, National Rifle Association, and Citizens against Handguns). As before, instructions were designed to maximize the motivation to be accurate and minimize partisan bias. The proportion of proattitudinal selections out of the eight arguments each participant looked at provides our measure of confirmation bias. Figure 7.6 displays these data by study, issue, and sophistication. For all groups examined, proponents of the issue sought out more supporting than opposing arguments, and this difference was quite substantial for sophisticates in both studies and for both issues. Given the chance, sophisticated respondents selected arguments from like-minded groups 70–75 percent of the time. For example, on average, sophisticated opponents of stricter gun control sought out six arguments of the NRA or the Republican Party and only two arguments from the opposition.

To directly test the confirmation hypothesis, we regressed this measure of biased search on t_1 attitude extremity for both studies and both issues, with results reported in Table 7.2. Clearly, participants were more likely to read the arguments of a sympathetic source than to expose themselves to an opposing point of view. Supporters of gun control or affirmative action were significantly more likely to search out the arguments of "their" issue groups (e.g., Citizens Against Handguns or the NAACP). As expected, these results are particularly

TABLE 7.2. *Test of Confirmation Bias: Regressions of Proportion of Proattitudinal Hits on Prior Attitudes*

	All Participants	Least Sophisticated	Most Sophisticated	Weak Priors	Strong Priors
			Study 1		
Affirmative Action	.326 (.107)*	.338 (.284)	.778 (.116)***	.055 (.247)	.402 (.161)
Gun Control	.360 (.099)**	.170 (.171)	.594 (.099)**	.041 (.218)	.693 (.106)***
			Study 2		
Affirmative Action	.328 (.074)**	.226 (.080)	.721 (.146)***	.242 (.143)	.389 (.137)
Gun Control	.560 (.072)***	.406 (.164)	.711 (.089)***	.541 (.113)**	.499 (.148)*

Cells report unstandardized coefficients and standard errors. *** $p < 0.001$; ** $p < 0.01$; * $p < 0.05$.

pronounced for sophisticates, where, for example, every 10 percent increase in support for affirmative action in study 1 led to a 7.78 percent increase in the proportion of proaffirmative action hits on the information board. We did not obtain consistent results for the strength of prior attitudes hypothesis.

Because we also recorded the processing times for participants in the information board task, we were able to replicate our disconfirmation bias for participants who opted to open and read a counterattitudinal argument. On average, across both experiments, we found that participants spent about two seconds longer reading an argument from the opposition, and sophisticates spent more than five seconds longer when considering such challenging arguments. This implies that they were actively processing this information, and likely finding reasons to denigrate and discredit it.

Results for attitude polarization. The prior attitude effect, the disconfirmation bias, and the confirmation bias should all theoretically lead down a path of attitude polarization, because they consistently deposit more supportive evidence and affect in long term memory. *JQP* predicts that those on either side of a political issue should become more attitudinally extreme over time, even when exposed to the same balanced stream of information. A regression of t_2 attitude extremity on t_1 extremity provides a simple test of this polarization hypothesis. In this regression, coefficients significantly greater than 1 indicate attitude polarization, because they show that posterior scores are more extreme than prior scores. Table 7.3 contrasts these regression results for groups of participants defined by sophistication and strength of prior attitude, as well as the top and bottom thirds of the sample in degree of processing bias. A tertile split on the variables that measure confirmation and disconfirmation biases – the proportion of proattitudinal hits in the information board task and the average

TABLE 7.3. *Test of Attitude Polarization, Studies 1 and 2 Combined: Regressions of Posterior on Prior Attitudes*

	Least Sophisticated	Most Sophisticated	Weak Priors	Strong Priors	Least Biased	Most Biased
Argument Strength Task (Disconfirmation Bias)						
Affirmative Action	1.195 (.090)**	1.268 (.079)***	1.024 (.079)	1.297 (.091)***	1.072 (.114)	1.237 (.082)***
Gun Control	.755 (.158)	1.149 (.086)*	.907 (.098)	1.214 (.132)*	.805 (.146)	1.164 (.086)*
Information Board Task (Confirmation Bias)						
Affirmative Action	.933 (.094)	1.330 (.068)***	1.097 (.097)	1.177 (.068)**	1.031 (.189)	1.191 (.073)**
Gun Control	1.044 (.153)	1.223 (.121)*	1.142 (.140)	1.177 (.115)	.626 (.492)	1.277 (.094)***

Cells report unstandardized coefficients and standard errors. Significance of coefficients is computed relative to a slope of 1.0. *** $p < 0.01$; ** $p < 0.05$; * $p < 0.10$.

pro minus average con ratings in the argument strength task, respectively – allows us to contrast the top and bottom thirds in degree of bias.

Pooling the data from both studies (for statistical power), we find strong evidence of attitude polarization for sophisticated participants, for those with strong priors, and, most importantly, for those who were the most biased in their argument ratings and information search. We find polarization across both tasks and both issues (indeed, only one of twelve expected cells in Table 7.3 fails to achieve significance – strong priors for gun control in the information board task). For example, the regression coefficient for the most sophisticated third of the sample who rated affirmative action arguments shows a 27 percent polarization of attitudes (slope of 1.27). Those who were most biased in rating gun control arguments, as measured by the difference between their strength ratings of pro and con arguments, show a highly significant 28 percent polarization (slope of 1.28). Unsophisticates and those with weak priors did not generally polarize, though the low knowledge participants who rated affirmative action arguments present an exception.

These findings directly and clearly link the *processes* of motivated skepticism to attitude polarization as theory predicts, something that to our knowledge has not been demonstrated before. Those participants whose argument strength ratings were most skewed by disconfirmation biases had significantly more extreme attitudes on affirmative action and gun control *after* rating the arguments, while those whose ratings were more evenhanded showed no significant attitude polarization. Similarly, confirmation biases – seeking out attitudinally consistent arguments while avoiding inconsistent arguments in the information board – led to more extreme attitudes as compared to the least biased participants for both issues.

In sum, despite repeated instructions designed to encourage the evenhanded treatment of policy arguments, we find consistent evidence of motivated bias – the prior attitude effect, disconfirmation bias, and confirmation bias – with a substantial attitude polarization as the result. We believe our participants undoubtedly tried to be evenhanded, but they found it impossible to be fair-minded.

Procedures and participants, Study 3. The 164 participants for Study 3 were drawn from the same student population as our earlier studies (49% male, 42% white, 47% Democrat, 20% Republican), and the experiment was conducted in our Laboratory for Experimental Research in Political Behavior.

Given the evidence we have reported for confirmation, disconfirmation, and selective exposure biases, each of which contributes to attitude polarization, we thought it prudent to carry out a set of conceptual replications (Taber, Cann, and Kucsova, 2009) to test the generalizabilty of motivated skepticism. This was especially important given that the information board highlighted the source of messages – political parties and advocacy groups – each known to influence attitude change and persuasion (Petty and Cacioppo, 1981). The first change was to eliminate source cues by focusing solely on disconfirmation

TABLE 7.4. *Example Arguments for Study 3*

Short Argument	Long Argument	Two-Sided Argument
Smoking marijuana is a stepping stone to harder drugs, including cocaine and heroin.	Smoking marijuana is a stepping stone to harder drugs, including cocaine and heroin. Most serious addicts began by smoking pot. Experience shows that serious drug addiction usually starts with marijuana.	Smoking marijuana is a stepping stone to harder drugs, including cocaine and heroin. Some argue that legalizing marijuana would at least help move drug abusers from hard drugs to marijuana. But experience shows that serious drug addiction usually starts with marijuana.
Freedom of speech is a cherished democratic value that is meant to protect everyone, not just those we like or agree with.	Freedom of speech is a cherished democratic value that is meant to protect everyone, not just those we like or agree with. Tolerance of others' views is required in a democracy. Allowing individual students to silence those they dislike by refusing to pay the mandatory student activity fee goes against the very values this country stands for.	Freedom of speech is a cherished democratic value that is meant to protect everyone, not just those we like or agree with. Some might argue that the refusal to finance the freedom of speech of others is itself an expression of free speech. Nevertheless, allowing individual students to silence those they dislike by refusing to pay the mandatory student activity fee goes against the very values this country stands for.

biases in the argument strength rating task. In addition, we asked participants to evaluate the strength of pro and con arguments to a much broader range of local and national issues: legalization of marijuana, animal testing by drug companies, gays in the military, the Electoral College, U.S. foreign aid, university funding of unpopular groups on campus, punishing cheaters in college, and a tuition hike. A third change had participants make their argument strength ratings to three types of argument formats: short one-sided arguments (like those in many attitude scales), long, relatively complex one-sided arguments (of the type often found in attitude surveys), and long, relatively complex arguments with a counterargument (similar to those in framing and counterfactual studies). Table 7.4 illustrates two examples of each argument type. At issue here is whether the prior attitude effect, disconfirmation bias, and polarization hold across a wider range of argument types and formats found in survey research and in more general political discourse.

Other aspects of the experimental design were the same as in the initial study: strong encouragement to be objective in argument strength ratings, t_1 and t_2 measures of prior attitudes on the issues, measures of sophistication and argument strength, a stop-and-think thought listing task for some arguments to test for a disconfirmation bias, and a t_2-t_1 measure of attitude change to test for polarization.

Results for Prior Attitude Effect. As in our initial studies, the expectation is that participants will judge counterattitudinal arguments to be weaker than pro-attitudinal ones. Average strength ratings for the arguments, broken down by argument type (short, long, and two-sided), for both supporters and opponents, participants' level of sophistication, and their strength of prior attitude on the issue, confirm a strong, consistent prior attitude effect: arguments that were congruent with prior attitudes were rated stronger than incongruent arguments, and this bias appears across all but one subgroup (weak supporters' ratings of long arguments show no bias).

Results for Disconfirmation Bias. We again have two tests of the disconfirmation hypothesis, which posits that participants will actively counterargue challenges to their priors, especially when they have strong prior attitudes and when they are politically knowledgeable. First, we recorded the time it took participants to rate each argument, where longer times indicate deeper processing and indirectly suggest counterarguing when in response to challenging arguments. Second, we asked participants to list their thoughts immediately following half of the argument rating trials so that we can analyze the content of these thoughts for direct evidence of counterarguing.

We find effortful disconfirmation processes, as indicated by longer processing times for arguments that are incongruent with the respondent's prior position, especially among the most knowledgeable participants and those with strong priors, who took 30 percent longer to process incongruent arguments across all argument types. As expected, these comparisons were consistently insignificant for unsophisticates and those with weak priors.

Longer rating times indicate deeper processing, but what exactly are participants doing with this extra time? We subjected the thoughts listed by participants to the same coding scheme used for Study 2, dividing all thoughts into three basic categories: *affective statements* (e.g., "I just don't like this argument"), *new information* (e.g., "this argument doesn't take into account the aggressiveness of some campus groups"), and *comments* about the source or evidence (e.g., "everyone knows that the *NY Times* is a liberal newspaper"). Each statement was also coded as denigrating or bolstering the argument. The expectation is that most thoughts about attitude-congruent arguments will be bolstering, while incongruent arguments will trigger denigrating comments, especially for sophisticates and those with strong prior attitudes.

Our results confirm this expectation: sophisticates more than unsophisticates and those with strong more than weak priors denigrated challenging arguments and bolstered supportive ones. Specific to the disconfirmation hypothesis, the interaction of argument congruence and response type was highly significant. Respondents in Study 3, like those in Studies 1 and 2, sought to disconfirm challenging arguments. Again confirming the initial study, despite our best efforts to motivate accurate and even-handed treatment of the evidence, across all argument types participants displayed a pronounced tendency to bolster attitude-consistent arguments while actively (and passionately) rejecting those that challenged their prior positions on the issues.

Polarization Results. Again in a third experimental study, we found polarization of attitudes as a result of biased information processing triggered by prior attitudes, with polarization stronger for sophisticates and those with strong prior attitudes across experimental conditions. First, those participants whose argument ratings were most affected by their prior attitudes, as measured by the average ratings for attitude-congruent arguments minus the average ratings for attitude-incongruent arguments, had significantly more extreme attitudes *after* rating the balanced set of arguments, while those who showed the least bias had more moderate post-test attitudes for all three argument types. Second, those who showed a strong disconfirmation bias, computed as the number of attitude-consistent thoughts (bolstering thoughts for pro arguments and denigrating thoughts for con arguments) generated in the thoughts listing task divided by the total number of thoughts, were also strongly polarized, while those in the bottom third of disconfirmation bias moderated.

Results for Argument Type. In addition to replicating the findings of Studies 1 and 2, we sought to test two expectations about how type of argument might influence processing bias. First, we predicted that longer, more complex one-sided arguments would generate more motivated bias than shorter, simpler arguments because the richer content should activate multiple connections. Studies 1 and 2, which used complex and evocative arguments like the long arguments in this study, uncovered stronger biases and polarization than did the simpler declarative statements typically used by social psychologists. Second, we predicted that two-sided arguments, which embed a weak counterargument, would generate less motivated bias than one-sided arguments of equal complexity. This expectation was based on suggestive evidence from social psychology that such arguments, which are found frequently in real-world discourse, may have greater credibility and therefore more pull than one-sided arguments.

We found, however, across a broad range of policies and argument types, no evidence that motivated biases are contingent on argument length, complexity, an explicitly available contrary argument, or participants knowing the partisan source of arguments.

General Discussion

Motivated, passionate, and knowledgeable citizens are the bedrock of democracy. And yet the very passions that motivate civic action drive biases and polarization. *JQP* predicts that feelings aroused outside awareness in the earliest stages of information processing systematically direct the course of subsequent thought and action. These intrinsic feelings and the affective contagion they arouse promote persistence of attitudes and motivated biases in the treatment of political arguments and evidence.

A primary goal of these three studies was to see if motivated biases stood up when people are confronted with spirited arguments confirming or challenging their positions on "hot" issues, which participants acknowledged were important and about which many held strong attitudes. The evidence is reliable, strong, and in line with *JQP*'s predictions in showing that people find it very difficult to escape the pull of their prior attitudes and beliefs, which guide the processing of new information in predictable and sometimes insidious ways. Contrary to hopeful anticipation, but not to *JQP*'s expectations, we found the prior attitude congruence effect to be similar to what we found when people make snap judgments about political leaders (Chapter 3), simple candidate issue statements (Chapter 4), groups (Chapter 5), policy recommendations (Chapter 6), and here when confronted with challenging arguments to established attitudes.

8

A Computational Model of the Citizen as Motivated Reasoner

Chapter 2 developed our *JQP* theory, grounded in social, cognitive, and neuropsychology, of how citizens develop and change their political beliefs and attitudes. It is a theory of the citizen as motivated reasoner, driven to rationalize the political thoughts and behaviors that are often caused by events and forces outside conscious awareness, some coming from within, as when prior attitudes motivate biases, and some coming from without, as when environmental cues trigger affective transfer or contagion. Chapters 3 through 7 presented empirical tests of our most basic assumptions as well as tests of several key implications of the theory. We now turn to a different kind of test, one that is common in cognitive science but less so in political science. In this chapter, we seek to establish the "completeness" of our theory as a functional description of human information processing, its internal coherence, its sensitivity to variations in basic assumptions, and its ability to perform as real citizens do in the fundamental task of democratic citizenship: the processing of information to create and update candidate preferences over the course of a political campaign. To accomplish this, we develop a formal computational model of our theory, test its internal processing mechanisms, and then test its empirical performance against that of a simpler Bayesian updating model in predicting the changing attitudes of real citizens in an actual political campaign (for full details, see Kim, Taber, and Lodge, 2010).

We should alert the reader at the outset that our purpose, and therefore our approach, differs from the norms of formal theory in political science. Instead of adopting the mathematical approach of classical physics, which has infiltrated the social sciences by way of economics, we embrace the formal methods and norms of cognitive science. That is, rather than pursuing a parsimonious model that can account for a particular phenomenon in isolation, we seek to build a model that can account for our current concern, preference updating, *while also accommodating what is known from social and cognitive psychology about other memory and information processes.* This is what is meant by theoretical "completeness": cognitive models must have sufficient scope to cover the phenomena of current interest while also covering already known phenomena about human cognition. Otherwise we elevate parsimony over validity in the desiderata of science and our formal models risk becoming isolated toys (Taber and Timpone, 1996).

A Model of Political Information Processing

As detailed in Chapter 2, our theory integrates cognitive and affective structures and mechanisms into a single framework: (1) an associative network representation of knowledge and attitudes in long-term memory (LTM), (2) activation and decay mechanisms for concepts in LTM, which determine what information is accessible for retrieval into conscious working memory (WM), (3) processes for the construction of attitudes from accessible information in memory, and (4) processes for the updating and expression of cognitive associations and attitudes. Here we develop each of these sets of mechanisms, both axiomatically and procedurally.

A theory of memory processes. The foundation for *JQP*'s memory processes is the classic cognitive architecture most closely associated with John R. Anderson (Anderson, 1983; Anderson et al. 2004), and we develop our model within the ACT-R modeling framework, which is used in cognitive science to model a wide range of learned behaviors, among them language comprehension, the recognition and recall of information, inferencing, the formation of beliefs, and the learning of complex skills (*The Adaptive Character of Thought – Rational*; Anderson, Bothell, Byrne, Douglass, Lebiere, and Qin 2004; open source modeling tools available at http://act-r.psy.cmu.edu/). However, while ACT-R provides comprehensive, integrated mechanisms for fundamental memory processes and learning, it lacks the affective mechanisms that are central to our theory. Consequently, much of our work developing *JQP* was devoted to building affect and updating mechanisms and integrating them with the cognitive processes in ACT-R.

Our theory can be expressed in seven axioms.

Axiom 1, Modularity: The human cognitive system consists of several separate, interdependent modules such as a central processing system, goal system, and memory systems.

Axiom 2, Adaptivity and Efficiency: The human cognitive mechanism is adaptive to the structures and challenges of the external environment and has evolved to be an efficient, though not necessarily parsimonious, information-processing machine.

Axiom 3, Parallel and Serial Processing: Cognitive mechanisms use a mixture of parallel and serial processes. Parallel processes operate rapidly and efficiently because they can operate simultaneously, while serial processes are slower and less efficient because only one process may occur at a time (as is characteristic of conscious attention and deliberation).

Axiom 4, Semantic Structure of Memory: Human long-term memory is structured associatively in semantic networks.

The ACT-R modeling framework, within which we have designed *JQP*, includes procedures to functionally represent these four axioms (see Anderson et al. 2004), though the memory structures and processes (Axiom 4) require further elaboration because of differences between our approach and the classic cognitive architecture built into ACT-R. In particular, *JQP* brings valence affect center stage; one's likes and dislikes for "objects" in memory (e.g., leaders, groups, and issues) play a central role in our theory.

Axiom 5, Hot Cognition: Concepts in memory are affectively charged (positive, negative, ambivalent, or neutral). Through repeated coactivation of sociopolitical concepts and affect, these concepts become positively and/or negatively charged. This affective evaluation is linked directly to the conceptual representation in long-term memory (Abelson, 1963; Lodge and Taber, 2005; Figure 2.1).

For example, citizens form impressions of candidates, parties, and issues spontaneously as part of the online processing of information, and these evaluations are stored as links in LTM, where they may be subsequently cued on exposure to new information (Lodge and Taber, 2000, 2005).

Figure 8.1 illustrates our theoretical framework for memory (Axioms 4 and 5), using part of the knowledge structure about George W. Bush of a typical, liberal survey respondent before the onset of the 2000 presidential campaign. (We use the example of former President Bush because our empirical data in this chapter come from the 2000 presidential election.) Each node or concept in memory is represented by an oval, the border thickness of which varies to indicate differences in accessibility. For the conflicted liberal shown in Figure 8.1, the traits "caring," "honest," "bumbler," and "hypocritical" are all quite accessible, while the issues "patients' rights" and "gays in the military" are less accessible. Associations between pairs of nodes are represented by connecting lines of varying thickness, which indicate their strength of association. So "conservative" and "Republican" are more closely associated with Bush in this respondent's belief system than are Bush's character traits. Plus and minus signs linked to the nodes represent positive and negative feelings about the memory objects. A summary evaluation of an object may be obtained by combining the positive and negative valences (as when a survey respondent is asked for a thermometer rating of a candidate), but the theory can also represent ambivalence in cases where a node (e.g., "small government") carries both positive and negative affect. Finally, every aspect of the initial knowledge structure — the particular object nodes and associations, the strengths of these nodes and associations, and the valences and strengths of evaluative tags attached to the

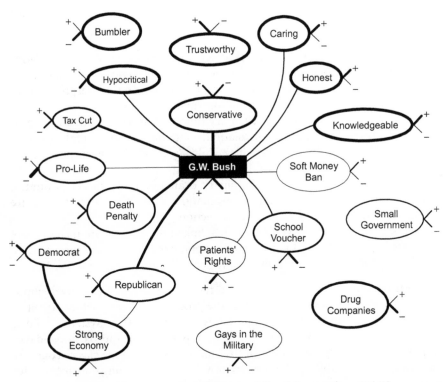

FIGURE 8.1. Memory Representation of Average Liberal Respondent, NAES 2000

nodes – change as citizens and agents respond to information throughout the campaign.

Objects in long-term memory (LTM) vary in how easily and quickly they may be retrieved to influence current processing. In our theory, this memory accessibility is a function of (1) how frequently and recently they have been retrieved in the past (practice and order effects), (2) how much momentary activation they receive from current processing (as when reading the word "Bush" activates the "Bush" concept node), (3) the amount of activation spread to the node from associated concepts that are currently being processed (as when reading "Bush" activates an associated concept, "Conservative"), (4) the degree of affective congruency between the memory node and currently processed information (as when thinking about "terrorism" activates other negative concepts), and (5) the decay of activation levels through time and disuse (forgetting effects). All five of these processes occur automatically, outside of awareness, and are not under conscious control.

Four of these influences on memory accessibility, excepting affective congruency, are built into the ACT-R modeling framework and are part of the classic associative network model of memory. But the addition of affective systems requires we propose several new axioms and develop additional model procedures. First, the axioms:

Axiom 6, Primacy of Affect: Valence affect enters the processing stream prior to the retrieval of semantic considerations, cognitive associations, and emotional appraisals, thereupon influencing the retrieval and interpretation of these and other forms of subsequent information.

Axiom 7, Affective Congruency: Memory objects that are affectively congruent with currently processed information, including environmental and internal stimuli, become more accessible, while affectively incongruent concepts in memory become less accessible.

Axiom 8, Attitude Construction: Summary evaluations of objects (attitudes) are constructed by integrating the evaluations of memory objects that are accessible at the time of attitude construction.

Axiom 9, Online Processing: Evaluations linked to objects in memory are updated continually and automatically upon exposure to new information, reflecting the influence of momentarily accessible information in WM.

In earlier chapters, we have reviewed research and presented novel empirical evidence that valence affect enters the processing stream before cognitive considerations. Neurological studies show that the "affect system" follows "quick and dirty" pathways that rapidly prepare us for approach-avoidance responses. The incorporation of affective mechanisms into the classic cognitive architecture will enable *JQP* to represent motivated reasoning and account for both persistence and responsiveness in political information processing, which provides a critical formal validation for our underlying theory.

Computational procedures to represent our theory. Our modeling task, made somewhat less daunting by the use of the ACT-R programming environment, entails specifying algorithms to (1) calculate the momentary accessibilities of memory objects; (2) compute longer term baseline levels of activation of memory objects, including the effects of rehearsal and decay; (3) construct attitudes toward the objects of thought; and (4) update affect in memory.

JQP's activation mechanism, which determines the accessibilities of all concepts in LTM at any moment in time, operationalizes the classical mechanisms of human recall (axiom 4), modified by affective congruency (axiom 6). The momentary accessibility of a given concept node is formally a function of residual past activation, spreading activation from associated concepts, affective congruency, and external stimulation.

More precisely,

$$A_i = B_i + \sum_{j=1}^{n} W_j \left[(S_{ji} - \ln(F_j)) + \gamma C_{ji} \right] + \sigma M_i + N\left(0, \frac{\pi s}{\sqrt{3}}\right) \qquad (1)$$

where A_i is the activation level of node i, B_i is the base level activation of node i (given in Equation 2), W_j is the attention weight for node j (for $j = 1$

TABLE 8.1. *Variables and Parameters*

Variables		Values
A_i	Activation of node i	Given in Equation 1
B_i	Residual activation of node i	Given in Equation 2
CA_i	Constructed evaluation of node i	Given in Equation 3
OL_i	Affective tag attached to node i	Given in Equation 4
W_i	Attention weight for node i	$1/n$, where n is number of objects in WM
S_{ji}	Strength of association from j to i	f(Number of times j has sent activation to i)
F_i	"Fan" dilution of activation from i	Number of nodes linked to i
C_{ji}	Indicator of affective congruency	1 if OL_i and OL_j same valence -1 if OL_i and OL_j different valence 0 if either OL_i or OL_j are neutral (0)
M_i	Indicator of external match to i	1 if external information matches i 0 if no match to i
T_{ij}	Processing time for activation decay	Time since i was processed jth time

Parameters		Values
γ	Affective congruence	2, estimated on NAES data
σ	External stimuli	5, after sensitivity analyses
s	Random noise in activation	0.1, from cognitive research
d	Memory decay	0.5, from cognitive research
δ	Online vs. memory-based processing	0.56, estimated on NAES data
ρ	Recency vs. primacy in updating	0.94, estimated on NAES data

to n, where n is the number of nodes currently being processed), S_{ji} is the strength of association between nodes j and i, F_j is the number of nodes linked to node j, γ is a parameter governing the weight given to affective congruence, C_{ji} is a trichotomous indicator of affective congruency between nodes j and i, σ is a parameter governing the weight given to external activation, M_i is a binary variable indicating whether node i matches external information being processed, and $N(0, \pi s/\sqrt{3})$ is normally distributed noise with a mean of 0 and standard deviation determined by the parameter s (see Table 8.1 for notation).

Equation 1 can be understood in terms of its three primary subcomponents: B_i captures the residual effects of past processing and memory decay; the term following the summation sign represents the cumulative effects of other memory nodes, broken into spreading activation from semantic associations and affective congruency; and σM_i is the algorithm to activate concepts that semantically match external information (e.g., reading "Bush" activates the "Bush" node). The effects of both spreading activation and affective congruency are limited by the amount of processing attention (W_j) that may be given to node j, which is a diminishing function of the number of concepts currently being processed. The fan effect (F_j) represents another cognitive limitation, which restricts the amount of activation that can be spread to any one concept from densely linked nodes. By establishing the momentary accessibilities of all memory objects, Equation 1 essentially forms the basis of the distinction between LTM and WM, with only the most accessible objects entering WM.

Baseline activation is calculated as follows:

$$B_{it} = \ln \left(\sum_{j=1}^{m} T_{ij}^{-d} \right) \tag{2}$$

where B_{it} is the baseline activation of node i at time t, m is the number of times node i has been processed in the past, T_{ij} is the elapsed time since node i was processed the jth time, and d is a parameter representing the rate of memory decay over time. As desired, B_{it} increases with the frequency and recency of processing of node i and decays over time and disuse.

Given the primacy of affect (Axiom 6), it is clear that the construction of an attitude toward an object of thought will be influenced by the evaluative tag attached to the object. The constructed evaluation will be further influenced by the considerations about the object that come to mind as part of the activation process (Axiom 8). In *JQP*, this attitude construction process is implemented as a weighted average of accessible evaluative tags.

$$CA_i = (1 - \delta)OL_i + \delta \left[\sum_{j=1}^{n} a_j OL_j \right], \quad \text{for } j \neq i \tag{3a}$$

$$a_j = \frac{(A_j / A_i)}{\sum_j (A_j / A_i)}, \quad \text{for } j \neq i \text{ and } A_j > 0 \tag{3b}$$

where CA_i is the constructed attitude toward object i, δ is a parameter that controls the influence of other currently accessible considerations (the js) relative to the evaluative tag already stored for object i (OL_i), OL_j is the existing evaluative tag for node j, A_i and A_j are the accessibilities of nodes i and j, a_j is the normalized accessibility of j relative to i, and n is the number of other accessible considerations at the moment of attitude construction.

The objects that are associated in LTM with node i or held in WM at the time of construction form the set of n considerations that enter this attitude construction process. Each consideration is weighted by its relative accessibility (a_i), however, so effectively this set only includes objects with positive current activation $(A_j > 0)$. As a result, the considerations that enter the attitude construction process change as a function of external events and current information processes. If no considerations are retrieved from memory at the time of attitude construction (i.e., $n = 0$), because either none are accessible at the moment or the attitude object has no associations in memory, then $CA_i = OL_i$. Importantly, the parameter δ controls the degree to which *JQP* represents online and/or memory-based models of information processing: $\delta = 0$ yields a purely OL model; $\delta = 1$ yields a purely MB model; $0 < \delta < 1$ yields hybrid models. This fact highlights one of the advantages of computational analyses on our theoretical model: it is possible to (1) determine the behavior of the model under variations in δ, and (2) estimate model fit to empirical data under variations in δ. Both of these procedures help to illuminate the roles of memory-based and online processing in attitude updating.

Previous experimental research shows that attitudes and cognitive associations are routinely updated online, at the time that relevant information is encountered, with the affective implications stored back to memory as OL tallies (Hastie and Pennington, 1989; Lodge, Steenbergen, and Brau 1995). Equation 4 offers an updating rule for OL affect in the form of an anchoring and adjustment process. In our model, attitudes constructed by Equations 3 are automatically integrated back into the affective tag associated with the object of thought.

$$OL_{ir} = \sum_{k=1}^{r} \rho^k CA_{jk}, \quad \text{for } j \neq i \tag{4}$$

where OL_{ir} is the evaluative tag for node i that exists after processing the rth piece of information, ρ is a parameter that governs the weight of new relative to old information, and CA_{jk} is the attitude toward object j (as constructed by Equations 3), which is the new piece of information associated with node i at processing stage k. Note that $\rho < 1$ implies the evaluative tag for node i becomes more persistent as more information about the object is processed.

When new information is presented as English text input, *JQP* performs a cascade of computations through these equations. To be precise, new external information causes *JQP* to compute levels of momentary activation (Equation 1) and baseline activation (Equation 2) for all nodes in LTM. Following this initial round of memory processing, the object nodes that have the highest momentary activation levels enter working memory (WM). In the simulations that follow, WM is set at five objects, though this could be varied as a way of manipulating cognitive limitations. Memory retrieval is followed by an evaluation of the information in WM (Equation 3). Finally, the affective tags associated with these objects in WM are updated (Equation 4). Processing stops and WM is cleared when there is no new external information. Note that momentary and baseline activation levels of memory objects and the associated affects that resulted from all of this processing *remain* in LTM, so the model's representations of beliefs and attitudes is responsive to environmental information over time.

The set of cognitive/affective mechanisms that we have described for *JQP* is consistent with the distinction between automatic and deliberative processes. That is, these processes initialize and operate spontaneously. For example, when *JQP* "reads and responds" to the sentence "Bush supports school-vouchers," the underlying memory processes – the spreading of activation to associated nodes, the affective congruence effects, the computation of an attitude, and the updating of affect – occur automatically. The model becomes "consciously" aware of only the most accessible concepts and their associated attitudes when they are retrieved into working memory. The computational agents represented in *JQP*, just like human agents, become "aware" *only* of the outputs of the process, not of the process itself.

Motivated reasoning is captured in *JQP* under the following conditions. First, there must be prior attitudes in LTM as represented by affective tags, and these attitudes must be minimally coherent to trigger defensive processing. For example, if the feelings associated with Bush and with the objects that are closely linked to Bush in LTM are very inconsistent, with positive and negative associations of approximately equal strength, constructed attitudes toward Bush will be very influenced by environmentally induced affect (mood?) but will *not* be consistently biased in either direction by prior affects. This resonates with empirical findings that strong, relatively univalent prior attitudes are the driving force behind motivated reasoning. Second, affective congruency, as captured when the parameter $\gamma > 0$, is central to motivated processing. With no affective contagion effect on activation levels in Equation 1 (i.e., $\gamma = 0$), there will be no affective biases in memory retrieval that might drive attitude perseverance. Third, motivated reasoning relies on both online and memory-based processing. Attitude construction that mixes OL and MB processing promotes motivated reasoning because it is responsive both to the prior itself and to the biased set of retrieved considerations that can strengthen or even polarize that attitude. Procedurally, this means that $0 < \delta < 1$ in Equations 3. Fourth, the updating of attitudes, as captured in Equation 4, must weight old information more strongly than new information (i.e., $0 < \rho < 1$). Attitude updating that favors priors promotes persistence, while updating that favors novel information promotes moderation and eventually persuasion. These parameter ranges are not only reasonable, they are to be expected based on empirical research that we have reviewed or reported in earlier chapters.

If *JQP* agents initialized with attitudes and parameter values that promote motivated reasoning closely simulate the behavior of real citizens, even outperforming alternative specifications, this will be additional evidence for the fundamental hypotheses of our theory and for the overall coherence and completeness of our *JQP* theory.

Parameters. Model parameters are used in several different ways by computational modelers: (1) parameters relevant to a hypothesis under examination may be manipulated experimentally; (2) where suitable data exist, parameters may be estimated based on model fit with empirical data; or (3) sensitivity analyses may be conducted to find parameter ranges within which a model behaves as expected. For the simulations reported here, we used all three strategies.

There are six free parameters in *JQP* (see Table 8.1). Two parameters are a standard part of any model constructed using ACT-R, and these were simply set to values that have previously been estimated on empirical data in the cognitive science literature (Anderson et al. 2004): s, which governs the amount of random noise in Equation 1, was set to 0.1; and d, which regulates the rate of memory decay in Equation 2, was set to 0.5. Three parameters are unique to *JQP*, and these needed to be estimated on novel empirical data, in this case the NAES 2000 data on candidate evaluations: γ, which governs the influence of affective congruence in Equation 1, was found to optimize model fit at a value of 2.00; δ, which controls the degree of online versus memory-based processing in Equation 3, provided best model fit at 0.56; and ρ, which controls the relative weight of early versus recent information in Equation 4, optimized fit at 0.94. The final parameter, σ, which governs the direct influence of external stimuli on activation in Equation 1, was set to a value of 5 after detailed sensitivity analyses.

Model behavior in *JQP* is *not* very sensitive to reasonable variation around these parameter values, so in some sense the precision of the selected values is misleading. The findings we report are not sensitive to knife-edge variation in these parameters, and the pattern of results remains the same for all parameter ranges capable of producing reasonable memory processes and affective contagion. Of course, the degree of model fit degrades as parameter values depart from these values. Finally, we should note that the optimized values for γ, δ, and ρ will produce motivated reasoning for agents that possess reasonably univalent and strong prior attitudes toward the current object of thought (candidate or issue, for example). This constitutes a first empirical finding from the simulation analyses: *best model fit is achieved for parameters that instantiate motivated reasoning processes.*

Two illustrations. Campaign information or survey questions can be presented to *JQP* as simple declarative or interrogative English sentences, respectively, and the model parses them into words or phrases that may match concepts in memory. Note that this is not a complete linguistic parser (such models do exist), so *JQP* must be fed input that can be directly matched to concepts in LTM. For the current illustrations, *JQP* is initialized as a liberal agent with the beliefs and feelings shown in Figure 8.1.

What happens when *JQP* is asked, in much the same way a citizen might be asked by a pollster, "How do you feel about George W. Bush?"

- First, the phrase "How do you feel about" is recognized as a request for an evaluation of the object, in this case "George W. Bush."
- On reading "George W. Bush," the node for Bush receives activation as computed by Equation 1. Because the Bush node matches the input "Bush,"

M_{Bush} resets from o to 1, causing A_{Bush} to increase. The node Bush enters WM along with its directly associated affect.

- With Bush held in WM, other concepts associated with Bush (e.g., conservative, Republican, death penalty) now become more accessible because of the spread of activation from Bush (computed by a round of Equation 1 for all nodes), with the increase dependent on the strength of association and degree of affective congruence between Bush and these nodes. So in addition to the cognitively associated concepts listed above, such affectively consonant nodes as hypocritical and bumbler also become more accessible, while evaluatively incongruent nodes – honest, pro-abortion, strong economy – become less accessible. Note that the influence of affective congruence is independent of semantic association. Some of these concepts, especially those that are both strongly associated and affectively congruent (e.g., conservative) will receive enough activation to enter WM.
- Using Equations 3, *JQP* now constructs an attitude toward Bush that integrates the evaluative tags attached to Bush and other currently accessible information. Given the just-discussed spread of activation from Bush and affective contagion, such concepts as conservative, Republican, and hypocritical would significantly influence the attitude that is constructed, while others such as knowledgeable, caring, and strong-economy have less influence. *JQP* would report a highly negative attitude in response to the question.

Note that we treated this example as a single isolated question. Survey questions, however, are generally embedded in an instrument with multiple items and influences (e.g., previous questions or interviewer effects), and the recent history of processing would normally affect how a given question is answered by *JQP*. The overall flow of processing through a full survey would change the associations and attitudes stored in *JQP*'s long-term memory. In addition, the act of processing a survey question like the one in this example would influence the largely negative feelings tagged to the Bush node because the newly constructed attitude will be integrated back into the online tally through Equation 4.

Now consider an example that illustrates rudimentary motivated reasoning in *JQP*. Again starting with the attitudes and beliefs represented in Figure 8.1, consider what would happen if *JQP* were presented with the campaign statement, "Bush is honest."

- Reading "Bush" increases the activation level of the Bush node and deposits it in WM as described previously. Associated concepts and affectively congruent concepts again receive activation from Bush, and some of these concepts enter WM. This first step is essentially the same as in our survey question example.
- After recognition and processing of the word "Bush," *JQP* recognizes that the word "is" signifies that what follows will be about Bush.

- When *JQP* reads "honest," the node honest will receive activation and be deposited in WM along with Bush and his close associates. Upon retrieval, the concept honest will influence the accessibilities of other objects in LTM in the same way that Bush did, and some of these associates may enter WM. Note, however, that "honest" will trigger associations through Equation 1 after Bush has already been activated, so the negative feelings associated with Bush will influence the retrieval of considerations in response to "honest."
- *JQP* will now construct an evaluation of honest, *but in the context of Bush*. That is, if *JQP* were asked "How do you feel about honest?" in a vacuum, the response would likely be univalently positive. But an evaluation of honest computed by Equations 3 in the context of an activated Bush (and the mostly negative concepts associated with Bush in our example) will be very different indeed. The evaluation constructed in this context is the *subjective* implication of the campaign information "Bush is honest." For the liberal *JQP* in Figure 8.1, this evaluative implication would certainly be less positive and perhaps even somewhat negative.
- Finally, the online tag attached to Bush is updated using Equation 4 and the evaluation constructed in the previous step for honest in the context of Bush.

When the liberal *JQP* of our example reads the evaluatively inconsistent statement "Bush is honest," negative considerations such as "Bush is a conservative" and "Bush is a Republican" conspire with the preexisting negative attitude toward Bush to weaken or reverse the positive implication of the information. An evaluatively consistent statement like "Bush supports school vouchers" would feed into the already negative attitude toward Bush. Given strong enough negative priors for Bush and a dense network of consistently negative associations to Bush, a liberal *JQP* would likely *polarize* in the direction of her negative priors in response to any mildly positive statement. A conservative *JQP* would exhibit the opposite pattern of motivated bias.

Note, finally, that enough consistently cross-cutting information about an object will eventually overturn priors, in which case *JQP* will be persuaded. How much is "enough" depends on the strength and univalence of priors for the object and the density of affectively consistent associations to the object.

Simulating the Dynamics of Candidate Evaluation in the 2000 U. S. Presidential Election

Earlier chapters have provided "granular" empirical tests, mostly experimental, of key postulates and assumptions of our theory of citizen information processing. This chapter has a quite different purpose in focusing on the internal coherence and completeness of the theory taken as a whole as measured by the ability of our computational representation of *JQP* to "behave" like a real citizen in producing evaluations of political objects. The 2000 National Annenberg

Election Survey provides the data for this "global" test of *JQP*. Using a rolling cross-sectional design, the 2000 NAES conducted daily telephone interviews from November 8, 1999 to January 19, 2001 with an average daily sample of 50–300 adults and a full random sample of over 100,000 citizens (Romer, Kenski, Waldman, Adasiewicz, and Jamieson, 2003). Figure 8.2 shows the changing "feeling thermometer" evaluations of Republican George W. Bush (Panel a) and Democrat Al Gore (Panel b) across four periods of the campaign, broken down by ideological self-placement. These trajectories of changing attitudes are the "dependent variables" we seek to simulate using a set of artificial citizens.

Evaluations of political candidates, groups, or ideas over the course of a political campaign are determined in *JQP* by the set of affective/cognitive *information-processing mechanisms* that we described in the last section, which are constant for all agents; initial *knowledge structures*, which may vary by individual agent; and exposure to *campaign information* over time, which may also vary individually due to selective attention and exposure. Because two of these dimensions vary across individuals, we need to create multiple *JQP* agents in the simulation.

Initial knowledge structures. Beliefs and attitudes are represented in our theory in terms of a set of concepts and associations among concepts, with evaluative tags linked to each, and all of these objects and associations vary in strength (Figure 8.1). We rely on the early cross-sectional data in the 2000 NAES as a source for the initial beliefs and attitudes of our *JQP* agents. These data were collected during the primary season between December 1999 and July 2000, before the GOP convention, which effectively kicked off the general election campaign. We created 100 *JQP* agents that replicated the distributional properties of the empirical NAES sample.

For each of the five self-identified ideological groups – very liberal, liberal, moderate, conservative, and very conservative – we obtained the means and standard deviations for attitudes toward the two candidates, two parties, and major political issues, as well as perceptions of the candidates' traits and issue positions. Because these data do not include ratings of the positivity or negativity of the traits attributed to candidates (how positive is "sincere"?), we turned to another well-known data set, which provides ratings of hundreds of traits normed to large samples of U.S. respondents. The distribution of evaluative tags for traits in our simulation is taken from the Affective Norms for English Words (ANEW; Bradley and Lang, 1999).

To create the 100 agents in our simulated sample, we followed a stochastic process. First, each agent was randomly selected into one of the ideological groups according to the frequencies found in the NAES sample, yielding on average seven strong conservatives, twenty-nine conservatives, forty-one moderates, nineteen liberals, and four strong liberals. Next, each agent's beliefs and attitudes were randomly generated for every political and trait concept found in the NAES 2000 survey. A concept node was created for every candidate,

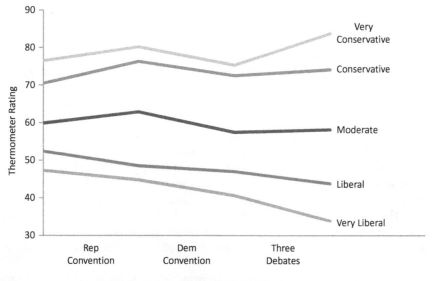

(a) Evaluations of George W. Bush

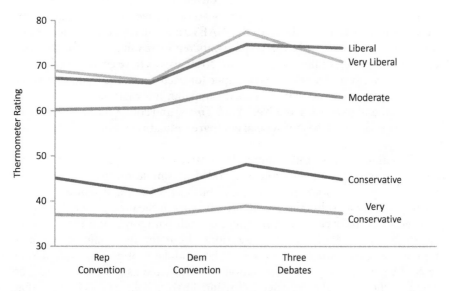

(b) Evaluations of Al Gore

FIGURE 8.2. Candidate Evaluations from the 2000 NAES

party, issue, and trait. Links among nodes were created for every question about an association (e.g., Does Bush support tax cuts?), and the strength of this association was assigned as a random variable based on the means and standard deviations for responses to the NAES question for the given ideological group. Affective tags were assigned to each concept node based on the means and standard deviations of feeling thermometers reported for the candidates, groups, and issues by the given ideological group (e.g., Do you support tax cuts?), with trait evaluations taken from the ANEW data. Initial baseline accessibilities of the political memory objects were set using the response rates for each survey item as a proxy for the frequency and recency of use. In short, initial accessibilities, associations, and evaluative tags were generated stochastically following the distributional properties (mean and standard deviation) from the survey data for the given ideological group. Though agents fall within the "normal" range of beliefs and attitudes for their ideological group, they vary in their specific beliefs (links and accessibilities) and attitudes (evaluative affects), so that each draw of 100 agents forms a unique sample.

Campaign information. Campaign information was obtained from *Newsday*, *New York Times*, and *Wall Street Journal* accounts of the Republican Convention (7/31–8/3), the Democratic Convention (8/14–8/17), and the three debates (10/3, 10/11, 10/17). These news accounts, we assume, roughly represent the information available to the NAES 2000 survey respondents. Since only about 10 percent of NAES respondents report reading "a great deal of" newspaper coverage of the campaign, our strategy was to select the single most extensive news story from the given paper for each event and code that story for the simulation. Note that we coded campaign information as reported in reputedly liberal (*Newsday* and *New York Times*) and conservative (*Wall Street Journal*) news sources, so that we can compare simulations using different news flows.

JQP is able to parse only simple declarative or interrogative English sentences, so campaign information was coded as simple campaign statements attributable to some known actor (e.g., "Bush says Gore is dishonest"). Recognizing that many subtleties are smoothed away in the process, we developed a procedure to recover the gist meaning of each paragraph of a news article. We scanned each paragraph for assertions about the two major candidates that may be clearly attributed to one of the candidates or groups evaluated in the NAES survey, and that information was extracted as gist statements. For example, when *Newsday* reported following the third debate (10/18/2000) that "Gore pointed to Bush and said, 'If you want someone who will spend a lot of words describing a whole convoluted process and then end up supporting legislation that is supported by the big drug companies, this is your man,'" the statement was coded "Gore said Bush supports Drug Companies." All qualifications were ignored, all modifiers excised, reducing the complex text to its gist meaning.

While understating the complexity of campaign information that was available in the 2000 campaign, this coding procedure has several benefits for our purposes. First, given the reportedly meager media consumption of the modal NAES respondent, this approach likely captures their processing better than a rich, detailed, semantic content analysis. Second, this procedure minimizes the subjective interpretation process, which is the part of human content coding most fraught with error. Finally, there is empirical evidence that citizens do indeed process the gist meaning of campaign statements and ignore even not-so-subtle qualifications (Hamill and Lodge, 1986; Lodge, Steenbergen, and Brau, 1995; Taber and Steenbergen, 1995).

The agent-based simulation. The empirical dynamics to be explained in this chapter are the changes in feeling thermometer ratings of the two major presidential candidates in 2000 for each of the five ideological groups over the course of the campaign, and in particular across four time points: before the campaign began, after the Republican Convention, after the Democratic Convention, and after the three candidate debates. We will compare the trajectories of candidate evaluations for our simulated agents to the trajectories for NAES respondents shown in Figure 8.2. Simulated agents are initialized as described previously, and then they are asked to evaluate George Bush and Al Gore. They are then presented with the stream of campaign statements coded from coverage of the Republican Convention, and asked again to evaluate the candidates. Coverage of the Democratic Convention follows, after which they again evaluate the candidates. And finally, the agents process coverage of the three debates and give their last evaluations of the candidates.

Because of the stochastic procedures used to initialize our agents as well as the random error introduced in the model equations, we repeat the simulation 100 times. One may think of the 100 simulations as representing the sampling distribution and each simulation as representing an individual sample. The computational demands of this procedure were truly daunting, and so we ran the simulation on the Teragrid Supercomputer System (http://www.teragrid.org), which distributes its 2.5 petaflop computational capacity across eleven partner sites in the United States.

In addition to the candidate evaluations of Gore and Bush taken at four time points in the simulated campaign, on which we will focus, we also stored the complete trace of all internal dynamics in *JQP* (such as momentary changes in internal attitudes on reading each new piece of information), and these detailed processing dynamics can be further explored.

Simulation results. We will focus on the degree of fit between the changing candidate evaluations of the simulated agents and those of the NAES respondents, using the *New York Times* and *Newsday* coverage of campaign events (we will later compare simulations based on *Wall Street Journal* coverage). Figure 8.3 shows the simulated and real trajectories, with *JQP* evaluations averaged across the 100 simulated samples (i.e., across 10,000 agents). We will first examine the simulated and empirical trajectories in qualitative terms,

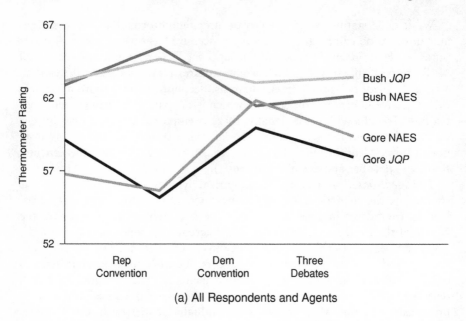

(a) All Respondents and Agents

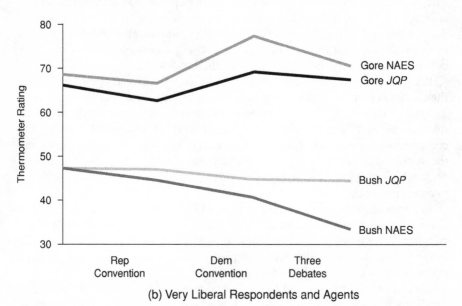

(b) Very Liberal Respondents and Agents

FIGURE 8.3. Real and Simulated Candidate Evaluations, 2000 Presidential Election

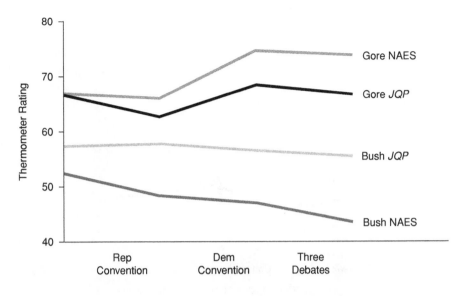

(c) Liberal Respondents and Agents

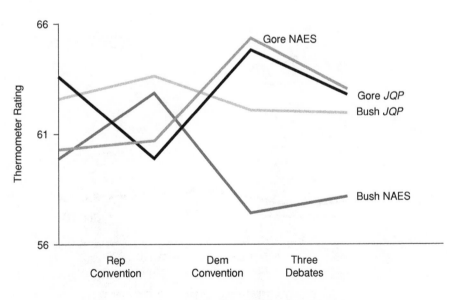

(d) Moderate Respondents and Agents

FIGURE 8.3. (*continued*)

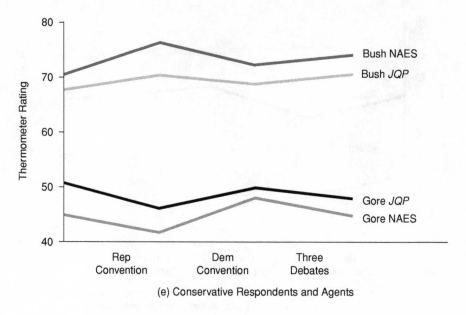

(e) Conservative Respondents and Agents

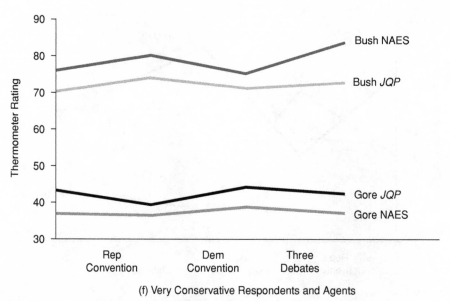

(f) Very Conservative Respondents and Agents

FIGURE 8.3. (*continued*)

comparing starting positions, direction and magnitude of changes, polarization of evaluations, and ending positions.

Across all ideological subsamples, *JQP* got the relative initial ordering of Bush and Gore right. This is essentially a "static" test of our initialization procedures before any campaign information has been given to the agents, but it is not a trivial exercise since it might fail if the activation and attitude construction procedures misrepresent the actual psychological mechanisms at work in NAES respondents or the raw initialization data (evaluations of, associations among, and accessibilities of the key political objects and trait concepts). Recall that *JQP* does not simply retrieve its evaluation of Bush when asked "How do you feel about George Bush?" As detailed in our example of *JQP* answering a survey question, the reported attitude is constructed from an integration of accessible feelings triggered by this question.

Moreover, with the exception of the forty-one moderate agents, who on average liked both candidates better than the survey respondents did at the start of the campaign, simulated evaluations were very close to actual evaluations after initialization. Looking at these data in Figure 8.3, it is clear that the stochastic initialization procedures produced a simulated sample that replicates the NAES sample reasonably well before the start of the campaign.

The critical test for *JQP* is how well the comparison of candidate evaluations holds up as the *JQP* agents and NAES respondents process campaign information. Because the degree of model fit over the course of the simulation depends on (1) the quality of initialization, which we have just examined on a qualitative level, (2) the selection of appropriate campaign information sources, and (3) the reliability and accuracy of the coding procedure for campaign information, in addition to (4) the "behavioral" validity of the model itself, this is a stringent test. And yet the qualitative behavior of the *JQP* agents holds up quite well, especially for the nonmoderates in the sample.

At the most general level, when comparing the direction of movement for all agents with all NAES respondents, there is a strong qualitative fit. For all six points of comparison (three time points by two candidates) the average *JQP* agent moved in the same direction as the average NAES participant. Now turning to the ideological groups in the sample and leaving aside the moderates for the moment, we see that for twenty-three out of twenty-four points of comparison, the *JQP* agents moved in the same direction as the NAES respondents upon exposure to coverage of the relevant campaign event. The sole exception was a very slight positive reaction (almost flat) of liberal *JQP* agents to the Republican Convention, while real liberal survey respondents reacted negatively. This is a quite remarkable result given the difficulty of this global test of our model.

And even the trajectories for moderates generally support the model, showing changes in the right direction for four out of six comparisons. One of the two "misses" is clearly a failure of initialization, as moderate *JQP* agents evaluated Gore too highly at initialization, but then corrected following the GOP

Convention. The other movement in the "wrong" direction, for evaluations of Bush after the three debates, actually brought *JQP* agents closer to their NAES counterparts and seems a correction for the insufficient adjustment of Bush evaluations after the Democratic Convention. In any case, we should recognize that the moderates in the NAES sample are a mixed bag, including uninformed and disinterested as well as involved but ambivalent citizens, and as such they may simply be less predictable for a model like *JQP* in which much of the "action" builds from early affective reactions. We should also note that the scale for the Y-axis for moderate agents is considerably more compressed than the other panels of Figure 8.3, so that the differences we see are actually not greater in magnitude than what is found for other groups.

In addition to being in the same direction, most changes in the simulated trajectories are of comparable magnitude to changes in the real world. For the ten comparison paths – Bush and Gore over the five ideological groups – five remain within two thermometer points of their initial spread, one converges, and four diverge by more than two points from the initial spread. All four divergent paths occur because *JQP* is less responsive than survey respondents were to campaign information (or the campaign information we coded was less arousing than the information real citizens get).

In all cases where NAES participants' candidate evaluations polarized over the course of the campaign, moving to a more extreme position in the direction of their initial inclination, so did the *JQP* agents, although often to a lesser degree. The groups that polarized included very liberal respondents and agents for both candidates, liberal respondents and agents for Gore, conservative respondents and agents for both candidates, and very conservative respondents and agents for Bush. Liberals and liberal agents moderated for Bush, and very conservative participants and agents moderated for Gore.

Finally, all simulated ideological groups finished the campaign as they started, with the candidates ordered correctly. To summarize, all simulation groups properly ordered the candidates after initialization, responded in the same direction as real citizens and with comparable magnitude to information about key campaign events, polarized or moderated exactly as did NAES respondents, and approached Election Day with the candidates properly ordered.

Table 8.2 reports several correlational measures of overall model fit to the NAES data, averaged across the 100 simulations using the *New York Times* and *Newsday* coverage of the campaign events. The top section of the table reports correlations between real and simulated candidate evaluations over the course of the campaign, broken down by ideological group. These correlations show a very robust fit between the simulated and real evaluations, supporting our qualitative conclusion that the simulation tracks real trajectories of evaluations quite closely. Very conservative respondents and agents, however, show substantially lower correlations, and we note at this point that there likely is a mismatch between the news coverage processed by the very conservative agents

TABLE 8.2. *Average Correlations between NAES and Simulated Evaluations*

Correlations Across Time		
Ideological Group	Bush	Gore
Very Liberal	0.89	0.87
Liberal	0.90	0.89
Moderate	0.90	0.76
Conservative	0.96	0.93
Very Conservative	0.50	0.55
All Voters	0.91	0.89
Correlations Across Ideological Groups		
Time	Bush	Gore
Initial	0.88	0.92
GOP Convention	0.92	0.91
Dem. Convention	0.92	0.92
Debates	0.92	0.91
Average	0.91	0.92

in these simulations, based on reputedly liberal media, and the media coverage very conservative citizens actually consume, a point we will address more fully when we discuss the *Wall Street Journal* simulations. The lower section of Table 8.2 reports correlations between simulated and actual evaluations across the ideological groups, broken down by time period. This analysis, which measures how tightly the simulation fits the empirical distribution of candidate evaluations across the ideological spectrum at each point in the campaign, also shows a very strong model fit.

We can also report that the distribution of results across the 100 simulations clustered quite tightly, with only a few outlier simulation runs (the worst fitting run had a 0.69 correlation over time and 0.56 across groups; the standard deviations for the distribution of correlations across time and across groups in the 100 simulations was 0.04 and 0.08 respectively). This close clustering of simulation runs speaks to the internal validity of the model (for other tests of internal validity, see Kim, 2005); that is, it gives us some confidence that the average agent behavior across simulation runs that we analyze represents the theoretical model.

Of course, real citizens have potentially richer and more diverse sources of media information than did *JQP*, and they exert control over their own media exposure. In the 100 simulations just described, all *JQP* agents processed the relatively liberal newspapers *Newsday* and the *New York Times*, but real-world voters undoubtedly read different newspapers, watched TV news, talked to their friends, and browsed the internet. One might expect liberal and conservative citizens to read different newspapers (or other media) and get a different slant from them, and indeed we found strong empirical evidence of this sort of selective exposure in Chapter 7. Table 8.3 looks at how closely *JQP* reproduces the dynamics of observed candidate evaluations when agents read *Newsday* and the *New York Times* versus when they read the *Wall Street Journal*.

Results averaged across the 100 simulation runs for each type of media are reported in Table 8.3 for three measures of attitude change. The first two columns present average correlations as a measure of the *responsiveness* of *JQP* agents to the information coded from liberal versus conservative news reports. This is the measure of model fit to the NAES data that we have focused on so far, and the differences in model fit by media source are striking. As expected, strong liberals and liberal agents track better when reading the reputedly liberal sources *Newsday* and the *New York Times*, while strong conservative agents do appreciably better when reading the more conservative *Wall Street Journal*. That is, the model performs best when the media sources processed by the agents *match* the types of sources we can expect NAES respondents select in the wild. This finding corroborates expectations about media slant and selective exposure.

The three middle columns of Table 8.3 compare the *persistence* (i.e., inertia) in candidate evaluations across campaign events for real and simulated voters, as measured by the standard deviations of the trajectories of evaluations across time for each media source, broken down by ideological group. Small standard deviations indicate relative "stickiness" in evaluations over time, where priors impose a heavier anchor on attitude change, while larger standard deviations indicate more change in response to campaign information. Though the evaluations of real voters in the NAES survey changed somewhat more than those of simulated agents, especially for liberal respondents, the striking finding is the overall similarity in persistence. When averaged across all ideological groups, NAES respondents showed a standard deviation on a 100 point thermometer scale of 2.24 compared to 1.96 and 1.95 for *JQP* agents using liberal and conservative media respectively. There were no real differences in the persistence of *JQP* agents' evaluations based on liberal versus conservative media, which is not surprising because persistence in our theory is largely a function of the heavy weight of prior attitudes rather than the impact of new information. Real and simulated voters show substantial persistence in their evaluations over the course of the campaign, indeed far more than a purely responsive model would predict (as we will show in the next section).

The third set of columns in Table 8.3 reports the changing candidate differentials for George W. Bush and Al Gore as a measure of *polarization*. The candidate differential, or spread, is the thermometer rating of Bush minus the rating of Gore. We are interested in whether the differential increases over the course of the campaign, which would indicate polarization, or whether it moderates, so we compute the difference between the candidate differential before and after the campaign (the differential computed after the three debates minus

TABLE 8.3. *Comparison of Liberal and Conservative Media*

	Responsiveness Correlations Across Time		Persistence Standard Deviations of Evaluations			Polarization Candidate Differentials (After–Before)		
	ND/NYT	WSJ	NAES	ND/NYT	WSJ	NAES	ND/NYT	WSJ
Very Liberal	0.88	0.66	5.27	2.71	2.28	15.5	6.4	3.3
Liberal	0.90	0.72	4.00	2.63	2.27	15.4	5.6	2.8
Moderate	0.83	0.69	2.39	2.06	1.99	4.5	2.1	−0.5
Conservative	0.94	0.86	2.51	2.00	2.01	3.9	2.2	3.8
Very Conservative	0.52	0.79	2.39	2.10	2.18	7.0	3.9	5.1
All Voters	0.90	0.77	2.24	1.96	1.95	9.3	4.1	2.9

the differential collected before the GOP Convention). In support of one of our most demanding hypotheses, we find polarization almost across the board. Every group of citizens in the sample polarized to some degree, on average 9.3 points. We also see polarization on average for all *JQP* agents, regardless of media source, though less than what was observed for real citizens. All ideological groups of agents polarized, with the exception of moderate agents exposed to the *Wall Street Journal*, who moderated by 0.48 points. Here, media source did matter. Liberal and very liberal agents polarized most when fed liberal media, while conservative and very conservative agents polarized most in response to a conservative source. Confirming another implication of our theory, strength of priors predicts degree of polarization. In every case, those agents with larger candidate differentials at the outset of the campaign polarized more over the course of the campaign than did those with lower initial differentials. And the more extreme ideological groups (very liberal and very conservative) always polarized more than less ideological groups, both in the NAES data and in the simulations.

Overall, these simulation results fit the data very well, both qualitatively and quantitatively. The *JQP* agents reproduce the observed responsiveness, persistence, and polarization of candidate evaluations of the survey respondents. Correlations between simulated and actual changes in candidate evaluations over time were consistently strong, especially when we take into account selective exposure to preferred media. Moreover, the changes in simulated evaluations over time were of comparable magnitude to the changes in NAES evaluations. Finally, like the survey respondents, the simulated agents' candidate differentials became more extreme over the election campaign, showing clear evidence of polarization. This was true for nearly all ideological groups, despite the fact that no individual-specific or ideological group-specific parameters were employed in the simulations; that is, *the mechanisms themselves and the parameter values were the same across all individual agents and all ideological groups for both sets of 100 simulations.* The campaign messages processed by all agents were also identical within a given media simulation. Only the initial knowledge structures for agents differed, and those were stochastically generated based on empirical data. In short, a single theoretical model replicated the critical changes in evaluations of the two candidates over the course of a presidential campaign across five ideological groups.

Moreover, these results are not sensitive to reasonable variations in parameter values (see Kim 2005). For all $\sigma > 0$, $\delta < 1$, and $\rho > 0$, *JQP* responds to external information, adjusting candidate evaluations to reflect the subjective tenor of each new piece of information. For all $\delta > 0$ and $\gamma > 0$, prior beliefs and attitudes bias the processing of information in the direction of priors. As γ and δ increase, motivated biases become stronger and prior attitudes become more persistent. As σ and ρ decrease, the responsiveness of the model to new external information weakens. The parameters s and d do not play a significant role in the results we report, though both are important to other cognitive functions not discussed in this chapter. The most important point for present purposes is that the qualitative results of the simulations we report hold for a wide range of parameter values. That is, the theoretical model is quite robust to variation in model parameters.

Comparisons of JQP with a Bayesian Learning Model

We believe the evidence we report of the qualitative and quantitative correspondence between the behavior of *JQP* agents and NAES respondents in the 2000 presidential election is compelling, but one might wonder how *JQP*'s performance compares to other theoretical models of belief updating. A family of Bayesian learning models has been proposed to explain changes in citizens' views of the political parties in response to the flow of information over time (Achen, 1992, 2002; Bartels, 2002; Gerber and Green 1998; Green et al., 2002; Grynaviski, 2006). This group of models represents the most sophisticated application of Bayesian ideas to the problems of attitude updating in response to political information. In order to comparatively evaluate *JQP*'s performance against the current "state-of-the-art" model of preference updating, we will now simulate a set of 100 Bayesian agents for the 2000 presidential election, following the same procedures as our two simulations of *JQP* agents.

Bayesian learning models theorize that people update their beliefs or attitudes by assimilating new information with their prior beliefs and attitudes. In this most general sense, *JQP* is a Bayesian model. However, most models based on Bayesian updating emphasize the rational nature of an unbiased assimilation process in which new information stands independently of priors (Achen 1992; Bartels, 2002; Bullock, 2009; Evans and Over, 1996; Gerber and Green, 1998). Though this requirement of "rational" updating is neither necessary nor implied by Bayes' Rule, which makes no stipulations about how new information is subjectively perceived and is therefore consistent with motivated reasoning models like *JQP*, it is the case that the applications of Bayesian learning in political science have largely assumed unbiased updating (for an excellent critique of "rational" updating models, see Bartels, 2002). We adapt the most prominent such model, Gerber and Green's (1998; Achen 1992) "rational" learning model, for comparison with *JQP*. The Gerber and Green model has the advantage of being a perfect theoretical foil for *JQP*, because it includes no mechanisms that would allow motivated reasoning. This comparison, then, will test our claim that *JQP* can replicate the responsiveness, persistence, and polarization of candidate evaluations over the course of a real election campaign *because* it includes motivated reasoning mechanisms not present in the Bayesian rational learning model. This is the striking difference between the models.

Here we develop the Gerber/Green model informally and then compare simulations of the 2000 presidential election based on it with the two *JQP* simulations and with NAES data (for a formal discussion, see Kim, Taber, and Lodge, 2010). The Bayesian model assumes that citizens seek to estimate some potentially changing, underlying quality of a candidate, which forms the basis of their evaluations (perhaps the candidate's competence, likeability, or position in issue space). Given a stream of information about candidates, citizens will update their estimates to reflect each new piece of information. In general, they update their estimates by averaging their current estimates with the new information, but how they weight this new information depends on their uncertainty, both about their current estimate and about the new information. Gerber and Green employ a Kalman filter algorithm to formalize their assumption that citizens assimilate new information in optimal fashion, by which we mean they minimize the expected squared error of their estimates over time. The Kalman filter is applied recursively to estimate an unknown quantity based on an uncertain prior for that quantity and a stream of noisy data. In our case, the unknown is the underlying candidate quality, the uncertain prior is the most recent candidate evaluation (starting with some initial evaluation), and the noisy data are the campaign statements coded from news reports of campaign events. As the Kalman filter is applied over time, its weights for priors and new information eventually should converge to a steady state value in the [0,1] interval, such that when this weight is equal to one, only new information matters for evaluations, and when it is equal to zero, only priors matter. When the weight converges on a value between zero and one, evaluations will update as a weighted average of the prior estimate and the new information. Without adding additional mechanisms for the subjective perception of new information, this model cannot produce polarization, and it can only predict persistence when the weight on new information approaches zero, in which case it becomes unresponsive.

To parallel the *JQP* simulations, we applied the Gerber/Green model to the NAES 2000 data as follows: (1) 100 agents were initialized into ideological groups following the same stochastic procedure as described for the *JQP* simulations; (2) initial priors were the thermometer ratings of the candidates collected before the GOP Convention; (3) the Bayesian agents processed the coded news reports from liberal news sources, and in a second separate simulation they processed reports from conservative media; (4) evaluations were updated using the Kalman filter; (5) 100 simulation runs were conducted for each media source; and (6) five parameters governing uncertainties and the variances of normally distributed error terms were empirically estimated to provide best model fit to the actual NAES candidate evaluations (Kim, 2005; Kim, Taber, and Lodge, 2010). Here we will compare the candidate evaluations based on the best-fitting Bayesian learning model to the average evaluations of the *JQP* agents and NAES respondents, for both media sources broken down by ideological group.

Table 8.4 presents this comparative analysis, broken down into columns for responsiveness, persistence, and polarization. To take into account the selective

TABLE 8.4. *Comparison of Bayesian Rational Learning Model and JQP, Matched Media*

	Responsiveness Correlations Across Time		Persistence Standard Deviations of Evaluations			Polarization Candidate Differentials (After-Before)		
	JQP	Bayesian	NAES	JQP	Bayesian	NAES	JQP	Bayesian
Very Liberal	0.88	0.41	5.27	2.71	13.83	15.5	6.4	−9.7
Liberal	0.90	0.55	4.00	2.63	12.65	15.4	5.6	−6.2
Moderate	0.83	0.55	2.39	2.06	12.08	4.5	2.1	−4.9
Conservative	0.86	0.20	2.51	2.01	11.86	3.9	3.8	−23.5
Very Conservative	0.79	0.32	2.39	2.18	13.30	7.0	5.1	−35.8
All Voters	0.90	0.62	2.24	1.95	11.82	9.3	4.1	−14.1

exposure that was almost certainly observed in the NAES data, we report analyses for "matched" simulations: liberal media were used for all very liberal, liberal, and moderate agents, while conservative media were used for conservative and very conservative agents. The Bayesian model did reasonably well in tracking the observed changes in candidate evaluations over the course of campaign events, as measured by the correlations to NAES data reported in column two, but *JQP* clearly was more responsive. This is particularly important because the Bayesian approach is intended to maximize responsiveness to data. Compared to real citizens, however, the Bayesian model *over*-responded to the stream of campaign information. We can see this clearly in the middle columns, which present the standard deviations of the distributions of evaluations over time. While *JQP* agents are slightly too persistent, the Bayesian model fluctuates far more than NAES respondents did in response to campaign information.

It turns out that the Bayesian learning model generates much more volatile changes in candidate evaluations over time than were observed for the survey respondents, while *JQP* produces changes of comparable magnitude to the NAES data. And the candidate differentials of Bayesian agents moderated over the course of the campaign, quite substantially for conservative agents. That is, the spread between Bush and Gore decreased over time so that, on average, Bayesian agents began the campaign favoring Bush by 20.4 points, but ended favoring Bush by only 6.3 points. Very conservative Bayesian agents dropped from a differential of 40.9 to only favoring Bush by 5.1 points! NAES respondents and *JQP* agents, by contrast, polarized over the campaign. As noted earlier, it was especially the most ideological agents and citizens who polarized the most, but these were the groups that moderated the most in the Bayesian simulations.

The NAES 2000 data show that evaluations of both Bush and Gore responded to the flow of campaign information, but within a relatively narrow range constrained by priors, and eventually preferences became more extreme. *JQP* closely reproduces this balance among responsiveness, persistence, and polarization in candidate evaluations, but the Bayesian model does not. This difference in performance obtains despite the fact that both models are initialized using the same stochastic procedures and receive the same set of campaign information.

We do not argue that it is impossible to account for the persistence and responsiveness of political attitudes using a Bayesian learning model. In fact, in a general sense, *JQP* is a Bayesian learning model in that prior beliefs play a critical role in learning in the model. Like Bartels (2002), however, we believe that any model that cannot produce differential subjective interpretations of information based on priors cannot account for the empirical balance among persistence, responsiveness, and polarization. Without motivated reasoning, it would be difficult if not impossible to provide a psychologically realistic account of why and how voters with opposing ideological structures could

TABLE 8.5. *Correlations of Online, Memory-Based, and Hybrid Models of Attitude Construction with NAES 2000 Data*

Model	δ	Bush	Gore	Overall
Online	0	0.52	0.83	0.68
Memory Based	1	0.34	0.73	0.53
Hybrid	0.56	0.91	0.89	0.90

simultaneously maintain or even strengthen their candidate evaluations while responding to a common information stream.

Online, Memory-Based, and Hybrid Models of Updating

Information processing theories of political evaluation processes – most notably the online and memory based models – have not been represented as formal models and directly tested against empirical data. However, given the theoretical mechanisms underlying *JQP* discussed previously, it is straightforward to implement a pure online, a pure memory-based, and a hybrid model of attitude updating within *JQP*. This allows us to test the empirical validity of these models against the NAES 2000 data.

Recall that the parameter δ in Equation 3 controls the degree to which the model represents online or memory-based attitude updating. A pure online processing model can be implemented by setting $\delta = 0$, in which case the constructed evaluation of an object is determined solely by the value of its prior online tally. Conversely, a purely memory-based model of attitude updating can be implemented by setting $\delta = 1$, which constructs an attitude as a simple average of the valences of considerations, weighted by their strength of association with the target object. Finally, a mixture of online and memory-based processing occurs for $0 < \delta < 1$, with the weight given memory-based considerations estimated by δ. In essence, the optimal estimate for δ tells us how heavy an anchor the prior attitudes toward the candidates were in the 2000 presidential election relative to other considerations triggered by new information, and thereby provide data to address the debate over the relative validities of online and memory based models of attitude updating.

Table 8.5 reports average over-time correlations between the candidate evaluations of artificial agents and NAES respondents for the purely online, purely memory based, and optimal hybrid models. First, it is clear that the online model outperforms the purely memory-based model, but, as expected, a hybrid model provides the best overall model fit. This is especially true for evaluations of George Bush. Most interesting, the best fitting hybrid model weights memory-based considerations only slightly more than the prior attitude. That is, all other considerations together account for 0.56 of the constructed attitude, while the prior attitude toward the candidate accounts for 0.44. This fits quite nicely with several recent conjectures that hybrid updating models should outperform pure models (Lavine 2002; Taber 2004). There is also a strong suggestion in these data that the relative mix of new considerations and the online tally will vary across attitude objects and perhaps across time and situation.

Simulating the Survey Respondent's Beliefs about Candidates

How does a survey respondent answer questions that ask for beliefs about a candidate's issue positions or personal traits? That is, when asked questions of the form, "Does candidate Soandso support issue Whatisit?" what determines the response? Our *JQP* theory of political information-processing proposes that the accessibility of the concept "Whatisit" in memory at the moment of answering the survey question (that is, having just activated the "Soandso" node) determines the response. In particular, we suggest that the answer to such political belief questions is driven by the momentary accessibility of the relevant issue or trait concept in LTM, which is formalized in Equation 1 as a function of: (1) its base-level activation; (2) the strength of the semantic association between the candidate and the issue or trait; (3) the degree of affective congruence between the candidate and the issue or trait; and (4) the number of considerations that are associated with the concept (the fan effect, which reduces the impact of any one consideration when there are many linked considerations). The strength of this reported belief as measured by explicit strength questions or by implicit reaction time measures will be a direct function of this accessibility.

This *JQP* model captures a number of well-known biases in survey responses, including question order effects, interviewer effects, and framing effects from question wording. The model has memory for question order since baseline activation responds to the entire history, and especially the recent history of concept activation. Race or gender of interviewer affect current activation of concepts associated with these categories. Frames presented in the survey questions influence baseline activation, semantic associations, and affective congruence. For example, if a female interviewer asks questions about gender equality, *JQP*'s answers will be colored by considerations linked to the concept female in long-term memory. And the model is subject to affective biases in survey response through the influence of affective congruency on current accessibility of considerations.

We conducted a unique test of this theory of the survey response by simulating experimental data originally collected by Richard Lau and David Redlawsk (2001; Redlawsk, 2001). Using their innovative dynamic process tracing procedure, Lau and Redlawsk immersed 199 undergraduate student subjects into a complex though controlled political environment, entailing both a primary and general election among fictitious candidates. We will focus just on the primary campaign for our simulation.

At the beginning of the experimental session, each participant's attitude toward and knowledge about a range of political issues and groups were surveyed, including questions about the issue stands of prominent political groups. Each participant then registered for either the Republican or Democratic primary to select a presidential candidate for their party. Next, they entered a dynamic information environment in which they were exposed to a stream of campaign information about four fictitious primary candidates from each party. In the Lau/Redlawsk dynamic process tracing procedure, campaign "headlines" scroll by on a computer screen and subjects may click on the headlines that interest them in order to read a brief story. As in the real world, information exposure is partially controlled by the subject. During the primary campaign, which lasted on average thirty minutes, participants also responded to four opinion polls, which collected their evaluations of the eight candidates. The first of these polls was used to identify each subject's initially most and least liked candidates.

In this complex campaign environment, each subject processed a unique set of campaign information about each candidate (different in amount, content, and order) and responded to the four polls at different points in time. Following the primary, each participant completed a survey about all the candidates, including their beliefs about where their most and least liked candidates stood on four policy issues: affirmative action, military spending, progressive taxation, and environmental regulation. We will focus on these beliefs about candidate issue positions as the key variables our simulated agents will predict.

To summarize, the Lau/Redlawsk experiment includes 199 participants with unique but known personal stands on and knowledge about the issues, who have been exposed to unique but known streams of campaign information about fictitious candidates, and who are asked the same set of questions about where the candidates stand on four issues. Our approach to simulating this experiment is straightforward. We conducted an individual-level, multiple-agent simulation of the primary phase of the experiment in which we initialized 199 *JQP* agents to represent the experimental participants, exposed each agent to a stream of campaign information and opinion polls that exactly matches the information experienced by the given subject, and then asked each agent the set of postcampaign questions, including the issue positions of their most and least liked candidates. The initial knowledge structure of each agent is obtained from the pre-test questionnaire for the corresponding actual subject. Then, each of the 199 agents "read" the same pieces of (coded) campaign information and answered the same survey questions as each corresponding, actual subject did in the experiment. There was no sampling procedure and no random component in the initialization of these 199 agents because we wanted to match the experimental sample exactly.

This procedure simulates the knowledge structures about each of the fictitious candidates over the course of the experiment, and, in particular, those knowledge structures that exist just as the survey questions about issue stands are asked. We cannot observe directly the real subjects' mental processing as they answer survey questions, but we can observe in considerable detail the information processing of their artificial twins from the simulation, and this gives us unique leverage on the problem.

To determine appropriate parameter values for the simulation, we followed two procedures that will be familiar from our earlier discussion. First, for the parameters that govern classical cognitive processing in the ACT-R environment, we assigned default values from the cognitive literature as described above. Second, for the three parameters that are unique to *JQP* (δ, ρ, and γ), we estimated optimal values for the Lau/Redlawsk data, finding that $\gamma = 2$, $\rho = 1$, and $\delta = 0.4$ maximized model fit in terms of match between subjects' and agents' preferences for the candidates. The rank order correlations between subjects' and agents' candidate preferences were .86 for the four Democrats and .83 for the four Republicans, which gives us confidence in the overall validity of the simulation and provides additional validation on a second data set of the *JQP* model of candidate evaluations. But our interest here is in the answers to survey questions about candidate issue positions.

Our theory claims that a survey response is based on an internal, transient psychological factor, the accessibility of the issue concept in LTM at the moment the survey respondent is thinking about the survey question. This accessibility is a function of the issue concept's baseline activation, the strength of semantic association between the candidate and the issue concept, the affective congruence between the candidate and the issue concept, and the fan effect. All of these variables are recorded in *JQP*'s processing runs in the simulation of the Lau/Redlawsk data, and so we can subject our claim to a direct test using the variables from the 199 simulated agents to predict the matched real subjects' survey responses to the candidate issue position questions. With reference to Equation 1, which computes the activation level of concepts in *JQP*, we estimate the following model using simulated independent variables and empirical dependent variables.

$$Response_{ijk} = \beta_1 + \beta_2 \text{Baseline}_{jk} + \beta_3 [\text{Association}_{ijk} - \ln(\text{Fan}_{ik})]$$
$$+ \beta_4 \text{AffCong}_{ijk} + \varepsilon_{ijk} \qquad (5)$$

Response$_{ijk}$ is subject k's response to the question about candidate i's position on issue j (measured on a seven-point scale), where there are 199 subjects, each of whom is asked about their most preferred and least preferred candidates' positions on the four policy issues listed earlier as well as their ideological placement. Since the independent variables are drawn from the simulation, the subscript k on the right hand side of the model refers to the matching agent for the given subject. To recap these independent variables, Baseline$_{jk}$ refers to the baseline accessibility of issue j, Association$_{ijk}$ denotes the strength of association between candidate i and issue j, Fan$_{ik}$ is the number of concepts linked to candidate i (under the fan effect, the more associations there are to a

TABLE 8.6. *Ordered Logit Results for Predictions of Survey Responses Using Simulated Predictors of Issue Accessibility*

Group	Baseline Accessibility of Issue Concept	Association of Issue and Candidate Minus Fan Effect	Affective Congruence between Issue and Candidate
Democrats	8.89***	0.47***	1.13***
	(1.86)	(0.09)	(0.17)
Independents	4.45*	0.30**	0.79***
	(2.38)	(0.14)	(0.22)
Republicans	6.05*	0.31	0.43*
	(3.46)	(0.22)	(0.26)
Liberal	7.38***	0.47***	1.13***
	(2.09)	(0.10)	(0.19)
Moderate	8.40***	0.35***	0.68***
	(1.97)	(0.11)	(0.16)
Conservative	4.90	0.16	0.90**
	(4.32)	(0.32)	(0.37)
Low Knowledge	6.11***	0.55***	1.05***
	(2.67)	(0.15)	(0.24)
Mid Knowledge	8.35***	0.45***	1.09***
	(1.83)	(0.10)	(0.16)
High Knowledge	9.14***	0.29*	0.32
	(2.83)	(0.15)	(0.25)
All Subjects	7.99***	0.44***	0.92***
	(1.32)	(0.07)	(0.12)

Note: Cells report coefficients and standard errors. *** $p < 0.01$; ** $p < 0.05$; * $p < 0.10$.

concept, the less activation may be spread to any particular one of these associated concepts), and $AffCong_{ijk}$ is the degree of affective congruency between issue i and candidate j. These simulated psychological variables are recorded immediately upon agent k's having processed the relevant survey question, and after k has processed exactly the same stream of information and questions that were presented to their human survey twin from the Lau/Redlawsk data.

Table 8.6 reports ordered logit results for this model. First, pooling all subjects/agents, we find strong support for our *JQP* model of issue accessibility at the time of the survey question. All hypothesized psychological components simulated within the 199 agents are highly significant predictors of the actual survey responses. In short, we were able to predict real subjects' responses to questions like "Does Donald support increased military spending?" by referring to the processing mechanisms of their artificial twins from the simulation. We also estimated the model on nine subsamples, finding all coefficients in the expected direction, with twenty-three of these twenty-seven coefficients statistically significant. Interestingly, the model did less well for Republican and conservative respondents than for other groups. Because *JQP* performed quite well in earlier tests on conservative respondents, it is unlikely this is due to any particular mismatch between the processing mechanisms in the model and conservative thought processes.

These results offer three forms of confirmation for our theory. First, they provide another global test of *JQP*'s ability to perform information processing tasks in parallel with real humans. Just as with the NAES 2000 data, *JQP* agents initialized to represent human respondents processed political information and produced candidate evaluations that correspond to their real twins' preferences. Second, in simulating the Lau/Redlawsk data we have shown strong support for the theory we have advanced to account for the formation and reporting of political beliefs. All three psychological components of our processing model – baseline activation, semantic association minus fan effect, and affective congruency – were significant predictors of actual political beliefs. This result tells us that concept accessibility is critical to understanding survey responses and that our particular model of the dynamics of concept accessibility is sufficient to explain these dynamics. Third, we have shown that *JQP* provides a compelling theoretical framework for analyzing the behavior of experimental subjects. This gives us traction on the difficult problem of the unobservable nature of internal mental processes. By creating artificial twins for experimental participants we can "observe" their mental processing while simulated agents perform experimental tasks (for an earlier discussion of this analytic approach, see Taber and Steenbergen, 1995).

General Discussion

We set out in this book to develop and test a comprehensive theory of political information processing, so it is fitting that our final empirical chapter presents a complete working model of the theory. The benefits of formal theory are manifest, and computational modeling allows us to capitalize on the precision of expression and communication, the clarity and transparency of assumptions, and the power, rigor, and fertility of deductions of formal approaches while relaxing some of the restrictions on complexity and "process realism" found in mathematical modeling (Taber and Timpone, 1996). In this chapter, we have formalized our *JQP* theory, used the theory to simulate changing candidate evaluations over the 2000 presidential election campaign, analyzed the processing of liberal and conservative media within the model, evaluated model performance against a Bayesian rational learning model, examined online, memory-based, and hybrid versions of our model, and applied *JQP* to simulate the formation and reporting of political beliefs in an electoral experiment. The model has been remarkably successful across all of these applications in replicating the processing and behavior of real citizens.

It is clear from the NAES 2000 data that evaluations of George W. Bush and Al Gore responded to the flow of campaign information, but within a relatively narrow range constrained by priors, and eventually preferences became more extreme. *JQP* closely reproduces these observed dynamics, while the Bayesian learning model can account for neither persistence nor polarization. Both models start with the same distribution of initial knowledge structures and receive the same set of campaign information, but only *JQP* captures the full range of dynamics in the trajectories of evaluations. Our model replicates the responsiveness, persistence, and polarization of the NAES candidate evaluation *because it models motivated reasoning.* In contrast to the Bayesian model, *JQP* is a motivated skeptic in how it weighs new information. Specifically, in *JQP* the prior belief structure for an attitude object determines how incoming information will be perceived (through the patterns of activation in memory), and when attitudes are updated, information that favors priors is weighted more heavily. This motivated reasoning is the direct consequence of the processing mechanisms that define *JQP*. Without motivated reasoning, it would be difficult if not impossible to provide a psychologically realistic account for why and how voters with opposing ideological structures could simultaneously maintain their candidate evaluations while responding to a common information stream.

We also applied *JQP* to explain how a survey respondent answers questions about a political candidate's positions on political issues and traits. We hypothesized that an internal, transient psychological factor, namely the accessibility of the issue concept in LTM, will determine perceptions about a candidate's issue positions. In *JQP*, this accessibility is a function of the issue concept's baseline activation, the strength of semantic association between the candidate and the issue concept minus the fan effect, and the affective congruence between the candidate and the issue concept. These predictions, which emerged through the process of formalizing our theory, were tested against the Lau-Redlawsk experimental data in a unique form of computational experimentation (Taber and Steenbergen, 1995). This test was also successful, as we found that all of the hypothesized processes were significant predictors of the survey response.

JQP has passed this most stringent set of tests. The theory has the internal coherence to enable formalization; it has the comprehensiveness to cover a wide range of information processing dynamics, including online, memory-based, and hybrid processes of attitude formation, learning and belief updating, and responsiveness and resistance to new information; it has the deductive power to generate testable hypotheses; it has global empirical validity in the sense of close correspondence with the behavioral dynamics of survey and experimental participants. If one makes the assumption that long term memory processes are automatic, while working memory processes are conscious, then it implements a dual processing framework. In these senses, our motivated reasoning theory of political cognition is now complete, and we may turn to a final discussion of its theoretical implications.

9

Affect, Cognition, Emotion

Which Way the Causal Arrow?

JQP posits that motivated reasoning and the ensuing rationalization of beliefs, attitudes, and intentions is built into our basic neurocognitive architecture, propelled by the seven principles described in Chapter 2 that drive the sampling, comprehension, interpretation, and evaluation of information in ways that systematically bias thinking and behavior. Our model brings affect center stage in proposing that all thinking, reasoning, and decision making is affectively charged, and our research program tested for the direct, spontaneous effects of prior attitude and unnoticed affective cues on the appraisal of sociopolitical objects and on subsequent reasoning and behavior.

The central tenet of *JQP* is that affect enters into the decision stream spontaneously at every stage of the process. Cognition is hot; across numerous experiments we found that social and political concepts evoke an instantaneous experience of positive and/or negative affect. At the moment an object is registered, an evaluative tally is automatically called up, triggering a series of largely unconscious, sometimes somatically embodied processes that drive the perception and evaluation of events in defense of one's prior attitudes. This uncontrolled affective reaction directly signals the desirability of one object or choice over another and thereupon systematically guides the encoding, search, retrieval, interpretation, and evaluation of information in ways that promote affectively congruent rationalization effects. Because people are perceptually aware of their feelings moments before they are cognizant of an object's meanings, the activated attitude proves to be a powerful determinant of what citizens think and say when they talk to themselves or others, answer a pollster's questions, or act in accord with their intentions.

The robust implicit priming effects reported here reflect how beliefs, feelings, intentions, and behaviors that were contiguously associated in the past or momentarily joined in a situational context are automatically activated on mere exposure to an environmental trigger or situational cue. Across dozens of tests we found that consciously unnoticed events systematically impact the way people think about candidates, groups, and issues, and how they evaluate complex policy proposals. In broad summary we found support for *JQP*'s basic expectations:

- Positive and/or negative affect is evoked automatically by the preconscious appraisal of leaders and groups, as well as the evaluation of issues and their anticipated consequences.
- This affective experience represents the relative desirability of one outcome over another.
- Such evaluative responses are constructed online, at the very instant attention is momentarily fixed on the object and this affective response can be activated without conscious awareness of the triggering event, even when the affective cue is substantively unrelated to the object.
- Once this spontaneously activated response becomes automatic, it cannot be readily accessed or easily modified by introspection.
- If the affective connection is strong enough, somatic responses lend visceral support to recollections and preferences and in so doing turn cold "as-if" responses into more powerfully felt experiences.
- This affective experience feeds back on the appraisal process itself, routinely promoting a selective search of long term memory for belief-confirming evidence and thereby informing the conscious expression of opinion, choice, and action in affectively-congruent ways.

These results confirm the power of System 1 processing on a range of conscious processes from cursory snap judgments characteristic of candidate evaluations to in-depth if-then appraisals of policy evaluations. Three basic processes appear to promote the judgmental biases we and others uncover. First and foremost is the hardwired associative architecture of long-term memory where following Hebb's law bundles of neurons ("objects") that frequently fire together become wired together to create a network of connections that bring thoughts, feelings, and intentions into the decision stream spontaneously on their mere exposure. Secondly, the associations in LTM are sculpted by experience: rich experiences build the dense interconnected networks characteristic of sophisticates. And finally, priming is the key mechanism guiding the activation process as these associations – weighted by one's experience – become the considerations that spontaneously inform both conscious and unconscious judgment and choice. A key take-home point is that all conscious (System 2) thinking and reasoning is constructed from the biased sampling of associations generated automatically by the associative structure of LTM.

In our experiments we routinely used simple, nonpolitical words or images to prime affect and concepts in LTM. From what we have learned, activated concepts do far more than make cognitive connections. Concepts are embodied cognitions. Thinking nudges attitudes and behavioral intentions in complementary ways (Buonomano, 2011). The following are two more examples supporting our contention that cognition *and* affect *and* behavioral intentions are so interconnected in knowledge structures that concepts prime consistent feelings and behavior. Jostmann and colleagues (2009) had experimental subjects estimate the value of foreign currencies while holding either a heavy or light clipboard. From what we have learned about ideomotor behavior you know the result. In an even more subtle demonstration, Miles and colleagues (2010) found that subjects asked to think about the future leaned forward.

Granted, there are more gaps in our theory than in Nixon's tapes, chief among them:

- We have too weak an understanding of how concepts in LTM are matched to environmental events.
- We only superficially grasp how new information is integrated into OL Tallies.
- We have insufficient evidence for the claim that one's OL Tally is a summing up, albeit biased, of the perceived costs and benefits of one's prior experiences.
- We lack direct measures of somatic response and therefore do not directly test how the viscera impact attitudes and motivate affectively congruent behavior.

Despite these gaps in theory, we find moderate to strong empirical support across numerous empirical tests of the model. On average, across all our candidate and issue experiments, unnoticed and unappreciated priming events moved participants' evaluations about one third of a standard deviation on five- and six-point scales. This is remarkable given that we purposely used simple affective prime words and pictures *devoid* of any direct cognitive relevance to the political objects being judged. The finding that affectively charged, semantically *un*related primes produce systematic facilitation and inhibition effects on the thoughts people have and how they reason implies a generalized *affective contagion* effect that seriously challenges conventional as well as normative models of the formation and expression of political beliefs, attitudes, and behavioral intentions. More troublesome still, these unobtrusive processes appear to be effective across multiple contexts and are not easily detected in persuasive messages.

Had we chosen substantively related primes, say "slum" or "ghetto" on racial evaluations instead of "grief" or "funeral," the combined effects of both cognitive and affective associations would surely promote stronger results. Had we joined the affective primes with party or ideological labels or endorsements – as is real-world practice (Cobb and Kuklinski, 1997; Kuklinski and Hurley, 1994; Kuklinski et al., 2000; Zaller, 1994) – the effects would predictably be many times stronger still. But, our aim was theoretical – to test for the unconscious effects of affect on political evaluations – not to demonstrate that consciously unnoticed affective primes can override partisanship or any of the other variables known to affect public opinion and political behavior.

Rather, what we show is that unnoticed priming effects systematically bolster or undermine the expression of one's prior attitudes and identifications and thereupon influence subsequent evaluations.

We also found strong, systematic individual differences in this affect-driven susceptibility to biased reasoning, with the greatest prejudice among those with the strongest prior attitudes and most knowledge. Those citizens who know the most and feel the strongest are most prone to confirmation and disconfirmation biases and least likely to integrate new, contrary information into their thinking in ways the good Reverend Bayes would approve (Stroud, 2008). We interpret this susceptibility to preconscious priming effects on those citizens with the strongest attitudes and most knowledge as due to two factors: first, sophisticates are the most likely to have repeatedly connected their beliefs to feelings to intentions, and then their rich, highly interconnected knowledge structure provides them the facts, figures, and cognitive wherewithal to rationalize away disconfirming evidence and better defend their prior attitudes.

In the studies in which we manipulated candidate similarity we found that the affective primes had an independent, statistically significant main effect on candidate evaluations comparable to the effect of issue proximity. Then, when we encouraged participants to think long and hard about public policy proposals we found a direct effect of the affective primes on the retrieval of supportive thoughts about the issues, which in turn bolstered support for policies. As demonstrated in the information search experiments, prior attitude triggers confirmation and disconfirmation biases that lead to belief and attitude polarization. Again, we see this as evidence supporting the hot cognition and affective congruence postulates of *JQP* and confirming the predicted difficulty if not impossibility of separating affect from cognition.

Perhaps most impressive is *JQP*'s success, when instantiated in a computational model, to track the 2000 presidential election and integrate media coverage of the major campaign events into the knowledge structures of artificial agents, who then succumbed to motivated reasoning and the rationalization of political beliefs, attitudes, and vote intention. The virtual agents closely simulated the information processing of real citizens across an actual election, and modeled their responsiveness *and* their resistance to campaign information, thereupon promoting the polarization of both real and simulated opinion.

At this juncture then there is a wealth of empirical evidence demonstrating affective priming and contagion effects, and some emerging consensus as to how this priming effect works. One perspective that has certainly influenced *JQP* was advanced by Robert Zajonc (1980, 1984), who argues that the cognitive and affective systems are somewhat independent (though architecturally interrelated as depicted in our Figure 2.1). There is neurological evidence (e.g., LeDoux, 1996) that the affect system is easily and swiftly activated and once set in motion generates a "quick and dirty" approach-avoidance reaction to the situation, with conscious, deliberative appraisal following moments later. From this perspective the automatic affective response is primary, entering the decision stream first, and may or may not (depending on individual and situational factors) be modified by a later conscious, cognitive assessment (Devine, 1989; Murphy and Zajonc, 1993).

A related perspective that has also influenced *JQP*, this following John Dewey, sees response competition as a plausible explanation for the attitudinal contagion effect (Hermans, De Houwer, and Eelen, 1994; Wentura, 1999). By this and our account, implicit attitudes directly and inexorably link feelings to behavior. Attitudinal objects automatically potentiate an immediate approach-avoidance behavioral response, which on mere exposure to the attitudinal object readies a bivalent "go–no go" behavioral response (Nosek, 2004). When the prime and target are affectively congruent, behavioral responses to the target are speeded up, but when the juxtaposition is incongruent the automatic response must first be inhibited, then redirected, and consequently is slowed down. In this light, a negative attitudinal object readies an "avoidance" response, which, were it followed by a contrary signal (a "false alarm" as with an incongruent prime), the prepared action must first be stopped and an alternative forward-looking "go" response initiated.

Both Zajonc's two-independent-systems perspective and the response competition explanation accomplish a long sought-after desideratum of social science in linking affect to cognition, thoughts to feelings and attitudes to behavior. What is critical from our perspective is that political beliefs, feelings, intentions, and actions will, if repeatedly associated in everyday thinking, become tightly interconnected in a Hebbian network of interdependencies that only become disassociated in pathological cases (Gazzaniga, 1992, 1998).

We believe in a decade's time there will be compelling evidence extending our findings in demonstrating:

- There are affective neural connections – now established most clearly for fear in rats (LeDoux, 1996) and in contemporary work on mirror neurons (Oberman and Ramachandran, 2007) – confirming hard-wired pathways linking seeing to feeling to thinking to action.
- It will prove impossible, despite the best efforts of rational choice theorists, to tease apart feelings from the expression of beliefs, goals and behavior, *or* keep affect independent of the evaluation of evidence.
- Further, because of the temporal and motivational primacy of affect, we expect that feelings will prove to be the strongest predictors of behavior. Were there such a thing as affect-free cognitions, any such "cool" links from belief to feeling to behavior would be weak because of their lack of motivational thrust.

To the extent that "some" (Fazio, 1992) or "all" (Bargh, Chaiken, Govender, and Pratto, 1992) sociopolitical concepts spontaneously invoke unconscious affective responses that biases subsequent judgments, then our discipline's focus and reliance on conscious, introspectively accessible considerations will fail to correctly model the whys and wherefores for how citizens think, reason, and act politically. A dual process model of attitude formation and expression that incorporates both conscious and implicit mechanisms, as does *JQP*, cannot but help advance our understanding of how citizens form, update, express, and act upon their political beliefs and preferences.

Key questions – danced around in Chapters 5 and 6 but at this juncture still a long way from being answered to anyone's satisfaction – are how, when, and for whom will the spontaneously evoked unconscious effects we found in our experiments impact the expression of political judgments, evaluations, intentions, and actions elicited in questionnaires and the real world. We know that unconscious processing drives the sampling, comprehension, interpretation, and evaluation of information in ways that systematically bias thinking and behavior, but we need to better specify the underlying mechanisms and processes if we are to learn the ins and outs of political persuasion both inside and outside the lab. Antonio Damasio (2002) was right in claiming "the brain is a feeling machine for thinking," as was William James (1890) in believing that "thinking is for doing." But how?

To the extent that our seven-postulate model approximates the mechanisms and processes guiding the expression of attitudes, we foresee a number of important consequences for the practice of political science and, more specifically, political psychology.

JQP and the Survey Response

The impressive body of empirical knowledge that political scientists have cumulated about political beliefs, attitudes, and behavior is based almost entirely on some form of verbal self-report, which is conventionally understood as "the product of the deductive integration of an individual's beliefs about an object's attributes" (Krosnick et al., 1992: 152). In both surveys and experiments, we routinely ask people factual questions, ask for their beliefs, their attitudes, past behaviors, intentions, and actions. The questions and context – more specifically the concepts they invoke – determine how memory is searched and consequently what information is retrieved and reported. From this perspective one can think of a pollster's questions as complex primes, causing some feelings, thoughts, goals, and behaviors to become more accessible. How people respond explicitly – what they say, how they say it, the speed of their response, and what they choose to censure – is a function of whatever considerations from long term memory are made momentarily available to working memory.

But here is the rub: only a small sample of the cognitive and affective associations activated in LTM become available for conscious processing. Consequently, there is always some disassociation between implicit and explicit measures of beliefs and attitudes. Usually, the correlations between explicit and implicit measures are positive (Wattenberg, Judd, and Park, 1997), though sometimes negative (Nosek, 2004), and on other occasions the relationship disappears (Zajonc, 2000). Moreover, implicit and explicit measures will routinely differ in content if not direction (Cunningham, Preacher, and Banaji, 2001; Gawronski and Bodenhausen, 2006; Karpinski, Steinman, and Hilton, 2005; Nosek, 2004).

Specific to the expression of attitudes in a survey setting, it appears to be the case that the simple act of asking questions promotes an intellectualization process that dampens the affective connection between thoughts and feelings (Epstein, 1972; 1992). These "cool" responses are no longer heartfelt, but rather are affect-deprived *beliefs about the experience, not the experience itself.* Absent a visceral connection to the experience itself, the response is not embodied, but becomes what Paula Niedenthal and her colleagues call "cold, as-if emotional responses" (Niedenthal, Halberstadt, and Innes-Ker, 1999; Niedenthal, Halberstadt, and Setterlund, 1997). Online processing may (repeat "may") help us get around this problem if (repeat "if") as we argue evaluative tallies reflect a summing up of the costs and benefits of one's past experiences and if voiced quickly will be less context dependent than memory-based judgments. Then again, we have also presented evidence that embodied affective tallies are also undermined by systematic biases.

There are methodological questions as well: where, when, why, and how will implicit and explicit responses differ? As shown in Chapters 5, 6, and 7, because implicit processes are more responsive than conscious appraisals to subtle, context cues that easily escape cognitive awareness, implicit and explicit responses will most likely diverge in complex decision environments where much more information enters the decision stream than can be accessed or appraised consciously. While the explicit expression of a belief or attitude depends crucially on what conscious *and* unconscious considerations entered the response, the individual is only privy to what comes consciously to mind, a problem endemic to much social science research, both survey and experimental.

JQP versus Prominent Models of Candidate Evaluation and Vote Choice

Having empirically tested the predictions of our model as best we can, let us briefly compare *JQP* to the most prominent models of public opinion and attitude change: first, Zaller's (1992) "Receive-Accept-Sample" (RAS) model that informs *The Nature and Origins of Mass Opinion* (1992), as well as Zaller and Feldman's (1992) important application of the model to the survey response; next, Lau and Redlawsk's (2006) political decision-making models and their process tracing methodology for testing these models; and finally, the Marcus, Neuman, and MacKuen (2000) model of emotions in *Affective Intelligence and Political Judgment*, along with Brader's (2006) experimental test of AI.

Each of these models is among the very best that political psychologists have developed to date and each makes a unique, positive contribution to our understanding of how citizens process campaign information to inform their political behavior. *JQP* shares much with these prominent models at the general, descriptive level, but our research program differs significantly in theoretical description, in the focus on process, in many key predictions, but most importantly in the manner of hypothesis testing and in how we explain the results, both ours and theirs.

Zaller and Feldman's (1992) *Model of the Survey Response.* In his classic, *The Nature and Origins of Mass Opinion*, John Zaller challenges the idea that voters have fixed preferences. Instead he presents a model where individuals have conflicting "considerations" (facts, values) in long-term memory on many specific political issues, with their expressed preferences determined by the mix of considerations made accessible to conscious memory. The process generating an attitudinal response is based on Zaller's "Receive-Accept-Sample" (RAS) model: your stated opinions reflect considerations that you have received (heard or read about and stored in memory), which are sampled from the most salient considerations (that come momentarily to mind), which will be more likely accepted (if they are consistent with one's prior beliefs and partisan persuasion). A key axiom of the model is that when asked their opinion by a pollster, a voter's explicitly expressed preference is said to be constructed on the fly from a small non-random sample of these top of the head associations.

We too see the expression of beliefs and attitudes as a constructive process generating top-of-the-head opinions. There is no "point" in memory representing a "true attitude" or single opinion, so "most of what gets measured as public opinion does not exist except in the presence of a pollster" (Zaller, 1992: 265). All well and good; an important point lost on many analysts. Accordingly, when NES respondents are explicitly asked to think about what they like about a candidate or issue, they can recall a couple of facts, figures, or reasons and compute a preference by averaging across the sample of considerations. In general, the greater an individual's level of political awareness, the more likely she is to receive campaign messages and the more able she will be to resist evidence that is inconsistent with her partisan or other dispositions. But be careful here as the modal number of open-ended responses in the NES survey of congressional candidates is one.

In one sense, Zaller's take on the formation of public opinion is in line with our unconscious versus conscious dual processing perspective, implying as it does that the process that brings considerations into conscious memory is unconscious. But unlike *JQP*, the RAS model is a cognitively centered, memory-based depiction of preferences, as only those considerations now in conscious memory drive the reported response. As expressed in Zaller's "Reception Axiom," affective information is likely to affect respondents "only insofar as it leads to intellectual – which is to say, cognitive – engagement" (42–43).

This axiom is contrary to *JQP* on three counts: first, our hot cognition postulate challenges the very notion of a purely cognitive response. All the "objects" we have tested so-far (political leaders, groups, hard and easy issues, symbols, as well as concrete and abstract concepts) have been found to be affectively

charged in memory. Second, our primacy of affect and affective contagion postulates claim and we find that one's prior affect – be it for a political figure,
group, issue, or policy proposal – systematically biases the retrieval of considerations from memory. Third, the Reception Axiom ignores the Type 1 and
Type 2 contextual cues long known to escape conscious awareness, but which
nonetheless systematically bias the sampling of considerations.

There are also direct challenges to Zaller's key Resistance Axiom, which proposes that arguments inconsistent with citizens' predispositions will be rejected
"only to the extent that they (the respondents) possess the contextual information necessary to perceive a relationship between the message and their predispositions" (44). Here, "contextual information" refers to the considerations
currently in conscious Working Memory. In *JQP*, we theorize that motivated
reasoning is triggered by the spontaneous activation of an extant attitude and
need not be summoned up by any in-depth evaluation of campaign information.
More troublesome still, asking people to "stop and think," to ruminate before
responding, which is the major manipulation in the Zaller-Feldman (1992)
analysis of the survey response, will bring *less*-important cognitive considerations to mind and thereupon deflect the evaluation off its online trajectory.
This is empirically demonstrated in Chapters 7 and 8, as well as by Gigerenzer
(2007), Wilson (2002), and in Forgas's (1995) experiments testing his affect-
infusion model. In short, we see the Zaller model as having the causal arrow
going the wrong way in modeling the retrieval of cognitive considerations as the
"chariot driver" explaining preferences. In *JQP* by contrast, a spontaneously
evoked affective preference steers the retrieval of considerations and thereupon
promotes motivated reasoning.

Lau and Redlawsk's (2006) Process Tracing Approach. In a series of experiments using a dynamic information board, Lau and Redlawsk (1997, 2001,
2006) monitor what information participants read about hypothetical political candidates and track their search patterns in simulated primary and general election campaigns. In contrast to the information board we employed in
the Chapter 7 experiments on motivated skepticism, the scrolling method is
designed to mimic the ebb and flow of political campaigns over time in presenting information about candidate demographics, trait information, interest
group endorsements, poll results, and the candidates' issue positions.

This method allows participants to self-select what campaign information
to click on and read as it streams down and disappears off the computer
screen. Data collected in this way sheds light on decision and information
processing strategies citizens use in the complex information environment of
a political campaign. Participants can choose to or not to click on colored
boxes labeling the type of information (e.g., "Roger's position on Iraq") which
pop open to reveal policy-specific information. The computer collects data on
what types and pieces of information were selected, and the length of time
each window was open, thereby allowing Lau and Redlawsk to show how
different decision-making strategies depend on different campaign factors and

such individual differences as political knowledge, motivation, and cognitive ability. Tests of decision models using this method focus on the breadth and depth of search as a function of one's goals (e.g., accuracy) and the complexity of the decision context (e.g., the number of candidates, their similarity, and the number of ascribed attributes), with analyses examining compensatory and non-compensatory decision rules for the integration of information into candidate evaluations and vote choice.

By and large, Lau and Redlawsk characterize the decision process as a conscious, reflective search for reasons to compare and choose among political candidates. Their Model 1, "Dispassionate Decision Making," is described as an explicit search and conscious calculation of tangible consequences to self and family. Model 2, "Confirmatory Decision," is a conscious search for candidate information consistent with early childhood socialization, most commonly party identification. Model 3, "Fast and Frugal Decision Making," is the active search for one or two candidate attributes that matter most, prototypically a single issue. And Model 4, "Intuitive Decision Making," follows a satisficing strategy in seeking out just enough information to make a "good-enough" vote choice. Were they not cast exclusively in terms of conscious memory search, we would have little objection to the models.

More central to our theoretical focus on the role of affect in political information processing is the Redlawsk (2001) and Redlawsk, Civettini, and Lau (2007) analyses, which employ the scrolling procedure in simulated campaigns to compare memory-based to online information processing and try to disentangle cognitive from affective processing. In principle, this approach might provide useful data for testing hypotheses about underlying conscious and unconscious processing, but in practice we have concerns about the method. This art-mimicking-life advantage is offset by an experimental design with thousands of moving parts that makes it difficult to observe when, where, and how biases creep into the decision stream. The dynamic information board, in which all sorts of campaign and nonpolitical information stream by at a fast pace, places unique and we believe undue demands on information processing as compared to real-world voter decision making (a view shared by McGraw, 2011; and Kruglanski and Sleeth-Keppler, 2007). Experimental participants in these simulated campaigns face a highly fluid environment in which political candidates state preferences and take sides on multiple policy preferences. As described by Redlawsk, Civettini, and Lau (2007: 152):

evaluative expectations are often violated and emotional responses to candidates are heightened. An initially preferred candidate becomes suddenly and unexpectedly less attractive, while a rejected candidate begins taking positions that are very close to their own. The result should be conflict between the initial evaluation and new information.

This "chaotic" electoral campaign (their descriptor) may be the way it is seen in the quaint towns of Iowa and central New Jersey but is nothing like the far more predictable, narrative-based structure we New Yorkers face.

Explicit here and in their characterization and analyses of campaign information processing is the privileging of memory-based processing. It is instructive to review the postexperimental design used by Redlawsk, Civettini, and Lau (2007: 162). After completing the search portion of the study, participants take a ten- to fifteen-minute "Memory Test," in which they are asked to "List everything remembered about each of the four candidates and indicate affective reactions to these memories to the experimenter." This is followed by a ten-minute "Decision Process," in which participants "Describe how the decision to support one candidate was made, [and] list [their] likes and dislikes for the chosen candidate." And finally a twenty- to thirty-minute "Information Review" where they "review the title of each piece of information examined . . . indicating whether the item can be recalled and if so whether it was accessed by mistake, and the affective reaction to the information." To our knowledge, this is the most retrospective memory-based procedure citizens might encounter outside a fifty-minute psychotherapy session.

Redlawsk (2001) finds strong correlations (averaging 0.56) predicting vote choice from the mix of recalled likes and dislikes about the candidates. We too (Lodge, Steenbergen, and Brau, 1995) find moderate to strong positive correlations between the respondent's recollected likes and dislikes and vote choice, as would any similar analysis on NES data (e.g., Zaller and Feldman, 1992). Recall however that information decays exponentially so tapping memory within minutes of reading the campaign information dramatically inflates the relationship. Oddly, Redlawsk does not find much evidence of false memories, with about 80 percent of the recollections coded as accurate, whereas Lodge, Steenbergen, and Brau, as well as Zaller and Feldman find that about half the recollections were partisan-based rationalizations. One reason for this discrepancy may well be that each of the individual information screens presented in the Lau and Redlawsk simulations presented a single atomized idea, not as in Lodge, Steenbergen, and Brau or the NES, general policy statements (e.g., Candidate X opposes abortion) perhaps with a qualifier (e.g., "except in the cast of rape and incest"). Recollecting the gist is of course easier than recalling the more complex policy statement but it is the evaluation of the gist *and* qualifier, not simply recollection of the gist, that better tests the role of memory on judgment and choice. True enough, people vote for the candidate they say they like best! But *JQP* differs in the explanation of this well-documented, tautological correlation.

Redlawsk (2001) argues – this central to the argument for why memory-based processing trumps online processing – that the online processing people engage in when forming and updating their candidate impressions is distinct from the processing engaged in when people are called on to choose between candidates. The vote choice, Redlawsk assumes, is based on the retrieval, evaluation, and integration of evidence differentiating the candidates, rather than on a simpler comparison of the respective evaluative tallies that they and we agree were formed online during the (simulated) campaign. In *JQP*, vote choice is often a relatively simple decision: choose the candidate with the most positive OL evaluative tally.

Moreover, to reject the primacy of online processing on the basis of these studies, we must assume that any extant affective impression formed online during exposure to the campaign information does not influence the encoding, interpretation, comprehension, and, yes, the recall, integration, and evaluation of sampled information in tally-consistent ways. Unfortunately, the research design makes it impossible to directly compare memory-based to online processing because there is no direct test of the effects of an OL Tally on the motivated retrieval and evaluation of recollections. The inability to test for order effects makes it impossible to distinguish the primacy effect found in impression formation from the recency effect characteristic of memory-based recall. In *JQP* both the encoding *and* retrieval processes are influenced significantly by an affective contagion effect that theoretically should and empirically does impact the observed correlation between the retrieved considerations and candidate evaluation. This then is rationalization, and the causal arrow flies from evaluative tally to the selective encoding and retrieval of considerations.

A better, albeit imperfect, test of how and when new information is integrated into a candidate evaluation was carried out by Cassino (2005) in a series of clever experiments employing an indirect measure of online evaluations. In a between-subject experimental design, participants read twelve policy statements by a hypothetical congressman, which they had previously evaluated. In one condition the congressman first voiced three policy positions known from pretests to be favored by the participant, followed by six neutral statements, and finally three stands that the participant opposed. The order of favorable and opposing statements was reversed for the second experimental group. After reading each policy statement, an unambiguous positive or negative "target" word (e.g., cancer, sunshine) appeared on the screen, and participants were instructed to indicate as quickly as possible with a button response whether the word was positive or negative. Note, the task was *not* to say whether they currently liked or disliked the congressman's position, but whether the target word was positive or negative. In this design, the candidate's statement – whether attitudinally favored or opposed – serves as a positive or negative prime, and reaction times to evaluate the unrelated target words are indirect measures of online evaluations of the congressman. Note that this is a dynamic version of our own hot cognition studies, reported in Chapter 3, but here allowing Cassino to better track changing online evaluations as participants process information about the hypothetical congressman.

The information integration curves from Cassino's study are plotted in Figure 9.1. The top line depicts average responses over time (the twelve issue statements) in the initially positive experimental group, and the bottom line shows the initially negative group. Two characteristics of the evaluative integration curves stand out: first, even in this low-salient, purposely bland evaluative situation, candidate evaluations are created on the first through third

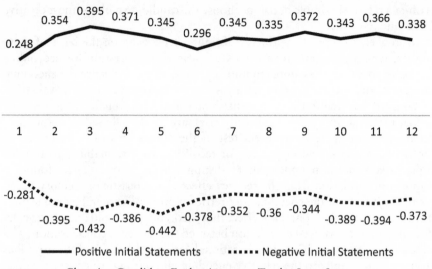

FIGURE 9.1. Changing Candidate Evaluations over Twelve Issue Statements

pieces of information and stay steady for the six neutral pieces of information. Secondly, and more importantly, the affectively *in*congruent information presented at the tail-end of the information flow (statements ten to twelve) should, normatively speaking, reduce support for the candidate but do not; the evaluation is stable from the initial impression onward, unaffected by the incongruent policy statements. Once an initial preference is established, the contrary statements had no discernable impact on the evaluative tally. This we see as evidence of the primacy of affect and the ensuing anchoring of evaluations with insufficient adjustment to later information. Additional tests by Cassino (2005) found that the initial evaluative tallies predicted well the ultimate candidate preference ($R^2 = .368$). A simple additive rule, as suggested by Redlawsk (2001; see also Betsch et al., 2001), would correlate as well but would show an effect for contrary information on candidate evaluation at the tail end of the campaign.

Now, surely it is the case that some incontrovertible piece of incongruent evidence, a smoking gun – Nixon and Watergate, Clinton with "that woman" Monica, Senator Edwards fathering a child with his mistress while his wife is in cancer remission, Gingrich delivering divorce papers to his wife recovering from surgery in the hospital – can tip an evaluation.

Redlawsk, Civettini, and Emmerson (2010), for example, found just such a "tipping point" when study participants were confronted with 40 percent of campaign information contrary to their initial candidate evaluations. These reasonable people switched from support to opposition on the basis of this onslaught of contrary information. Their initial impressions held steady at 20 percent incongruent information (as did the evaluations in the Cassino study with 25 percent incongruent information). It appears to take a lot of contrary information to override a first impression, but it can be done (McGraw, 1987).

Apparently, after but two or three evaluations the online tally behaves as a *likeability heuristic* which may if explicitly challenged prompt the citizen to ask "why do I (dis)like him/her/it?" (Isbell and Ottati, 2002). What follows naturally from this "how do I feel?" heuristic are confirmation and disconfirmation biases that conspire to weaken if not override the accuracy goals that characterize appraisal of the first few bits of information *before* an evaluation crystallizes. From this point onward the search, comprehension, and integration of information into a preference is strongly biased in defense of one's attitude.

Telltale evidence of this was captured in a second wave of Cassino's (2005) study when participants were explicitly asked why they liked or disliked the candidate. As did Gazzaniga's split-brain patients, these "normals" from New Jersey almost universally offered up sensible reasons which were overwhelmingly congruent with their affective evaluations, although about a third of the given reasons could not be directly linked or liberally inferred from any of the candidate's actual statements. A major unanticipated effect of asking for reasons in this follow-up assessment was to bolster the participant's candidate evaluation above their originally expressed OL Tally. In other tests looking at the evaluation-to-recall relationship, Lodge, Steenbergen, and Brau (1995) also found memory-based recall effects on evaluation, and here too the correlation was inflated by rationalizations, the misremembering of campaign information in line with one's partisanship. Accordingly, the positive relationship between recall and evaluation is in part a consequence of a biased search and retrieval of memory and the ensuing confirmation and disconfirmation biases characteristic of motivated reasoning.

We believe *JQP*'s affect heuristic is the most basic and immediate of heuristics, entering the decision stream unconsciously before the application of such cognitively-based shortcuts as endorsements, campaign ads, candidate policy statements, or ideological label (though even these seemingly cognitive cues are demonstrably affective in operation). As memory fades, rationalizations come more strongly to the fore. Let's take this one step further (a discussion point we will soon address more fully): if personally important attitudes are the most readily accessible from memory (a well-documented effect), and if summary evaluations reflect the integration of the anticipated cost-and-benefit consequences of one's preferences and choices (a hallmark of rational choice theory), then the OL Tally represents a rough summing up of one's assessments of the positive and negative consequences of past experiences. On the other hand, while most of us would agree that the integration of attitudinally incongruent evidence is normatively desirable, we are not yet convinced that lesser mortals than Ben Franklin are constitutionally able to overcome our well-deserved reputation as *homo-not-so-sapiens*.

Marcus, Newman, and MacKuen's Theory of Affective Intelligence. The Affective Intelligence (AI) model developed by Marcus, Neuman, and MacKuen (2000) is among the most influential theories political scientists have developed to date on the effects of emotion on political judgments, albeit not without its critics (Basinger and Lavine, 2005; Huddy, Feldman, Taber, and Lahav, 2005; Johnston, Lavine, Lodge, and Woodson, 2010; Ladd and Lenz, 2008; 2011; Valentino, Brader, Gregorowicz, Groenendyk, and Hutchings, 2011).

The empirically untested neuropsychological underpinnings of the AI model come from Jeffrey Gray's (1984, 1987) theory of emotion. Within this framework, the limbic system is divided into somewhat independent positive and negative motivational subsystems that respond to reward and punishment and regulate coping strategies. Central to the AI model is the role played by two discrete emotions, enthusiasm and anxiety, in how citizens think about and evaluate political candidates and make their vote choice. The key prediction of the AI model is that anxiety about one's own party candidate *directly* triggers "surveillance" of the political domain, a heightened attention to campaign information that motivates voters to seek out information, which in turn inhibits voters' habitual reliance on such electoral heuristics as partisanship. In their analyses of the 1980, 1984, and 1988 NES election data, Marcus, Newman, and MacKuen do find that attention to the campaign, political learning, and a weakened reliance on partisanship are related to respondents' self-reported anxiety, while self-reported enthusiasm correlates with greater reliance on such heuristics as partisan identification.

These data certainly are consistent with the AI causal story, as well as with dissonance theory, the ELM, and *JQP*, in proposing that challenges to beliefs and attitudes promote in-depth search, but we see the process differently: affective incongruency between encountered information and one's preexisting evaluation of *either* candidate, *either* party, or *any* salient issue spontaneously motivates a search, both internal and external, for information. In *JQP*, a challenge to any preexisting political evaluation or attitude automatically evokes an affectively negative reaction, which if strong enough will promote the search and seizure of information in defense of one's prior attitude. Affectively congruent information, by contrast, will be accepted and integrated effortlessly into an updated evaluative tally. This is the thrust of the seven postulates guiding *JQP* and the basic finding of our motivated reasoning and attitude priming experiments: the evaluation of social objects – be they political candidates, groups, issues, or abstract ideas – facilitates the fishing and netting of like-valenced information and inhibits the selection and processing of incongruent information.

Specific to the measurement of discrete emotions, there is clear evidence that a simple, good-bad, approach-avoid response enters the decision stream *before* any conscious appraisal of the situation could define and label the emotion as anger, fear, anxiety, hope, or enthusiasm (Russell, 2003). This temporal primacy of affect is critical in understanding the causal processes

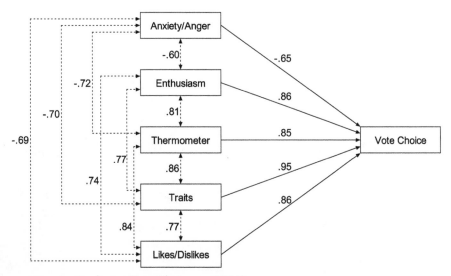

FIGURE 9.2. Predicting Vote Choice on NES Data

behind political behavior, because it orients all subsequent processing and response, including the appraisal of feelings and the labeling of an emotion. We believe this is the reason social scientists have found it so difficult to discriminate specific, like-valenced emotional responses one from another: self-reports of within-valenced emotions routinely correlate in the .60 to .80 range. *Once valence is controlled for there is precious little remaining variance to be explained by discrete emotion labels.* This makes perfect sense from our theoretical perspective, but poses a serious problem for AI where causation is theorized to occur late in the processing stream.

Consider, for example, some simple analyses on NES data (using the cumulative data file for presidential years 1984–2004 (N = 4,733, which excludes participants with missing data). We ran a probit model predicting presidential vote choice from comparative measures of simple valence affect toward the major candidates (where thermometer ratings are our proxy for an OL Tally), anxiety/anger, enthusiasm, trait attributions, and likes/dislikes. Before we proceed, it is worth noting that, like Marcus and colleagues, we combine the two negative emotion words and the two positive emotion words because they simply are not independent in the data, which itself suggests that simple good-bad valence is very powerful in determining subsequent emotional responses.

Figure 9.2 shows two different types of information about these variables. On the left, indicated by dotted lines, are correlations among the independent variables. These correlations are consistently strong, suggesting an underlying pattern of interconnections that we believe supports our theoretical expectation that valence affect occurs early and guides the *subsequent* appraisal of emotions, attribution of traits, and generation of considerations. On the right,

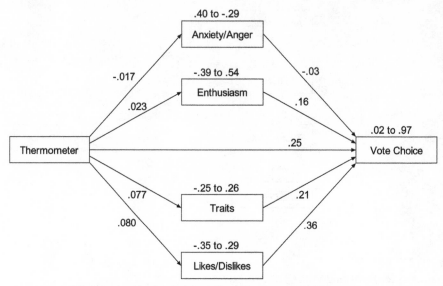

FIGURE 9.3. Multivariate Path Model of Vote Choice on NES Data

shown with solid lines, are the changes in predicted probabilities of voting Republican that emerge from five separate probit models, one for each independent variable, not controlling for any of the other variables. Changes in predicted probabilities are reported for a movement from the twenty-fifth to the seventy-fifth percentile of the given independent variable (i.e., from the Democratic end to the Republican end of the scale). While each of these independent variables, taken alone, is significantly related to vote choice, the effect is larger for simple affect (thermometer ratings), trait attributions, and likes/dislikes. Moving from −40 (i.e., the Democrat rating is forty points warmer than the Republican rating) to +40 (Republican forty points warmer than Democrat) on the comparative thermometer rating, for example, moves respondents from a very likely Democratic vote to a very likely Republican one. By contrast, moving the same percentile distance on the anxiety/anger scale makes respondents just 65 percent more likely to vote Democratic.

Arguably, trait attributions and retrieval of likes and dislikes are forms of what we have called affect contagion (retrieval of considerations driven by prior affect toward the candidates), which we would argue occurs earlier in the processing stream than the more deliberative appraisals of emotion, so from our perspective this result is not at all surprising. But the analysis in Figure 9.2 neither controls for multiple independent variables, nor considers theoretical sequence in the production of a vote choice. We need to model these sequenced, perhaps cascading processes.

To examine this hypothesized sequence, we ran a path analysis on the same data (Figure 9.3). Since vote choice is binary while the predictors and mediators are continuous (treating the five-point emotion variables as continuous), this analysis combines OLS and probit regression. At the first stage, represented by the arrows from thermometer ratings to the intermediate variables, the OLS path coefficients report the relationship between thermometer ratings and anxiety/anger, enthusiasm, trait attributions, and likes/dislikes, all of which are significant at the .001 level (no surprise given the just reported correlations). At the second stage, represented by the arrows to vote choice, we report the change in predicted probability of voting Republican from a probit analysis of the relationships between thermometer and the intermediate variables on the one hand and vote choice. These changes in predicted probability are computed for each variable holding all other variables at their means when thermometer is varied from the twenty-fifth to seventy-fifth percentiles. To aid interpretation, we also report the change in predicted values for each intermediate variable (above each variable label), rescaled to [-1, 1], and the total direct and indirect change in the predicted probability of voting Republican, as thermometer varies from the twenty-fifth to seventy-fifth percentiles.

In Figure 9.3, we can see that when comparative thermometer ratings move from −40 to 40 (warm toward the Democrat to warm toward the Republican), anxiety/anger shifts from the Republican candidate to the Democrat, and this change from .40 to −.29 on the comparative anxiety/anger measure (on a −1 to 1 scale) leads to a slight decline in the predicted probability of voting Republican (−.03 change, holding all other predictors at their means). The same change in feelings from Democratic warmth to Republican warmth (−40 to 40) generates a more positive balance of likes/dislikes for the Republican as compared to the Democrat (−.35 to .29 on the comparative index, rescaled to range from −1 to 1), and this shift in the balance of considerations leads to a large increase in the probability of voting Republican (.36 change, holding other predictors at their means).

We would like to highlight three findings from this analysis. First, the total effect on the probability of voting Republican of moving from the twenty-fifth to the seventy-fifth percentile on the thermometer ratings, including the direct effect of thermometer on vote choice (.25) and all indirect effects through the four intermediate variables, is enormous. Respondents move from almost certain Democratic voters (.02) to almost certain Republican voters (.97) with this shift in affect. Second, the variables we theorized to be intermediate in the causal cascade from early affect to final vote choice – negative emotions, positive emotions, trait attributions, and cognitive considerations – are all significantly driven by simple affect, as measured by the comparative thermometer ratings. Finally, the share of the overall shift in Republican vote propensity that can be explained by discrete emotions is very small, suggesting again that discrete emotions are likely to be late appraisals (or rationalizations) of earlier valence feelings.

There is a similar distinction between primary and secondary appraisals in the psychology literature on emotions (see Forgas, 2003, for instance). Primary appraisals are preconscious, evoked automatically (JUMP before you know if it is a snake or a stick), whereas secondary appraisals are conscious, occurring some moments later. Primary appraisals promote highly intercorrelated secondary appraisals that help explain the variance not accounted for by the automatic primary response. However, in most data sets once you control for valence there is little unexplained variance left over.

Support for this causal sequence was found in the studies of motivated skepticism (Chapters 5, 6, and 7), where participants who were confronted with attitudinally inconsistent information spent significantly more time processing and counterarguing the incongruent information. In contrast to the Affective Intelligence model (but more in line with Ladd and Lenz, 2008 and Basinger and Lavine, 2005), in *JQP* anxiety is *not* a direct causal factor promoting in-depth processing or changes in the judgmental criteria used to evaluate leaders, parties, or issues, but at best anxiety is a relatively weak mediating factor. A la William James (1890), the expressed emotion, here anxiety, is a *post-hoc appraisal* spawned by the discordant evaluation. If as we see it anxiety is not causal but is a mediator, then in theory we could (as depicted in Figure 9.3) substitute any negative evaluation of either candidate or either party, or any issue and get the same AI effects (see Ladd and Lenz, 2008).

From *JQP*'s perspective the emotional response (be it the labeling of one's feeling as anxiety or anger, hope, or enthusiasm) is a post-hoc rationalization triggered by spontaneously activated online evaluations. Such post-hoc appraisals are shown routinely in the NES open-ended like-dislike questions about candidate evaluations (Rahn, Aldrich, and Borgida, 1994; Lodge, Steenbergen, and Brau, 1995) and perceptions of the economy (Bartels, 2002; Kinder and Kiewiet, 1979; Sears and Lau, 1983). From our perspective the online tally (as may be captured by the thermometer response in survey research) is "a neurophysiological barometer of the individual's relation to an event at a given point in time, and self-reported affect is the barometer reading" (Barrett, 2006: 48).

Here again, as in our critique of Zaller and Redlawsk, we are essentially reordering the time course of processes and reversing the causal direction posited by AI theory. In *JQP* any negative sentiment may evoke anxiety, be it one's own party taking an antithetical position, or the opposing party or candidate echoing your preference. Leading scholars of emotion (Forgas, 1995; 2000; Lazarus, 1995; Johnson-Laird and Oatley, 1989; Scherer, Schoor, and Johnstone, 2001; Scherer, 2004) see the causal chain similarly in arguing that emotions are elicited by, and follow upon, the evaluations of objects, here parties, candidates, issues, or campaign events.

Emotions are always about something; one cannot experience fear without being aware of the gun, be angry without seeing the opponent's sneer, or not be depressed on seeing the pictures of starving children. Once triggered by this immediate affective response, appraisal of the cause and potential consequences of the event produces the emotion. *If* experienced viscerally, the secondary, subjective report of an emotional experience labels one's affective response and motivates a search for clarity (Lerner and Keltner, 2000). You may feel aroused but the emotion itself requires a reason for the feeling. The actual label given the somatic ("gut") experience is context dependent, culturally based, and we believe strongly influenced by folkloric explanations for how people respond in such situations (Robinson and Clore, 2000).

Even more problematic in the study of emotions are attempts to differentiate the effects of specific emotions, say anger from anxiety, especially in survey research where we have no direct measure of the precipitating event or the emotional experience itself and routinely rely on retrospective assessments. But the problem is challenging in experimental settings as well, where our manipulations of emotions are typically very weak – inducing sadness, for example, by having participants listen to a recording of the second movement of Schubert's *Death of a Maiden* or manipulating anxiety by informing respondents that a hypothetical candidate takes an issue position at odds with their own. At best such manipulations promote tepid, as-if emotional responses that are indistinguishable from simple valence affect.

Ted Brader's (2006) central experiment in *Campaigning for Hearts and Minds* provides a stronger test of the effect of emotion on the processing of political information than can be had from a cross-sectional or even a panel survey. In a between-subjects design, Brader embedded an election campaign ad from a real, previously broadcast local news show. The newscast and product advertising remained the same for all participants, but the campaign ad was manipulated in the following ways. Two ads, designed to evoke positive emotions (e.g., enthusiasm, hope, confidence), used a verbal script about improving neighborhoods and protecting children; two ads, designed to evoke negative emotions (e.g., fear, anxiety, worry), followed a different verbal script about threats to neighborhoods and children. One ad in each pair was accompanied by "evocative" images and music, while the other was served on white-bread imagery with no music, and it was this bland versus spicy within-valence comparison that Brader focused on. To maximize external validity, Brader's experiment was conducted on potential Massachusetts voters during the 1998 gubernatorial primary race using two known Democratic candidates.

Brader finds, as predicted by AI theory, that those who saw menacing images of crime scenes, a woman being assaulted, handguns, and crack pipes, all accompanied by discordant music, were more attentive to information in the news broadcast and incorporated more information from the campaign ad into their vote preferences than those exposed to tepid images and no music, while heightened "enthusiasm," triggered by hopeful images of children and schools and "sentimental" symphonic music, promoted greater reliance on prior attitudes than in the bland positive condition. In short, the major finding is that "Fear Ads Unsettle Voting Choices, Enthusiasm Ads Stabilize Voting Choices and Increase Certainty" (Brader, 2006: 120). We do not challenge this finding, but rather Brader's interpretation of these results as evidence of the failure of the endogenous affect hypothesis, which you recall posits a strong influence of prior attitudes on the search and seizure of information and a *direct* effect of priors on evaluations. We see reasons to be cautious here as Brader's experiments are not well designed to capture the influence of prior affect.

The election used as the test bed in Brader's study was an "impressively lackluster" two-candidate Democratic primary, so we think it unlikely that many experimental participants – 38 percent Democrats, 13 percent Republicans, and 49 percent "unenrolled" in a party – were motivated enough to form a candidate preference worth defending before viewing the candidate ads as part of this study. Indeed, as reported by Brader, participants held lukewarm positive feelings toward both candidates (means of 55 and 54 on a 100-point scale) prior to the experimental manipulations. There were very slight changes in the direction of the scale neutral point across all but one experimental group after viewing the campaign ads, which Brader interprets as a refutation of affect transfer. But both endogenous affect and our hot cognition postulate *require* an affective prior, the stronger the better. Given that the ads are for two Democratic candidates – thereby denying participants a valuable affective cue that could create an evaluative tally – why would the Republicans and Independents give a hoot, or for that matter even Democrats in this low impact newscast? This interpretation is also supported by the finding that participants provided just 1.2 thoughts on average in a free thought-listing task about the ads, far fewer than subjects in our studies routinely report in more engaging tasks. In short, Brader's participants simply had little prior affect that might influence their processing of the campaign ads, and so the experiment does not allow a reasonable test of the hot cognition hypothesis or a strong comparative test of the sequence of processes proposed by *JQP* and AI.

To the extent that most participants had any priors at all, they were mildly positive toward both Democrats in the study, so it is hardly surprising that the minor changes from these "predispositions" observed in Brader's experiment came for those who saw emotive negative ads. For most participants, positive ads would be in line with their weakly positive priors and so maintenance of these weak attitudes should be expected. Negative ads, however, would have some potential to trigger deeper processing and greater influence of campaign information because they challenge the weak positive priors of most participants. Both of these predictions follow from our theory as comfortably as from AI theory. Moreover, Brader did not measure affect or emotions as participants viewed the ads but rather at the end of the experiment, *after* the attitudinal and behavioral dependent variables were collected. Thus, we do not have direct measures of the mediating emotional responses which are theorized to have caused the attitudes and behavior.

In sum, we suspect that Brader's basic finding that fear cues promote more weight given to the message than to prior preferences follows directly from innocuous candidate statements and weak predispositions. From this perspective, the only factors capable of eliciting a bona fide response were the imagery and sound tracks. We suspect that Brader obtained an indirect effect for enthusiasm and fear, but no direct effect of prior evaluations, because these were the only engaging elements in an otherwise affect-free experimental setting. Recall that when we delivered affectively negative primes or exposed participants to "hot" candidates – Hilary, Giuliani – or policies they cared about – immigration, affirmative action, energy conservation – or challenged their initial attitudes with affectively incongruent primes, our participants did much the same as Brader's: they attended more to the attitudinally contrary information, recalled more information about the dissimilar candidates and issues, and subsequently revised their evaluations.

Leaving aside what we see as serious measurement problems and design flaws, the basic AI prediction – held in common with dissonance theory, the ELM, and *JQP* – that challenges the notion that beliefs and attitudes promote in-depth processing, finds support in recent experiments using different samples, different participants, different measures, and different research designs (Huddy, et al., 2005; MacKuen et al., 2010; Valentino, et al., 2008). Our major theoretical objection to the AI perspective is the assumption that anxiety-induced search will lead to a fair and more balanced evaluation of information. Across multiple experiments we find no evidence of an even-handed integration of new-found information into evaluations, finding instead affect-driven systematic confirmation and disconfirmation biases in judgment leading to attitude polarization.

JQP and the Rationality of the American Voter

Throughout this book we have called attention to the problems we bounded rationalists face in following Franklin's Rule or more problematic still trying to work our way through Bayes' Theorem. Looking across the experimental evidence, what we find is biased processing at every stage of the evaluative process, with the strength of associative priming effects far exceeding our expectations and truth be told far beyond our comfort zone. Even when we ask participants to stop and think, to be even handed in their appraisal of evidence and arguments, we find precious little evidence that they can overcome their prior attitudes or override the effects of incidental primes. Maybe had we explicitly presented more forceful counterarguments or offered monetary incentives we would see more objective appraisals or better evidence-based evaluative updating, but we are not optimistic about the effectiveness of such incentives.

We believe the chief reason we find bias everywhere is because it is rooted in the very architecture of memory, specifically (as depicted in Figure 2.1) in the associative nature of long-term memory. The associative structures and processes of memory are *hard wired* into the very architecture of the brain, as is the mechanism of spreading activation, which "moves" associations in LTM into consciousness. It is the relational nature of human memory that promotes coherent thinking and behavior. This "implicit-association effect is a product of both nature and nurture. Nature, because no matter what we learn, it is stored as a web of associations. Nurture, because the specific associations we learn are a product of our environment, culture, and education" (Buonomano, 2011: 41), and much of the storage, retrieval, and construction of responses occurs outside conscious awareness. People of course do learn new concepts and associations and can override their habitual ways of thinking and behaving, but this is unlikely unless people become aware of a *consequential* flaw in their reasoning and are motivated to counter its influence on perceptions and evaluations (Devine, 1989; Kahneman, 2011; Mendelberg, 2001).

But when the sources of bias are unnoticed or unappreciated, there may be no conscious appraisal of the event and hence no dissonance to motivate a correction. We see no easy way to fully overcome this vulnerability, other than by one or another form of classical or operant conditioning where repeated exposure to contrary messages establishes countervailing considerations and repeated conjoining of new associations creates new beliefs and attitudes. And this may not be a practical solution since most of us live in self-imposed echo chambers, which reverberate with attitudinally congruent beliefs and attitudinally reinforcing messages.

This focus on bias is a common theme throughout social and political psychology, and hundreds of *cognitive strategies* have been proposed to get people to be more critically responsive to the evidence (Cialdini, Petty, and Cacioppo, 1981; Chaiken, Liberman, and Eagly, 1989; Wilson, 2011). The dominant theory of attitude change today is the Elaboration Likelihood Model (ELM) developed by Petty and Cacioppo (1981; 1986), which has been tested many times across multiple domains (Petty, Fazio, and Briñol, 2009). A key premise of the ELM and earlier cognitive response models (Eagly and Chaiken, 1993; McGuire, 1966) is that attitude change is a function of the thoughts that come to mind when thinking consciously about the message, with persuasion likely when prochange considerations trump the cons.

Central to the ELM is an "elaboration continuum" which ranges from low to high, from superficial to in-depth thinking about an issue. When considering facts, figures, or arguments, people can take a *peripheral route* which does not involve much cognitive effort, with choices made on but a cursory look-see at the evidence and evaluations based on source cues, the attractiveness of the messenger, or some other readily available heuristic. But, if one is motivated and has the opportunity to scrutinize the evidence, people can follow a *central route* in which they appraise the evidence more closely so as to determine its merits. If on taking the central route the thoughts generated by elaboration are favorable the evidence will likely be accepted, and the individual persuaded. So, any persuasion factor, be it source, message, recipient, or context, can influence attitude change, and this influence will depend on the route taken, with the same factor sometimes acting as a simple heuristic and other times promoting more careful consideration. Research on the ELM routinely finds that in taking the central route people are likely to change their attitudes in response to strong, credible arguments on issues they care about, while the peripheral course leads to susceptibility to weak arguments and superficial cues.

Many people, academics in particular, place great faith in the central route and feel very comfortable recommending it to others. We are less sure. Note, in particular, that both the ELM and *JQP* hold that the thoughts that come to mind, whether due to a superficial cue or careful reasoning, determine the attitudinal response. But the models differ in the supposed process. We see spontaneous affective responses, sometimes due to prior attitudes and sometimes driven by irrelevant cues, systematically biasing the mix of thoughts that enter the decision stream. The ELM, being at heart a metacognitive (thoughts about thoughts) response model (Petty and Briñol, 2010), sees evaluations as more strongly biased by "preexisting pro and con ideas" than by positive and negative feelings. The ELM is driven by belief biases; *JQP* is driven by affective biases.

Numerous studies show that by *explicitly* calling attention to contrary evidence (Meliema and Bassili, 1995; Sniderman, Brody, and Tetlock, 1991) or by alerting people to potential biases in their thought processes (Strathman, et al., 1994), people may be made more responsive to credible sources and plausible evidence. However, even under these ideal central-route conditions, such direct intervention strategies oftentimes go awry in provoking an ironic boomerang effect, in which people overcorrect, giving the focal information more weight than it deserves (Denzler, Foerster, Liberman, and Rozenman, 2010; Shelton, Richeson, Salvatore, and Trawalter, 2009; Wegner, Ansfield, and Pilloff, 1998).

How often or how much such experimenter-induced dissonance would influence the attitudes of ordinary citizens, who appear to be highly tolerant if not oblivious to simultaneously held discrepant beliefs, incompatible attitudes, and discordant behavior, is uncertain. Be that as it may, note that in our studies we promoted central-route processing by choosing issues which our participants thought important, motivated them to think seriously about the arguments, encouraged them to be evenhanded, and in some studies upped the ante by informing them that they would have to publically defend their attitudes. These experimental manipulations did not override the prior attitude or priming effects that sparked confirmation, disconfirmation, and selective exposure biases and attitude perseverance as opposed to responsiveness to the evidence and persuasion.

Based on our own and others' experimental work, we have little confidence in such cognitively mediated strategies for changing strong attitudes and habits. Admittedly, we have not explored ways to correct the errors our participants make, in part because we have become increasingly pessimistic about the ability of citizens to override their biases when defending a strong prior attitude. Open-mindedness is possible, but it is not our natural inclination.

But what about relying on gut feelings? Should we, as George W. Bush claimed, be confident in his ability to look Vladimir Putin in the eye and see a trustworthy soul? Or, should we put our faith in Carl Sagan, a more skeptical observer:

I'm often asked the question, 'Do you think there is extraterrestrial intelligence?' I give the standard arguments – there are lots of places out there, and use the term *billions*, and so on. And then I say it would be astonishing to me if there weren't extraterrestrial intelligence, but of course there is no compelling evidence for it. And then I'm asked, 'Yeah, but what do you really think?' I say, 'I just told you what I really think' 'Yeah, but what's your gut feeling?' But I try not to think with my gut. Really, it's okay to reserve judgment until the evidence is in. (Sagan, *The Burden of Skepticism*, 1987)

From our perspective the key word here is "try."

The psychological battle between intellect and intuition was played out throughout the *Star Trek* series, where in its original incarnation the ultra-rational Mr. Spock and the hyperemotional Dr. McCoy served as foils, with Captain Kirk the near perfect synthesis of "intellect is driven by intuition, intuition is directed by intellect." Michael Shermer (2002), the editor of *Skeptic Magazine*, recounts the October 6, 1966 episode in which the transporter beaming Captain Kirk back to the space ship malfunctions and splits Captain Kirk into two beings, one like Spock, the cool epitome of emotion-free rationality, the other like the excitable McCoy, impulsive and irrational. Kirk is paralyzed by indecision, bemoaning the McCoy within him: "I can't survive without him. I don't want to take him back. He's like an animal – thoughtless, a brutal animal. And yet it is me!" Admittedly, this is a rather extreme case of hot cognition!

Where to draw the boundary between rational skepticism and irrational bias is a critical normative question, but one that our research and perhaps empirical research in general may not be able to address. We can demonstrate how, when, and to some extent why people's decision processes go awry, but we as well as others have little success in correcting for errors. Thinking systematically about the pros and cons is not a panacea. When can relying on one's OL Tally (intuition/gut response) be reasonable, if not rational? When should we follow the adage of high-stakes professional poker players – "think long, think wrong"?

An implication of *JQP*, empirically supported in Chapter 7, is that relying on one's OL Tally, rather than ruminating on the pros and cons, appears to work best when the decision maker confronts a complex, multidimensional choice. When the decision is simple people can work through the pros and cons reasonably well. But when the number of alternatives and their implications exceed two to three integrations, thinking hard and long before choosing appears to bring less important considerations into the mix and consequently muddles the choice (Gigerenzer, 2007). That such decisions need not be as monumental as Darwin's choice of Emma is captured in an experiment by Wilson and his colleagues (1993) in which they offered undergraduate women a poster for their dorm room. One group simply picked their favorite from a set of five, while the second group was asked to give reasons for liking or disliking each poster before selecting her favorite. Four weeks later the women were asked how much they enjoyed their poster. Here and in similar experiments contrasting snap judgments to deliberate ones on postchoice satisfaction (Dijksterhuis, 2004), thinking carefully about the reasons for one's preferences promotes *less* satisfaction than making a gut choice. In this case, 75 percent of those who gave reasons regretted their decision, while none of those who chose "unthinkingly" suffered buyer's remorse.

In a related study (Wilson and Schooler, 1991), this time looking at the tastiness of strawberry jams, those asked to simply taste and then state a preference produced a better correlation (.55) with food experts from *Consumer Reports* than did the group asked to taste and evaluate the jams on such dimensions as sweetness, texture, fruitiness, and spreadability before making their choice. Judgments become even worse when people are asked for the important attributes they like in jams before tasting. Respondents gave perfectly good reasons for their preferences when asked to do so, and yet these reasons were clearly not the things that actually made them happy. "Introspection," say Wilson and colleagues " . . . can change an optimal weighting scheme into a suboptimal one. When people analyze reasons, they seem to focus on those attributes of the attitude object that seem like plausible causes of their evaluations but were not weighted heavily before" (1993: 332).

Apparently, thinking of reasons brings to mind a host of extraneous factors that overwhelm the spontaneous evaluative response and bring into the calculus those factors that are most easily verbalized. Searching for reasons to (dis)like something brings secondary considerations to mind: an easily spreadable jam seems like a good thing and gets a high rating but doesn't contribute much to one's satisfaction. Intuition is successful because implicit preferences work best when simply acted upon rather than scrutinized. Socrates' famous dictum, "the unexamined life is not worth living," clearly doesn't apply to taste in posters or jams or the evaluation of political candidates and issues, or we suspect in mate selection. In many such complex decision tasks, gut feelings steer behavior along well-trodden associative pathways outside of conscious awareness. "Fast and frugal" action appears to suppress marginal considerations and can better assess preferences (Gigerenzer and Goldstein, 1996; Lehrer, 2009).

Where, when, how, if at all, would "first thought, best thought" be rational? Despite its long history and links to such concepts as intelligence, logic, problem solving, probability theory, and a host of normative precepts, few ideas are as difficult to nail down as rationality. So, if by rational we would be content in following Franklin's Rule, then lesser beings than Ben are rarely found to be rational decision makers. The normative question, it seems, turns on the source of our affect-driven likeability heuristic and whether the processing of new information and the updating of beliefs and attitudes can be evaluated independently of one's priors. Relying on one's OL Tally *would* prove a better strategy if it were the case (as of yet unproven to our satisfaction) that the OL

Tally is a more faithful representation of one's accrued approach-avoidance experiences than is reliance on the recall of pros and cons. If the summary evaluation is an accretion of one's past experiences, then relying on this running tally makes good sense; it has after all worked satisfactorily in the past.

But, there is a subtle and yet very troubling problem here – affect contagion triggered by hot cognition. Built into *JQP* and we suppose hard wired in each and every one of us – attitudes are weakened or strengthened on each evaluation of an object, thoughtlessly when new information is affectively congruent, actively counterargued or grudgingly accepted when incongruent. Equally if not more problematic, those of us living in an echo chamber will rarely confront contrary facts and perspectives. Basing an evaluation on one's OL Tally, whether responsive to past experience or not, feels like common sense and is easy to act on. Common sense, however, is a fallible guide (Watts, 2011), and strong feelings and ignorance are not orthogonal because the former often motivates the latter.

So, how and when will reliance on affectively triggered snap judgments be rational? From one point of view (with which are sympathetic), it can be argued that the prior-attitude effect and resulting disconfirmation biases are reasonable responses to attitude-relevant information. If it is true that OL Tallies reflect a cumulative summing up of one's prior positive and negative evaluations, then isn't it appropriate to weigh heavily one's attitudinal experiences? Think of the OL Tally metaphorically as a possession to be protected (Abelson and Prentice, 1989). This belief, this feeling, is mine! For all but ill-gotten possessions we paid a purchase price in terms of time and cognitive resources spent forming and updating our impressions. From this perspective, many political attitudes are worthy of such defense in their own right. To the extent one's attitude reflects a tallying up of the consequences of prior evaluations, it could well be more trustworthy than new contrary information, which is why Mother Nature made online processing so fast and frugal and we believe the default mode of evaluative processing. If, as is so often the case in the political realm, new information is "iffy" and could well reflect the strategic behavior of political opponents, why put much stock in contrary information? Could it be then that Republican and Democratic partisans, motivated reasoners to the core, are behaving rationally?

From another perspective (with which in true social scientist fashion we are also sympathetic), all rational updating decision strategies require the evaluation of new evidence to be at least somewhat independent of one's priors (Bartels, 2002; Evans and Over, 1996; Green and Shapiro, 1994; but see Gerber and Green, 1998). Ideally, evidence must be evaluated even-handedly *before* being integrated into a judgment or choice. In the extreme case, for which we found multiple instances, if one distorts new information so that it bolsters priors, the decision maker is not being rationally responsive to the environment (Nie et al., 2010; Stroud, 2008). Worse yet, manipulating the information stream to avoid any threat to one's priors by selective exposure to congruent information sources defrocks the good Reverend Bayes and all rational-man theories (McGrayne, 2011; Navarro et al., 2008).

For many citizens, perhaps the bias may be less extreme, but we all know ideologues, die-hard partisans, and bigots in both high and low places that fit both of these descriptions. Luker (1984), for example, found that attitudes among abortion activists are so linked to their beliefs and feelings about sexuality, gender, religion, and family, that they are incapable of entertaining points of view that challenge their own. Sears and Whitney (1973) found similar stubborn adherence to prior attitudes among those watching a political debate.

Of course, for the 66 percent of Americans who acknowledge the staying power of *homo sapiens* over millions of years of evolutionary time, there *must* be real-life situations where people can evaluate the evidence dispassionately enough to override the momentary thrust of prior feelings on snap judgments, reflection, and forethought. One contender in the political realm is those involved individuals who are both knowledgeable and capable enough to conjure up both good and bad aspects of a candidate, group, or issue. While no doubt true that many citizens have good reasons to be politically ambivalent, we repeatedly found that subtle, unnoticed cues systematically skewed the sampling of pros and cons for sophisticates in line with their priors, an effect bolstered we suspect by their uneasy feeling of dissonance.

Obviously, pushing either side of the rationality argument too strongly is a fool's gambit. So how do we reconcile these positions? Truth be told, not all that well! Skepticism is valuable and well-grounded attitudes should have inertia. But skepticism becomes bias when it encourages one to avoid discomforting news via the confirmation bias and selective exposure. It is also the case that the biases promoting attitude polarization are difficult to square with a normatively acceptable model (especially because in our experiments the supporters and opponents diverged after processing *exactly* the same information). Moreover, up to some tipping point for persuasion (Cassino, 2005; Redlawsk, Civettini, and Emmerson, 2010), *JQP* predicts and we found evidence of motivated reasoning even from counterattitudinal streams of information (see too Rahn, Aldrich, and Borgida, 1994), at least among the most sophisticated. True enough, if one is made aware of a biased message it is possible, albeit difficult (Devine, 1989; Mendelberg, 2001), to make a correction, but when the influential event comes and goes unnoticed or its influence is unappreciated, there is little dissonance generated that can fuel a reappraisal.

The most worrisome implication of our research program, we believe, is the ubiquity of consciously *un*noticed and *un*appreciated priming events in the media. Our conservative estimate is that implicit cues are embedded in virtually all political communications and cannot be purged from text or image because they are part and parcel of the message. Affective primes, whether incidental or deliberately embedded in political messages, produce strong affective contagion. The most effective political symbols, slogans, and events, however, will be those that trigger *both* feelings and concepts in mutually reinforcing ways, and our theory of motivated political reasoning provides an explanation for why this is so (recall Figure 1.4). A politician announcing her candidacy with the Statue of Liberty as the backdrop will gain the advantage of positive feelings through direct affect transfer and the indirect influence of affective contagion, as well as the reinforcing conceptual activation of "freedom," "liberty," "egalitarianism," and other semantic associates of Lady Liberty. Of course, we would anticipate that citizens from the opposing party would view the event as "transparently strategic" and experience the countervailing force of a negative prior attitude effect and motivated bias in the construction of considerations.

On the rationality question, we are not sure whether or not to join the doomsayers union. For what it is worth, we are not of the romantic, postmodernist school that sees intuition as somehow superior to careful thought. Nor are we in the classics camp that sees feelings as inherently dangerous. Rather, we see affect as a necessary, inescapable aspect of all deliberations, promoting bias, yes, yet vital to good decision making (Lerner and Loewenstein, 2004; Marcus, 2002; McDermott, 2004; Thagard, 2000).

Where we stand – uneasily on the razor's edge where the *Katha Upanishad* tells us the path to "salvation is hard" – is that *JQP* need not be and is not conceived by us as implacably hostile to normative, rational choice models in so far as we share a common assumption: rational decision makers aim to experience positive outcomes and avoid negative ones. This being the case, the summing up of our positive and negative experiences in an evaluative OL Tally drives both our model and rational choice models. In *JQP* the linking of affect to appraisal is a spontaneous process integrating one's good versus bad past evaluations and automatically linking positive or negative feelings to the options at hand. Where we differ is in spelling out how, when, and why feelings are linked to evidence in suboptimal ways and routinely create overly confident preferences.

We end this quest for a meaningful answer to an impossible question, as did T.S. Eliot in *The Hollow Men*, "not with a bang but a whimper." Maybe *JQP* is as rational as we *homo sapiens* can be.

Bibliography

Abelson, Robert. 1963. "Computer Simulation of 'Hot' Cognition." In *Computer Simulation of Personality, Frontier of Psychological Theory*, eds. Silvan Tomkins and Samuel Messick, 277–298, New York: John Wiley and Sons, Inc.

Abelson, Robert, Elliot Aronson, William McGuire, Theodore Newcomb, Milton Rosenberg, and Percy Tannenbaum. 1968. *Theories of Cognitive Consistency: A Sourcebook*. Chicago: Rand McNally.

Abelson, Robert, and Deborah Prentice. 1989. "Beliefs as Possessions: A Functional Perspective." In *Attitude Structure and Function*, eds. Anthony Pratkanis, Steven Breckler, and Anthony Greenwald, 361–381, Hillsdale, NJ: Erlbaum.

Achen, Christopher. 2002. "Parental Socialization and Rational Party Identification." *Political Behavior* 24 (2): 151–170.

Achen, Christopher. 1992. "Social Psychology, Demographic Variables, and Linear Regression: Breaking the Iron Triangle in Voting Research." *Political Behavior* 14 (3): 195–211.

Achen, Christopher, and Larry Bartels. 2006. "It Feels Like We're Thinking: The Rationalizing Voter and Electoral Democracy." Paper presented at the Annual Meeting of the American Political Science Association, Philadelphia, PA, August 31–September 3.

Acker, Felix. 2008. "New Findings on Unconscious Versus Conscious Thought in Decision Making: Additional Empirical Data and Meta-Analysis." *Judgment and Decision-Making* 3 (4): 292–303.

Ailes, Roger, and Jon Kraushar. 1989. *You Are the Message: Getting What You Want by Being Who You Are*. New York: Crown Business.

Albertson, Bethany. 2011. "Religious Appeals and Implicit Attitudes." *Political Psychology* 32 (1): 109–130.

Aldrich, John, John Sullivan, and Eugene Borgida. 1989. "Foreign Affairs and Issue Voting: Do Presidential Candidates 'Waltz Before a Blind Audience'?" *American Political Science Review* 83 (1): 123–142.

Amodio, David, and Patricia Devine. 2006. "Stereotyping and Evaluation in Implicit Race Bias: Evidence for Independent Constructs and Unique Effects on Behavior." *Journal of Personality and Social Psychology* 91 (4): 652–661.

Amodio, David, and Saaid Mendoza. 2010. "Implicit Intergroup Bias: Cognitive, Affective, and Motivational Underpinnings." In *Handbook of Implicit Social Cognition: Measurement, Theory, and Applications*, Bertram Gawronski and Keith Payne, 353–374, New York: Guliford.

Anderson, John. 1983. *The Architecture of Cognition*. Cambridge, MA: Harvard University Press.

Anderson, John. 1993. *Rules of the Mind*. Hillsdale, NJ: Erlbaum.

Anderson, John, Daniel Bothell, Michael Byrne, Scott Douglass, Christian Lebiere, and Yulin Qin. 2004. "An Integrated Theory of Mind." *Psychological Review* 111 (4): 1036–1060.

Anderson, Norman. 1965. "Averaging Versus Adding as a Stimulus-Combination Rule in Impression Formation." *Journal of Experimental Psychology* 70 (4): 394–400.

Anderson, Norman. 1968. "Likableness Ratings of 555 Personality-Trait Words." *Journal of Personality and Social Psychology*, 9 (3): 272–279.

Anderson, Norman. 1981. *Foundations of Information Integration Theory*. San Diego, CA: Academic Press.

Anderson, Norman, and Stephen Hubert. 1963. "Effects of Concomitant Verbal Recall on Order Effects in Personality Impression Formation." *Journal of Verbal Learning and Verbal Behavior* 2 (5–6): 379–391.

Ansolabehere, Stephen, and Shanto Iyengar. 1995. *Going Negative: How Political Advertisements Shrinks and Polarize the Electorate*. New York: Simon and Schuster.

Ansolabehere, Stephen, and Shanto Iyengar, Adam Simon, and Nicholas Valentino. 1994. "Does Attack Advertising Demobilize Electorate?" *American Political Science Review* 88 (4): 829–838.

Antonakis, John, and Olaf Dalgas. 2009. "Predicting Elections: Child's Play!" *Science* 323 (5918): 1183.

Ariely, Dan. 2008. *Predictably Irrational: The Hidden Forces That Shape Our Decisions*. New York: HarperCollins.

Ariely, Dan, and George Loewenstein. 2006. "The Heat of the Moment: The Effect of Sexual Arousal on Sexual Decision Making." *Journal of Behavioral Decision Making* 19: 87–98.

Aronson, Elliot. 1992. "The Return of the Repressed: Dissonance Theory Makes a Comeback." *Psychological Inquiry* 3 (4): 303–311.

Asch, Solomon. 1946. "Forming Impressions of Personality." *Journal of Abnormal and Social Psychology* 41: 258–290.

Atkinson, Matthew, Ryan Enos, and Seth Hill. 2009. "Candidate Faces and Election Outcomes: Is the Face-Vote Correlation Caused by Candidate Selection?" *Quarterly Journal of Political Science* 4 (3): 229–249.

Babad, Elisha. 1999. "Preferential Treatment in Television Interviewing: Evidence From Nonverbal Behavior." *Political Communication* 16 (3): 337–358.

Babad, Elisha. 2005. "The Psychological Price of Mass Media Bias." *Journal of Experimental Psychology: Applied* 11 (4): 245–255.

Banducci, Susan, Michael Thrasher, Colin Rallings, and Jeffrey Karp. 2003. "Candidate Appearance Cues in Low-Information Elections." Paper presented at the Annual

Conference of the American Political Science Association, Philadelphia, PA, August 28–31.

Bargh, John. 1989. "Conditional Automaticity: Varieties of Automatic Influence in Social Perception and Cognition." In *Unintended Thought*, eds. James Uleman, and John Bargh, 3–51, New York: Guilford.

Bargh, John. 1994. "The Four Horseman of Automaticity: Awareness, Intention, Efficiency, and Control in Social Cognition." In *Handbook of Social Cognition: Basic Processes*, eds. Robert Wyer and Thomas Srull, 1–40, Hillsdale, NY: Erlbaum.

Bargh, John. 1997. "The Automaticity of Everyday Life." In *Advances in Social Cognition*, ed. Robert Wyer, 1–61, Mahwah, NJ: Erlbaum.

Bargh, John. 1999. "The Cognitive Monster: The Case Against Controllability of Automatic Stereotype Effects." In *Dual Process Theories in Social Psychology*, eds. Shelly Chaiken and Yaacov Trope, 361–382, New York: Guilford.

Bargh, John. 2007. *Social Psychology and the Unconscious: The Automaticity of Higher Mental Processes*. Philadelphia, PA: Psychology Press.

Bargh, John, Shelly Chaiken, Rajen Govender, and Felicia Pratto. 1992. "The Generality of the Automatic Attitude Activation Effect." *Journal of Personality and Social Psychology* 62 (6): 893–912.

Bargh, John, Mark Chen, Lara Burrows. 1996. "Automaticity of Social Behavior: Direct Effects of the Trait Construct and Stereotype Activation." *Journal of Personality and Social Psychology* 71 (2): 230–244.

Bargh, John, Tanya L. Chartrand. 1999. "The Unbearable Automaticity of Being." *American Psychologist* 54 (7): 462–479.

Bargh, John, and Tanya Chartrand. 2000. "Studying the Mind in the Middle: A Practical Guide to Priming and Automaticity Research." In *Handbook of Research Methods in Social and Personality Psychology*, eds. Harry Reis and Charles Judd, 253–285, New York: Cambridge University Press.

Bargh, John, Peter Gollwitzer, Annette Lee-Chai, Kimberly Barndollar, and Roman Troetschel. 2001. "The Automated Will: Nonconscious Activation and Pursuit of Behavioral Goals." *Journal of Personality and Social Psychology* 81 (6): 1014–1027.

Baron, Reuben, and David Kenny. 1986. "The Moderator-Mediator Variable Distinction in Social Psychological Research: Conceptual, Strategic, and Statistical Considerations." *Journal of Personality and Social Psychology* 51 (6): 1173–1182.

Barrett, Lisa. 2006. "Are Emotions Natural Categories?" *Perspectives on Psychological Science* 1 (1): 28–58.

Barrett, Lisa. 2006. "Solving the Emotion Paradox: Categorization and the Experience of Emotion." *Perspectives on Psychological Science* 1 (1): 20–46.

Barrett, Lisa, Paula Niedenthal, and Piotr Winkielman. 2005. *Emotion and Consciousness*. New York: Guilford Press.

Barrett, Lisa, and James Russell. 1998. "Independence and Bipolarity in the Structure of Current Affect." *Journal of Personality and Social Psychology* 74 (4): 967–984.

Barsalou, Lawrence. 1992. *Cognitive Psychology: An Overview for Cognitive Scientists*. Hillsdale, NJ: Erlbaum.

Bartels, Larry. 1993. "Messages Received: The Political Impact of Media Exposure." *American Political Science Review* 87 (2): 267–285.

Bartels, Larry. 2000. "Partisanship and Voting Behavior, 1952–1996." *American Journal of Political Science* 44 (1): 35–50.

Bartels, Larry. 2002. "Beyond the Running Tally: Partisan Bias in Political Perceptions." *Political Behavior* 24 (2): 117–150.

Bartlett, Frederic. 1932. *Remembering: A Study in Experimental and Social Psychology.* Cambridge: Cambridge University Press.

Basinger, Scott, and Howard Lavine. 2005. "Ambivalence, Information, and Electoral Choice." *American Political Science Review* 99 (2): 169–184.

Bassili, John. 1989. *On-Line Cognition in Person Perception.* Hillsdale, NJ: Erlbaum.

Bassili, John, and Jean-Paul Roy. 1998. "On the Representation of Strong and Weak Attitudes About Policy in Memory." *Political Psychology* 19 (4): 669–681.

Baumeister, Roy, Mark Muraven, and Dianne Tice. 2000. "Ego Depletion: A Resource Model of Volition, Self-Regulation, and Controlled Processing." *Social Cognition* 18 (2): 130–150.

Baumeister, Roy, and Leonard Newman. 1994. "Self-Regulation of Cognitive Inference and Decision Processes." *Personality and Social Psychology Bulletin* 20 (1): 3–19.

Bechara, Antoine, Antonio Damasio, Hanna Damasio, and Steven Anderson. 1994. "Insensitivity to Future Consequences Following Damage to Human Prefrontal Cortex." *Cognition* 50 (1): 7–15.

Bechara, Antoine, Hanna Damasio, Daniel Tranel, and Antonio Damasio. 1997. "Deciding Advantageously Before Knowing the Advantageous Strategy." *Science* 275 (5304): 1293–1295.

Bechara, Antoine, Antonio Damasio, and Hanna Damasio. 2000. "Emotion, Decision Making and the Orbitofrontal Cortex." *Cerebral Cortex* 10 (3): 295–307.

Bechara, Antoine, Hanna Damasio, Daniel Tranel, and Antonio Damasio. 2005. "The Iowa Gambling Task and the Somatic Marker Hypothesis: Some Questions and Answers." *Trends in Cognitive Sciences* 9 (4): 159–162.

Bem, Darly. 1967. "Self Perception: An Alternative Interpretation of Cognitive Dissonance Phenomena." *Psychological Review* 74 (3): 183–200.

Berelson, Bernard, Paul Lazarsfeld, and William Mcphee. 1954. *Voting: A Study of Opinion Formation in a Presidential Campaign.* Chicago: University of Chicago Press.

Berger, Jonah, Mark Meredith, and Christian Wheeler. 2008. "Contextual Priming: Where People Vote Affects How They Vote." *PNAS* 105 (26): 8846–8848.

Berggren, Niclas, Henrik Jordahl, and Panu Poutvaara. 2010. "The Looks of a Winner: Beauty, and Electoral Success." *Journal of Public Economics* 94 (1–2): 8–15.

Berinsky, Adam, and Donald Kinder. 2006. "Making Sense of Issues through Media Frames: Understanding the Kosovo Crisis." *Journal of Politics* 68 (3): 640–656.

Berridge, Kent, and Julia Winkielman. 2003. "What Is an Unconscious Emotion? The Case for Unconscious 'Liking'." *Cognition and Emotion* 17 (2): 181–211.

Betsch, Tilmann, Henning Plessner, Katja Hoffmann, Robert Gütig, and Christiane Schwieren. 2001. *Different Mechanisms of Information Integration in Implicit and Explicit Attitude Formation.* Research paper, University of Heidelberg.

Betsch, Tilman, Henning Plessner, Christiane Schwieren, and Robert Guetig. 2001. "I Like It but I Don't Know Why: A Value-Account Approach to Implied Attitude Formation." *Personality and Social Psychology Bulletin* 27 (2): 242–253.

Biddle, Jeff, and Daniel Hamermesh. 1998. "Beauty, Productivity, and Discrimination: Lawyers' Looks and Lucre." *Journal of Labor Economics* 16 (1): 172–201.

Bishop, George F. 2004. *The Illusion of Public Opinion: Fact and Artifact in American Public Opinion Polls.* New York: Rowman & Littlefield.

Bishop, Melissa. 2005. "Language Codeswitching and Advertising: The Overlooked Communication Alternative." Paper presented at the American Marketing Association Summer Educator's Conference, San Francisco, July 29–August 1.

Black, Duncan. 1948. "On the Rationale of Group Decision-Making." *Journal of Political Economy* 56 (1): 23–34.

Black, Earl, and Merle Black. 1987. *Politics and Society in the South.* Cambridge, MA: Harvard University Press.

Blair, Irene. 2001. "Implicit Stereotypes and Prejudice." In *Cognitive Social Psychology: On the Tenure and Future of Social Cognition*, ed. Gordon Moskowitz, 359–374, Mahwah, NJ: Erlbaum.

Bobo, Lawrence. 1988. "Attitudes Toward the Black Political Movement: Trends, Meaning, and Effects on Racial Policy Preferences." *Social Psychology Quarterly* 51: 287–302.

Bobo, Lawrence. 2001. "Racial attitudes and Relations at the Close of the Twentieth Century." In *Racial Trends and Their Consequences*, eds. Neil Smelser, William Wilson, and Faith Mitchell, 264–301, Washington, DC: National Academy Press.

Bobo, Lawrence, and James Kluegel. 1993. "Opposition to Race-Targeting: Self-Interest, Stratification Ideology, or Racial Attitudes?" *American Sociological Review* 58: 443–464.

Bodenhausen, Galen. 1993. "Emotions, Arousal, and Stereotypic Judgments: a Heuristic Model of Affect and Stereotyping." In *Affect, Cognition, and Stereotyping: Interactive Processes in Group Perception*, eds. Donald Mackie and David Hamilton, 13–37, San Diego: Academic Press.

Bodenhausen, Gordon, and Andrew Todd. 2010. "Automatic Aspects of Judgment and Decision Making." In *Handbook of Implicit Social Cognition: Measurement, Theory, and Applications*, eds. Bertram Gawronski and Keith Payne, 278–294, New York: Guilford.

Bosson, Jennifer, William Swann, and James Pennebaker. 2000. "Stalking the Perfect Measure of Implicit Self-esteem: The Blind Men and the Elephant Revisited?" *Journal of Personality and Social Psychology* 79 (4): 631–643.

Bower, Gordon. 1981. "Mood and Memory." *American Psychologist* 36 (2): 129–148.

Bower, Gordon, and Joseph Forgas. 2001. "Affective Influences on the Content of Cognition." In *Handbook of Affect and Social Cognition*, ed. Joseph Forgas, 95–120, Hillsdale, NJ: Erlbaum.

Boynton, G. Robert, and Milton Lodge. 1994. "Computational Modeling: A Computational Model of a Survey Respondent." In *Political Judgment: Structure and Process*, eds. Milton Lodge and Kathleen McGraw, 229–248, Ann Arbor: University of Michigan Press.

Brader, Ted. 2005. "Striking a Responsive Chord: How Political Ads Motivate and Persuade Voters by Appealing to Emotions." *American Journal of Political Science* 49 (2): 388–405.

Brader, Ted. 2006. *Campaigning for Hearts and Minds: How Emotional Appeals in Political Ads Work.* Chicago: University of Chicago Press.

Brader, Ted. 2011. "The Political Relevance of Emotions: 'Reassessing' Revisited." *Political Psychology* 32 (2): 337–346.

Brader, Ted, and Nicholas Valentino. 2007. "Identities, Interests, and Emotions: Symbolic Versus Material Wellsprings of Fear, Anger, and Enthusiasm." In *The Affect*

Effect: Dynamics of Emotion in Political Thinking and Behavior, eds. Russell Neuman, George Marcus, Ann Crider, and Michael MacKuen, 180–201, Chicago: University of Chicago Press.

Brader, Ted, Nicholas Valentino, and Elizabeth Suhay. 2008. "What Triggers Public Opposition to Immigration? Anxiety, Group Cues, and Immigration Threat." *American Journal of Political Science* 52 (4): 959–978.

Bradley, Margaret, and Peter Lang. 1999. "Affective Norms for English Words (ANEW): Instruction Manual and Affective Ratings." Technical Report C-1. The Center for Research in Psychophysiology, University of Florida.

Brewer, Marilynn, and Rupert Brown. 1998. "Intergroup Relations." In *The Handbook of Social Psychology*, eds. Daniel Gilbert, Susan Fiske and Gardner Lindzey, 554–594, New York: McGraw-Hill.

Briñol, Pablo, Richard Petty, and Michael McCaslin. 2009. "Changing Attitudes on Implicit Versus Explicit Measures: What is the Difference?" In *Attitudes: Insights from the New Implicit Measures*, eds. Richard Petty, Russell Fazio, and Pablo Briñol. 285–326, New York: Psychology Press.

Browne, Janet. 2002. *Charles Darwin: The Power of Place*. Princeton, NJ: Knopf.

Bullock, John. 2009. "Partisan Bias and the Bayesian Ideal in the Study of Public Opinion." *Journal of Politics* 71 (3): 1109–1124.

Buonomano, Dean. 2011. *How the Brain's Flaws Shape Our Lives*. New York: W.W. Norton & Co.

Burdein, Inna. 2007. "Principled Conservatives or Covert Racists: Disentangling Racism and Ideology through Implicit Measures." Ph.D. Dissertation. *Stony Brook University*.

Burdein, Inna, Milton Lodge, and Charles S. Taber. 2006. "Experiments On the Automaticity of Political Beliefs and Attitudes." *Political Psychology* 27 (3): 359–371.

Burdein, Inna, and Charles Taber. 2004. "What are they really thinking? Implicit Measures of Ideology and Racism." Paper presented at the the Midwest Political Science Association. Chicago, IL, April 15–18.

Bushman, Brad, and Craig Anderson. 1998. "Methodology in the Study of Aggression: Integrating Experimental and Nonexperimental Findings." In *Human Aggression: Theories, Research and Implications for Social Policy*, eds. Russell Geen and Edward Donnerstein, 23–48, San Diego, CA: Academic Press.

Butz, David. 2009. "National Symbols as Agents of Psychological and Social Change." *Political Psychology* 30 (5): 779–804.

Byrne, Donn, Oliver London, and Keith Reeves. 1968. "The Effects of Physical Attractiveness, Sex, and Attitude Similarity on Interpersonal Attraction. " *Journal of Personality* 36 (2): 259–272.

Cacioppo, John, Gary Berntson, Jeff Larsen, Kristen Poehlmann, and Tiffany Ito. 2000. "The Psychophysiology of Emotion." In *The Handbook of Emotion*, eds. Michael Lewis, Jeannette Haviland, and Lisa Barrett, 173–191, New York: Guilford.

Cacioppo, John, and Gary Berntson. 1994. "Relationship between Attitudes and Evaluative Space: A Critical Review, with Emphasis on the Separability of Positive and Negative Substrates." *Psychological Bulletin* 115 (3): 401–423.

Cacioppo, John, and Wendi Gardner. 1999. "Emotion." *Annual Review of Psychology* 50: 191–214.

Cacioppo, John, Wendi Gardner, and Gary Berntson. 1997. "Beyond Bipolar Conceptualizations and Measures: The Case of Attitudes and Evaluative Space." *Personality and Social Psychology Review* 1 (1): 3–25.

Cacioppo, John, Carol Glass, and Thomas Merluzzi. 1979. "Self-Statements and Self-Evaluations: A Cognitive-Response Analysis of Heterosocial Anxiety." *Cognitive Therapy and Research* 3 (3): 249–262.

Callan, Mitchell, Nathaniel Powell, and John Ellard. 2007. "The Consequences of Victim Physical Attractiveness on Reactions to Injustice: The Role of the Observers' Belief In a Just World." *Social Justice Research* 20 (4): 433–456.

Campbell, Donald. 1958. "Common Fate, Similarity, and Other Indices of the Status of Aggregates of Persons as Social Entities." *Behavioural Sciences* 3 (1): 14–25.

Cardinal, Rudolph, John Parkinson, and Jeremy Everitt. 2002. "Emotion and Motivation: The Role of the Amygdala, Ventral Striatum, and Prefrontal Cortex." *Neuroscience and Biobehavioral Reviews* 26 (3): 321–352.

Carlston, Don. 2010. "Models of Implicit and Explicit Mental Representations." In *Handbook of Implicit Social Cognition: Measurement, Theory, and Applications*, eds. Bertram Gawronski and Keith Payne, 38–61, New York: Guilford.

Cassino, Dan. 2005. "Standing Water: The Causes and Consequences of Affective Intransitivity." Ph.D. Dissertation. Stony Brook University.

Cassino, Dan, and Milton Lodge. 2007. "The Primacy of Affect in Political Evaluations." In *The Affect Effect: Dynamics of Emotion in Political Thinking and Behavior*, eds. Russell Neuman, George Marcus, Ann Crider, and Michael MacKuen, 101–123, Chicago: University of Chicago Press.

Cassino, Dan, Charles Taber, and Milton Lodge. 2007. "Information Processing and Public Opinion." *Political Psychology* 48 (2): 205–220.

Chaiken, Shelly, Akiva Liberman, and Alice Eagly. 1989. "Heuristic and Systematic Information Processing within and beyond Persuasion." In *Unintended Thought*, eds. James Uleman and John Bargh, 212–252, New York: Guilford Press.

Chaiken, Shelly and Yaacov Trope, eds. 1999. *Dual Process Theories in Social Psychology*. New York: Guilford Press.

Chaiken S. and Yates S. 1985. "Affective-Cognitive Consistency and Thought-Induced Attitude Polarization." *Journal of Personality and Social Psychology* 49 (6): 1470–1481.

Chartrand, Tanya, and John Bargh. 2002. "Nonconscious Motivations: Their Activation, Operation, and Consequences." In *Self and Motivation: Emerging Psychological Perspectives*, eds. Abraham Tesser, Diederik Stapel, and Joanne Wood, 13–41, Washington, DC: American Psychological Association.

Chen, Mark, and John Bargh. 1999. "Consequences of Automatic Evaluation: Immediate Behavior Predispositions to Approach or Avoid the Stimulus." *Personality and Social Psychology Bulletin* 25 (2): 215–224.

Chen, Serena, and Annette Lee-Chai, and John Bargh. 2001. "Relationship Orientation as a Moderator of the Effects of Social Power." *Journal of Personality and Social Psychology* 80: 173–187.

Cialdini, Robert. 2001. *Influence: Science and Practice*. Boston: Allyn and Bacon.

Cialdini, Robert, Richard Petty, and John Cacioppo. 1981. "Attitude and Attitude Change." *Annual Review of Psychology* 32 (1): 357–404.

Clore, Gerald, Andrew Ortony, and Mark Foss. 1987. "The Psychological Foundations of the Affective Lexicon." *Journal of Personality and Social Psychology* 53 (4): 751–766.

Clore, Gerald, Norbert Schwarz, and Michael Conway. 1994. "Affective Causes and Consequences of Social Information Processing." In *Handbook of Social Cognition*, eds. Robert Wyer and Thomas Srull, 323–417, Hillsdale, NJ: Erlbaum.

Clore, Gerald and Linda Isbell. 2001. "Emotion and Virtue and Vice." In *Political Psychology in Practice*, ed. James Kuklinski. 103–123, New York: Cambridge University Press.

Coats, Susan, Eliot Smith, Heather Claypool, and Michele Banner. 2000. "Overlapping Mental Representations of Self and In-Group: Reaction Time Evidence and its Relationship to Explicit Measures of Group Identification." *Journal of Experimental Social Psychology* 36 (3): 304–315.

Cobb, Michael, and James Kuklinski. 1997. "Changing Minds: Political Arguments and Political Persuasion." *American Journal of Political Science* 41 (1): 88–121.

Collins, Allan, and Elizabeth Loftus. 1975. "A Spreading-Activation Theory of Semantic Processing." *Psychological Review* 82 (6): 407–428.

Collins, Allan, and M. Ross Quillian. 1969. "Retrieval Time from Semantic Memory." *Journal of Verbal Learning and Verbal Behavior* 8 (2): 240–247.

Conover, Pamela. 1988. "The Role of Social Groups in Political Thinking." *British Journal of Political Science* 18 (1): 51–76.

Converse, Philip. 1964. "The Nature of Belief Systems in Mass Publics." In *Ideology and Discontent*, ed. David Apter, 206–261, New York: Free Press.

Cooper, Joel, and Russell Fazio. 1984. "A New Look at Dissonance Theory." *Advances in Experimental Social Psychology* 17: 229–266.

Coser, Lewis. 1956. *The Functions of Social Conflict*. New York: Free Press.

Craemer, Thomas. 2008. "Nonconscious Feelings of Closeness toward African Americans and Support for Pro-Black Policies." *Political Psychology* 29 (3): 407–436.

Crawford, Matthew, Steven Sherman, and David Hamilton. 2002. "Perceived Entitativity, Stereotype Formation, and the Interchangeability of Group Members." *Journal of Personality and Social Psychology* 83 (5): 1076–1094.

Cunningham, William, Kristopher Preacher, and Mahazarin Banaji. 2001. "Implicit Attitude Measures: Consistency, Stability, and Convergent Validity." *Psychological Science* 12 (2): 163–170.

Cunningham, William and Jay Van Bavel. 2009. "Varieties of Emotional Experience: Differences in Object or Computation?" *Emotion Review* 1 (1): 56–57.

Custers, Ruud, and Henk Aarts. 2010. "The Unconscious Will: How the Pursuit of Goals Operates Outside of Conscious Awareness." *Science* 329 (5987): 47–50.

Damasio, Antonio. 1994. *Descartes' Error: Emotion, Reason and the Human Brain*. New York: Putnam.

Damasio, Antonio. 1996. "The Somatic Marker Hypothesis and the Possible Functions of the Prefrontal Cortex." *Proceedings of The Royal Society* 351: 1413–1420.

Damasio, Antonio. 1999. *The Feeling of What Happens: Body and Emotion in the Making of Consciousness*. New York: Harcourt Brace.

Damasio, Antonio. 2002. "How the Brain Creates the Mind," *Scientific American*, 12 (1): 4–9.

Damasio, Antonio. 2010. *Self Comes to Mind: Constructing the Conscious Brain*. New York: Pantheon Books.

Damasio, Antonio, Daniel Tranel, and Hanna Damasio. 1991. "Somatic Markers and the Guidance of Behaviour." In *Frontal lobe function and dysfunction*, eds. Harvey Levin, Howard Eisenberg, and Arthur Benton, 217–228, New York: Oxford University Press.

Davidson, Richard, Klaus Scherer, and H. Hill Goldsmith. 2003. *Handbook of the Affective Sciences*. New York: Oxford University Press.

Dawson, Michael. 1994. *Behind the Mule: Race and Class in African American Politics*. Princeton, NJ: Princeton University Press.

Deaux, Kay, Anne Reid, Kim Mizrahi, and Kathleen Ethier. 1995. "Parameters of Social Identity." *Journal of Personality and Social Psychology* 68 (2): 280–291.

Degner, Juliane, and Dirk Wentura. 2011. "Types of Automatically Activated Prejudice: Assessing Possessor -Versus Other-Related Valence in the Evaluative Priming Task." *Social Cognition* 29 (2): 183–211.

De Houwer, Jan. 2001. "A Structural and Process Analysis of the Implicit Association Test." *Journal of Experimental Social Psychology* 37 (6): 443–451.

De Houwer, Jan. 2006. "What are Implicit Measures and Why Are We Using Them?" In *The Handbook of Implicit Cognition and Addiction*, eds. Reinout Wiers and Alan Stacy, 11–28, Thousand Oaks, CA: Sage Publishers.

De Houwer, Jan. 2009. "Comparing Measures of Attitudes at the Functional and Procedural Level: Analysis and Implications." In *Attitudes: Insights from the New Implicit Measures*, eds. Richard Petty, Russell Fazio, and Pablo Briñol, 361–390, New York: Psychology Press.

De Houwer, Jan, Dirk Hermans, and Adriaan Spruyt. 2001. "Affective Priming of Pronunciation Responses: Effects of Target Degradation." *Journal of Experimental Social Psychology* 37 (1): 85–91.

De Houwer, Jan, Sarah Teige-Mocigemba, Adriaan Spruyt, and Agnes Moors. 2009. "Implicit Measures: A Normative Analysis and Review." *Psychological Bulletin* 135 (3): 347–368.

De Houwer, Jan, and Agnes Moors. 2010. "Implicit Measures: Similarities and Differences." In *Handbook of Implicit Social Cognition: Measurement, Theory, and Applications*, eds. Bertram Gawronski and Keith Payne, 176–193, New York: Guilford.

Delli Carpini, Michael, and Scott Keeter. 1991. "Stability and Change in the U.S. Public's Knowledge of Politics." *Public Opinion Quarterly* 55 (4): 583–612.

De Marchi, Scott. 2005. *Computational and Mathematical Modeling in the Social Sciences*. New York: Cambridge University Press.

Dennett, Daniel. 1991. *Consciousness Explained*. New York: Little, Brown and Company.

Denzler, Marcus, Jens Foerster, Nira Liberman, and Merav Rozenman. 2010. "Aggressive, Funny, and Thirsty: A Motivational Inference Model (MIMO) Approach to Behavioral rebound." *Personality and Social Psychology Bulletin*, 36 (10): 1385–1396.

De Steno, David, Richard Petty, Derek Rucker, Duane Wegener, and Julia Braverman. 2004. "Discrete Emotions and Persuasion: The Role of Emotion-Induced Expectancies." *Journal of Personality and Social Psychology* 86 (1): 43–56.

Deutsch, Roland, and Fritz Strack. 2010. "Building Blocks of Social Behavior: Reflective and Impulsive Processes." In *Handbook of Implicit Social Cognition: Measurement, Theory, and Applications*, eds. Bertram Gawronski and Keith Payne, 62–79, New York: Guilford.

Devine, Patricia. 1989. "Stereotypes and Prejudice: Their Automatic and Controlled Components." *Journal of Personality and Social Psychology* 56 (1): 5–18.

Dijksterhuis, Ap., and Ad van Knippenberg. 1998. "The Relation Between Perception and Behavior, or How to Win a Game of Trivial Pursuit." *Journal of Personality and Social Psychology* 74 (4): 865–877.

Dijksterhuis, Ap., and Henk Aarts. 2003. "On Wildebeests and Humans: The Preferential Detection of Negative Stimuli." *Psychological Science* 14 (1): 14–18.

Dijksterhuis, Ap. 2004. "Think Different: The Merit of Unconscious Thought in Preference Development and Decision Making." *Journal of Personality and Social Psychology* 87 (5): 586–598.

Dijksterhuis, Ap, Henk Aarts, and Pamela Smith. 2005. "The Power of the Subliminal: On Subliminal Persuasion and Other Potential Applications." In *The New Unconscious*, eds. Ran Hassin, James Uleman, and John Bargh, 77–106, New York, NY: Oxford University Press.

Dijksterhuis, Ap, Maarten Bos, Loran Nordgren, and Rick van Baaren. 2006. "On Making the Right Choice: The Deliberation-Without-Attention Effect." *Science* 311 (5763): 1005–1007.

Dijksterhuis, Ap, and Zeger van Olden. 2006. "On the Benefits of Thinking Unconsciously: Unconscious Thought Can Increase Post-Choice Satisfaction." *Journal of Experimental Social Psychology* 42 (5): 627–631.

Dijksterhuis, Ap, Luuk Albers, and Karin Bongers. 2009. "Digging For the Real Attitude: Lessons From Research on Implicit and Explicit Self-Esteem." In *Attitudes: Insights from the New Wave of Implicit Measures*, eds. Richard Petty, Russell Fazio and Pablo Briñol, 229–250, New York: Psychology Press.

Dion, Karen, Ellen Berscheid, and Elaine Walster, 1972. "What Is Beautiful is Good." *Journal of Personality and Social Psychology* 24 (3): 285–290.

Ditto, Peter, and David Lopez. 1992. "Motivated Skepticism: Use of Differential Decision Criteria for Preferred and Nonpreferred Conclusions." *Journal of Personality and Social Psychology* 63 (4): 568–584.

Ditto, Peter, James Scepansky, Geoffrey Munro, Anne Marie Apanovitch, and Lisa Lockhart. 1998. "Motivated Sensitivity to Preference-Inconsistent Information." *Journal of Personality and Social Psychology* 75 (1): 53–69.

Dovidio, John, Nancy Evans, and Richard Tyler. 1986. "Racial Stereotypes: The Contents of Their Cognitive Representations." *Journal of Experimental Social Psychology* 22 (1): 22–37.

Dovidio, John, Kerry Kawakami, and Kelly Beach. 2001. "Implicit and Explicit Attitudes: Examination of the Relationship Between Measures of Intergroup Bias." In *Blackwell Handbook of Social Psychology: Intergroup Processes*, eds. Rupert Brown and Samuel Gaertner, 175–197, Malden, MA: Blackwell.

Dovidio, John, Kerry Kawakami, Natalie Smoak, and Samuel Gaertner. 2009. "The Nature of Contemporary Racial Prejudice: Insights from Implicit and Explicit Measures of Attitudes." In *Attitudes: Insights from the New Implicit Measures*, eds. Richard Petty, Russell Fazio, and Pablo Briñol, 165–192, New York: Psychology Press.

Downs, Anthony. 1957. *An Economic Theory of Democracy*. New York: Harper & Bros.

Duckitt, John. 1992. "Patterns of Prejudice: Group Interests and Intergroup Attitudes." *South African Journal of Psychology* 22 (3): 147–156.

Duckworth, Kimberly, John Bargh, Magda Garcia, and Shelly Chaiken. 2002. "The Automatic Evaluation of Novel Stimuli." *Psychological Science* 13 (6): 513–519.

Dunbar, Kevin, and Johnathan Fugelsang. 2005. "Casual Thinking in Science: How Scientists and Students Interpret the Unexpected." In *Scientific and Technological Thinking*, eds. Michael Gorman, Ryan Tweney, David Goodling, 57–79, Mahwah, NJ: Erlbaum.

D'Souza, Dinesh. 1995. *The End of Racism*. New York, NY: Free Press.

Eagly, Alice. 1996. "Differences Between Women and Men: Their Magnitude, Practical Importance, and Political Meaning." *American Psychologist* 51 (2): 158–159.

Eagly, Alice, Richard Ashmore, Mona Makhijini, and Laura Longo. 1991. "What is Beautiful is Good, but...: A Meta-Analytic Review of the Research on the Physical Attractiveness Stereotype." *Psychological Bulletin* 110 (1): 109–128.

Eagly, Alice, and Shelly Chaiken. 1993. *The Psychology of Attitudes*. Orlando, FL: Harcourt Brace Jovanovich College Publishers.

Eagly, Alice, and Shelly Chaiken. 1998. "Attitude Structure and Function." In *The Handbook of Social Psychology*, eds. Daniel Gilbert, Susan Fiske, and Gardner Lindzey, 269–322. New York: McGraw-Hill.

Ebbinghaus, Hermann. 1885/1913. *Memory: A Contribution to Experimental Psychology*. New York: Dover Publications Inc.

Eberhardt, Jennifer, Phillip Atiba Goff, Valerie Purdie, and Paul Davis. 2004. "Seeing Black: Race, Crime, and Visual Processing." *Journal of Personality and Social Psychology* 87 (6): 876–893.

Edsall, Thomas, and Mary Edsall. 1992. *Chain Reaction: The Impact of Race, Rights, and Taxes on American Politics*. New York: W.W. Norton and Company.

Edwards, Kari, and Edward Smith. 1996. "A Disconfirmation Bias in the Evaluation of Arguments." *Journal of Personality and Social Psychology* 71 (1): 5–24.

Ehrlinger, Joyce, Ashby Plant, Richard Eibach, Corey Columb, Joanna Goplen, Jonathan Kunstman, and David Butz. 2011. "How Exposure to the Confederate Flag Affects Willingness to Vote for Barack Obama." *Political Psychology* 32 (1): 131–146.

Ekman, Paul. 2003. *Emotions Inside Out: 130 Years After Darwin's the Expression of the Emotions in Man and Animals*. New York: Annals of the New York Academy of Science.

Ekman, Paul. 2007. *Emotions Revealed: Recognizing Faces and Feelings to Improve Communication and Emotional Life*. New York: Henry Holt and Company.

Elliot, Andrew, and James Fryer. 2007. "The Goal Construct in Psychology." In *Handbook of Motivation Science*, eds. James Shah and Wendi Gardner, 235–250. New York: Guilford Press.

Elsworth, Phoebe, and Klaus Scherer. 2003. "Arousal Processes in Emotion." In *Handbook of Affective Sciences*, eds. Richard Davidson, Klaus Scherer, and H. Hill Goldsmith, 572–595, New York: Oxford.

Epstein, Seymour. 1972. "The Nature of Anxiety With Emphasis Upon its Relationship to Expectancy." In *Anxiety: Current Trends in Theory and Research*, ed. Charles Spielberger, 292–338, Oxford: Academic Press.

Epstein, Seymour. 1992. "Constructive Thinking and Mental and Physical Well-Being." In *Life Crises and Experiences of Loss in Adulthood*, eds. Leo Montada, Sigrun-Heide Filipp, Melvin Lerner, 385–409, Hillsdale, NJ: Erlbaum.

Erikson, Erik. 1950. *Childhood and Society*. New York: W.W. Norton.

Erisen, Cengiz, Milton Lodge, and Charles Taber. 2008. "Affective Contagion in Political Thinking." Paper Presented at the Annual Meetings of American Political Science Association, Boston, MA, August 28–31.

Erskine, Hazel. 1963. "The Polls: Exposure to Domestic Information." *Public Opinion Quarterly* 27 (3): 658–662.

Evans, Jonathan, and David Over. 1996. *Rationality and Reasoning*. Hove, UK: Psychology Press.

Eysenck, Michael, and Mark Keane. 2005. *Cognitive Psychology: A Student's Handbook*. East Sussex, UK: Psychology Press.

Farah, Martha. 1990. *Visual Agnosia: Disorders of Object Recognition and What They Tell Us About Normal Vision*. Cambridge: MIT Press/Bradford Books.

Fazio, Russell. 1989. "On the Power and Functionality of Attitudes: The Role of Attitude Accessibility." In *Attitude Structure and Function*, eds. Anthony Pratkanis, Steven Breckler, and Anthony Greenwald, 153–179, Hillsdale, NJ: Erlbaum.

Fazio, Russell. 1990. "A Practical Guide to the Use of Response Latency in Social Psychological Research." In *Research Methods in Personality and Social Psychology, Volume 11*, eds. Clyde Hendrick and Margaret Clark, 74–97, Thousand Oaks, CA: Sage.

Fazio, Russell. 1992. "Variability in the Likelihood of Automatic Attitude Activation: Data Reanalysis and Commentary on Bargh, Chaiken, Govender and Pratto (1992)." *Journal of Personality and Social Psychology* 64 (5): 753–758.

Fazio, Russell. 1995. "Attitudes as Object-Evaluation Associations: Determinants, Consequences, and Correlates of Attitude Accessibility." In *Attitude Strength: Antecedents and Consequences*, eds. Richard Petty and Jon Krosnick, 247–282, Hillsdale, NJ: Erlbaum.

Fazio, Russell. 2001. "On the Automatic Activation of Associated Evaluations: An Overview." *Cognition and Emotion* 15 (2): 115–41.

Fazio, Russell. 2007. "Attitudes as Object-Evaluation Associations of Varying Strength." *Social Cognition* 25 (5): 603–637.

Fazio, Russell, and Mark Zanna. 1978a. "On the Predictive Validity of Attitudes: The Roles of Direct Experience and Confidence." *Journal of Personality* 46 (2), 228–243.

Fazio, Russell, and Mark Zanna. 1978b. "Attitudinal Qualities Relating to the Strength of the Attitude-Behavior Relationship." *Journal of Experimental Social Psychology* 14, 398–408.

Fazio, Russell, and Carol Williams. 1986. "Attitude Accessibility as a Moderator of the Attitude-Perception and Attitude-Behavior Relations: An Investigation of the 1984 Presidential Election." *Journal of Personality and Social Psychology* 51 (13): 505–514.

Fazio, Russell, David Sanbonmatsu, Martha Powell, and Frank Kardes. 1986. "On the Automatic Activation of Attitudes." *Journal of Personality and Social Psychology* 50 (2): 229–238.

Fazio, Russell, Joni Jackson, Bridget Dunton, and Carol Williams. 1995. "Variability in Automatic Activation as an Unobtrusive Measure of Racial Attitudes: A Bona Fide Pipeline?" *Journal of Personality and Social Psychology* 69 (6): 1013–1027.

Feingold, Alan. 1992. "Gender Differences in Mate Selection Preferences: A Test of the Parental Investment Model." *Psychological Bulletin* 112 (1): 125–139.

Feinstein, Justin, Melissa Duff, and Daniel Tranel. 2010. "Sustained Experience of Emotion after Loss of Memory in Patients with Amnesia." *PNAS* 107 (17): 7674–7679.

Feldman, Jack, and John Lynch Jr. 1988. "Self-Generated Validity and Other Effects of Measurement on Belief, Attitude, Intention, and Behavior." *Journal of Applied Psychology* 73 (3): 421–435.

Feldman, Lisa. 1995. "Variations in the Circumplex Structure of Mood." *Personality and Social Psychology Bulletin* 21 (8): 806–817.

Ferejohn, John, and Morris Fiorina. 1974. "The Paradox of Not Voting: A Decision Theoretic Analysis." *American Political Science Review*, 68 (2): 525–536.

Ferguson, Melissa, and John Bargh. 2003. "The Constructive Nature of Automatic Evaluation." In *The Psychology of Evaluation: Affective Processes in Cognition and Emotion*, eds. Jochen Musch and Karl Klauer, 169–188. Hilldale, NJ: Erlbaum.

Ferguson, Milissa, and Ran Hassin 2007. "On the Automatic Association between America and Aggression for News Watchers." *Personality and Social Psychology Bulletin* 33 (12): 1632–1647.

Ferguson, Mellisa, and Shanette Porter. 2010. "What is Implicit about Goal Pursuit?" In *Handbook of Implicit Social Cognition: Measurement, Theory, and Applications*, eds. Bertram Gawronski and Keith Payne, 311–331, New York: Guilford.

Festinger, Leon. 1957. *A Theory of Cognitive Dissonance*. Stanford, CA: Stanford University Press.

Festinger, Leon, and James Carlsmith. 1959. "Cognitive Consequences of Forced Compliance." *Journal of Abnormal and Social Psychology* 58 (2): 203–210.

Fishbein, Martin, and Icek Ajzen. 1975. *Belief, Attitude, Intention, and Behavior: An Introduction to Theory and Research*. Reading, MA: Addison-Wesley.

Fiske, Susan. 1981. "Social Cognition and Affect." In *Cognition, Social Behavior, and the Environment*, ed. James Harvey, 227–264, Hillsdale, NJ: Erlbaum.

Fiske, Susan. 1982. "Schema-Triggered Affect: Applications to Social Perception." In *Affect and Cognition: The 17th Annual Carnegie Symposium on Cognition*, eds. Margaret Clark, and Susan Fiske, 55–78, Hillsdale, NJ: Erlbaum.

Fiske, Susan. 1998. "Stereotyping, Prejudice and Dscrimination." In *The Handbook of Social Psychology*, eds. Daniel Gilbert, Susan Fiske, and Gardner Lindzey, 357–411, Boston: McGraw-Hill.

Fiske, Susan, and Mark Pavelchak. 1986. "Category-Based versus Piecemeal Affective Responses: Developments in Schema-Triggered Affect." In *Handbook of Motivation and Cognition: Foundations of Social Behavior*, eds. Richard Sorrentino, and Tory Higgins, 167–203, New York: Guilford Press.

Fiske, Susan, and Shelley Taylor. 1991. *Social Cognition*, 2nd ed. New York: McGraw-Hill.

Forgas, Joseph. 1995. "Mood and Judgment: The Affect Infusion Model (AIM)." *Psychological Bulletin* 117 (1): 39–66.

Forgas, Joseph, ed. 2000. *Feeling and Thinking: The Role of Affect in Social Cognition*. New York: Cambridge University Press.

Forgas, Joseph. 2003. "Affective Influences on Attitudes and Judgments." In *Handbook of the Affective Sciences*, eds. Richard Davidson, Klaus Scherer, and H. Hill Goldsmith, 596–618, New York: Oxford University Press.

Forgas, Joseph, Arie Kruglanski, and Kipling Williams, eds. 2011. *The Psychology of Social Conflict and Aggression*. New York: Psychology Press.

Fowler, James, and Darren Schreiber. 2008. "Biology, Politics, and the Emerging Science of Human Nature." *Science* 322 (5903): 912–914.

Franklin, Benjamin. Letter to Jonathon Williams. April 8, 1779. Papers of Benjamin Franklin. Microfilm Collection. Library of Congress. Washington, D.C.

Franklin, Charles. 1991. "Eschewing Obfuscation? Campaigns and the Perception of U.S. Senate Incumbents." *American Political Science Review* 85 (4): 1193–1214.

Freedman, Jonathan, and David Sears. 1965. "Selective Exposure." In *Advances in Experimental Social Psychology, Volume 19*, ed. Leonard Berkowitz, 57–97, New York: Academic Press.

Frey, Dieter. 1986. "Recent Research on Selective Exposure to Information." In *Advances in Experimental Social Psychology, Volume 19*, ed. Leonard Berkowitz, 41–80, New York: Academic Press.

Friedman, Howard, M. Robin DiMatteo, and Timohy Mertz. 1980. "Nonverbal Communication on Television News." *Personality and Social Psychology Bulletin* 6 (3): 427–435.

Fuller, Raymond, and Alan Sheehy-Skeffington. 1974. "Effects of Group Laughter on Responses to Humorous Material: A Replication and Extension." *Psychological Reports* 35: 531–534.

Funk, Carolyn. 1999. "Bringing the Candidate into Models of Candidate Evaluation. " *Journal of Politics* 61 (3): 700–720.

Gamson, William. 1992. *Talking Politics*. Cambridge: Cambridge University Press.

Gawronski, Bertram, and Keith Payne, eds. 2010. *Handbook of Implicit Social Cognition: Measurement, Theory, and Applications*. New York: Guilford.

Gawronski, Bertram, and Galen Bodenhausen. 2006. "Associative and Propositional Processes in Evaluation: An Integrative Review of Implicit and Explicit Attitude Change." *Psychological Bulletin* 132 (5): 692–731.

Gawronski, Bertram, and Galen Bodenhausen. 2007. "Unraveling the Processes Underlying Evaluation: Attitudes From the Perspective of the APE Model." *Social Cognition* 25 (5): 687–717.

Gawronski, Betram, Galen Bodenhausen, and Andrew Becker. 2007. "I Like It, Because I Like Myself: Associative Self-Anchoring and Post-Decisional Change of Implicit Evaluations." *Journal of Experimental Social Psychology* 43 (2): 221–232.

Gawronski, Bertram, Fritz Strack, and Galen Bodenhausen. 2009. "Attitudes and Cognitive Consistency: The Role of Associative and Propositional Processes." In *Attitudes: Insights from the New Wave of Implicit Measures*, eds. Richard Petty, Russell Fazio, and Pablo Briñol, 85–117, New York: Psychology Press.

Gawronski, Bertram, and Rajees Sritharan. 2010. "Formation, Change, and Contextualization of Mental Associations: Determinants and Principles of Variations in Implicit Measures." In *Handbook of Implicit Social Cognition: Measurement, Theory, and Applications*, ed. Bertram Gawronski and Keith Payne, 216–240, New York: Guilford.

Gazzaniga, Michael. 1992. *Nature's Mind*. New York: Basic Books.

Gazzaniga, Michael. 1998. *The Mind's Past*. Berkeley: University of California Press.

Gazzaniga, Michael. 1998. "The Split Brain Revisited." *Scientific American* 279 (1): 50–55.

Gazzaniga, Michael. 2005. "Forty-Five Years of Split-Brain Research and Still Going Strong." *Nature Reviews: Neuroscience* 6 (8): 653–659.

Gazzaniga, Michael. 2009. "Humans: The Party Animal." *Daedalus* 138 (3): 21–34.

George, Alexander, and Juliette George. 1956. *Woodrow Wilson and Colonel House: A Personality Study.* New York: John Day.

Gerber, Alan, and Donald Green. 1998. "Misperceptions about Perceptual Bias." Paper presented at the Annual Meeting of the Midwest Political Science Association, Chicago, April 23–25.

Gerber, Alan, and Donald Green, 1998a. "Rational Learning and Partisan Attitudes." *American Journal of Political Science* 42 (3): 794–818.

Gibson, James, and Gregory Caldeira. 2009. *Citizens, Courts, and Confirmations: Positivity Theory and the Judgments of the American People.* Princeton, NJ: Princeton University Press.

Gibson, James, Milton Lodge, and Benjamin Woodson. 2010. "Inter-Cultural Differences in the Meaning and Influence of the Symbols of Legal Authority and Legitimacy." Paper presented at the Annual Meeting of the Midwest Political Science Association, Chicago, IL, April 22–26.

Gigerenzer, Gerd. 2007. *Gut feelings: The Intelligence of the Unconscious.* New York: Viking Penguin.

Gigerenzer, Gerd and Daniel Goldstein. 1996. "Reasoning the Fast and Frugal Way: Models of Bounded Rationality." *Psychological Review* 103: 650–669.

Gilbert, Daniel. 2006. *Stumbling on Happiness.* New York: Random House. 2006.

Gilens, Martin. 1995. "Racial Attitudes and Opposition to Welfare." *Journal of Politics* 57 (4): 994–1014.

Gilens, Martin. 2000. *Why Americans Hate Welfare: Race, Media, and the Politics of Antipoverty Policy.* Chicago: University of Chicago Press.

Gilliam, Franklin, Shanto Iyengar, Adam Simon and Oliver Wright. 1996. "Crime in Black and White: The Violent, Scary World of Local News." *Press/Politics* 1 (3): 6–23.

Gilliam, Franklin, and Shanto Iyengar. 2000. "Prime Suspects: The Influence of Local Television News on the Viewing Public." *American Journal of Political Science* 44 (3): 560–573.

Gilliam, Franklin, Nicholas Valentino and Matthew Beckmann. 2002. "Where You Live and What You Watch: The Impact of Racial Proximity and Local Television News on Attitudes About Race and Crime." *Political Research Quarterly* 55 (4): 755–780.

Giner-Sorolla, Roger. 2011. *Moral Emotions in Persons and Groups.* New York: Psychology Press.

Gladwell, Malcolm. 2005. *BLINK: The Power of Thinking without Thinking.* New York: Little, Brown, and Company.

Glanz, James. 2000. "Survey Finds Support is Strong for Teaching 2 Origin Theories." *The New York Times*, March 11. Sec. A, p. 1.

Gollwitzer, Peter, and John Bargh, eds. 1996. *The Psychology of Action: Linking Cognition and Motivation to Behavior.* New York: The Guilford Press.

Goren, Paul, Christopher Federico, and Miki Kittilson. 2009. "Source Cues, Partisan Identities, and Political Value Expression." *American Journal of Political Science* 53 (4): 805–820.

Gosnell, Harold. 1927. *Getting Out the Vote*. Chicago: University of Chicago Press.

Gould, Madelyn and David Shaffer. 1986. "The Impact of Suicide in Television Movies: Evidence of Imitation." *New England Journal of Medicine* 319 (24): 690–694.

Granberg, Donald, and Soren Holmberg. 1986. "Political Perception among Voters in Sweden and the US: Analyses of Issues with Explicit Alternatives." *Political Research Quarterly* 39 (1): 7–28.

Gray, Jeffrey. 1984. "The Contents of Consciousness: A Neuropsychological Conjecture." *Behavioral and Brain Sciences* 18 (4): 659–722.

Gray, Jeffrey. 1987. *The Psychology of Fear and Stress*. 2nd ed. Cambridge: Cambridge University Press.

Green, Donald, Bradley Palmquist, and Eric Schickler. 2002. *Partisan Hearts and Minds: Political Parties and the Social Identity of Voters*. New Haven, CT: Yale University Press.

Green, Donald and Ian Shapiro. 1994. *Pathologies of Rational Choice Theory: A Critique of Applications in Political Science*. New Haven, CT: Yale University Press.

Greenwald, Anthony, Catherine Carnot, Rebecca Beach, and Barbara. 1987. "Increasing Voting Behavior by Asking People if They Expect to Vote." *Journal of Applied Psychology* 72, 315–318.

Greenwald, Anthony, and Mahzarin Banaji. 1995. "Implicit Social Cognition: Attitudes, Self-Esteem, and Stereotypes." *Psychological Review* 102 (1): 4–27.

Greenwald, Anthony, Mahzarin Banaji, Laurie Rudman, Shelly Farnham, Brian Nosek, and Deborah Mellott. 2002. "Unified Theory of Implicit Attitudes, Stereotypes, Self-Esteem, and Self-Concept." *Psychological Review* 109 (1): 3–25.

Greenwald, Anthony, and Brian Nosek. 2009. "Attitudinal Dissociation: What Does It Mean?" In *Attitudes: Insights from the New Implicit Measures*, eds. Richard Petty, Russell Fazio, and Pablo Briñol, 65–118, New York: Psychology Press.

Greenwald, Anthony, Andrew Poehlman, Eric Uhlmann, and Mahzarin Banaji. 2009. "Understanding and Using the Implicit Association Test: III. Meta-Analysis of Predictive Validity." *Journal of Personality and Social Psychology* 97 (1): 17–41.

Gregory, Stanford, and Timothy Gallagher. 2002. "Spectral Analysis of Candidates' Nonverbal Vocal Communication: Predicting U.S. Presidential Elections Outcomes." *Social Psychology Quarterly* 65 (3): 298–308.

Grynaviski, Jeffrey. 2006. "A Bayesian Learning Model with Applications to Party Identification." *Journal of Theoretical Politics* 18 (3): 323–346.

Hagen, Michael. 1995. "References to Racial Issues." *Political Behavior* 17: 49–88.

Haidt, John. 2001. "The Emotional Dog and its Rational Tail: A Social Intuitionist Approach to Moral Judgment." *Psychological Review* 108 (4): 814–834.

Hamann, Stephan. 2001. "Cognitive and Neural Mechanisms of Emotional Memory." *Trends in Cognitive Science* 5 (9): 394–400.

Hamill, Ruth, and Milton Lodge. 1986. "Cognitive Consequences of Political Sophistication." In *Political Cognition*, eds. Richard Lau and David Sears, 69–93, Hillsdale, NJ: Erlbaum.

Hamilton, David, Steven Sherman, and Luigi Castelli. 2002. "A Group by Any Other Name – The Role of Entitativity in Group Perception." *European Review of Social Psychology* 12 (1): 139–166.

Hamilton, David, and Steven Sherman. 1994. "Stereotypes." In *Handbook of Social Cognition*, eds. Robert Wyer, Jr. and Thomas Srull, 1–68, Hillsdale, NJ: Erlbaum.

Hamilton, David and Steven Sherman. 1996. "Perceiving Persons and Groups." *Psychological Review* 103: 336–355.

Harmon-Jones, Eddie, Jack Brehm, Jeff Greenberg, Linda Simon, and David Nelson. 1996. "Evidence That the Production of Aversive Consequences Is Not Necessary to Create Cognitive Disonance." *Journal of Personality and Social Psychology* 70 (1): 5–16.

Hart, William, Victor Ottati, and Nathanial Krumdick. 2011. "Physical Attractiveness and Candidate Evaluation: A Model of Correction." *Political Psychology* 32 (2): 181–203.

Harton, Helen, and Bibb Latané. 1997. "Information and Thought-induced Polarization: The Mediating Role of Involvement in Making Attitudes Extreme." *Journal of Social Behavior and Personality* 12 (2): 271–299.

Hassin, Ran, Mellisa Ferguson, Danielle Shidlovsky, and Thomas Gross. 2007. "Waved by Invisible Flags: The Effects of Subliminal Exposure to Flags on Political Thought and Behavior." *Proceedings of the National Academy of Sciences* 104 (50): 19757–19761.

Hassin, Ran, James Uleman, and John Bargh, eds. 2005. *The New Unconscious*. New York, Oxford University Press.

Hastie, Reid. 1984. "Causes and Effects of Causal Attribution." *Journal of Personality and Social Psychology* 46 (1): 44–56.

Hastie, Ried, and Bernadette Park. 1986. "The Relationship Between Memory and Judgment Depends on Whether the Judgment is Memory-Based or On-line." *Psychological Review* 93: 258–268.

Hastie, Reid, and Nancy Pennington. 1989. "Notes on the Distinction Between Memory-Based versus On-Line Judgments." In *On-Line Cognition in Person Perception*, ed. John Bassilli, 1–19, Hillsdale, NJ: Erlbaum.

Healy, Andrew, Neil Malhotra, and Cecillia Hyunjung Mo. 2010. "Irrelevant Events Affect Voters' Evaluation of Government Performance." *Proceedings of the National Academy of the Sciences of the United States of America* 107 (29): 12804–12809.

Heider, Fritz. 1958. *The Psychology of Interpersonal Relations*. New York: Wiley.

Hermans, Dirk, Jan De Houwer, and Paul Eelen. 1994. "The Affective Priming Effect: Automatic Activation of Evaluative Information in Memory." *Cognition and Emotion* 8 (6): 515–533.

Heuer, Friderike, and Daniel Reisberg. 1990. "Vivid Memories of Emotional Events: The Accuracy of Remembered Minutiae." *Memory & Cognition* 18 (5): 496–506.

Hibbing, John, and Elizabeth Theiss-Morse. 2002. *Stealth Democracy: American's Beliefs About How Government Should Work*. New York: Cambridge University Press.

Higgins, Tory. 1989. "Knowledge Accessibility and Activation: Subjectivity and Suffering from Unconscious Sources." In *Unintended Thought: The Limits of Awareness*, eds. James Uleman and John Bargh, 75–123, New York: Guilford Press.

Hofmann, Wilhelm, and Timothy Wilson. 2010. "Consciousness, Introspection, and the Adaptive Unconscious." In *Handbook of Implicit Social Cognition: Measurement, Theory, and Applications*, eds. Bertram Gawronski and Keith Payne, 197–215, New York: Guilford.

Hofmann, Wilhelm, Betram Gawronski, Tobias Gschwendner, Huy Le and Manfred Schmitt. 2005. "A Meta-Analysis on the Correlation between the Implicit Association Test and Explicit Self-Report Measures." *Personality and Social Psychology Bulletin* 31: 1369–1385.

Hofstadter, Douglas. 2010. *I Am a Strange Loop*. New York: Basic Books.

Huang, Li-Ning and Vincent Price. 2001. "Motivations, Goals, Information Search, and Memory About Political Candidates." *Political Psychology* 22 (4): 665–692.

Huber, Gregory, and John Lapinski. 2006. "The 'Race Card' Revisited: Assessing Racial Priming in Policy Contests." *American Journal of Political Science* 50 (2): 421–440.

Huckfeldt, Robert, T.K. Ahn, Matthew Pietryka, and Jack Reilly. 2011. "Noise, Bias, and Expertise in the Political Communication Process." Paper presented at the Midwest Political Science Association, Chicago, IL, April 12–15.

Huckfeldt, Robert, Jeffrey Levine, William Morgan, and John Sprague. 1999. "Accessibility and the Political Utility of Partisan and Ideological Orientations." *American Journal of Political Science* 43 (3): 888–911.

Huddy, Leonie. 2002. "Context and Meaning in Social Identity Theory: A Response to Oakes." *Political Psychology* 23 (4): 825–838.

Huddy, Leonie, Stanley Feldman, Charles Taber, and Galya Lahav. 2005. "Threat, Anxiety, and Support of Antiterrorism Policies." *American Journal of Political Science* 49 (3): 593–608.

Huddy, Leonie, Stanley Feldman, and Erin Cassese. 2007. "On the Distinct Effects of Anxiety and Anger." In *The Affect Effect: Dynamics of Emotion in Political Thinking and Behavior*, eds. Russell Neuman, George Marcus, Ann Crider, and Michael MacKuen, 202–230, Chicago: University of Chicago Press.

Huddy, Leonie, and Anna Gunnthorsdottir. 2000. "The Persuasive Effect of Emotive Visual Imagery: Superficial Manipulation or the Product of Passionate Reason." *Political Psychology* 21 (4): 745–778.

Huddy, Leonie, and Nadya Terkildsen. 1993. "The Consequences of Gender Stereotypes for Women Candidates at Different Levels and Types of Office." *Political Research Quarterly* 46 (3): 503–525.

Hurwitz, Jon, and Mark Peffley. 2005. "Playing the Race Card in the Post-Willie Horton Era: The Impact of Racialized Code Words on Support for Punitive Crime Policy." *Public Opinion Quarterly* 69 (1): 99–112.

Isbell, Linda, and Victor Ottati. 2002. "The Emotional Voter: Effects of Episodic Affective Reactions on Candidate Evaluation." *The Social Psychology of Politics: Social Psychological Applications to Social Issues* 5: 55–74.

Ito, Tiffany. 2010. "Implicit Social Cognition: Insights from Social Neuroscience." In *Handbook of Implicit Social Cognition: Measurement, Theory, and Applications*, eds. Bertram Gawronski and Keith Payne, 80–92, New York: Guilford.

Ito, Tiffany, and John Cacioppo. 1999. "The Psychophysiology of Utility Appraisals." In *Well Being: The Foundations of Hedonic Psychology*, eds. Daniel Kahneman, Edward Diener, Norbert Schwarz, 470–488, New York: Russell Sage Foundation.

Ito, Tiffany, and John Cacioppo. 2005. "Variations on a Human Universal: Individual Differences in Positivity Offset and Negativity Bias." *Cognition and Emotion* 19 (1): 1–26.

Iyengar, Shanto, and William McGuire, eds. 1993. *Explorations in Political Psychology*. Durham, NC: Duke University Press.

Jackman, Simon, and Paul Sniderman, 2002. "The Institutional Organization of Choice Spaces: A Political Conception of Political Psychology." In *Political Psychology*, ed. Kristen Monroe, 209–224, Mahway, NJ: Erlbaum.

Jacoby, Larry, Colleen Kelley, Judith Brown, and Jennifer Jasechko. 1988. "Becoming Famous Overnight: Limits on the Ability to Avoid Unconscious Influences of the Past." *Journal of Personality and Social Psychology* 56 (3): 326–338.

James, William. 1884. "What is an Emotion?" *Mind* 9 (34): 188–205.

James, William. 1890. *Principles of Psychology*. New York: Holt.

Jamieson, Kathleen, and David Birdsell. 1988. *Presidential Debates: The Challenge of Creating an Informed Electorate*. New York: Oxford University Press.

Johnson, Laird, and Keith Oatley. 1989. "The Language of Emotions: An Analysis of a Semantic Field." *Cognition and Emotion* 3: 81–123.

Johnston, Chris, and Howard Lavine, Milton Lodge and Benjamin Woodson. 2010. *Affective Intelligence, Endogenous Affect, or Ambivalence? A Test of Three Theories*. Paper presented at the Annual Meeting of the Midwest Political Science Association. Chicago, IL, April 22–25.

Jost, John, Brian Nosek, and Samuel Gosling. 2008. "Ideology: Its Resurgence in Social, Personality, and Political Psychology." *Perspectives on Psychological Science* 3 (2): 126–136.

Jostmann, Nils, Daniel Lakens, and Thomas Schubert. 2009. "Weight as an Embodiment of Importance." *Psychological Science* 20 (9): 1169–1174.

Judd, Charles, and Jon Krosnick. 1989. "The Structural Bases of Consistency Among Political Attitudes: Effects of Political Expertise and Attitude Importance." In *Attitude Structure and Function*, eds. Anthony Pratkanis, Steven Breckler, and Anthony Greenwald, 99–128, Hillsdale, NJ: Erlbaum.

Judd, Charles and Cynthia Lusk. 1984. "Knowledge Structures and Evaluative Judgments: Effects of Structural Variables on Judgmental Extremity." *Journal of Personality and Social Psychology* 46 (6): 1193–1207.

Just, Marion, Ann Crigler and Todd Belt. 2007. "Don't Give up Hope: Emotions, Candidate Appraisals and Votes." In *The Affect Effect: Dynamics of Emotion in Political Thinking and Behavior*, eds. Russell Neuman, George Marcus, Ann Crigler and Michael MacKuen, 231–259, Chicago, IL: University of Chicago Press.

Kahneman, Daniel. 2011. *Thinking, Fast and Slow*. New York: Farrar, Straus, and Giroux.

Kahneman, Daniel, Paul Slovic, and Amos Tversky. 1982. *Judgment Under Uncertainty: Heuristics and Biases*. New York: Cambridge University Press.

Kahneman, David, and Amos Tversky. 1974. "Judgment under Uncertainty: Heuristics and Biases." *Science* 185 (4157): 1124–1131.

Karpinski, Andrew, Ross Steinman, and James Hilton. 2005. "Attitude Importance as a Moderator of the Relationship between Implicit and Explicit Attitude Measures." *Personality and Social Psychology Bulletin* 31 (7): 949–962.

Karremans, Johan, Wolfgang Stroebe, and Jasper Claus. 2006. "Beyond Vicary's Fantasies: The Impact of Subliminal Priming and Brand Choice." *Journal of Experimental Social Psychology* 42 (6): 792–798.

Kay, Aaron, Christian Wheeler, James Bargh and Lee Ross. 2004. "Material Priming: The Influence of Mundane Physical Objects on Situational Construal and Competitive Behavioral Choice." *Organizational Behavior and Human Decision Processes* 95 (1): 83–96.

Kelley, Stanley, and Thad Mirer. 1974. "The Simple Act of Voting." *American Political Science Review* 68 (2): 572–591.

Keltner, Dacher, and Paul Ekman. 2003. "Introduction: Expression of Emotion." In *Handbook of Affective Sciences*, eds. Richard Davidson, Klaus Scherer, and Hill Goldsmith, 411–456, New York: Oxford University Press.

Keppel, Geoffrey, and Thomas Wickens. 2004. *Design and Analysis: A Researcher's Handbook*. 4th ed. Upper Saddle River, NJ: Pearson/Prentice Hall.

Kibria, Nazli. 2000. "Race, Ethnic Options, and Ethnic Binds: Identity Negotiations of Second-Generation Chinese and Korean Americans." *Sociological Perspectives* 43 (1): 77–95.

Kim, Sung-youn. 2005. *A Model of Political Information Processing: The Dynamics of Candidate Evaluation and Strategic Behaviors in Social Dilemma Games*. Ph.D. Dissertation, Stony Brook University.

Kim, Sung-youn, Charles Taber, and Milton Lodge. 2010. "A Computational Model of the Citizen as Motivated Reasoner: Modeling the Dynamics of the 2000 Presidential Election." *Political Behavior* 32 (1): 1–28.

Kinder, Donald. 1986. "The Continuing American Dilemma: White Resistance to Racial Change 40 Years after Myrdal." *Journal of Social Issues* 42, 151–171.

Kinder, Donald. 1998. "Opinion and Action in the Realm of Politics." In *The Handbook of Social Psychology*, eds. Daniel Gilbert, Susan Fiske, and Gardner Lindzey, 778–876, Boston: McGraw-Hill.

Kinder, Donald, and D. Roderick Kiewiet. 1979. "Economic Discontent and Political Behavior: The Role of Personal Grievances and Collective Economic Judgments in Congressional Voting." *American Journal of Political Science* 23 (3): 495–527.

Kinder, Donald, Mark Peters, Robert Abelson, and Susan Fiske. 1980. "Presidential Prototypes." *Political Behavior* 2 (4): 315–337.

Kinder, Donald, and Lynn Sanders. 1996. *Divided by Color: Racial Politics and Democratic Ideals*. Chicago: University of Chicago Press.

Kinder, Donald, and David Sears. 1981. "Prejudice and Politics: Symbolic Racism Versus Racial Threats to the Good Life." *Journal of Personality and Social Psychology* 40 (3): 414–431.

King, Amy and Andrew Leigh. 2010. "Bias at the Ballot Box? Testing Whether Candidates' Gender Affects Their Vote." *Social Science Quarterly* 91 (2): 324–343.

King, Eden, Jenessa Shapiro, Michelle Hebl, Sarah Singletary, and Stacey Turner. 2006. "The Stigma of Obesity in Customer Service: A Mechanism for Remediation and Bottom-Line Consequences of Interpersonal Discrimination." *The Journal of Applied Psychology* 91 (3): 579–593.

Kleinnijenhuis, Jan, Anita van Hoof, and Dirk Oegema. 2006. "Negative News and the Sleeper Effect of Distrust." *International Journal of Press/Politics* 11 (2): 86–104.

Knowles, Eric, Brian Lowery, and Rebecca Schaumberg. 2010. "Racial Prejudice Predicts Opposition to Obama and His Heath Care Reform Plan." *Journal of Experimental Social Psychology* 46 (2): 420–423.

Kollman, Ken, John Miller, and Scott Page. 1992. "Adaptive Parties in Spatial Elections." *American Political Science Review* 86 (4): 929–937.

Kramer, Roderick, Geoffrey Leonardelli, and Robert Livingston. 2011. *Social Cognition. Social Identity, and Intergroup Relations*. New York: Psychology Press.

Krosnick, John, and Robert Abelson. 1992. "The Case for Measuring Attitude Strength in Surveys." In *Questions about Questions: Inquiries into the Cognitive Bases of Surveys*, ed. Judith Tanur, 177–203, New York: Sage.

Krosnick, Jon, Andrew Betz, Lee Jussim, and Ann Lynn. 1992. "Subliminal Conditioning of Attitudes." *Personality and Social Psychology Bulletin* 18 (2): 152–162.

Krosnick, Jon, and Richard Petty. 1995. "Attitude Strength: An Overview." In *Attitude Strength: Antecedents and Consequences*, eds. Richard Petty and Jon Krosnick, 1–24, Hillside, NJ: Erlbaum.

Krueger, Joachim, ed. 2011. *Social Judgment and Decision Making*. New York: Psychology Press.

Kruglanski, Arie and Donna Webster. 1996. "Motivated Closing of the Mind: 'Seizing' and 'Freezing.'" *Psychological Review* 103 (2): 263–283.

Kruglanski, Arie and Davis Sleeth-Keppler. 2007. "The Principles of Social Judgment." In *Social Psychology. Handbook of Basic Principles*, eds. Arie Kruglanski and Tory Higgins, 116–137, New York: Guilford Press.

Kuhn, Deanna, and Joseph Lao. 1996. "Effects of Evidence on Attitudes: Is Polarization the Norm?" *Psychological Science* 7 (2): 115–120.

Kuklinski, James, Norman Hurley. 1994. "On Hearing and Interpreting Political Messages: A Cautionary Tale of Citizens' Cue taking." *Journal of Politics* 56 (3): 729–751.

Kuklinski, James, and Paul Quirk. 2000. "Reconsidering the Rational Public: Cognition, Heuristics, and Mass Opinion." In *Elements of Reason: Cognition, Choice, and the Bounds of Rationality*, eds. Arthur Lupia, Mathew McCubbins, and Samuel Popkin, 154–187, Cambridge: Cambridge University Press.

Kuklinski, James, Paul Quirk, Jennifer Jenet, David Schwieder, and Robert Rich. 2000. "Misinformation and the Currency of Democratic Citizenship." *Journal of Politics* 63 (3): 790–816.

Kunda, Ziva. 1987. "Motivated Inference: Self-serving Generation and Evaluation of Causal Theories." *Journal of Personality and Social Psychology* 53 (4): 636–647.

Kunda, Ziva. 1990. "The Case for Motivated Reasoning." *Psychological Bulletin* 108 (3): 480–498.

Kunda, Ziva. 1999. *Social Cognition: Making sense of People*. Cambridge, MA: MIT Press.

Lachman, Roy, Janet Lachman, and Earl Butterfield, eds. 1979. *Cognitive Psychology and Information Processing: An Introduction*. Hillsdale, NJ: Erlbaum

Ladd, Jonathan, and Gabriel Lenz. 2008. "Regressing the Role of Anxiety in Vote Choice." *Political Psychology* 29 (2): 275–296.

Ladd, Jonathan, and Gabriel Lenz. 2011. "Does Anxiety Improve Voters' Decision Making?" *Political Psychology* 32 (2): 347–361.

Laird, James. 1974. "Self-Attribution of Emotion: The Effects of Expressive Behavior on the Quality of Emotional Experience." *Journal of Personality and Social Psychology* 29 (4): 475–486.

Lakoff, George. 1991. "Metaphors of War," At http://www2.iath.virginia.edu/sixties/HTML_docs/Texts/Scholarly/Lakoff_Gulf_Metaphor_1.html.

Lakoff, George. 2001. "Metaphors of Terror." At http://www.press.uchicago.edu/NEWS/911Lakoff/.

Lane, Robert. 1969. *Political Thinking and Consciousness: The Private Life of the Political Mind*. Chicago: Markham Publishers.

Lang, Peter, Mark Greenwald, Margaret Bradley, and Alfons Hamm. 1993. "Looking at Pictures: Affective, Facial, Visceral, and Behavioral Reactions." *Psychophysiology* 30 (3): 261–273.

Langlois, Judith, Lisa Kalakanis, Adam Rubenstein, Andrea Larson, Monica Hallam, and Monica Smoot. 2000. "Maxims or Myths of Beauty? A Meta-Analytic and Theoretical Review." *Psychological Bulletin* 126 (3): 390–423.

Langlois, Judith, Jean Ritter, Lori Roggman and Lesley Vaughn. 1991. "Facial Diversity and Infant Preferences for Attractive Faces." *Developmental Psychology* 27 (1): 79–84.

Langlois, Judith, Lori Roggman, Rita Casey, Jean Ritter, Loretta Reiser-Danner, and Vivian Jenkins. 1987. "Infant Preferences for Attractive Faces: Rudiments of a Stereotype?" *Developmental Psychology* 23 (3): 363–369.

Larson, Axel. 1996. "A Template-Matching Pandemonium Recognizes Unconstrained Handwritten Characters with high Accuracy." *Memory and Cognition* 24 (2): 136.

Lasswell, Harold. 1930. *Psychopathology of Politics*. Chicago: University of Chicago Press.

Lau, Richard. 1985. "Two Explanations for Negativity Effects in Political Behavior." *American Journal of Political Science* 29 (1): 119–138.

Lau, Richard. 1989. "Construct Accessibility and Electoral Choice." *Political Behavior* 11 (1): 5–32.

Lau, Richard, and David Redlawsk. 1997. "Voting Correctly." *American Political Science Review* 91 (3): 585–598.

Lau, Richard R. and David P. Redlawsk. 2001. "An Experimental Study of Information Search, Memory, and Decision-making during a Political Campaign." In *Citizens and Politics: Perspectives from Political Psychology*, ed. James Kuklinski, 136–159, New York: Cambridge University Press.

Lau, Richard, and David Redlawsk. 2006. *How Voters Decide*. New York: Cambridge University Press.

Lau, Richard, Lee Sigelman, and Ivy Rovner. 2007. "Effects of Negative Political Campaigns: A Meta-Analytic Reassessment." *Journal of Politics* 69 (4): 1176–1209.

Lavine, Howard. 2001. "Electoral Consequences of Ambivalence Toward Presidential Candidates." *American Journal of Political Science* 45 (4): 915–929.

Lavine, Howard. 2002. "On-Line versus Memory-Based Process Models of Political Evaluation." In *Political Psychology*, ed. Kristin Monroe, 225–248, Mahwah, NJ: Erlbaum.

Lavine, Howard, Cynthia Thomsen, and Marti Gonzales. 1997. "The Development of Interattitudinal Consistency: The Shared-Consequences Model." *Journal of Personality and Social Psychology* 72 (4): 735–749.

Lavine, Howard, Eugene Borgida, and John Sullivan. 2000. "On the Relationship between Attitude Involvement and Attitude Accessibility: Toward a Cognitive-Motivational Model of Political Information Processing." *Political Psychology* 21 (1): 81–106.

Lavine, Howard, Milton Lodge, Jamie Polichak, and Charles Taber. 2002. "Explicating the Black Box through Experimentation: Studies of Authoritarianism and Threat." *Political Analysis* 10 (4): 343–361.

Lavine, Howard, Marco Steenbergen, and Christopher Johnson, C. (forthcoming). *The Ambivalent Partisan: How Critical Loyalty Promotes Democracy*. New York: Oxford University Press.

Lazarus, Richard. 1995. "Vexing Research Problems Inherent in Cognitive-Mediational Theories of Emotion and Some Solutions." *Psychological Inquiry* 6 (3): 183–196.

LeDoux, Jospeh. 1994. "Emotion, Memory and the Brain." *Scientific American* 270 (6): 32–39.

LeDoux, Joseph. 1996. *The Emotional Brain: The Mysterious Underpinnings of Emotional Life.* New York: Simon & Schuster.

LeDoux, Joseph. 2003. *Synaptic Self: How Our Brains Become Who We Are.* London: Penguin Books.

Lebo, Matthew, and Daniel Cassino. 2007. "The Aggregated Consequences of Motivated Reasoning and the Dynamics of Partisan Presidential Approval." *Political Psychology* 28 (6): 719–746.

Lehrer, Jonah. 2009. *The Decisive Moment: How the Brain Makes Up Its Mind.* Melbourne, Australia: The Text Publishing Company.

Lenz, Gabriel, and Chappell Lawson. 2007. "Looking the Part: Television Leads Less Informed Citizens to Vote on Candidate's Appearance." Unpublished manuscript, Department of Political Science, MIT.

Lerner, Jennifer, and Dacher Keltner. 2000. "Beyond Valence: Toward a Model of Emotion-Specific Influences on Judgment and Choice." *Cognition and Emotion* 14 (4): 473–493.

Lerner, Jennefer, Deborah Small, George Loewenstein. 2004. "*Heart Strings and Purse Strings,* Carryover Effects of Emotions on Economic Decisions." *Psychological Science* 15 (5): 337–341.

Levenson, Robert. 2003. "Autonomic Specificity and Emotion." In *Handbook of the Affective Sciences,* eds. Richard Davidson, Klaus Scherer, and Hill Goldsmith, 212–224, New York: Oxford University Press.

Libet, Benjamin. 1985. "Unconscious Cerebral Initiative and the Role of Conscious Will in Voluntary Action." *Behavioral and Brain Science* 8 (4): 529–539.

Libet, Benjamin. 1993. "The Neural Time Factor in Conscious and Unconscious Events." In *Experimental and Theoretical Studies of Consciousness,* CIBA Foundation Symposium 174: 123–146. Chichester: Wiley.

Libet, Benjamin. 2004. *Mind Time: The Temporal Factor in Consciousness.* Cambridge, MA: Harvard University Press.

Lichtenstein, Meryl and Thomas Srull. 1987. "Processing Objectives as a Determinant of the Relationship Between Recall and Judgment." *Journal of Experimental Social Psychology* 23 (2): 93–118.

Lindsay, Peter, and Donald Norman. 1977. *Human Information Processing: An Introduction to Psychology.* New York: Academic Press.

Lickel, Brian, David Hamilton, Grazyna Wieczorkowska, Amy Lewis, Steven Sherman, and Neville Uhles. 2000. "Varieties of Groups and the Perception of Group Entitativity." *Journal of Personality and Social Psychology* 78 (2): 223–246.

Lindstrom, Martin, and Paco Underhill. 2008. *Buyology: Truth and Lies about Why We Buy.* New York. Doubleday.

Little, Anthony. Robert Burriss, Benedict Jones and Craig Roberts. 2007. "Facial Appearance Affects Voting Decision." *Evolution and Human Behavior* 28 (1): 18–27.

Lodge, Milton, Kathleen McGraw, and Patrick Stroh. 1989. "An Impression Driven Model of Candidate Evaluation." *American Political Science Review* 83 (2): 399–420.

Lodge, Milton, Marco Steenbergen, and Shawn Brau. 1995. "The Responsive Voter: Campaign Information and the Dynamics of Candidate Evaluation." *American Political Science Review* 89 (2): 309–326.

Lodge, Milton, and Patrick Stroh. 1993. "Inside the Mental Voting Booth: An Impression-Driven Model." In *Explorations in Political Psychology*, eds. Shanto Iyengar and William McGuire, 225–263, Durham: Duke University Press.

Lodge, Milton, and Charles Taber. 2000. "Three Steps toward a Theory of Motivated Political Reasoning." In *Elements of Reason: Cognition, Choice, and the Bounds of Rationality*, eds. Arthur Lupia, Mathew McCubbins, and Samuel Popkin, 183–213, New York: Cambridge University Press.

Lodge, Milton, and Charles Taber. 2005. "The Automaticity of Affect for Political Leaders, Groups, and Issues: An Experimental Test of the Hot Cognition Hypothesis." *Political Psychology* 26 (3): 455–482.

Lodge, Milton, Charles Taber and Brad Verhulst. 2011. "Conscious and Unconscious Information Processing with Implications for Experimental Political Science." In *Handbook of Experimental Political Science*, eds. James Druckman, Donald Green, James Kuklinski, and Arthur Lupia, 155–170. New York: Cambridge University Press.

Loewenstein, George. 2007. "Affect Regulation and Affective Forecasting." In *Handbook of Emotion Regulation*, ed. James Gross, 180–203, New York: Guilford.

Loewenstein, George, and Jennifer Lerner. 2003. "The Role of Affect in Decision Making." In *Handbook of the Affective Sciences*, eds. Davidson, Richard, Klaus Scherer, and Hill Goldsmith, 619–642, New York: Oxford University Press.

Loewenstein, George, Elke Weber, Christopher Hsee, and Ned Welch. 2001. "Risk as Feelings." *Psychological Bulletin* 127 (2): 267–286.

Lord, Charles. 1992. "Was Cognitive Dissonance Theory a Mistake?" *Psychological Inquiry* 3 (4): 339–342.

Lord, Charles, Lee Ross, and Mark Lepper. 1979. "Biased Assimilation and Attitude Polarization: The Effects of Prior Theories on Subsequently Considered Evidence." *Journal of Personality and Social Psychology* 37 (11): 2098–2109.

Luker, Kristin. 1984. *Abortion and the Politics of Motherhood*. Berkeley: University of California Press.

MacKuen, Michael, Jennifer Wolak, Luke Keele, and George Marcus. 2010. "Civic Engagements: Resolute Partisanship or Reflective Deliberation?" *American Journal of Political Science* 54 (2): 440–458.

MacLeod, Colin, and Lynlee Campbell. 1992. "Memory Accessibility and Probability Judgments: An Experimental Evaluation of the Availability Heuristic." *Journal of Personality and Social Psychology* 63 (6): 890–902.

Maison, Dominika, Anthony Greenwald, and Ralph Bruin. 2004. "Predictive Validity of the Implicit Attitude Test in Studies of Brands, Consumer Attitudes, and Behavior." *Journal of Consumer Psychology* 14 (4): 405–415.

Marcus, George. 1991. "Emotions and Politics: Hot Cognitions and the Rediscovery of Passion." *Social Science Information* 30 (2): 195–232.

Marcus, George. 2002. *The Sentimental Citizen: Emotion in Democratic Politics*. University Park: The Pennsylvania State University Press.

Marcus, George, Michael MacKuen, and Russell Neuman. 2011. "Parsimony and Complexity: Developing and Testing Theories of Affective Intelligence." *Political Psychology* 32 (2): 323–336.

Marcus, George, W. Russell Neuman, and Michael MacKuen. 2000. *Affective Intelligence and Political Judgment*. Chicago: University of Chicago Press.

Markus, Helen, and Robert Zajonc. 1985. "The Cognitive Perspective in Social Psychology." In *The Handbook of Social Psychology* (Vol. 1), eds. Gordon. Lindzey and Eliot Aronson, 137–230, New York: Random House.

Martin, Leonard, and Abraham Tesser eds. 1992. *The Construction of Social Judgments*. Hillsdale, NJ: Erlbaum.

Mast, Fred, and Gerald Zaltman. 2005. "A Behavioral Window on the Mind of the Market: An Application of the Response Time Paradigm." *Brain Research Bulletin* 67 (5): 422–427.

McConahay, John. 1986. "Modern Racism, Ambivalence, and the Modern Racism Scale." In *Prejudice, Discrimination, and Racism*, ed. John Dovidio and Samuel Gaertner, 91–125, Orlando, FL: Academic Press.

McDermott, Rose. 2004. "The Feeling of Rationality: The Meaning of Neuroscientific Advances for Political Science." *Perspectives on Politics* 2(4): 691–706.

McGraw, Kathleen. 1987. "Guilt Following Transgression: An Attribution of Responsibility Approach." *Journal of Personality and Social Psychology* 53 (2): 247–256.

McGraw, Kathleen. 2000. "Contributions to the Cognitive Approach to Political Psychology." *Political Psychology* 21 (4): 805–832.

McGraw, Kathleen M. (2011). "Candidate Impressions and Evaluations". In *Handbook of Experimental Political Science*, eds. James N. Druckman, Donald P. Green, James H. Kuklinski and Arthur Lupia, 187–200. Cambridge: Cambridge University Press.

McGraw, Kathleen, Mark Fischle, Karen Stenner, and Milton Lodge. 1996. "What's in a Word? Bias in Trait Descriptions of Political Leaders." *Political Behavior* 18 (3): 263–287.

McGraw, Kathleen, Milton Lodge, and Patrick Stroh. 1990. "On-Line Processing in Candidate Evaluation: The Effect of Issue Order, Salience, Issue Importance, and Sophistication." *Political Behavior* 12 (1): 41–58.

McGraw, Kathleen M., and Marco Steenbergen. 1995. "Pictures in the Head: Memory Representations of Political Candidates." In *Political Judgment: Structure and Process*, eds. Milton Lodge and Kathleen M. McGraw, 15–42, Ann Arbor: University of Michigan Press.

McGraw, Kathleen, Milton Lodge, and Jeffery Jones. 2002. "The Pandering Politicians of Suspicious Minds." *Journal of Politics* 64 (2): 362–383.

McGrayne, Sharon. 2011. *The Theory That Would Not Die: How Bayes Rule Cracked the Enigma Code, Hunted Down Russian Submarines, and Emerged Triumphant from Two Centuries of Controversy*. New Haven, CT: Yale University Press.

McGuire, William. 1966. "Attitudes and Opinions." *Annual Review of Psychology* 17 (1): 475–515.

McGuire, William, and Claire McGuire. 1991. "The Content, Structure, and Operation of Thought Systems." In *Advances in Social Cognition, Volume IV*, eds. Robert Wyer and Thomas Srull, 1–78, Hillsdale, NJ: Erlbaum.

McGuire, William, and Alice Padawer-Singer. 1976. "Trait Salience in the Spontaneous Self-Concept." *Journal of Personality and Social Psychology* 33 (6): 743–754.

Meffert, Michael, Michael Guge, and Milton Lodge. 2004. "Good, Bad, and Ambivalent: The Consequences of Multidimensional Political Attitudes." In *Studies in Public Opinion: Attitudes, Nonattitudes, Measurement Error, and Change*, eds. Willem Saris and Paul Sniderman, 63–92, Princeton, NJ: Princeton University Press.

Meliema, Amgelika, and John Bassili. 1995. "On the Relationship between Attitudes and Values: Exploring the Moderating Effects of Self-Monitoring and Self-Monitoring Schematicity." *Personality and Social Psychology Bulletin* 21: 885–892.

Mendelberg, Tali. 2001. *The Race Card: Campaign Strategy, Implicit Messages, and the Norm of Equality*. Princeton, NJ: Princeton University Press.

Merikle, Philip, and Meredyth Daneman. 1998. "Psychological Investigations of Unconscious Perception." *Journal of Consciousness Studies* 5: 5–18.

Miles, Lynden, Louise Nind, and Neil Macrae. 2010. "Moving Through Time." *Psychological Science* 21 (2): 222–223.

Millar, Murray, and Abraham Tesser. 1986. "Thought-Induced Attitude Change: The Effects of Schema, Structure and Commitment." *Journal of Personality and Social Psychology* 51 (2): 259–269.

Miller, Arthur, John McHoskey, Cynthia Bane, and Timothy Dowd. 1993. "The Attitude Polarization Phenomenon: Role of Response Measure, Attitude Extremity, and Behavioral Consequences of Reported Attitude Change." *Journal of Personality and Social Psychology* 64 (4): 561–574.

Miller, Arthur, Martin Wattenberg, and Oksana Malanchuk. 1986. "Schematic Assessments of Political Candidates." *American Political Science Review* 80 (2): 521–540.

Miller, George. 1956. "The Magic Number Seven, Plus or Minus Two: Some Limits on Our Capacity for Processing Information." *Psychological Review* 63 (2): 81–97.

Mondak, Jeffery. 1994. "Policy Legitimacy and the Supreme Court: The Sources and Contexts of Legitimization." *Political Research Quarterly* 47 (3): 675–692.

Moors, Agnes, Adriaan Spruyt and Jan De Houwer. 2010. "In Search of a Measure that Qualifies as Implicit: Recommendations Based on a Decompositional View of Automaticity." In *Handbook of Implicit Social Cognition: Measurement, Theory, and Application*, eds. Bertram Gawronski and Keith Payne, 19–37, New York: Guilford.

Morris, James, Nancy Squires, Charles Taber, and Milton Lodge. 2003. "Activation of Political Attitudes: A Psychophysiological Examination of the Hot Cognition Hypothesis." *Political Psychology* 24 (4): 727–745.

Mueller, Ulrich and Allan Mazur. 1996. "Facial Dominance in West Point Cadets Predicts Military Rank 20 +Years Later." *Social Forces* 74 (3): 823–850.

Mullen, Brian, David Futrell, Debbie Stairs, Dianne Tice, Roy Baumeister, Kathryn Dawson, Catherine Riordan, Christine Radloff, George Goethals, John Kennedy, and Paul Rosenfeld. 1986. "Newscasters' Facial Expressions and Voting Behavior of Viewers: Can a Smile Elect a President?" *Journal of Personality and Social Psychology* 51 (2): 291–295.

Munro, Geoffrey, Peter Ditto, Lisa Lockhart, Angela Fagerlin, Michael Gready, and Elizabeth Peterson. 2002. "Biased Assimilation of Sociopolitical Arguments: Evaluating the 1996 U.S. Presidential Debate." *Basic and Applied Social Psychology* 24 (1): 15–26.

Murphy, Fionnuala, Ian Nimmo-Smith, and Andrew Lawrence. 2003. "Functional Neuroanatomy of Emotion: A Meta-Analysis." *Cognitive, Affective, & Behavioral Neuroscience* 3 (3): 207–233.

Murphy, Sheila, and Robert Zajonc. 1993. "Affect, Cognition and Awareness: Affective Priming with Optimal and Suboptimal Stimulus Exposures." *Journal of Personality and Social Psychology* 64 (5): 723–729.

Navarro, Daniel, Michael Lee, Matthew Dry, and Benjamin Schultz. 2008. "Extending and Testing a Bayesian Theory of Generalization." *Proceedings of the 30th Annual Conference of the Cognitive Science Society*, 1746–1751. The Cognitive Science Society: Austin, TX.

Neely, James. 1976. "Semantic Priming and Retrieval from Lexical Memory: Evidence for Facilitatory and Inhibitory Processes." *Memory & Cognition* 4 (5): 648–654.

Neely, James. 1977. "Semantic Priming and Retrieval from Lexical Memory: Roles of Inhibitionless Spreading Activation and Limited-capacity Attention." *Journal of Experimental Psychology: General* 106 (3): 226–254.

Neisser, Uric. 1976. *Principles and Implications of Cognitive Psychology*. New York: W.H. Freeman.

Neuman, Russell. 1986. *The Paradox of Mass Politics: Knowledge and Opinion in the American Electorate*. Cambridge, MA: Harvard University Press.

Neuman, Russell, Marion Just, and Ann Crigler. 1992. *Common Knowledge: News and the Construction of Political Meaning*. Chicago: University of Chicago Press.

Newman, Leonard, and Uleman, James. 1989. "Spontaneous Trait Inference." In *Unintended Thought*, eds. Jens Uleman, and James Bargh, 155–188, New York: Guilford.

Nie, Norman, Darwin Miller, Saar Golde, Daniel Butler, and Kenneth Winneg. 2010. "The World Wide Web and the U.S. Political News Market." *American Journal of Political Science* 54 (2): 428–439.

Niedenthal, Paula, and Carolyn Showers. 1991. "The Perception and Processing of Affective Information and Its Influences on Social Judgment." In *Emotion and Social Judgments*, ed. Joseph Forgas, 125–143, Elmsford, NY: Pergamon Press.

Niedenthal, Paula, and Marc Setterlund. 1994. "Emotion Congruence in Perception." *Personality and Social Psychology Bulletin* 20 (4): 401–411.

Niedenthal, Paula, Jamin Halberstadt, and Marc Setterlund. 1997. "Being Happy and Seeing "Happy": Emotional State Mediates Visual Word Recognition." *Cognition and Emotion* 11 (4): 403–432.

Niedenthal, Paula, Jamin Halberstadt, and Ase Innes-Ker. 1999. "Emotional Response Categorization." *Psychological Review* 106 (2): 337–361.

Niedenthal, Paula, and Jamin Halberstadt. 2000. "Grounding Categories in Emotional Response." In *Feeling and Thinking: The Role of Affect in Social Cognition*, ed. Joseph Forgas, 357–386, New York: Cambridge University Press.

Niedenthal, Paula, Lawrence Barsalou, Piotr Winkielman, Silva Krauth-Gruber, and Francois Ric. 2005. "Embodiment in Attitudes, Social Perception, and Emotion." *Personality and Social Psychology Review* 9 (3): 184–211.

Nisbett, Richard, and Lee Ross. 1980. *Human Inference: Strategies and Shortcomings of Social Judgment*. Englewood Cliffs, NJ: Prentice-Hall.

Norretranders, Tor. 1998. *The User Illusion: Cutting Consciousness Down to Size*. New York: Penguin Books.

Norris, Catherine, Amanda Dumville, and Dean Lacy. 2011. "Affective Forecasting Errors in the 2008 Election: Underpredicting Happiness." *Political Psychology* 32 (2): 235–249.

Nosek, Brian. 2004. *Moderators of the Relationship Between Implicit and Explicit Attitudes.* Unpublished manuscript, University of Virginia, Charlottesville.

Nosek, Brian, Jesse Graham, and Carlee Hawkins. 2010. "Implicit Political Cognition." In *Handbook of Implicit Social Cognition: Measurement, Theory, and Applications,* eds. Bertram Gawronski and B. Keith Payne, 548–564, New York: Guilford.

Nosek, Brian, Anthony Greenwald, and Mahzarin Banaji. 2005. "Understanding and Using the Implicit Association Test: II. Method Variables and Construct Validity." *Personality and Social Psychology Bulletin* 31 (2): 166–180.

Nosek, Brian, and Frederick Smyth. 2007. "A Multitrait-Multimethod Validation of the Implicit Association Test: Implicit and Explicit Attitudes are Related but Distinct Constructs." *Journal of Experimental Psychology* 54 (1): 14–29.

Nyhan, Brendan, and Jason Reifler. 2010. "When Corrections Fail: The Persistence of Political Misperceptions." *Political Behavior* 32 (2): 303–330.

Oakhill, Jane, and Phillip Johnson-Laird. 1985. "The Effect of Belief on the Spontaneous Production of Syllogistic Conclusions." *Quarterly Journal of Experimental Psychology* 37 (4): 553–570.

Oatley, Keith. 2002. "Creative Expression and Communication of Emotions in the Visual and Narrative Arts." In *Handbook of the Affective Sciences,* eds. Richard Davidson, Klaus Scherer, and Hill Goldsmith, 481–502, New York: Oxford University Press.

Oberman, Lindsay, and Vilayanur Ramachandran. 2007. "The Simulating Social Mind: The Role of the Mirror Neuron System and Simulation in the Social and Communicative Deficits of Autism Spectrum Disorders." *Psychological Bulletin* 133 (2): 310–327.

Olivola, Christopher, and Alexander Todorov. 2010. "Fooled by First Impressions? Re-examining the Diagnostic Value of Appearance-Based Inferences." *Journal of Experimental Social Psychology* 46: 315–324.

Olson, Kristina, and Yarrow Dunham. 2010. "The Development of Implicit Social Cognition." In *Handbook of Implicit Social Cognition: Measurement, Theory, and Applications,* eds. Bertram Gawronski and Keith Payne, 241–254, New York: Guilford.

Olson, Michael, and Russell Fazio. 2004. "Reducing the Influence of Extrapersonal Associations on the Implicit Association Test: Personalizing the IAT." *Journal of Personality and Social Psychology* 86 (5): 653–667.

Olson, Michael, and Russell Fazio. 2009. "Implicit and Explicit Measures of Attitude: The Perspective of the MODE Model." In *Attitudes: Insights From the New Implicit Measures,* eds. Richard Petty, Russell Fazio and Pablo Briñol, 19–64, New York: Psychology Press.

Olson, James, and Mark Zanna. 1993. "Attitudes and Attitude Change." *Annual Review of Psychology* 44: 117–154.

Ongur, Dost, and Joseph Price. 2000. "The Organization of Networks within the Orbital and Medial Prefrontal Cortex of Rats, Monkeys and Humans." *Cerebral Cortex* 10 (3): 206–219.

Ortony, Andrew, and Terrence Turner. 1990. "What's Basic About Basic Emotions?" *Psychological Review* 97 (3): 315–331.

Orwell, George. 1949. *1984.* New York: Harcourt, Brace, and Company.

Oskamp, Stuart, and Wesley Schultz. 2005. *Attitudes and Opinions* (3rd ed.). Mahwah, NJ: Erlbaum.

Page, Benjamin, and Robert Shapiro. 1992. *The Rational Public: Fifty Years of Trends in Americans' Policy Preferences*. Chicago: University of Chicago.

Panksepp, Jaak. 1998. *Affective Neuroscience: The Foundations of Human and Animal Emotions*. New York: Oxford University Press.

Park, Bernadette. 1989. "Trait Attributes As On-line Organizers in Person Impressions." In *Online Cognition in Person Perception*, ed. John Bassilli, 39–60, Hillsdale, NJ: Erlbaum.

Pascal, Blaise. 1670 (2010). *Pensées*. New York: Penguin Books. Translated by A. J. Krailsheimer.

Pascalis, Oliver, and Alan Slater, eds. 2003. *The Development of Face Processing in Infancy and Early Childhood: Current Perspectives*. New York: Nova Science Publishers.

Payne, John. 1982. "Contingent Decision Behavior." *Psychological Bulletin* 92 (2): 382–402.

Payne, Keith, Clara Cheng, Olesya Govorun, and Brandon Stewart. 2005. "An Inkblot for Attitudes: Affect Misattribution as Implicit Measurement. *Journal of Personality and Social Psychology* 89 (3): 277–293.

Pennington, Nancy, and Reid Hastie. 1992. "Explaining the Evidence: Tests of the Story Model for Juror Decision Making." *Journal of Personality and Social Psychology* 62 (2): 189–206.

Pennington, Nancy, and Reid Hastie. 1993. "Reasoning in Explanation-Based Decision Making." *Cognition* 49 (1–2): 123–163.

Perdue, Charles, John Dovidio, Michael Gurtman, and Richard Tyler. 1990. "Us and Them: Social Categorization and the Process of Intergroup Bias." *Journal of Personality and Social Psychology* 59 (3): 475–486.

Perkins, Andrew, and Mark Forehand. 2010. "Implicit Social Cognition and Indirect Measures in Consumer Behavior." In *Handbook of Implicit Social Cognition: Measurement, Theory, and Applications*, eds. Bertram Gawronski and Keith Payne, 535–547, New York: Guilford.

Perugini, Marco, Juliette Richetin, and Cristina Zogmaister. 2010. "Prediction of Behavior." In *Handbook of Implicit Social Cognition:Measurement, Theory, and Applications*, eds. Bertram Gawronski and Keith Payne, 255–277, New York: Guilford.

Pettigrew, Thomas and Roel Meertens. 1995. "Subtle and Blatant Prejudice in Western Europe." *European Journal of Social Psychology* 25 (1): 57–75.

Petty, Richard, and Pablo Briñol. 2008. "Persuasion: From Single to Multiple to Meta-Cognitive Processes." *Perspectives on Psychological Science* 3 (2): 137–147.

Petty, Richard, and Pablo Briñol. 2010. "Attitude Structure and Change: Implications for Implicit Measures." In *Handbook of Implicit Social Cognition:Measurement, Theory, and Applications*, eds. Bertram Gawronski and Keith Payne, 335–352, New York: Guilford.

Petty, Richard, and John Cacioppo. 1981. *Attitudes and Persuasion: Classic and Contemporary Approaches*. Dubuque, IA: Brown and Benchmark.

Petty, Richard, and John Cacioppo. 1986. *Communication and Persuasion: Central and Peripheral Routes to Attitude Change*. New York: Springer.

Petty, Richard, Russell Fazio, and Pablo Briñol, eds. 2009. *Attitudes: Insights from the New Implicit Measures*. New York: Psychology Press.

Petty, Richard. and Jon Krosnick, eds. 1995. *Attitude Strength: Antecedents and Consequences*. Hillsdale, NJ: Erlbaum.

Petty, Richard, Zakary Tormala, Pablo Briñol, and Blair Jarvis. 2006. "Implicit Ambivalence from Attitude Change: An Exploration of the PAST Model." *Journal of Personality and Social Psychology* 90 (1): 21–41.

Petty, Richard, and Duane Wegener. 1998. "Attitude Change: Multiple Roles for Persuasion Variables." In *The Handbook of Social Psychology*, eds. Daniel Gilbert, Susan Fiske, and Gardner Lindzey, 323–390, Boston: McGraw-Hill.

Petty, Richard, Duane Wegener, and Leandre Fabrigar. 1997. "Attitudes and Attitude Change." *Annual Review of Psychology* 48: 609–647.

Petty, Richard, David Schumann, Steven Richman, and Alan Strathman. 1993. "Positive Mood and Persuasion: Different Roles for Affect under High and Low Elaboration Conditions." *Journal of Personality and Social Psychology* 64 (1): 5–20.

Phan, Luan, Tor Wager, Stephan Taylor, and Israel Liberzon. 2002. "Functional Neuroanatomy of Emotion: A Meta-Analysis of Emotion Activation Studies in PET and fMRI." *NeuroImage* 16 (2): 331–348.

Piliavin, Jane Allyn, John Dovidio, Samuel Gaertner, and R.D. Clark. 1981. *Emergency Intervention*. New York: Academic Press.

Plato. 2000. *The Republic*. Cambridge: Cambridge University Press.

Pratkanis, Anthony. 1989. "The Cognitive Representation of Attitudes." In *Attitude Structure and Function*, eds. Anthony Pratkanis, Steven Breckler, and Anthony Greenwald 70–98, Hillsdale, NJ: Erlbaum.

Price, Vincent and Mei-Ling Hsu. 1992. "Public Opinion About AIDS Policies: The Role of Misinformation and Attitudes toward Homosexuals." *Public Opinion Quarterly* 56 (1): 29–52.

Pomerantz, Eva, Shelly Chaiken, and Rosalind Tordesillas. 1995. "Attitude Strength and Resistance Processes." *Journal of Personality and Social Psychology* 69 (3): 408–419.

Posner, Michael, and Charles Snyder. 1975a. "Attention and Cognitive Control." In *Information Processing and Cognition: The Loyola Symposium*, ed. Robert Solso, 55–85, Hillsdale, NJ: Erlbaum.

Posner, Michael, and Charles Snyder. 1975b. "Facilitation and Inhibition in the Processing of Signals." In *Attention and Performance V.*, eds. P.M.A. Rabbitt, and Stanislav Dornic, 669–698, New York: Academic Press.

Pyszczynski, Thomas, and Jeffrey Greenberg. 1987. "Self-Regulatory Perseveration and the Depressive Focusing Style: A Self-Awareness Theory of Reactive Depression." *Psychological Bulletin* 102 (1): 122–138.

Pyszczynski, Thomas, Sheldon Solomon, and Jeff Greenberg. 2003. *In the Wake of 9/11: The Psychology of Terror*. New York: American Psychological Association.

Rabinowitz, George and Stuart MacDonald. 1989. "A Directional Theory of Issue Voting." *American Political Science Review* 83 (1): 93–121.

Rahn, Wendy, John Aldrich, and Eugene Borgida. 1994. "Individual and Contextual Variations in Political Candidate Appraisal." *American Political Science Review* 88 (1): 193–199.

Rahn, Wendy, John Aldrich, Eugene Borgida, and John Sullivan. 1990. "A Social Cognitive Model of Candidate Appraisal." In *Information and Democratic Processes*, eds. John Ferejohn and James Kuklinski, 136–159, Urbana: University of Illinois Press.

Rahn, Wendy, Jon Krosnick, and Michael Breuning. 1994. "Rationalization and Derivation Processes in Survey Studies of Political Candidate Evaluation." *American Journal of Political Science* 38 (3): 582–600.

Rapport, Ronald, Kelly Metcalf, and Jon Hartman. 1989. "Candidate Traits and Voter Inferences: An Experimental Study." *Journal of Politics* 51 (4): 917–932.

Ratcliff, Roger and Gail McKoon. 1996. "Bias Effects in Implicit memory Tasks." *Journal of Experimental Psychology: General* 125 (4): 403–421.

Razran, Gregory. 1938. "Conditioning Away Social Bias by the Luncheon Technique." *Psychological Bulletin* 37: 481.

Read, Stephen, and Lynn Miller. 1998. *Connectionist Models of Social Reasoning and Social Behavior*. Mahwah, NJ: Erlbaum.

Redlawsk, David. 2001. "You Must Remember This: A Test of the On-Line Model of Voting." *Journal of Politics* 63 (1): 29–58.

Redlawsk, David. 2002. "Hot Cognition or Cool Consideration? Testing the Effects of Motivated Reasoning on Political Decision Making." *Journal of Politics* 64 (4): 1021–1044.

Redlawsk, David. 2004. "What Voters Do: Information Search During Election Campaigns." *Political Psychology* 25 (4): 595–610.

Redlawsk, David, Andrew Civettini, and Karen Emmerson. 2010. "The Affective Tipping Point: Do Motivated Reasoners Ever 'Get It'?" *Political Psychology* 31 (4): 563–593.

Redlawsk, David, Andrew Civettini, and Richard Lau. 2007. "Affective Intelligence and Voting: Information Processing and Learning in a Campaign." In *The Affect Effect: Dynamics of Emotion in Political Thinking and Behavior*, eds. Russell Neuman, George Marcus, Ann Crider, and Michael MacKuen, 152–179, Chicago: Chicago University Press.

Reyes, Robert, Thompson, William, and Gordon Bower. 1980. "Judgmental Biases Resulting From Differing Availabilities of Arguments." *Journal of Personality and Social Psychology* 39 (1): 2–12.

Rich, Frank. 2006. *The Greatest Story Ever Sold: The Decline and Fall of the Truth From 9/11 to Katrina*. New York: The Penguin Press.

Riggle, Ellen, Victor Ottati, Robert Wyer, James Kuklinski, and Norbert Shwarz. 1992. "Bases of Political Judgments: The Role of Stereotypic and Nonstereotypic Information." *Political Behavior* 14 (1): 67–87.

Riker, William, and Peter Ordeshook. 1968. "A Theory of the Calculus of Voting." *American Political Science Review* 62 (1): 25–42.

Risen, Jane, and Clayton Critcher. 2011. "Visceral Fit: While in a Visceral State, Associated States of the World Seem More Likely." *Journal of Personality and Social Psychology* 100 (5): 777–793.

Rhodes, Gillian. 2006. "The Evolutionary Psychology of Facial Beauty." *Annual Review of Psychology* 57: 884–887.

Robinson, Michael, and Gerald Clore. 2002. "Belief and Feeling: Evidence for an Accessibility Model of Emotional Self-Report." *Psychological Bulletin* 128 (6): 934–960.

Roccato, Michele, and Cristina Zogmaister. 2010. "Predicting the Vote through Implicit and Explicit Attitudes: A Field Research." *Political Psychology* 31 (2): 249–274.

Rolls, Edmund. 1999. *The Brain and Emotion*. New York: Oxford University Press.

Romer, Daniel, Kate Kenski, Paul Waldman, Christopher Adasiewicz, and Kathleen Hall Jamieson. 2003. *Capturing Campaign Dynamics: The National Annenberg Election Survey*. New York: Oxford University Press.

Rosar, Ulrich, Markus Klein, and Tilo Beckers. 2008. "The Frog Pond Beauty Contest: Physical Attractiveness and Electoral Success of the Constituency Candidates at the North Rhine-Westphalia State Election of 2005." *European Journal of Political Research* 47 (1): 64–79.

Rosch, Eleanor. 1975. "Cognitive Representations of Semantic Categories." *Journal of Experimental Social Psychology* 104 (3): 192–233.

Rosch, Eleanor. 1978. "Principles of Categorization." In *Cognition and Categorization*, eds. Eleanor Rosch and Barbara Lloyd, 28–50, Hillsdale, NJ: Erlbaum.

Roseman, Ira. 1991. "Appraisal Determinants of Discrete Emotions." *Cognition and Emotion* 5 (3): 161–200.

Roseman, Ira. 2001. "A Model of Appraisal in the Emotion System: Integrating Theory, Research, and Applications." In *Appraisal Processes in Emotion: Theory, Methods, Research*, eds. Klaus Scherer, Angela Shorr, and Tom Johnstone, 68–91, New York: Oxford University Press.

Roseman, Ira, Robert Abelson, and Michael Ewing. 1986. "Emotions and Political Cognition: Emotional Appeals in Political Communication." In *Political Cognition*, eds. Richard Lau and David Sears, 279–294, Hillsdale, NJ: Erlbaum.

Rosenberg, Shawn. 2002. *The Not So Common Sense: Differences in How People Judge Social and Political Life*. New Haven, CT: Yale University Press.

Rosenberg, Shawn, Lisa Bohan, Patrick McCafferty, and Kevin Harris. 1986. "The Image and the Vote: The Effect of Candidate Presentation on Voter Preference." *American Journal of Political Science* 30 (1): 108–127.

Roth, Byron. 1994. *Prescription for Failure: Race Relations in the Age of Social Science*. New Brunswick, NJ: Transaction.

Rucker, Derek, and Richard Petty. 2004. "Emotion Specificity and Consumer Behavior: Anger, Sadness, and Preference for Activity." *Motivation and Emotion* 28 (1): 3–21.

Rumelhart, David, and Andrew Ortony. 1977. "The Representation of Knowledge in Memory." In *Schooling and the Acquisition of Knowledge*, eds. Robert Anderson, Rand Spiro, and William Montague, 99–135, Hillsdale, NJ: Erlbaum.

Russell, James. 1980. "A Circumplex Model of Affect." *Journal of Personality and Social Psychology* 39 (6): 1161–1178.

Russell, James. 1991. "Culture and the Categorization of Emotions." *Psychological Bulletin* 110 (3): 426–450.

Russell, James. 2003. "Core Affect and the Psychological Construction of Emotion." *Psychological Review* 110 (1): 145–172.

Russell, James, Jo-Ann Bachorowski, and Jose Fernández-Dols. 2003. "Facial and Vocal Expressions of Emotion." *Annual Review of Psychology* 54: 329–349.

Russell, James, and Lisa Barrett. 1999. "Core Affect, Prototypical Emotional Episodes, and Other Things Called Emotion: Dissecting the Elephant." *Journal of Personality and Social Psychology* 76 (5): 805–819.

Ruys, Kristen, and Diederik Stapel. 2008. "The Secret Life of Emotions." *Psychological Science* 19 (4): 385–391.

Sagan, Carl. 1987. "The Burden of Skepticism." *The Skeptical Inquirer* 12 (1): 38–46.

Sanbonmatsu, David, and Russell Fazio. 1990. "The Role of Attitudes in Memory-Based Decision Making" *Journal of Personality and Social Psychology* 59 (4): 614–622.

Sanford, Anthony. 1987. *The Mind of Man: Models of Human Understanding.* New Haven, CT: Yale University Press.

Sassenberg, Kai,and Gordon Moskowitz. 2005. "Don't Stereotype, Think Different! Overcoming Automatic Stereotype Activation by Mindset Priming." *Journal of Experimental Social Psychology* 41 (5): 506–514.

Schachter, Stanley, and Jerald Singer. 1962. "Cognitive, Social, and Physiological Determinants of Emotional State." *Psychological Review* 69 (5): 379–399.

Schatz, Robert, and Howard Lavine. 2007. "Waving the Flag: National Symbolism, Social Identity, and Political Engagement." *Political Psychology* 28 (3): 329–355.

Scherer, Klaus. 1999. "On the Sequential Nature of Appraisal Processes: Indirect Evidence from a Recognition Task." *Cognition and Emotion* 13 (6): 763–793.

Scherer, Klaus. 2004. "What Emotions Can Be Induced by Music? What are the Underlying Mechanisms? And How Can We Measure Them?" *Journal of New Music Research* 33 (3): 239–251.

Scherer, Klaus, Angela Schorr, and Tom Johnstone, eds. 2001. *Appraisal Processes in Emotion: Theory, Methods, Research.* New York: Oxford University Press.

Schnabel, Konrad, and Jens Asendorph. 2010. "The Self-Concept: New Insights from Implicit Measurement Procedures." In *Handbook of Implicit Social Cognition:Measurement, Theory, and Applications*, eds. Bertram Gawronski and Keith Payne, 408–425. New York: Guilford.

Schneider, Daniel, Jon Krosnick, Eyal Ofir, Claire Milligan, and Alexander Tahk. 2008. "The Psychology of Voting: How and Why the Order of Candidate Names on the Ballot and Election Laws Influence Election Outcomes." *Society for Personality and Social Psychology Annual Meeting*, Albuquerque, New Mexico, January 26–28.

Schneider, Daniel, Alexander Tahk, and Jon Krosnick. 2007. "Reconsidering the Impact of Behavior Prediction Questions on Illegal Drug Use: The Importance of Using Proper Analytic Methods." *Social Influence* 2 (3): 178–196.

Schuman, Howard, and Stanley Presser. 1981. *Question and Answers in Attitude Surveys: Experiments on Question Form, Wording, and Context.* New York: Academic Press.

Schwarz, Norbert, and Herbert Bless. 1992. "Scandals and the Public's Trust in Politicians: Assimilation and Contrast Effects." *Personality and Social Psychology Bulletin* 18 (5): 574–579.

Schwarz, Norbert and Gerald Clore. 1983. "Mood, Misattribution, and Judgments of Well-Being: Informative and Directive Functions of Affective States." *Journal of Personality and Social Psychology* 45 (3): 513–523.

Schwarz, Norbert and Gerald Clore. 1988. "How Do I Feel about It? Informative Functions of Affective States." In *Affect, Cognition, and Social Behavior: New Evidence and Integrative Attempts*, eds. Klaus Fiedler and Joseph Forgas, 44–62, Goettingen, Federal Republic of Germany: Hogrefe.

Schwitzgebel, Eric. 2008. "The Unreliability of Naïve Introspection." *Philosophical Review* 117 (2): 242–273.

Schwitzgebel, Eric. 2011. *Perplexities of Consciousness.* Cambridge, MA: MIT Press.

Sears, David. 2001. "The Role of Affect in Symbolic Politics." In *Citizens and Politics: Perspectives from Political Psychology*, ed. James Kuklinski, 14–40, Cambridge: Cambridge University Press.

Sears, David, and Jonathan Freedman. 1967. "Selective Exposure to Information: A Critical Review." *Public Opinion Quarterly* 31 (2): 194–213.

Sears, David, Jonathan Freedman, and Edward O'Connor, Jr. 1964. "The Effects of Anticipated Debate and Commitment on the Polarization of Audience Opinion." *The Public Opinion Quarterly* 28 (4): 615–627.

Sears, David, and P.J. Henry. 2003. "The Origins of Symbolic Racism." *Journal of Personality and Social Psychology* 85 (2): 259–275.

Sears, David, Leonie Huddy, and Lynitta Schaffer. 1986. "A Schematic Variant of Symbolic Politics Theory, as Applied to Racial and Gender Equality." In *Political Cognition*, eds. Richard Lau and David Sears, 159–202, Hillsdale, NJ: Erlbaum.

Sears, David, and Richard Lau. 1983. "Inducing Apparently Self-Interested Political Preferences." *American Journal of Political Science* 27 (2): 223–252.

Sears, David, and Robert Whitney. 1973. *Political Persuasion*. Morristown, NJ: General Learning Press.

Sekaquaptewa, Denise, Partick Vegas, and William von Hippel. 2010. "A Practical Guide to Paper and Pencil Implicit Measures of Attitudes." In *Handbook of Implicit Social Cognition: Measurement, Theory, and Applications*, eds. Bertram Gawronski and Keith Payne, 140–155, New York: Guilford.

Shabbir, Haseeb, and Des Thwaites. 2007. "The Use of Humor to Mask Deceptive Advertising: It's No Laughing Matter." *Journal of Advertising* 36 (2): 75–85.

Shanteau, James. 1992. "How Much Information Does an Expert Use? Is it Relevant?" *Acta Psychologica* 81 (1): 75–86.

Shelton, Nichole, Jennifer Richeson, Jessica Salvatore, and Sophie Trawalter. 2009. "Ironic Effects of racial bias During Interracial Interactions." *Psychological Science* 16 (5): 397–402.

Shepard, Roger. 1967. "Recognition Memory for Words, Sentences, and Pictures." *Journal of Verbal Learning and Verbal Behavior* 6 (1): 156–163.

Sherman, Jeffrey. 2009. "Controlled Influences on Implicit Measures: Confronting the Myth of Process Purity and taming the Cognitive Monster." In *Attitudes: Insights from the New Implicit Measures*, eds. Richard Petty, Russell Fazio, and Pablo Briñol, 391–428, New York: Psychology Press.

Shermer, Michael. 2002. "The Captain Kirk Principle." *Scientific American* 287 (6): 39.

Shih, Margaret, Todd Pittinsky, and Nalini Ambady. 1999. Stereotype Susceptibility: Identity Salience and Shifts in Quantitative Performance. *Psychological Science* 10 (1): 81–84.

Sidanius, Jim, Felicia Pratto, and Lawrence Bobo. 1996. "Racism, Conservatism, Affirmative Action and Intellectual Sophistication: A Matter of Principled Conservatism or Group Dominance?" *Journal of Personality and Social Psychology* 70: 476–490.

Sigelman, Lee, Carol Sigelman, and Christopher Fowler. 1987. "A Bird of a Different Feather? An Experimental Investigation of Physical Attractiveness and the Electability of Female Candidates." *Social Psychology Quarterly* 50 (1): 32–43.

Simon, Herbert. 1957. *Models of Man: Social and Rational: Mathematical Essays on Rational Human Behavior in a Social Setting*. New York: Wiley.

Simon, Herbert. 1967. "Motivational and Emotional Controls of Cognition." *Psychological Review* 74 (1): 29–39.

Simon, Herbert. 1969. *The Sciences of the Artificial.* Boston: MIT Press.

Simon, Herbert. 1985. "Human Nature in Politics: The Dialogue of Psychology and Political Science." *American Political Science Review* 79 (2): 293–304.

Simons, Daniel. 1996. "In Sight, Out of Mind: When Object Representations Fail." Psychological Science 7 (5): 301–305.

Singer, Nancy. "Making Ads That Whisper." *The New York Times*, November, 14, 2010, p. 4.

Sleeth-Keppler, David. 2007. "Seeing the World in Black and White: The Effects of Perceptually Induced Mind-Sets on Judgment." *Psychological Science* 18 (9): 768–772.

Slovic, Paul. 1999. "Trust, Emotion, Sex, Politics, and Science: Surveying the Risk Assessment Battlefield." *Risk Analysis* 19: 689–701.

Slovic, Paul. 2002. "The Affect Heuristic." In *Heuristics and Biases*, eds. Thomas Gilovich, Dale Griffin, and Daniel Kahneman, 397–420, New York: Cambridge University Press.

Slovic, Paul, Melissa Finucane, Ellen Peters, and Donald McGregor. 2004. "Risk as Analysis and Risk as Feelings: Some Thoughts about Affect, Reason, Risk, and Feelings." *Risk Analysis* 24: 1–12.

Slovic, Paul, Melissa Finucane, Ellen Peters, and Donald MacGregor. 2007. "The Affect Heuristic." *European Journal of Operations Research* 177 (3): 1333–1352.

Small, Deborah A., and Jennifer S. Lerner. (2008). "Emotional Policy: Personal Sadness and Anger Shape Judgments About a Welfare Case." *Political Psychology* 29: 149–168.

Smith, Craig, Kelly Haynes, Richard Lazarus, and Lois Pope. 1993. "In Search of the Hot Cognitions: Attributions, Appraisals, and Their Relation to Emotion." *Journal of Personality and Social Psychology* 65 (5): 916–929.

Smith, Eliot. 1999. "Affective and Cognitive Implications of a Group Becoming Part of the Self: New Models of Prejudice and the Self-Concept." In *Social Identity and Social Cognition*, eds. Dominic Abrama and Michael Hoggs, 83–196, London: Blackwell Publishers.

Smith, Eliot. 1994. Procedural Knowledge and Processing Strategies in Social Cognition. In *Handbook of Social Cognition*, eds. Robert Wyer and Thomas Srull, 99–151, Hillsdale, NJ: Erlbaum.

Smith, Eric. 1989. *The Unchanging American Voter.* Berkeley: University of California Press.

Son Hing, Leanne, Greg Chung-Yan, Leah Hamilton, and Mark Zanna. 2008. "A Two-Dimensional Model that Employs Explicit and Implicit Attitudes to Characterize Prejudice. *Journal of Personality and Social Psychology* 94 (6): 971–987.

Sniderman, Paul. 1993. "The New Look in Public Opinion Research." In *Political Science: The State of the Discipline, Volume II*, ed. Ada Finifter, 218–223, Washington: The American Political Science Association.

Sniderman, Paul. 2000. "Taking Sides: A Fixed Choice Theory of Political Reasoning." In *Elements of Reason: Cognition, Choice, and the Bounds of Rationality*, eds. Arthur Lupia, Matthew McCubbins, and Samuel Popkin, 74–84, New York: Cambridge University Press.

Sniderman, Paul, and Philip Tetlock. 1986a. "Reflections on American Racism." *Journal of Social Issues* 42 (2): 173–187.

Sniderman, Paul, and Philip Tetlock. 1986b. "Symbolic Racism: Problems of Motive Attribution in Political Analysis." *Journal of Social Issues* 42 (2): 129–150.

Sniderman, Paul, and Thomas Piazza. 1993. *The Scar of Race.* Cambridge, MA: Harvard University Press.

Sniderman, Paul, and Edward Carmines. 1997. *Reaching beyond Race.* Cambridge, MA: Harvard University Press.

Sniderman, Paul, and Shawn Theriault. 2004. "The Structure of Political Argument and the Logic of Issue Framing." In *Studies in Public Opinion: Attitudes, Non-attitudes, Measurement Error and Change*, eds. Willem Saris and Paul Sniderman, 133–165, Princeton, NJ: Princeton University Press.

Sniderman, Paul, Richard Brody, and Philip Tetlock. 1991. *Reasoning and Choice: Explorations in Political Psychology.* Cambridge: Cambridge University Press.

Sniderman, Paul, Thomas Piazza, Philip Tetlock, and Ann Kendrick. 1991. "The New Racism." *American Journal of Political Science* 35 (2): 423–447.

Sniderman, Paul, and Philip Tetlock, and Edward G. Carmines, eds. 1993. *Prejudice, Politics and the American Dilemma.* Stanford, CA: Stanford University Press.

Solomon, Robert. 2003a. *Not Passion's Slave: Emotions and Choice.* New York: Oxford University Press.

Solomon, Robert. 2003b. *What is an Emotion: Classic and Contemporary Readings* (2nd ed.). New York: Oxford University Press.

Sroufe, Alan. 1979. "The Coherence of Individual Development: Early Care, Attachment, and Subsequent Development." *American Psychologist* 34 (10): 834–841.

Stagner, Richard. 1942. "Some Factors Related to Attitude toward War." *Journal of Personality and Social Psychology* 16, 131–142.

Steele, Claude, and Joshua Aronson. 1995. "Stereotype Threat and the Intellectual Test Performance of African-Americans." *Journal of Personality and Social Psychology* 69: 797–811.

Steenbergen, Marco, and Milton Lodge. 2003. "Process Matters: Cognitive Models of Candidate Evaluation." In *Electoral Democracy*, eds. Michael MacKuen and George Rabinowitz, 125–171. New York: Cambridge University Press.

Stevens, Laura, and Susan Fiske. 1995. "Motivation and Cognition in Social Life: A Social Survival Guide." *Social Cognition* 13 (3): 189–214.

Strack, Fritz, Leonard Martin, and Sabine Stepper. 1988. "Inhibiting and Facilitating Conditions of the Human Smile; A Nonobtrusive Test of the Facial Feedback Hypothesis." *Journal of Personality and Social Psychology* 54 (5): 768–777.

Strathman, Alam, Faith Gleicher, David Boninger, and Scott Edwards. 1994. "The Consideration of Future Consequences: Weighing Immediate and Distant Outcomes of Behavior." *Journal of Personality and Social Psychology* 66 (4): 742–752.

Stroud, Natalie Jomini. 2008. "Media Use and Political Predispositions: Revisiting the Concept of Selective Exposure." *Political Behavior* 30: 341–366.

Taber, Charles. 2003. "Information Processing and Public Opinion." In *The Handbook of Political Psychology*, eds. David Sears, Leonie Huddy, and Robert Jervis, 433–476, New York: Oxford University Press.

Taber, Charles, and Marco Steenbergen. 1995. "Computational Experiments in Electoral Behavior." In *Political Judgment: Structure and Process*, eds. Milton Lodge and Kathleen McGraw, 141–178. Ann Arbor: University of Michigan Press.

Taber, Charles, and Richard Timpone. 1996. *Computational Modeling. Sage University Paper Series on Quantitative Applications in the Social Sciences.* Newbury Park, CA: Sage.

Taber, Charles, and Milton Lodge. 2006. "Motivated Skepticism in the Evaluation of Political Beliefs." *American Journal of Political Science* 50 (3): 755–769.

Taber, Charles, Milton Lodge, and Jill Glather. 2001. "The Motivated Construction of Political Judgments." In *Citizens and Politics: Perspectives from Political Psychology*, eds. James Kuklinski, 198–226, London: Cambridge University Press.

Taber, Charles, Damon Cann, and Simona Kucsova. 2009. "The Motivated Processing of Political Arguments." *Political Behavior* 31 (2): 137–155.

Tajfel, Henri. 1981. *Human Groups and Social Categories.* Cambridge: Cambridge University Press.

Taylor, Shelly. 1981. "A Categorization Approach to Stereotyping." In *Cognitive Processes in Stereotyping and Intergroup Behavior*, ed. David Hamilton, 145–182, Hillsdale, NJ: Erlbaum.

Taylor, Shelly. 1982. "The Availability Bias in Social Perception and Interaction." In *Judgment under Uncertainty: Heuristics and Biases*, eds. Daniel Kahneman, Paul Slovic, and Amos Tversky, 190–200. New York: Cambridge University Press.

Teige-Mocigemba, Sarah, Karl Klauer, and Jeffery Sherman. 2010. "A Practical Guide to Implicit Association Tests and Related Tasks." In *Handbook of Implicit Social Cognition: Measurement, Theory, and Applications*, eds. Bertram Gawronski and Keith Payne, 117–139, New York: Guilford.

Tesser, Abraham. 1986. "Some Effects of Self-Evaluation Maintenance on Cognition and Action." In *The Handbook of Motivation and Cognition: Foundations of Social Behavior*, eds. Richard Sorrentino and Tory Higgins, 435–464, New York: Guilford Press.

Thagard, Paul. 2000. *Coherence in Thought and Action.* Cambridge, MA: MIT Press.

Thagard, Paul. 2005. *Mind: Introduction to Cognitive Science.* 2nd ed. Cambridge, MA: MIT Press.

Thagard, Paul. 2006. *Hot Thought: Mechanisms as Applications of Emotional Cognition.* Cambridge, MA: MIT Press.

Thomas, Eliot Stearns. 1925. "The Hollow Men." In *Collected Poems, 1909–1962.* 1991. 77–82. Orlando, FL: Harcourt Brace Jovanovich.

Thompson, Erik, Robert Roman, Gordon Moskowitz, Shelly Chaiken, and John Bargh. 1994. "Accuracy Motivation Attenuates Covert Priming: The Systematic Reprocessing of Social Information." *Journal of Personality and Social Psychology* 66 (3): 474–489.

Thompson, Megan, Mark Zanna, Dale Griffin. 1995. "Let's Not Be Indifferent About Attitudinal Ambivalence." In *Attitude Strength: Antecedents and Consequence*, eds. Richard Petty and Jon Krosnick, 361–386, Hillsdale, NJ: Erlbaum.

Tiedens, Larissa, and Susan Linton. 2001. "Judgment under Uncertainty: The Effects of Specific Emotions on Information Processing." *Journal of Personality and Social Psychology* 81 (6): 973–988.

Todd, Peter, and Gerd Gigerenzer. 2000. "Simple Heuristics That Make Us Smart." *Behavioral and Brain Sciences*, 23 (5): 727–741.

Todorov, Alexander, Anesu Mandisodza, Amir Goren, and Crystal Hall. 2005. "Inferences of Competence from Faces Predict Electoral Outcomes." *Science* 308 (5729): 1623–1626.

Todorov, Alexander, Sean Baron, and Nikolaas Oosterhof. 2008. "Evaluating Face Trustworthiness: A Model Based Approach." *Social, Cognitive, and Affective Neuroscience* 3 (2): 119–127.

Tourangeau, Roger, Lance Rips, and Kenneth Rasinski. 2000. *The Psychology of the Survey Response.* New York: Cambridge University Press.

Trawalter, Sophie, and Jenessa Shapiro. 2010. "Racial Bias and Stereotyping: Interpersonal Processes." In *Handbook of Implicit Social Cognition: Measurement, Theory, and Applications,* eds. Bertram Gawronski and Keith Payne, 375–406. New York: Guilford.

Trungpa, Chogyam. 1983. *First Thought, Best Thought. 108 Poems.* Boston: Shambhala Publications.

Turner, John. 1987. *Rediscovering the Social Group: A Self-Categorization Theory.* Oxford, UK: Blackwell Publishers.

Turner, John, and Andrew Ortony. 1992. "Basic Emotions: Can Conflicting Criteria Converge?" *Psychological Review* 99 (3): 566–571.

Tursky, Bernard, Milton Lodge, and Richard Reeder. 1979. "Psychophysical and Psychophysiological Evaluation of the Direction, Intensity, and Meaning of Race-Related Stimuli." *Psychophysiology* 16 (5): 452–462.

Tversky, Amos, and Daniel Kahneman. 1973. "Availability: A Heuristic for Judging Frequency and Probability." *Cognitive Psychology* 5 (2): 207–232.

Tversky, Amos, and Daniel Kahneman. 1974. "Judgment Under Uncertainty: Heuristics and Biases." *Science* 185 (4157): 1124–1131.

Uhlmann, Eric, David Pizarro, David Tannenbaum, and Peter Ditto. 2009. "The Motivated Use of Moral Principles." *Judgment and Decision Making* 4 (6): 476–491.

Uleman, James. 1999. "Spontaneous Versus Intentional Inferences in Impression Formation." In *Dual Process Theories in Social Psychology,* eds. Shelly Chaiken, and Yaacov Trope, 141–160, New York: Guilford.

Uleman, James, and John Bargh. 1989. *Unintended Thought.* New York: Guilford Press.

Uleman, James, Leonard Newman, and Gordon Moskowitz. 1996. "People as Flexible Interpreters: Evidence and Issues from Spontaneous Trait Inference." In *Advances in Experimental Social Psychology,* ed. Mark Zanna, 211–279, San Diego, CA: Academic Press.

Valentino, Nicholas, Antoine Banks, Vincent Hutchings, and Anne Davis. 2009. "Selective Exposure in the Internet Age: The Interaction between Anxiety and Information Utility." *Political Psychology* 30 (4): 591–613.

Valentino, Nicholas, Krysha Gregorowicz, and Eric Groenendyk. 2008. "Efficacy, Emotions, and the Habit of Participation." *Political Behavior* 31 (3): 307–330.

Valentino, Nicholas, Vincent Hutchings, Antoine Banks, and Anne Davis. 2008. "Is a Worried Citizen a Good Citizen? Emotions, Political Information Seeking, and Learning via the Internet." *Political Psychology* 29 (2): 247–273.

Valentino, Nicholas, Vincent Hutchings, and Ismail White. 2002. "Cues That Matter: How Political Ads Prime Racial Attitudes During Campaigns." *American Political Science Review* 96 (1): 91–110.

Valentino, Nicholas A., Ted Brader, Krysha Gregorowicz, Eric W. Groenendyk, and Vincent Hutchings. 2011. "Election Night's Alright for Fighting: The Participatory Impact of Negative Emotions." *Journal of Politics.* In Press.

Van Veen, Vincent, Marie Krug, Jonathan Schooler, and Cameron Carter. 2009. "Neural Activity Predicts Attitude Change in Cognitive Dissonance." *Nature Neuroscience* 12 (11): 1469–1474.

Verbruggen, Frederick, and Jan De Houwer. 2007. "Do Emotional Stimuli Interfere with Response Inhibition? Evidence From the Stop Signal Paradigm." *Cognition and Emotion.* 21 (2): 391–403.

Verhulst, Brad, Milton Lodge, and Howard Lavine. 2010. "The Attractiveness Halo: Why Some Candidates Are Perceived More Favorably Than Others." *Journal of Nonverbal Behavior* 34 (2): 111–117.

Verhulst, Brad, Milton Lodge, and Charles Taber. 2010. "The Effect of Unnoticed Cues and Cognitive Deliberation on Candidate Evaluation." Unpublished Manuscript.

Warshaw, Paul, and Fred Davis. 1985. "Disentangling Behavioral Intention and Behavioral Expectation." *Journal of Experimental Social Psychology* 21 (3): 213–228.

Watson, David, and Auke Tellegen. 1985. "Towards a Consensual Structure of Mood." *Psychological Bulletin* 98 (2): 219–235.

Wattenberg, Brend, Charles Judd, and Bernadette Park. 1997. "Evidence for Racial Prejudice at the Implicit Level and Its Relationship With Questionnaire Measures." *Journal of Personality and Social Psychology* 72 (2): 262–274.

Watts, Duncan. 2011. *Everything is Obvious Once You Know the Answer.* New York: Crown Press.

Webb, Eugene, Donald Campbell, Richard Schwartz, and Lee Sechrest. 1966. *Unobtrusive Measures: Nonreactive Research in the Social Sciences.* New York: Rand McNally.

Wegener, Duane, John Downing, Jon Krosnick, and Richard Petty. 1995 "Measures and Manipulations of Strength-related Properties of Attitudes: Current Practice and Future Directions." In *Attitude Strength: Antecedents and Consequences*, eds. Richard Petty and Jon Krosnick, 1–24, Hillsdale, NJ: Erlbaum.

Wegner, Daniel, and John Bargh. 1998. "Control and Automaticity in Social Life." In *The Handbook of Social Psychology*, eds. Daniel Gilbert, Susan Fiske, and Gardner Lindzey, 446–496, New York: McGraw-Hill.

Wegner, Daniel, Matthew Ansfield, and Dianiel Pilloff. 1998. "The Putt and the Pendulum: Ironic Effects of the Mental Control of Action." *Psychological Science* 9 (3): 196–199.

Wegner, Daniel. 2002. *The Illusion of Conscious Will.* Cambridge, MA: MIT Press.

Weinberger, Joel, and Drew Westen. 2008. "RATS, We Should Have Used Clinton: Subliminal Priming in Political Campaigns." *Political Psychology* 29 (5): 631–651.

Wentura, Dirk. 1999. "Activation and Inhibition of Affective Information: Evidence for Negative Priming in the Evaluation Task." *Cognition and Emotion* 13: 65–91.

Wentura, Dirk, and Juliane Degner. 2010a. "Automatic Evaluation Isn't that Crude! Moderation of Masked Affective Priming by Type of Valence." *Cognition and Emotion* 24 (4): 609–628.

Wentura, Dirk, and Juliane Degner. 2010b. "A Practical Guide to Sequential Priming and Related Tasks." In *Handbook of Implicit Social Cognition: Measurement, Theory, and Applications*, eds. Bertram Gawronski and Keith Payne, 95–116, New York: Guilford.

Wentura, Dirk, and Sabine Otten. 1999. "About the Impact of Automaticity in the Minimal Group Paradigm: Evidence From Affective Priming Tasks." *European Journal of Social Psychology* 9 (8): 1049–1071.

Westen, Drew. 2008. *The Political Brain: The Role of Emotion in Deciding the Fate of the Nation.* New York: Public Affairs.

Westen, Drew, and Pavel Blagov, 2007. "A Clinical-Empirical Model of Emotion Regulation: From Defense and Motivated Reasoning to Emotion Constraint Satisfaction." In *Handbook of Emotion Regulation*, ed. James Gross, 373–392, New York: Guilford Press.

Westen, Drew, Pavel Blagov, Kieth Harenski, Clint Kilts, and Stephan Hamann. 2006. "Neural Bases of Motivated Reasoning: An fMRI Study of Emotional Constraints on Partisan Political Judgment in the 2004 U.S. Presidential Election." *Journal of Cognitive Neuroscience* 18 (11): 1974–1958.

Whalen, Paul, Lisa Shin, Sean McInerney, Hakan Fischer, Christopher Wright, and Scott Rauch. 2001. "A Functional MRI Study of Human Amygdala Responses to Facial Expressions of Fear vs. Anger." *Emotion* 1 (1): 70–83.

Wicklund, Robert, and Jack. Brehm. 1976. *Perspectives on Cognitive Dissonance.* Hillsdale, NJ: Erlbaum.

Wiers, Reinout, Katrijn Houben, Anne Roefs, Peter de Jong, Wilheim Hofmann, and Alan Stacy. 2010. "Implicit Cognition in Health Psychology: Why Common Sense Goes Out the Window." In *Handbook of Implicit Social Cognition: Measurement, Theory, and Applications.* eds. Bertram Gawronski and Keith Payne, 462–488, New York: Guilford.

Wilson, James. 1996. "Forward." In *Fixing Broken Windows: Restoring Order and Reducing Crime in Our Communities*, eds. George and Kelling and Catherine Coles, i–xiii, New York: Touchstone.

Wilson, Paul. 1968. "Perceptual Distortion of Height as a Function of Ascribed Academic Status." *Journal of Social Psychology* 74 (1): 97–102.

Wilson, Timothy. 2002. *Strangers to Ourselves: Discovering the Adaptive Unconscious.* Cambridge, MA: Harvard University Press.

Wilson, Timothy. 2011. *Redirect.* New York: Little Brown.

Wilson, Timothy, and Jonathan Schooler. 1991 "Thinking Too Much: Introspection Can Reduce the Quality of Preferences and Decisions." *Journal of Personality and Social Psychology* 60 (2): 181–192.

Wilson, Timothy, and Sara Hodges. 1992. "Attitudes as Temporary Constructs." In *Construction of Social Judgments*, eds. Leonard Martin and Abraham Tesser, 37–65, Hillsdale, NJ: Erlbaum.

Wilson, Timothy, and Nancy Brekke. 1994. "Mental Contamination and Mental Correction: Unwanted Influences on Judgments and Evaluations." *Psychological Bulletin* 116 (1): 117–142.

Wilson, Timothy, Samuel Lindsey, and Tonya Schooler. 2000. "A Model of Dual Attitudes." *Psychological Review* 107 (1): 101–126.

Wilson, Timothy, Douglas Lisle, Jonathan Schooler, Sara Hodges, Kristen Klaaren, and Suzanne LaFleur. 1993. "Introspecting about Reasons Can Reduce Post-Choice Satisfaction." *Personality and Social Psychology Bulletin* 19 (3): 331–339.

Winkielman, Piort, and Kent Berridge. 2004. "Unconscious Emotion." *Current Directions in Psychological Science* 13 (3): 120–123.

Winkielman, Piotr, Robert Zajonc, and Norbert Schwarz. 1997. "Subliminal Affective Priming Resists Attributional Interventions." *Cognition and Emotion* 11: 433–465.

Wittenbrink, Bernd. 2007. "Measuring Attitudes Through Priming." In *Implicit Measures of Attitudes*, eds. Bernd Wittenbrink and Norbert Schwarz, 17–58, New York: Guilford.

Wittenbrink, Bernd, Charles Judd, and Bernadette Park. 1997. "Evidence for Racial Prejudice at the Implicit Level and Its Relationship with Questionnaire Measures." *Journal of Personality and Social Psychology* 72 (2): 262–274.

Wittenbrink, Bernd, Charles Judd and Bernadette Park. 2001. "Spontaneous Prejudice in Context: Variability in Automatically Activated Attitudes." *Journal of Personality and Social Psychology* 81 (5): 815–827.

Wyer, Natalie, Jeffrey Sherman, and Steven Stroessner. 2000. "The Roles of Motivation and Ability in Controlling the Consequences of Stereotype Suppression." *Personality and Social Psychology Bulletin* 26 (1): 13–25.

Wyer, Robert. 2007. "Principles of Mental representation." In *Handbook of Basic Principles*. (2nd ed.), eds. Arie Kruglanski and Tori Higgins, 285–331, New York, Guilford.

Wyer, Robert, and Thomas Srull. 1989. *Memory and Cognition in its Social Context*. Hillsdale, NJ: Erlbaum.

Yzerbyt, Vincent, Charles Judd, and Olivier Corneille, eds. 2004. *The Psychology of Group Perception: Perceived Variability, Entitativity and Essentialism*. New York: Psychology Press.

Zajonc, Robert. 1980. "Feeling and Thinking: Preferences Need No Inferences. " *America Psychologist* 35 (2): 117–123.

Zajonc, Robert. 1984. "On the Primacy of Affect." *American Psychologist* 39 (2): 117–123.

Zajonc, Robert. 2000. "Feeling and Thinking: Closing the Debate Over the Independence of Affect." In *Feeling and Thinking: The Role of Affect in Social Cognition*, ed. Joseph Forgas, 31–58, Cambridge, MA: Cambridge University Press.

Zajonc, Robert, and Daniel McIntosh. 1992. "Emotions Research: Some Promising Questions and Some Questionable Promises." *Psychological Science* 3 (1): 70–74.

Zaller, John. 1992. *The Nature and Origins of Mass Opinion*. New York: Cambridge University Press.

Zaller, John, and Stanley Feldman. 1992. "A Simple Theory of Survey Response: Answering Questions versus Revealing Preferences." *American Journal of Political Science* 36 (3): 579–616.

Zanna, Mark. 1990. "Attitude Function: Is it Related to Attitude Structure?" *Advances in Consumer Research* 17 (1): 98–100.

Zebrowitz, Leslie. 2004. "The Origin of First Impressions." *Journal of Cultural and Evolutionary Psychology* 2 (2): 93–108.

Zebrowitz, Leslie, and Susan McDonald. 1991. "The Impact of Litigants' Baby-Facedness and Attractiveness on Adjudications in Small Claims Courts." *Law and Human Behavior* 15 (6): 603–623.

Zebrowitz, Leslie, and Joann Montepare. 2008. "Social Psychological Face Perception: Why Appearance Matters." *Social and Personality Compass* 2 (3): 1497–1517.

Zebrowitz, Leslie, Judith Hall, Nora Murphy, and Gillian Rhodes. 2002. "Looking Smart and Looking Good: Facial Cues to Intelligence and Their Origins." *Personality and Social Psychology Bulletin* 28 (2): 238–249.

Index

Books in the Series